When Women Didn't Count

When Women Didn't Count

The Chronic Mismeasure and Marginalization of American Women in Federal Statistics

Robert Lopresti

An Imprint of ABC-CLIO, LLC

Santa Barbara, California • Denver, Colorado

Library of Congress Cataloging-in-Publication Data

Names: Lopresti, Robert, author.
Title: When women didn't count : the chronic mismeasure and marginalization of American women in federal statistics / Robert Lopresti.
Description: Santa Barbara, California : Praeger, [2017] | Includes bibliographical references and index.
Identifiers: LCCN 2017007032 (print) | LCCN 2017019865 (ebook) | ISBN 9781440843693 (ebook) | ISBN 9781440843686 (alk. paper)
Subjects: LCSH: United States—Statistics—History. | Women—United States—Statistics—History. | Government questionnaires—United States—History. | United States—Statistical services—History. | Sex discrimination—United States—History.
Classification: LCC HA214 (ebook) | LCC HA214 .L67 2017 (print) | DDC 305.402/1—dc23
LC record available at https://lccn.loc.gov/2017007032

ISBN: 978-1-4408-4368-6
EISBN: 978-1-4408-4369-3

21 20 19 18 17   1 2 3 4 5

This book is also available as an eBook.

Praeger
An Imprint of ABC-CLIO, LLC

ABC-CLIO, LLC
130 Cremona Drive, P.O. Box 1911
Santa Barbara, California 93116-1911
www.abc-clio.com

This book is printed on acid-free paper ∞
Manufactured in the United States of America

This book is dedicated to two people who were professors at the Graduate School of Library Service at Rutgers, the State University of New Jersey in the 1970s. Walt Fraser gave me the best advice I received there: "Take a course in government documents, if you can stand it. Most people can't, so there are always jobs." Patricia Reeling taught that course and has always been my model on how to explain government information sources to people. Without those two sages, my life would have been very different and this book would never have been written.

Contents

Illustrations   ix

Preface   xi

Acknowledgments   xiii

Chronology   xv

Part I   Why Care about Government Statistics?   1

Chapter 1   Introduction   3

Chapter 2   Statistical System of the United States   7

Part II   Demographics   13

Chapter 3   Population and Age   15

Chapter 4   Marriage, Divorce, and Cohabitation   21

Chapter 5   Motherhood   29

Chapter 6   Single Mothers   35

Part III   Women at Home   41

Chapter 7   Heads of Household, Heads of Family   43

Chapter 8   Housewives, Homemakers, and Housekeepers   49

Part IV   Concepts of Employment   61

Chapter 9   "Occupations Suitable for Women"   63

Chapter 10   "Gainful Employment"   75

Chapter 11   Income   83

Chapter 12   Unemployment during the Great Depression   93

Part V   Women at Work   99

Chapter 13   The Bureau of Labor Statistics and the
                  Women's Bureau   101

Chapter 14   Employment   111

Chapter 15   Women Factory Workers   129

Chapter 16   "Farm Females"   137

Chapter 17   Women Business Owners,
                  Women-Owned Businesses   149

Part VI   Women and Health   157

Chapter 18   Nonreproductive Health Issues   159

Chapter 19   Contraception   173

Chapter 20   Abortion   179

Part VII   Women and the Law   189

Chapter 21   Women as Criminals   191

Chapter 22   Prostitution   203

Chapter 23   Women as Crime Victims   211

Chapter 24   Rape   219

Part VIII   Women at War   229

Chapter 25   Rosie the Riveter: Civilian Women during
                  the World Wars   231

Chapter 26   Women in the Military   241

Part IX   Conclusion   249

Chapter 27   Conclusion   251

Notes   255

Bibliography   297

Index   341

Illustrations

Tables

5.1 The first appearances of certain subjects in U.S. Census Bureau's *Current Population Reports* and *Statistical Briefs*. 31

7.1 Women breadwinners and their relation to family heads, 1900. 44

8.1 Instructions to census-takers on how to count homemakers, housewives, grown daughters doing housework, and housekeepers. 50

9.1 Occupations of the 1970 *Intermediate Occupation Classification* list for only one sex. 73

13.1 *Handbook on Women Workers:* Subjects covered in different editions. 106

14.1 Selected tables from the 1924 to 1926 and 1941 editions of the *Handbook of Labor Statistics*. 120

17.1 Selected occupations from a 1933 Women's Bureau report. 150

18.1 *Health, United States*—Women's Health topics. 163

20.1 Data about abortions appearing in *Health, United States*, over five-year intervals. 184

21.1 Number of women in U.S. prisons in 1880, by offense. 192

21.2 Relevant crimes for which only men were in prison, 1880. 194

23.1 Domestic violence terminology: Earliest uses found in
federal reports.   213

24.1 "Forcible Rape" subcategories in the index of the
Sourcebook of Criminal Justice Statistics.   224

24.2 Characteristics of rape analyzed at the *Criminal
Victimization in the United States* website, 2016.   226

25.1 Women's war work during World War I.   239

26.1 Subjects researched by DACOWITS.   246

Figure

18.1 *Vital and Health Statistics* series. Percentage of titles
mentioning "women" or "mothers" in specific contexts.   160

Preface

Gathering, organizing, and reporting statistics involves making many subjective decisions. That is just as true in this book as it is in, say, a volume of the *Census of Population*. I want to be transparent about some of the choices I have made.

Each chapter of this book proceeds more or less chronologically. In some cases a subtopic appeared so often that it threatened to derail the main line and had to be split off into a chapter of its own. Therefore, for example, "Motherhood" is followed by "Single Mothers."

In the same way, the broader organization of the book involved value-laden choices. For example, does the chapter on prostitution belong in the section on "Law" or the section on "Work?"

In these cases I tried to adhere to the principle of "thinking like the government"; that is, I tried to put together things that the government publications themselves seemed to treat as similar.

Since the government has preferred the word "sex" to "gender," for clarity's sake I have done the same. The word "gender" appears here only when it is used in a quotation.

The government, and indeed the public, has changed over time the terms it uses for various racial groups. When I discuss a text I have generally stuck to the term found in that text. One exception: on occasion a source has used "negro," "colored person," or similar terms, without a capital letter. Rather than ignore it or silently correct it in the text, I have followed it with [sic] to indicate that the error is in the original. Similarly I have capitalized "Whites" and "Blacks" when referring to people, because that is the usage the Census Bureau prefers.

Most organizations mentioned in the text are federal agencies. When one is not and there seems to be a possibility of confusion, I mention that it is a nonprofit or the like (e.g., the National Council for Research on Women). If you are uncertain, check the footnotes; federal agency names there always begin with "U.S."

Other writers might have made other choices, but I wanted to acknowledge that I made these consciously.

Acknowledgments

I am triply indebted to my employer, Western Washington University. It would have been impossible to start this book, much less finish it, without the six months of professional leave that I was granted. Second, Western Libraries' large collection of federal documents was a gold mine for data. Finally, the professionals who work in the Libraries' Interlibrary Loan, Cataloging, and Circulation departments went above and beyond to track down material for me. For all of this I am truly grateful.

I can't imagine doing research in American history without the use of Hathi Trust. This free, full-text, digital library provided me with easy access to hundreds of publications. Since they only heard from me on the rare occasions I had a complaint, I am eager to thank them for their hard and excellent work.

I am also indebted to Mary Ellen Huls's two-volume bibliography, *United States Government Documents on Women, 1800–1990.* Standing on the shoulders of giants, indeed.

My life-long friend Robert Gerzoff, a retired federal statistician, was kind enough to reach out to colleagues on my behalf, and I thank all those who responded. I was particularly pleased to receive advice from Margo Anderson, whose work had already found its way into my bibliography several times. I am also grateful to Penelope Ciancanelli for answering some questions for me.

Extra thanks go out to Professors Paul Piper, Sylvia Tag, and Susan Weiner for useful suggestions.

Much thanks to Michael Millman, my editor at Praeger, who had faith in this book and, in addition to his editorial skills, showed both patience and persistence. Thanks also go to Ken Weiner for keeping it legal.

My wife, Terri, has put up with 40 years of my allegedly interesting anecdotes about government publications. She probably never expected to hear as many as she has in the last two years. I thank her for her encouragement, enthusiasm, and editing eye.

All mistakes, misunderstandings, and other failures herein are, of course, my own.

Most of this book was written on Coast Salish land.

Robert Lopresti

December 2016

Chronology

1848

Seneca Falls Convention, the first conference on women's rights in the United States.

1870

First census to record separate occupation figures for men and women.[1]

1880

First census with enumerators (census-takers) of both sexes.[2]

1907

Census Bureau published a book entitled *Statistics of Women at Work*.[3]

Congress authorized what became a 19-volume report on the effects of the workplace on women and children.[4]

1912

First minimum wage law for women and minors passed, Massachusetts.[5]

1918

As a war measure, the Women in Industry Service office was created in the Labor Department.[6]

1920

The Nineteenth Amendment was ratified, giving women the vote.

Women's Bureau was established in the Labor Department.[7]

1923

First of several Supreme Court decisions ruled minimum wage laws for women unconstitutional (*Adkins v. Children's Hospital*).[8]

1932

Frances Perkins became secretary of Labor, the first female member of the president's cabinet.[9]

1942
The armed forces created Women's Reserves to cope with wartime personnel strains.

1951
Defense Advisory Committee on Women in the Services (DACOWITS) created to advise Pentagon on women's issues in armed forces.[10]

1961
Kennedy created the President's Commission on the Status of Women.[11]

1963
Equal Pay Act ensured equal pay for women in federal employ.[12]

1964
Civil Rights Act prohibited discrimination in hiring based on sex.[13]

Supreme Court overturned a law banning the use of contraceptives by married couples (*Griswold v. Connecticut*).[14]

1967
Congress repealed law restricting number of women in the armed forces.[15]

1972
Congress passed the Equal Rights Amendment. It was not ratified by the states.[16]

The Equal Employment Opportunity Act expanded the 1964 Civil Rights Act to cover all aspects of employment, including wages and training.[17]

1973
The U.S. Supreme Court decided *Roe v. Wade,* overturning state laws against abortion.[18]

1980
The decennial census replaced "head of household" with the neutral "householder."[19]

1990
The General Accounting Office published a report detailing the gaps caused by women being left out of medical research, sparking a change in the system.[20]

1991
Sexual assaults at Tailhook '91 drew national attention to the dangers facing women in the armed forces.[21]

1994
The Violence Against Women Act became law. Among its results was the creation of federal agencies dedicated to studying the subject.[22]

1995
Clinton created the President's Interagency Council on Women, as well as the White House Office of Women's Initiatives and Outreach.[23]

2001

George W. Bush disbanded the President's Interagency Council on Women, and the White House Office of Women's Initiatives and Outreach.[24]

2002

George W. Bush changed the DACOWITS charter to include military families as well as military women.[25]

2009

Obama created the White House Council on Women and Girls.[26]

Obama changed the DACOWITS charter to again focus on military women.[27]

2016

The Democratic Party selected Hillary Rodham Clinton as the first female major party presidential candidate. She was defeated.

PART I

Why Care about Government Statistics?

CHAPTER ONE

Introduction

In the *Occupation Statistics* volume of the 1910 Census there is a section called "Peculiar Occupations for Women." It noted that the census-takers had reported females "following many occupations which are very peculiar or unusual for women." The report explained that "careful examination" revealed many errors "either of the sex or of the occupation" and most of these errors were then corrected before publication.[1]

Looking back with a century of hindsight, it is easy to wonder how many of those "errors" were actually accurate recordings of women pioneering in a field, innovators who were deleted from history by assumptions about what females can and can't do.

The U.S. government is one of the world's largest collectors of social statistics, and these numbers are neither natural (like the speed of sound) nor neutral. They do more than just fill history books; they can make history.

A few examples of how federal statistics can change our lives follow:

- The decennial census determines how many representatives your state has in Congress.
- Rising crime rates can cause property values to drop in a town and discourage people from moving there.
- Employment numbers—amid many other economic figures—cause rises and falls in the stock market.

Decisions about which statistics to collect and publish are political, in the broad sense of the word and sometimes in the narrower sense as well. For example, in 1996, at the request of the National Rifle Association,

Congress forbade the Centers for Disease Control and Prevention from gathering statistics on gun violence.[2]

This book illustrates how changes in the perception and roles of women have been reflected, and in some cases formed, by government statistics. It is *not* primarily a book of numbers, but it is concerned with the way numbers are collected, presented, and interpreted.

For example:

- When did the Census Bureau stop assuming that the "head of household" was always a man?
- When did the government start collecting statistics on domestic violence?
- How many women were locked up without trial during World War I for having a venereal disease?

Government statistics appear in many types of official publications such as reports, bulletins, hearings, and data compilations. The most important of the last group is the *Statistical Abstract of the United States,* an almanac of American life that the Census Bureau published from 1888 through 2012. Each volume offers a remarkable snapshot, not only of the country itself but of what data (from any source) the government thought was important enough to include in its main portrait of American life. Each chapter of this book will end with a look at its subject through the lens of the *Statistical Abstract.*

For the purposes of this book, there are three types of government statistics:

- Those collected and published by the federal government, such as the decennial census.
- Those gathered by other organizations but included in government statistical collections. For example, the government does not research the number of religious group members, so for many years the *Statistical Abstract* included figures borrowed from the Princeton Religion Research Center and other sources.
- Statistics without clear sources that enter the public record through the activity of government officials. For example, in 2011 Senator Jon Kyl stated in Congress that abortion was "well over ninety percent of what Planned Parenthood does."[3]

What might be considered a fourth category will not generally appear in this book: statistics that nongovernment officials bring into the realm of federal publications. For example, a witness at a congressional hearing might report that a certain percentage of women are survivors of domestic violence, but unless that data comes from a federal source, or is utilized in further government work, it will not be reported here. The book will also not typically include research that was paid for with government funds, but published by private companies.

This book will show women as they have appeared—and disappeared—in government statistics throughout U.S. history. The main focus is on the questions, not the answers. In other words, while numbers will sometimes appear, the book's central interest is in when, how, and why the government chose to collect them. The book will also point out public reactions to the government statistics, as well as some examples of published research that used the data.

The federal government collects statistics on many other groups of people, some of whom are occasionally mentioned in this book. It would be wonderful if they received similar treatment in their own right, but I had no time or space to discuss them adequately here. Some examples include:

- Children
- Different races and ethnic groups
- Disabled people
- The LGBTQ community
- Native Americans
- Senior citizens

For the same reasons of space and time limits, I have not tried to cover regions of the country or other parts of the world.

It is worth noting that until women are counted separately, American men are also lost in the fog of data. If we don't know what percentage of tailors were women in a given year, then we don't know how many tailors were men either.

I hope that this book will provide insight into life in our country and shed much-needed light on how statistics have helped to shape it.

CHAPTER TWO

Statistical System of the United States

The collecting of statistics is built into the nation's DNA. Title I, Section 2, of the U.S. Constitution states, in part:

> Representatives and direct Taxes shall be apportioned among the several States which may be included within this Union, according to their respective Numbers, which shall be determined by adding to the whole Number of free Persons, including those bound to Service for a Term of Years, and excluding Indians not taxed, three fifths of all other Persons.
>
> The actual Enumeration shall be made within three Years after the first Meeting of the Congress of the United States, and within every subsequent Term of ten Years, in such Manner as they shall by Law direct.[1]

In other words, to determine how many members of the House of Representatives should be allocated to each state, the population was to be counted every 10 years.

To carry out this obligation, Congress passed a law approving the first census on March 1, 1790.[2] This sparked a number of debates, some of which continue today. What questions should be asked in the census? Should it be limited to the information required for allocating congressional seats, or should the government take advantage of this chance to get more information about its citizens?

Congressman (and future president) James Madison was among the first to suggest adding more questions. He listed 30 occupations and wanted to find out how many people worked in each. This idea was rejected.[3]

In early times the census was conducted by assistant U.S. marshals going from door to door. The head of a household was asked her or his name and how many people lived in that place, and that was all. There was no standardized form and no follow-through. Records were not private and, in fact, were required to be posted in a public place.[4]

One critic of this process was President George Washington, who noted:

> One thing is certain our *real* numbers will exceed, greatly, the official returns of them; because the religious scruples of some, would not allow them to give in their lists; the fears of others that it was intended as the foundation of a tax induced them to conceal or diminish theirs, and thro' the indolence of the people, and the negligence of many of the Officers numbers are omitted.[5]

Suspicions about how the information would be used and laments about an undercount are trends that have continued to the present day.

As the decades passed more questions were added about manufacturing, occupations, and demographic details. Starting in 1850 individuals, rather than households, received individual lines in the census forms, and "social" information was gathered, such as data about schools, churches, and crime. This was also the first census for which the results were kept confidential.[6]

Four years later J.D.B. De Bow, the superintendent of the Census Office, first suggested that it needed to be a permanent agency. The practice had been to create a census office from scratch before the decennial year and disband it after the reports were published, but he argued that reinventing the wheel every decade was not the best approach: "Every ten years some one at Washington will enter the hall of a department, appoint fifty or a hundred persons under him, who, perhaps have never compiled a table before, and are incapable of combining a column of figures correctly. . . . If any are qualified it is no merit of the system."[7]

Unfortunately this point of view did not win out until 1902, when a permanent Census Bureau was created in the U.S. Interior Department. One statistician who worked there, Dr. Walter F. Willcox, stated many years later that this victory involved women in a surprising way:

> Director William R. Merriam handled Congress very cleverly; got a stunning group of girls on his staff, [and] nearly all of them, no doubt, wanted to remain in Washington, and in the Census Office (at least until they got married). These girls, I was told brought so much pressure on Congress

that in 1902, or thereabouts, the office was made permanent, not for any scientific reason, but to keep the staff from being disbanded.[8]

A year later the bureau was transferred to the new U.S. Commerce and Labor Department.[9]

The debate that started with James Madison, over how many questions should appear on the census, took another turn in 1940 when, for the first time, the census asked additional questions of a sample of the population. This became known as the "long form" and continued through the 2000 Census, after which it was replaced by the American Community Survey (ACS), taken in non-census years.

Members of the public have suggested many thousands of questions for the census. Among the many rejected have been the following:

- Do you own a piano?
- Have you ever had what is popularly known as a "paranormal" or "psychic" experience?
- Are you a blonde or brunette?
- Do you take vitamins and/or minerals to supplement your daily diet?
- If unmarried, are you a virgin?
- What kind of exterior building material is used for your residence?
- Do you believe in God?[10]

Another big change came in 1960 when, for the first time, the census was taken by mail. Enumerators (census-takers) were sent out to follow up only if forms were not returned.[11]

The debate on the census has never gone away. For example, in the run-up to the 2010 Census, Congresswoman Michele Bachmann (R-MN) said that her family would refuse to fill out any questions except the number of people in the household. She feared that the "very intricate, very personal" information requested by the Census Bureau could be misused by the government. Actually the types of questions she was worried about, most of which had been asked for decades, were no longer on the census form at all but had become part of the ACS.[12]

The Census Bureau, whatever questions it may ask, is not the federal government's only collector of statistics. In fact, the Committee on National Statistics noted that "the United States has one of the most decentralized statistical systems in the developed world."[13]

At one point it seemed that would not be the case. The law that created the U.S. Commerce and Labor Department in 1903 permitted the secretary of that agency to transfer statistical responsibilities from most other departments to the Census Bureau. However, according to a historian, the secretary of Commerce and Labor and the director of the Census immediately began to quarrel over "the authority to select and appoint temporary Bureau personnel, the name of the Bureau, the choice of a seal, centralization of the disbursing function, making census records available to the other agencies of the Department, and the failure of the Secretary to pass on to the Congress complaints from the Director."[14] Not surprisingly, the secretary did not choose to add to the bureau's powers.

The outcome is that, while some countries have a single entity collecting and disseminating numerical data (e.g., Statistics Canada[15]), the United States has many. Thirteen agencies have that as their primary job.[16] These agencies receive approximately 38 percent of the federal money spent on statistics and more if the decennial census is included.[17]

The following are the primary statistical agencies with their current parent departments arranged by what is generally recognized as their years of origin.

1862. Statistics of Income Division—U.S. Treasury Department, Internal Revenue Service.[18]

1867. National Center for Education Statistics—U.S. Education Department.[19]

1884. Bureau of Labor Statistics—U.S. Labor Department.[20]

1902. Census Bureau—U.S. Commerce Department.[21]

1935. Office of Research, Evaluation and Statistics—U.S. Social Security Administration.[22]

1950. National Center for Science and Engineering Statistics—U.S. National Science Foundation.[23]

1960. National Center for Health Statistics—U.S. Health and Human Services Department.[24]

1961. National Agricultural Statistics Service—U.S. Agriculture Department.[25]

1961. Economic Research Service—U.S. Agriculture Department.[26]

1972. Bureau of Economic Analysis—U.S. Commerce Department.[27]

1977. Energy Information Administration—U.S. Energy Department.[28]

1979. Bureau of Justice Statistics—U.S. Justice Department.[29]

1992. Bureau of Transportation Statistics—U.S. Transportation Department.[30]

The one agency on this list that will appear in this book almost as often as the Census Bureau is the Bureau of Labor Statistics (BLS). The BLS resides in the Labor Department but actually predates it. It was set up originally as the Bureau of Labor in the Interior Department in 1884.[31] The BLS quickly began producing figures on employment, unemployment, and consumer expenditure, among other subjects.

In 1997 the government created a website called FedStats, which was supposed to be a guide and index to the world of federal statistical agencies. Most of its functions were shorn away in 2014, but it still lists all the government agencies with significant statistical responsibilities—not just the 13 mentioned earlier but a total of 127. A sample of these include the following:

Agricultural Research Service—U.S. Agriculture Department

Federal Bureau of Investigation—U.S. Justice Department

Institute of Museum and Library Services—independent agency

National Institute on Aging—U.S. Health and Human Services Department

United States Geological Survey—U.S. Interior Department[32]

The most important agency on that broader list, as far as this book is concerned, is the Women's Bureau in the Labor Department. It has been conducting statistical surveys of working women since 1920.[33]

Entire books have been written about the federal statistical system, but this chapter is enough of an introduction for the sake of this book's subject. More will appear about some agencies as their duties come into focus.

Statistical Abstract

All of the chapters of this book will end with a reference to the *Statistical Abstract of the United States*. This almanac was published by the government annually from 1878 through 2012, when it was defunded. Commercial publishers now produce books with the same title, but since they are not government publications they fall outside the scope of this text.

Among the many useful aspects of the *Abstract* was that it generally gave the source of each statistical table, in effect serving as an index to a much broader array of government data. Also, in cases where the government itself did not collect statistics (e.g., church membership and certain abortion data), the *Abstract* gathered them from other sources.

But most crucially, the *Statistical Abstract* provided a snapshot of what the federal government considered important enough in a given year to include in this basic look at life in the United States. The early years focused mostly on manufacturing and commerce, but as time went on the book's interests varied with those of the nation's government and population. For example, here are the first years certain data appeared in the series:

Immigrants of each nationality. 1878.[34]

Public schools in the United States. 1879.[35]

Vessels wrecked. 1885.[36]

Area of Indian Reservations. 1888.[37]

Telephones, number. 1889.[38]

Civil Service, number of positions. 1910.[39]

Homicides in selected cities. 1922.[40]

Accidents and fatalities, aircraft. 1944–1945.[41]

Population using fluoridated water. 1965.[42]

Motor vehicle safety defect recalls. 1978.[43]

Firearm mortality among children, youth, and young adults. 1992.[44]

Student use of computers. 1995.[45]

Internet publishing and broadcasting. 2008.[46]

PART II

Demographics

CHAPTER THREE

Population and Age

In a Special Report on the 1900 Census the authors wrote with evident satisfaction that in regard to at least one question "there is no ambiguity of terms, and in the United States there is no unwillingness on the part of any race, age, or class of the population to give correct answers to the question of sex. Hence the amount of conscious and intentional error in the answers is probably infinitesimal."[1]

The next census made a similar claim: "The returns as to sex are probably more accurate than those of any other characteristic of the population. There is no ambiguity of terms, no motive to misrepresent the facts, and little or no opportunity for error in recording the sex of persons actually enumerated."[2]

A century later, readers living in a time when some universities offer applicants a choice of six "gender identity" terms[3] may wonder how accurate those statements were. However, the number and age of the population distributed by sex have long been considered an essential part of federal statistics-collecting.

The first federal census, conducted in 1790, recorded the name of only the head of household but counted the number of free White males, free White females, other free people, and slaves. There was a separate count of free White males aged 16 and up "to assess the country's industrial and military potential," as the Census Bureau explains it today.[4]

The next few censuses added a few more population details, including the ages of free Whites of both sexes, broken down into various age categories. In 1850, for the first time, the names of all free persons were recorded, not just the heads of households.[5]

In his *Compendium* of the 1850 head count, census superintendent J.D.B. De Bow provided the ratio of White females to males for each census. There were always more men than women.[6] He also gave the proportion by age, with the category of "old age" starting at 50.

But De Bow was especially interested in an oddity seen among younger people, one that would be mentioned repeatedly in census reports as decades rolled past: women seemed to lie about their age more than men. "Between fifteen and twenty," wrote De Bow, "there is a large and growing excess of females, attributable in some slight degree, as Prof. Tucker intimated, to the anxiety of the sex to retain this interesting age." On the same page, however, he noted the number of people who claimed to be between 20 and 30 seemed "to show a disposition to retain those ages on the part of both sexes."[7]

De Bow's report had data for the "Free Colored Population" broken down by state all the way back to the first census, but information data for that group by sex started only with the fourth census, in 1820.[8]

The year 1860 saw the start of another recurring theme: the special importance of counting men between ages 18 and 45. This was vital because they represented America's "fighting men."[9] The concept was explained more clearly in the 1870 report: "It is difficult to conceive of any species of information which can, from a practical point of view, have precedence in a census over the determination of the number of males between 18 and 45 . . . [in order] to ascertain the military strength of the people."[10]

The reports of that census also complained that earlier volumes

> have totally disregarded another fact of the highest value, namely, the number of males in the country above the age of 21 years. If any information in regard to the number of persons, according to age, might be supposed to be of interest to the political philosopher, it is the number of persons of voting age. . . . Twenty years means nothing more than any other period; but eighteen years, the age at which a man enters the militia of his country; twenty-one years, the age at which a man becomes a voter in every state of the union; these periods do mean something, and hold important relations to political science.[11]

The author of that report was the census superintendent Francis Amasa Walker. He was also responsible for the first *Statistical Atlas of the United States,* based on that census. In the introduction he attempted to explain the reasons his charts showed variance by sex, and the result is an interesting look at the differences in how men's and women's lives were perceived. The example he chose was on the number of blind people in the United States.

> We find the lines which stand for the males and females, severally, under 10 years of age, to be not far from equal, the liability of the sexes to blindness from birth being substantially equal, and the perils of the nursery and the play-ground being nearly the same for both, though still somewhat greater in the case of the boy than the girl. Up to 20 years the same proportion holds, but after this period, the liability to acquired blindness becomes greater on the part of the male. Perhaps the man goes into the machine-shop, the furnace, the mine, where his eyes are incessantly exposed to destructive accidents; perhaps he works all day in the direct glare of the sun; perhaps he rides much on the cars, as passenger or as railway employee; perhaps he engages in riots on the street or fights in the saloon, and through one or another of these means, loses his sight.
>
> All the while, the woman is, in a degree, protected by her place, her occupation and her disposition, from accidents involving loss of sight. But after middle life, say at 45 or 50 years of age, the liability of the man begins to diminish relatively, that of the woman to increase. He is less actively employed, less adventurous, less reckless, less quarrelsome. The woman is perhaps no more quarrelsome, reckless, adventurous or actively engaged, but her patient sewing and darning through long years, trying at the best, and often with insufficient or unfavorable light, now begins to tell. Moreover, her greater tenacity of life after 50 years of age until at 70 the number of the two sexes becomes about equal, while after this, the females remain distinctly in excess.[12]

The 1900 Census found, as others had, that there were more men in the country than women. But how accurate were the figures? The bureau worried that men might be undercounted because they were more likely to belong to "the homeless class."[13] They had, however, found a method for testing the calculations.

A recent election in Maryland had resulted in a partial census recount, "in the effort to gather evidence upon which indictments of the enumerators for false and fraudulent returns might be based." This study found that 2.6 percent of males and 2.5 percent of females had been missed on the first try. That happened despite the fact that "a strenuous effort was made, for political reasons, to make the first enumeration absolutely complete. The political henchmen employed as enumerators and their superiors doubtless had fuller information regarding the male population, and especially the potential voters than regarding the females."[14]

The 1900 Census report was also concerned with the unexpectedly large number of people whose ages were given as round numbers. This problem later became known as "age heaping."[15] Men were found to be more likely to "round" their age between 30 and 45, while women were more likely to do so at 25 and over 50. The report theorized that

> errors are made in larger proportion by illiterates than by persons possessing the rudiments of education, and the female sex is more illiterate than the male. Perhaps a larger proportion of women are unwilling to state their age. In such cases either the incorrect answers received or the estimated age entered by the enumerators would be probably a multiple of five. . . .
>
> The only tenable explanation of the excess of females at ages 16 to 25 is that it is an error. . . . [T]he best explanation is that a certain number of women not between 16 and 25 years old report themselves at ages between those limits. The probable reason is that many women prefer to pass as at the age at which marriage is most common.[16]

The 1910 Census reports found a startling difference between the sexes: there were almost 2,700,000 more men than women.[17] That was a greater difference than the last census by more than a million. This gap was especially clear in "the most important class of the native population, namely, the native whites of native parentage."[18] "Native" referred to people born in the United States, not necessarily to Native Americans.

The same report found it "incredible" that the figures showed almost three times as many native-born Chinese males in the country as females. They found an explanation in the report of the immigration commissioner: "He shows that perhaps the most important way which Chinese immigrants have devised for evading the exclusion laws is for the foreigner to enter the country from Canada or Mexico, submit to arrest for violation of the law, and on trial to present Chinese testimony that he was born in the United States and is thus by birthright a citizen to whom the exclusion law has no application."[19]

This census also found slightly more male Blacks than females, but many more female Mulattoes (the term they then used for people of mixed White and Black races) than males. The report speculated as to the reason for this: "It may be that the negro [sic] women with an admixture of white blood are anxious to be returned as mulattoes [sic], while the men are more indifferent in this respect." Alternatively, the report suggested, the enumerators recorded the women they saw accurately but guessed at the category of the men who were not home when the census-takers came by.[20]

The 1910 Census also recognized a significant social change. Persons aged 21 and over "have certain special legal rights with reference to property, the elective franchise, and other matters." In previous censuses "special statistics of this age class were presented only for males. At the present time, however, there are several states in which women have the right to vote in all elections, and a number of other states in which they have the right to vote in certain elections." As a result some statistics about the population of both sexes over the age of 21 was provided, "but much greater detail is given regarding males."[21]

Women in all states had the right to vote by 1919, and starting with the next year's census the questions asked and data published regarding number and age ceased to vary much by sex. The 2010 Census recorded 96.7 men for every 100 females, an increase from 96.3 a decade before.[22]

Statistical Abstract

The population of the individual states appeared in the first edition of the *Statistical Abstract,* published in 1878.[23] Population figures were not broken down by sex until the 1905 volume.[24]

Starting in 1898 the *Statistical Abstract* provided tables on the number of people of school age, voting age, and militia age. The school age figures were broken down by sex; the others counted only males.[25] This pattern continued unchanged through the 1922 edition;[26] 1923 introduced "Age Distribution" by five broad categories, and "Persons, 21 and Over" (i.e., of voting age). Both of these tables were separated by sex.[27]

A table on "Sex Ratio of Males to Females by Age" was available from 1976 through 1999.[28]

CHAPTER FOUR

Marriage, Divorce, and Cohabitation

"Marriage is something that virtually all Americans experience at some time in their lives," the Census Bureau noted in 1978. "Some may postpone marriage, while others enjoy it, endure it, or terminate it; but very few people can or wish to, escape it completely."[1]

Since until recently every legal marriage in the United States consisted of one man and one woman, it is reasonable to ask: Why does a book concerning statistics on women need a chapter on marriage and divorce? If the sexes had always been treated the same in law and in federal statistics, it would not be necessary, but that is not the case.

The first census to ask about marital status was that of 1880, but those figures were never tabulated or published.[2] Nonetheless, the subject was clearly on the minds of those in government because in 1887 Congress authorized Carroll D. Wright, the commissioner of Labor, to collect and publish statistics on marriage and divorce from 1867 through 1886.[3]

When it appeared two years later, the Wright Report, as the thousand-page book became known, shocked the nation. Wright had been remarkably detailed, covering, for example, the marriage guidelines of the major religions and comparative statistics from other countries.

Wright listed the rules for marriage in every state, which often varied by sex. For example, in Kansas a male could marry without parental consent at 15, a girl at 12.[4]

What he could not provide were complete marriage figures, because they were only available from 66 percent of U.S. counties.[5] Divorce data, on the other hand, was close to complete, and that was where the surprises were. Divorces had risen by 157 percent during a 20-year period, while population had grown by less than half that amount.[6] Wright also debunked the belief that states with more permissive divorce laws had more divorces.[7]

Of the 328,716 divorces granted during those 20 years, almost two-thirds were won by wives. The causes for which wives sought divorce more often than husbands were cruelty (more than seven times as frequently), desertion, and drunkenness. Wright noted that "of course, the wife only" can charge "failure to provide," since the wife is not expected to financially support her husband. The one cause for which more men than women won divorces was adultery.[8]

These first figures on divorce caused strong reactions. The *New York Times* commented: "If the elaborate tables of statistics accompanying it do not prove that marriage is a failure, they show at least that the number of cases in which it is not a success is very great, and what is still more alarming, they show that the number is constantly and rapidly increasing."[9]

The next census was the first to publish data on "the conjugal condition of the people of the United States." It noted that 79,000 more men were married than women but offered no explanation for that. It also observed that divorced men were more likely than women to remarry.[10]

The 1900 Census went into the "marital condition" in greater depth. A "Special Report" explained that "every person in the community at a given day, like the day for which a census speaks, is either married or not married. The not-married fall into two classes—those who have never been married, and those who have been married, but whose married life ended before the census day. The latter fall into two classes, according as their married life ended by death of the other party to the marriage or by divorce." There is a fifth category: "The unknown, a small class embracing those for whom the question is unanswered."[11]

The publication goes on to say that some people are incorrect in what they report about their own marital status or that of a household member. There is also the problem of

conscious misrepresentation. A man who reports himself as married admits thereby certain duties and obligations; a woman making a similar statement usually asserts a right rather than admits an obligation. A husband who has abandoned his wife and is living apart from her is tempted to report himself as single, while she is likely to report herself correctly as married, or incorrectly as widowed. . . . The married father of an illegitimate child is almost sure to report himself correctly as single; the mother is tempted to report herself incorrectly as married, widowed, or divorced.

Intentional misrepresentation thus affects returns for the two sexes in opposite directions, leading to an understatement of the true number of married men and an overstatement of the true number of married women.

The variance was masked by the fact that some male immigrants were married to women overseas. The report also noted that there were 21,494 more Black wives listed than husbands, adding "it is not likely that many of these were married to white [sic] men. A large majority were probably returned incorrectly."[12]

The report also suggested, rather dourly, that "the relatively small number of divorced women reported in cities is regarded as indicating little else than the inaccuracy of the returns."[13] The analysis concluded that there were probably more divorced people than was reported, because it is "the only marital condition which entails in most communities some social condemnation. It is likely not to be admitted in many cases where it actually exists."[14] Warnings of this type continued at each census through the 1950s.[15]

Finally, the Special Report observed another limitation on the data: if a man and a woman claimed to be married, the census-takers had no way of checking that information.[16]

The year 1907 saw the creation of a law that had a strange effect on some married couples. The Expatriation Act decreed that any woman who married a foreigner would lose her American citizenship and take on that of her husband. If her husband was later naturalized, she became a U.S. citizen as well.[17] It is difficult to measure how many women were affected since the first three censuses that gathered data on naturalization, starting in 1890, counted only adult males.[18]

In 1922 Congressman John L. Cable sponsored the Married Women's Independent Nationality Act, which severed the citizenship of spouses. Unfortunately, that meant women who had lost their citizenship before the new law passed had to apply for it again, even if their husband became a citizen.[19]

The first *Annual Report of the Commissioner of Naturalization* published after the new law reported that more than 6,000 women were granted certificates of naturalization that fiscal year and it was believed that most of them were married. The commissioner also noted that "among the human side lights" of this was "the aversion which women in this situation feel to the necessity of going through the customary 'naturalization' process" like "any lowly immigrant."[20]

In 1909 the Census Bureau published a follow-up to the Wright Report, and a second edition five years later. It discovered more cause for concern about marriage dissolution: "Apparently, the divorce rate, like the velocity of a falling body, is constantly increasing."[21]

It found that the main causes for divorces granted to women between 1887 and 1906 were abandonment or desertion (almost 250,000); cruelty (almost 210,000); adultery (73,000); neglect to provide (almost 73,000); and habitual drunkenness, intemperance, or intoxication (almost 50,000). The main causes for divorces granted to men were abandonment or desertion (167,000), adultery (100,000), and cruelty (34,000). "Sexual immorality" was a ground for divorce in almost one-third of those granted to husbands.[22] Two-thirds of all divorces were granted to women.

In no state was it possible to have a mutual divorce: someone had to be at fault. The report noted that "it is not at all unusual for alimony to be granted to the wife, although the husband is the person who sues for and obtains the divorce. It is, however, exceedingly unusual for the husband to obtain alimony from the wife, as the wife is under no legal obligation to support the husband." Alimony was asked for in 125,000 cases and granted in almost 70 percent.[23] Still assuming that women did not work, the report listed the occupations of husbands in divorce cases, but not wives.[24]

In 1910 a special census was conducted of the "Indian Population." Among the questions asked of the Native Americans was "whether now living in polygamy. If the Indian man is living with more than one wife, write 'Yes' in this column. . . . If living in polygamy, whether the wives are sisters."[25]

The standard 1910 Census was the first to refer to "those consensually married," essentially what is often called common-law marriage.[26] The next few censuses took similar approaches to the issues of marriage and divorce.

The 1950 Census report *Duration of Current Marital Status* covered only women. The original plan was to publish data for both sexes, but budget problems intervened.[27] The 1970 Census was the first to ask how the respondent's first marriage ended.[28]

About this time the Census Bureau began publishing a series of Current Population Reports related to this subject. It was common for the data on marriage and divorce to be much more detailed about women than men, with no explanation for this choice. For example, *Marriage, Divorce, Widowhood, and Remarriage by Family Characteristics, June 1975*, includes this data only for females:

- With children whose first marriage ended in divorce, by various characteristics.
- Children born before divorce, number of years divorced, and whether remarried.

- Those first marriage ended in divorce by age of youngest child at divorce, children born before divorce and whether remarried.

The same report also noted that women with five or more years of college were much more likely to be divorced than men with similar education.[29]

In 1973 the Centers for Disease Control started the National Survey of Family Growth (NSFG). Originally conducted every five years, the NSFG is now continuous. Its original focus was on fertility and family planning, but from the beginning it also tracked, for example, ever-married women.[30] In 2002 it began to survey men as well.[31] Among the relevant topics currently listed in the survey are cohabitation with opposite sex, divorce and marital disruption, marriage, remarriage, and sexual identity and attraction.[32]

In 1989 the National Center for Health Statistics published a report on *Remarriages and Subsequent Divorces*. It found that divorced men were more likely to remarry than divorced women at all ages above 25.[33]

A year later the Census Bureau published a report on remarriage, covering only women. It noted that almost half the marriages taking place in 1987 were remarriages for at least one partner.[34]

The 1990 Census showed government statisticians struggling, not for the first time, to keep up with shifts in society. They added the category of "unmarried partner." More surprisingly, if someone reported being the spouse of someone of the same sex, "the *relationship* category remained the same, but the *sex* of the partner was changed." Starting with the next census that same-sex person was reported as the right sex, but listed as an unmarried partner.[35]

A National Center for Health Statistics report on *Cohabitation, Marriage, Divorce, and Remarriage* noted that some sources of marriage data were changing or disappearing. For example, the Vital Statistics program stopped collecting marriage and divorce registration data in 1995. The Current Population Survey stopped publishing a supplement on marital history in the same year.[36]

As a response to the "diminished quality of vital statistics data on marriage and divorce," in 2008 the Census Bureau's American Community Survey began to ask questions about "marital events."[37] In previous years the ACS had asked if the subject were married and so on, but starting in 2008 it also asked if the status changed during the last year.[38]

In 2010 the National Center for Health Statistics used data from the NSFG to publish a report on "First Premarital Cohabitation." While the NSFG was by then including in-person interviews with members of both sexes, this publication was only about women. It found that almost half the females interviewed in the previous five years had "cohabitated with a partner as a first union, compared to 34% of women in 1995."[39] The average length of the first cohabitation had increased from 13 months in 1995 to 22 months in the 2006–2010 period.[40] Forty percent of women's first premarital cohabitations transitioned to marriage within three years. One-third remained intact; the rest dissolved.[41] The report also noted that cohabitation had "become a more frequent site for childbearing."[42]

The year 2011 saw the Census Bureau's first report on same-sex couple households, which made up 1 percent of all couple households. Approximately 20 percent of them had children in the home. As before, people who claimed to be spouses were reported as unmarried partners. No figures were given as to male versus female households.[43]

In 2015 the Census Bureau published a working paper that attempted to solve the confusion over same-sex couples. The example the authors offered was: "What is going on in cases where a couple is recorded as a same-sex married couple on the relationship item, but one person's sex is marked as male and the other's as female?"[44] They concluded that in most cases where the sexes reported disagreed with the relationship listed (same-sex married or unmarried, opposite-sex married or unmarried), the sexes were given correctly and the relationship was marked wrongly.[45]

The Census Bureau website now has a page about same-sex couples, offering data from the American Community Survey, the Current Population Survey, the Survey of Income and Program Participation, the Decennial Census, and the American Housing Survey.[46]

The American Community Survey provides a historic table with estimates on same-sex households back to 2005. Unfortunately, a change in estimation techniques made in 2008 to make the figures more compatible with the upcoming census resulted in a drastic drop in the numbers.[47] Therefore, for example, the estimated number of female–female spousal couples fell from 177,937 in 2005 to 80,301 in 2008 and as of 2014 has only risen to 171,590.[48]

In 2016 the Office of Tax Analysis published a working paper that attempted to calculate the number of same-sex marriages in the United States, by examining the number of such pairs filing taxes jointly. The result was an estimate of about 183,355 couples.[49] The paper also found that female–female couples averaged an adjusted gross income of $124,000, compared to $176,000 for male–male, and $113,000 for different-sex couples.[50]

Statistical Abstract

Marriage first appeared in the 1907 edition of *Statistical Abstract,* and only in the context of women breadwinners. In 1900 more than half of divorced women were breadwinners. Only 5.6 percent of married women were.[51] No similar table was given for adult male breadwinners.

"Marriage and Divorce" gained its own section of the book the next year, reporting that women were granted about two-thirds of all divorces. The book also listed the causes for divorce. Remarkably, three men were granted divorces between 1892 and 1906 for "neglect to provide."[52]

In 1912 the *Statistical Abstract* began to present the "Marital Conditions of Persons 15 Years of Age and Over," by state, and whether White or Colored.[53]

The 1953 edition was the first to offer the age of brides and grooms at first marriage and remarriage, but only for a few states. In 1950 no males under the age of 15 married but 254 females did, and one of that age remarried. The median age for new brides was 21.6 and for grooms 23.9.[54]

Two years later the *Abstract* added a table on the marital status of women (but not men) in the civilian labor force. In the most recent year, roughly 56 percent of female workers were married. A second table broke those figures down by age.[55]

In 1979 the *Statistical Abstract* introduced a table on "Interracial Married Couples." It reported that between 1970 and 1975 the number of "husband Black, wife White" couples rose by 131.7 percent, while the number of "wife Black, husband White" pairs rose by 25 percent. People of other races were listed only if they had a Black or White partner.[56]

The year 1977 saw the introduction of statistics about "sharing [a household] with person of the opposite sex."[57] Tables on "Cohabitation" began appearing in 1992 but typically gave figures only for women. The book defined cohabitation as "not married but living with a partner or boyfriend," and while "partner" is ambiguous, the assumption would be that there were an equal number of male and female cohabiters.[58] "Unmarried-Partner Household" arrived in 2001, but at first only for statistics from Puerto Rico.[59] A year later the term was used in data for the entire country, including counts for female–female and male–male couples.[60]

The year 2012, the last year of the federally published *Statistical Abstract*, saw the introduction of a table on "Sexual Identity." Males and females were identified as "heterosexual or straight, homosexual or gay, bisexual, something else," or "did not report."[61]

CHAPTER FIVE

Motherhood

In 1982 a Census Bureau publication noted that the "traditional family" of the 19th century was assumed to be "an extended family with several generations living and working together in rural America." On the other hand, the 1950s' traditional family was "pictured as a husband-wife family where the husband was usually the family wage earner and the wife characteristically stayed home and cared for the children." Finally, it concluded that "future generations may someday describe the 'traditional' family of the 1980s as one where both the husband and wife are employed and their young children are cared for by a nonfamily member while the mother and father are at work."[1]

The Census Bureau has been tracking the reality of American families for 150 years. The information it has produced has helped shape our views of what is "traditional" and "normal" in the home, and much of that has revolved around views of motherhood.

The book containing mortality statistics of the 1860 Census, solemnly described as the "Final Exhibit," also appears to provide the first federal statistical data related to motherhood. Specifically, it reported that childbirth killed 3,117 women in 1850 and 4,066 women in 1860. In each case that was around 2.5 percent of female deaths.[2]

Information related to living mothers first appeared in 1890. Specifically, all women who were or had ever been married were asked how many children they had had and how many were still living. Unfortunately, this data was neither tabulated nor published.[3] The question remained essentially unchanged for three more censuses, although in those cases the results did appear in the reports. The 1890 Census also asked about the "element of foreign parentage among the white population," recording the nationality of mothers and fathers born in other lands.[4]

The 1940 Census increased coverage dramatically with five reports on *Differential Fertility, 1940 and 1910*. The volume on *Women by Number of Children under Five* included data on the education and employment status of mothers but gave occupations only for the husbands. *Women by Number of Children Ever Born* provided more details but still did not list occupations for the mothers.[5]

The final volume of the quintet is *Fertility by Duration of Marriage*. This book contained statistics on "native white [sic] and Negro women by number of children ever born and duration of marriage in relation to social and economic characteristics."[6] "Native" here means people born in this country, not the modern sense of Native Americans.

"Duration of marriage" in this case did not refer to how long *all* marriages last. The report was interested only in "unbroken marriages," which it defined as those of women who "were married only once and whose husbands were reported as members of the household."[7]

According to the *Fertility* report of the 1950 Census, each census-taker was "instructed not to inquire about adopted children or stepchildren; but he was told that, if the question was raised he was not to count children who were not born to the women."[8] Only "natural children" (not adopted or stepchildren) were to be included.[9]

The same report noted what it saw as an emerging trend, working mothers: "If a woman has a baby she is likely to give up a job or not to look for a job, as the case may be. In the last decade or so, however, a life pattern seems to be developing among many married women in which they work until the arrival of the first baby, temporarily withdraw from the labor force while their children are young, and then return to the labor force after their children are old enough to require little care."[10]

By 1960 the term "own child" had been amended to include adopted and stepchildren.[11] The same report finally gave both the employment status and major occupation fields of mothers.[12]

After that point the interesting data about mothers moved away from the decennial census to other government products. Many of those were Current Population Reports (CPR), also from the Census Bureau. Table 5.1 shows the date of some of the first CPRs on certain subjects.

Moving away from the Bureau, it appears that the earliest federal statistical publication with a reference to motherhood in the title was *Maternal Mortality from all Conditions Connected with Childbirth in the United States and Certain Other Countries*, written by Grace L. Meets and published by the Children's Bureau in 1917. Meets reported that figures showed approximately 15,000 women died in the United States in 1913 from conditions

Table 5.1 The first appearances of certain subjects in U.S. Census Bureau's *Current Population Reports* and *Statistical Briefs*.

1946	Differential fertility
1950	Estimated net reproduction rates for the White population, by counties
1961	Marriage, fertility, and childspacing
1969	Women by number of own children under five years old
1971	Fertility variations by ethnic origin
1973	Birth expectations and fertility
1976	Premarital fertility
1978	Nursery school and kindergarten enrollment of children and labor force status of their mothers
1979	Divorce, child custody, and child support
1982	Trends in child care arrangements of working mothers
1989	Single parents and their children
1989	Stepchildren and their families
1990	Time off for babies: maternity leave arrangements
1990	Work and family patterns of American women
1995	Child support for custodial mothers and fathers (first to include fathers)
1995	Mothers who receive food stamps—fertility and socioeconomic characteristics

Source: U.S. Commerce Department, Economics and Statistics Administration, Census Bureau, *Subject Index to Current Population Reports,* 5, 6, 16. In some cases the publication dates were ascertained through *Worldcat.*

related to childbirth, but "physicians and statisticians agree that these figures are a great underestimate."[13]

In 1933 the same agency published a book titled *Mothers' Aid.* That was the current term for laws that provided "aid to families having young children that have become dependent through the loss or disability of the breadwinner and that may be expected to be dependent for a relatively long time, usually during the period when the children are too young to work." Most states that provided aid required that "the mother shall be a proper person to have the care of her children."[14] During 1921–1922 there were 45,825 families receiving aid in the United States. In 1931, during the Great Depression, that number rose to 93,620.[15]

In 1974 the Bureau of Labor Statistics' research journal, the *Monthly Labor Review,* dedicated an issue to "Women in the Workplace." One article observed that while the number of children in families had dropped by one and a half million since 1970, the number with working mothers had risen by more than a half million. The authors blamed this, in part, on the increase in "broken families," that is, divorcing parents.[16]

During the same year, the National Center for Health Statistics (NCHS) published a report on *Wanted and Unwanted Births*. "Wantedness" was measured strictly by "the woman's responses to questions about *her* feelings and not those of her husband." The authors concluded that one-fifths of all births "would not have occurred if these women had given birth only to those babies they reported as 'wanted' at the time of conception." However, they warned, it was wrong "to conclude that 'unwanted births' are the same as 'unwanted children,' for many unplanned or undesired pregnancies result in children who are cherished."[17]

In 1979 the NCHS published *Trends in Breast Feeding among American Mothers*. This first federal publication on the topic concluded that breast-feeding had fallen off "precipitously" in the last few decades. Less than 10 percent of the mothers whose first child was born between 1966 and 1973 had nursed their baby for three months or more.[18]

Five years later the same agency provided data on midwife use and out-of-hospital births. The report offered three reasons for nonhospital deliveries: (1) economic or geographic difficulties, (2) "desire for a more natural, family-centered birth experience and the opportunity for immediate bonding between baby and mother," and (3) accident.[19]

In 1987 the Centers for Disease Control and Prevention, in cooperation with state health agencies, created the Pregnancy Risk Assessment Monitoring Program (PRAMS), which gathers data about women's attitudes and experiences in the period around pregnancy. The data does not cover all states but reaches about 83 percent of births. Some of the main subjects PRAMS covers include feelings about the most recent pregnancy, types of prenatal care, alcohol and tobacco use, physical abuse, and contraceptive use.[20]

The year 1995 saw the NCHS using its National Survey of Family Growth to reveal information about how the health and behavior of pregnant women affected the likelihood of their babies to be born alive and at what birth rate. There were tables on when prenatal care began, where prenatal care was received (a private doctor, a hospital, etc.), whether women had smoked or drank during pregnancy, and how their deliveries were paid for.[21]

A year later the U.S. Education Department was surveying families as well. The National Household Education Survey studied the likelihood of mothers, fathers, and stepparents to participate in their children's schooling. For example, biological mothers living with stepfathers were "less likely to be highly involved in their children's schools than biological mothers in two-biological-parent families." However, biological fathers in stepmother families were "more likely to be highly involved in their children's schools than biological fathers in two-biological parent families."[22]

The Maternal and Child Health Bureau took its present form in the late eighties. It "develops, administers, directs, coordinates, monitors, and supports federal policy and programs pertaining to health care facilities, [and] health care promotion of mothers and children," among other duties.[23] In 2000 this bureau published a book entitled *A Snapshot of Mother and Child Health*. Among its many findings were that in 1998 61 percent of mothers with preschool-aged children were employed, and 70 percent of them were working full-time.[24]

In 2003 the Bureau of Labor Statistics published a working paper examining the possible correlation between mothers working during the first three years of their child's life and that child's tendency as an adolescent to "engage in a range of risky behaviors: smoking cigarettes, drinking alcohol, using marijuana and other drugs, engaging in sex and committing crimes." They found "little evidence" that it was true. As for adolescents with working mothers, they found a possible correlation with alcohol use.[25]

The NCHS began publishing its *Data Brief* series in 2007. While it published reports on births and contraception, the first brief specifically about mothers came in 2016. It revealed that the mean age of mothers at first birth had risen from 24.9 years in 2000 to 26.3 in 2014.[26]

Statistical Abstract

Mothers made their first appearance in *Statistical Abstract* in 1940. Unfortunately, it is not a very dramatic entrance: a table giving the number of births and deaths in various cities simply mentions that it is listing the place of delivery, not the regular residence of the mothers.[27]

The 1943 edition added a table about the "Number of Children Ever Born per 1,000 Women 15 to 74 Years Old, by Age and Color of Woman, Urban and Rural: 1940." The data was limited to women who had ever been married.[28]

The year 1954 saw the addition of data on old-age and survivors insurance. Recipients included widowed mothers.[29] There was also a table on birth rates, adjusted for underrepresentation by the race and age of the mother.[30]

Three years later a table on civilian employees of the federal government who had received veterans preference in hiring included "wives, widows, and mothers of veterans."[31]

In 1958 the table on "Number of Children Born per 1,000 Women" mentioned, for the first time, whether the mothers were in the labor force. As in previous years, it also mentioned the occupation group the husband belonged to.[32]

The year 1960 saw the first data concerning working mothers. It was limited to women with children under 12 years who worked 35 hours or more "for pay or profit or without pay on a family farm or business." It reported on the marital status: husband present, husband absent, and widowed or divorced. Single mothers were not considered.[33]

The same year that the U.S. Supreme Court decided *Roe v. Wade,* the *Statistical Abstract* for 1973 took up an interest in "unwanted fertility," unwanted and unplanned births, and "theoretical births per woman without unwanted births."[34]

The 1970s also saw coverage of preprimary school enrollment, but it wasn't until 1978 that data began to appear on the labor status of those children's mothers.[35]

The 1980 volume included several new tables about the family. This included data on female (but not male) householders by presence of children, and currently divorced, separated, remarried, or never-married women, by the amount of child support payments they were receiving.[36] A new table on children living with only one parent covered both mothers and fathers.[37]

In 1986 tables appeared on breast-feeding (by race, education, and region) and cesarean deliveries (by the mother's age). There is also detailed economic information on the families of women who had given birth in the last year.[38]

The year 1995 added tables on live births and low birthweight of children whose mothers smoked or drank during pregnancy.[39] A year later statistics appeared on births to teenage mothers.[40]

The last federally published edition of the *Statistical Abstract,* in 2012, featured several new tables. These included women who had a child in the last year by living arrangement, educational attainment, citizenship, and poverty status.[41]

CHAPTER SIX

Single Mothers

USA.gov is the official search engine of the federal government and an excellent place to find websites and publications of national, state, and local agencies. If one searches there for "illegitimate births," the first record retrieved is the National Center for Health Statistics' page on "Unmarried Childbearing." The word "illegitimate" does not appear there.[1]

Vocabulary changes dramatically over time on social issues, and this subject is a prime example.

The government began asking women how many children they had borne in the 1890 Census. The question has been asked each decade since, except in 1920 and 1930. However, for many decades it was only asked of married women.[2]

As part of that same 1890 Census, Frederick H. Wines wrote the *Report on Crime, Pauperism, and Benevolence*. It did not include tables on single mothers but had data on illegitimate children in various types of institutions.[3]

In 1926 the Labor Department's Children's Bureau issued a report on *Children of Illegitimate Birth*. Its work concluded that "a study of the histories of these children who have been deprived of their birthright indicates the mental suffering that may be more important to consider than any actual 'stigma' that might pertain to illegitimate birth."[4] In other words, the pain of being fatherless might cause more damage than people looking down on one for being illegitimate.

Two years later the same agency did a study of single women who kept their babies. It found that institutions for such women fell into two categories, based on their motives: "The spiritual reclamation of women who were immoral or the protection of women who sought to conceal their maternity." The former hoped that the mother would keep her offspring so that "the child may be a factor in holding the mother to the path of rectitude." The latter types were often for-profit businesses and expected to remove the child once it was born.[5]

The publications of the 1940 Census included four volumes on *Differential Fertility*, comparing the current data with that of 1910. One of these books, *Women by Number of Children Ever Born*, tracked the women by White or Negro, ever married, duration of marriage, and so on. Single women were not asked if they had any children. However, the report noted that in the case of unmarried births "there is a tendency to report such births as legitimate."[6]

This assumption continued through the 1960 Census, where it received its most complete explanation:

> Although the question of children ever born was asked only of women reported as having been married, the number of children reported undoubtedly includes some illegitimate births. It is likely that many of the unwed mothers living with an illegitimate child reported themselves as having been married and therefore were among the women who were expected to report the number of children ever born, and that many of the mothers who married after the birth of an illegitimate child counted that child (as they were expected to do). On the other hand, the data are, no doubt, less complete for illegitimate than for legitimate births. Consequently, the rates of children ever born per 1,000 total women may be too low.[7]

In 1970 the census questionnaire did not specify married women only, but the census-taker "was instructed to limit question 25 (children ever born) to mothers who were or had been married unless a son or daughter had been listed."[8]

Single mothers appeared in one volume of the 1970 Census reports: *Childspacing and Current Fertility:* "In this present report, all children ever born to single women are counted as well as those ever born to women ever married." On the other hand, a separate volume had "single women being treated as childless for the purpose of computing rates of children ever born to women of all marital classes combined."[9]

In 1973 the staff of Congress's Joint Economic Committee issued a briefing paper entitled *The Family, Poverty, and Welfare Programs: Factors Influencing Family Instability*. Such staff papers are intended to inform the members of Congress and do not represent official opinions of the committee.

One of the essays was by Phillips Cutright who noted that

> for both whites [sic] and nonwhites illegitimacy rates were relatively stable from 1920 through 1940. After 1940 the white [sic] illegitimacy rate gradually increased and reached a high in 1968—the last year for which national data are available. The nonwhite rate rose from 1940 through 1965, but declined between 1965 and 1968.
>
> Illegitimacy rates are determined by the degree to which a population of unmarried women in the childbearing years is subject to involuntary controls over conception and gestation, as well as by the amount of sexual activity, and use of effective contraception and induced abortion. The rise in U.S. illegitimacy rates after 1940 was not caused by decline in the use of effective contraception.[10]

Cutright found no parallel between Aid to Families with Dependent Children rates and illegitimacy, casting doubt on the idea that easy access to welfare programs encouraged single motherhood. "Economic theories of fertility may not apply to illegitimacy," he explained, "because those theories assume rational deliberate calculation by parents and access to perfect means of fertility control."[11]

In another report in the same book, Harry D. Krause lamented: "Welfare is our domestic Vietnam. Increased expenditures have brought diminishing returns. . . . The left wants double, the right wants half, and the result is deplorable. . . . The 10 years from 1961 to 1970 saw enough new illegitimate children to populate a city the size of Los Angeles."[12]

The following year the National Center for Health Statistics published *Trends in Illegitimacy United States 1940–1965*. It proposed two reasons for the increase in illegitimate births: abortion was decreasing and more teenage girls were having "premarital intercourse."[13]

In 1976 the Census Bureau published a Special Study on "premarital fertility." It reported on "the fertility of single women and of women who married while pregnant" and included data on women who gave birth "soon enough after marriage to imply a premarital conception."[14] However, it warned: "The true incidence of births before marriage is likely to be even higher because of misreporting of some dates or events. . . . [S]ome persons may have reported the approximate date when a consensual [i.e. common-law] marriage or an informal arrangement began."[15]

The year 1980 brought the first census in which all women who had never been married were asked how many children they had borne.[16]

A year later the National Center for Health Statistics issued *Trends in Teenage Childbearing: United States 1970–1981*. It reported that childbearing rates for unmarried teenagers had increased throughout the 1970s and by the end of the decade the trend was growing for all ages.[17]

The de-stigmatization of single motherhood had another effect. The Census Bureau noted in 1992 that premarital conceptions were becoming less likely to lead to a pre-birth marriage. The bureau speculated that "the increasing social acceptance of never-married mothers and the desire to avoid an unstable marriage may be involved in the decline of women marrying before the birth of their first child."[18]

The Violent Crime Control and Law Enforcement Act of 1994 required the Health and Human Services Department to prepare a report on the increase of "out-of-wedlock births." The result was almost 300 pages of statistics and expert opinions.[19] In the Executive Summary Kristin A. Moore noted:

> When they hear the phrase "unmarried parent," many Americans picture a teenage girl having a first child. However, there is no typical nonmarital birth. Nonmarital births can be first births, second births, or higher-order births. Nonmarital births can precede a first marriage; they can occur to a parent who is not married and who never marries; they can occur within a cohabiting relationship; or they can occur to a parent whose marriage has terminated. A woman with several children may have had one or more births within marriage and one or more births outside of marriage. It is important to note that more than 70 percent of single parent families have only one or two children.[20]

By 1998 the trend to premarital childbearing was visible among older women. The Census Bureau reported that more than half of first births to women under the age of 30 were "either born out-of-wedlock or conceived before the women's first marriage. About 60 years ago, only one of 6 births was born or conceived before marriage."[21]

In 2004 a Green Book (briefing material, not the official opinion of the committee), prepared for the House Ways and Means Committee contained an appendix on "Data on Nonmarital Births." This seems to contain the last use of the term "illegitimate birth" in federal publications, other than congressional speeches or testimony.[22]

In 2013 the Census Bureau's blog, *Random Samplings*, included an article that discussed newly released information on births to unmarried women. "As of 2011, 62 percent of women age 20 to 24 who gave birth in the previous 12 months were unmarried. This compares with 17 percent among women age 35 to 39." The report also showed that women who had graduated high school were much more likely to have an unmarried birth than women with bachelor degrees.[23]

Statistical Abstract

The 1935 edition of the *Statistical Abstract* was the first to mention "illegitimate children" but only in the context of children in institutional care.[24]

The year 1957 introduced a table on "Illegitimate Live Births by Age of Mother."[25] This data went away after 1991.[26]

"Homes for Unwed Mothers" first appeared in 1968, reporting that 2,000 females had dwelled in them in 1950 and 3,000 in 1960. Perplexingly, each of those years also found 1,000 males living in those homes.[27] Could they all have been newborn baby boys? In any case, the subject was no longer covered after 1991.[28]

"Births to Unmarried Women" first appeared in the 1977 edition. The footnotes warned that there were "no estimates included for misstatements on birth records or failures to record births." The same year introduced "Children Ever Born to Single Women, by Age of Woman."[29] In 1990 the notes for that table explained that, in the case of states that did not report on the parents' marital status, it was "inferred from a comparison of the child's and parents' surnames on the birth certificate."[30] Therefore, if a woman marrying in those states kept her original name, she would be recorded as a single mother.

The 100th edition of the *Statistical Abstract* (1979) was the first to abandon the use of the word "illegitimate."[31]

The 1996 volume saw the addition of "percent births to unmarried mothers."[32]

PART III

Women at Home

CHAPTER SEVEN

Heads of Household, Heads of Family

In late 2009 an unsigned editorial in *Between the Lines*, a weekly newspaper aimed at Michigan's lesbian, gay, bisexual, and transgender community, urged readers to fill out their census forms in the coming spring. The authors pointed out that, while there was no question on the form about sexual orientation, "we can show our relationships, and for the first time in the history of the U.S. census, we can show our marriages." Since the census asks for the truth "as we know it," the authors said, "If you consider yourself to be married, mark married. If not, don't. Simple as that."

The authors then offered advice for those in biracial relationships: "Make sure that the white [*sic*] member of the relationship is not written in as the head of household. Otherwise the entire household will be marked as white [*sic*]."[1]

This last assertion was not true; by that point the census had no trouble listing multiple-race households.[2] More to the point, the phrase "head of household" hadn't been used in the decennial census in 40 years, although it can still be found in some other government publications. The main reason this phrase became controversial was that in the view of the Census Bureau a woman could be the head only if no adult man was present.

In the first five decennial censuses the "head of family" was the only person whose name was recorded. The other members were merely counted. Starting in 1850 all members of the household were listed, but no head was designated.[3]

The 1880 Census was the first to list each person's relationship to the head of the household.[4] The next census provided a breakdown of how many families were headed by women.[5]

In 1900 a census study looked for the first time at women breadwinners in relation to the heads of their families in 27 cities:

Table 7.1   Women breadwinners and their relation to family heads, 1900.

Boarders (including living with employer)	35.2 percent
Themselves heads of families	11.9 percent
Living with father	26.3 percent
Living with mother	12.2 percent
Living with other relative (including husband)	14.5 percent[6]

Source: U.S. Commerce and Labor Department, Census Bureau, *Statistics of Women at Work,* 25.

"Living with mother" meant that the mother was not living with her husband, since if she were, he would automatically be counted as the head of that family. The Census Bureau noted that some married women were living with a parent rather than with their husband and observed: "To what extent this separation implies wife desertion or marital infidelity can not of course be determined from the census returns, as the occupation of the husband may have necessitated separation from his family."[7]

The 1930 Census *Abstract* included a table of families classified by the age of their head but stated, with no further explanation, that it "is limited to those with a man as head."[8] The same volume separated male-headed households into "married, wife present" and "other marital status," but there is no such division with families with a female head, since she would not have that title if her husband were present.[9]

The 1940 Census was the first to use the term "private household" to describe "the related family members and the unrelated lodgers and servants or hired hands who live in the same dwelling unit and share common housekeeping arrangements." The head of a private household was "usually a married man and the chief breadwinner of the family. In some cases, however, the head is a parent of the chief earner or is the only adult member of the household." In other words, a woman could not be the head if an adult male were present. The same publication also noted that more women were listed as "married women" than as "wives" because the term "wife" was applied only to the spouse of the head of the household.[10]

The instructions to enumerators (census-takers) for the 1950 Census were clear on this subject: "The head is the person so reported to the enumerator, with the exception that married women are not classified as heads if their husbands are living with them at the time of the census. In the small proportion of the cases where the wife is reported to the enumerator as the head, the husband is almost always an invalid; in order to avoid establishing a separate category for the small number of families with the wife reported as the head, such families are edited to show the husband as the head."[11] There was also a table listing major occupations, but only for the head of the household, so working wives (or daughters) were overlooked.[12]

The questions and definitions did not change significantly through the 1970 Census, but the winds of change were picking up. During the early years of that decade, the Census Bureau conducted several surveys asking a total of 940 married couples whom they considered to be the head of their household; 49 percent said the male. About one-third said they were joint heads, and most of the rest said the female. Interestingly, only 40 percent of the couples married to each other agreed that the man was the head.[13]

In 1974 the Census Bureau published its first report exclusively on "female family heads." It began by stating that the number of women who head their own families rose by 50 percent between 1955 and 1973, increasing from 4.2 million to 6.6 million, with almost half of that gain taking place in the last four years. The report noted "growing concern among social scientists and government planners" about the possible "general breakdown of family living arrangements in the United States."[14]

In 1976 a small group of feminists, many of them demographers, formed the Social Scientists in Population Research. Their goal, according to one of their members, Harriet B. Presser, was to "decapitate" the census, by removing all references to heads from their surveys and reports.[15] At a meeting with this group, Paul Glick, the senior demographer of the Census Bureau, was asked to explain the term "head of household." According to Presser, he replied: "It means who is top dog."[16]

Later that year Arthur Norton, the chief of the Marriage and Family Statistics Branch of the Census Bureau, spoke to a committee of the American Economic Association. According to meeting notes, he said:

> The Bureau faces a dilemma. It seems the Bureau is in the position of fostering a continuation of attitudes that imply superior/subordinate relationships within households by using the "head" concept. The Bureau does not want to be in that position. While it realizes that the roles of members in modern families are changing, it also is concerned as a data producer, with maintaining the ability to offer a data set that is responsive to a wide

variety of user needs. . . . For example, the Social Security Administration (SSA) and the Veterans Administration are extremely interested in how elderly people are living—e.g. "are they living in a dependency status, heading their own households, or living with someone else?" . . . The Department of Housing and Urban Development (HUD) insists that the Census Bureau remove the sexist connotations of its "relationship item" but retain the "head" concept because it is an important concept for many of its programs.[17]

While Norton was correct that some government agencies seemed committed to the phrase, there were many reasons why economists such as Barbara Bergmann called it "ambiguous, subjective, and invidious."[18] Presser pointed out that "if a grandmother and mother and child were living in a three-person household, and the grandmother were to report herself as the head, we have no idea what that means relative to a similar three-person household in which the mother reports herself as head."[19]

At a 1978 conference on *Issues in Federal Statistical Needs Relating to Women,* sponsored by the Census Bureau, Nancy Smith Barrett of the Urban Institute argued that

> the psychological aspects should not be ignored. For many people, the fact that the Federal Government categorizes husbands as household heads in official surveys contributes to a belief in male dominance and demeans wives. However, the problems posed for analytical use of the CPS [Current Population Survey] are also important. Many of the published data include information only on the head. For instance, much of the data provided in the *Current Population Reports,* Series P-60, provide income breakdowns by age, race, educational level and work experience of the head only. Since wives are excluded from headship by definition, this means that information on the characteristics of wives by family income category is unavailable, regardless of whether the wife's earnings are the principal or sole source of the family's income.[20]

In 1977 Janet L. Norwood, then the deputy commissioner of the Bureau of Labor Statistics (BLS), published an article in her agency's *Monthly Labor Review,* pointing out that the BLS also said married women could not be classified as heads if their husbands lived with them. In 1975, she noted, 11 percent of wives working outside the home earned more than their husbands. Also, many siblings or other relatives live together; how does one determine who is the head in such a household?[21]

By the following year the Census Bureau had resolved its dilemma: the problematic term would be replaced with "householder," a person of either sex, who would serve as the reference person for the others in the household (e.g., husband of the householder, daughter of the householder).[22] One bureau writer said that the agency was recognizing that "many households and families are no longer organized according to autocratic principles."[23]

In 1983 the BLS announced that the phrase "female-headed families" was also disappearing. The new terms were "women maintaining families" or "female family householder," defined as "a never-married, divorced, widowed, or separated woman with no husband present and who is responsible for her family."[24]

"Head of household" has mostly vanished from the vocabulary of the Census Bureau and the BLS, but vestigial traces still appear in other government publications. For example, the Bureau of Justice Statistics published a comprehensive study in 2003 entitled *Criminal Victimization in the United States*. The data arranged by sex included "relationship to head of household."[25]

The Federal Reserve Board, which governs the nation's Federal Reserve banks, manages the Survey of Consumer Finances (SCF), which is usually conducted every three years. The SCF uses the term "Primary Economic Unit" (PEU) to mean "the economically dominant single person or couple" and those in the household who are financially interdependent with them. A 2014 article in the *Federal Reserve Bulletin* explained that the SCF "also designates a head of the PEU, not to convey a judgment about how an individual family is structured but as a means of organizing the data consistently. If a couple is economically dominant in the PEU, the head is the male in a mixed-sex couple or the older person in a same-sex couple. If a single person is economically dominant, that person is designated as the family head in this report."[26] That article was published a few months after Janet L. Yellen became the first woman to head the Board of Governors of the Federal Reserve System. As of 2016, the term is still in use.[27]

One more government institution where "head of household" still appears is the tax form, but the Internal Revenue Service uses the term for any unmarried person who meets certain filing qualifications.[28]

Statistical Abstract

The term "family head" first appeared in the 1944–1945 edition of the *Statistical Abstract,* in which a "private family" is defined as consisting of "a family head and all other persons in the house who are related to the head by blood, marriage, or adoption, and who live together and share common housekeeping arrangements."[29] "Family head" showed up eight times in the last volume of the series (2012), usually in information taken from the SCF.[30]

"Head of Household" arrived, without definition, in the 1947 *Statistical Abstract,* in a table about "Migration Status of the Population." This was mainly concerned with movement between the states, not international immigration.[31] The term continued to make occasional appearances, still undefined, usually in relation to family wages.[32]

The 1980 edition replaced both "head of household" and "head of family" with "householder." It explained that "this policy contrasts with the Bureau's longtime practice of always classifying the husband as the head in married-couple families."[33] It included a table on "Female Family Householders, by Race and Presence of Children" and another on characteristics (e.g., presence of children and marital status) by race.[34] Male household heads did not get a table of their own until 2003.[35]

CHAPTER EIGHT

Housewives, Homemakers, and Housekeepers

In 1948 the Women's Bureau of the U.S. Labor Department held a conference timed to commemorate the centennial of the first women's rights meeting, the Seneca Falls Convention. In order to emphasize the importance of the event, the president of the United States made the opening address.

After being introduced by the bureau director Frieda S. Miller, Harry Truman said: "When Miss Miller opened her remarks she started off by saying that you represented workers, homemakers, citizens. I want to reverse that order. I want to say 'homemakers, workers, citizens,' for if it were not for the homemakers we would have neither the citizens nor the workers."[1]

"Homemaker" and its sister term "housewife" have always been problematic in government publications, especially statistics. Neither one seems to have been clearly defined by federal agencies, but context suggests that a housewife is a woman who takes care of her family's home without pay, while a homemaker is a person (usually female) who does the same but may also have other work for which she is paid. In 1961, for example, the U.S. Education Office published a book entitled *Management Problems of Homemakers Employed outside the Home.*[2]

One long-debated issue has been the fact that most economists do not consider people who take care of their own family's home and have no paid employment to be working. As Nancy Folbre and Marjorie Abel noted: "In 1800 women whose work consisted largely of caring for their families were considered productive workers. By 1900, they had been formally relegated to the census category of 'dependents,' a category that included infants, young children, the sick, and the elderly."[3]

The 1870 Census was the first for which occupational figures were published for women. Table 8.1 shows how the census-takers and statisticians

Table 8.1   Instructions to census-takers on how to count homemakers, housewives, grown daughters doing housework, and housekeepers.

	Unpaid Wives	Grown Daughters	Housekeepers
1870	Women keeping house for their own families or for themselves, without any other gainful occupation, will be entered as *keeping house*	Grown daughters assisting mothers will be reported as *without occupation*	Persons who receive distinct *wages* or *salary* for the service are reported as *housekeepers*
1880	Same	If they assist in the household duties without fixed remuneration: *housework without pay*	Same
1890	*Housewives* are women who keep house for their own families or for themselves, without any gainful occupation	If they assist in the household duties without fixed remuneration: *housework without pay*. But for "the large body of persons, particularly young women, who live at home and do nothing": *no occupation*	Same
1900	Make no entry for them	Make no entry for them	Same
1910	Woman doing housework in her own home, without salary or wages, and having no other employment, occupation to be listed as *none*.	Not mentioned	A woman working *at housework for wages* should be returned as *housekeeper, servant, cook*, or *chambermaid*, as

(Continued)

	Unpaid Wives	**Grown Daughters**	**Housekeepers**
	If a woman, in addition to doing her own housework *regularly* earns money by some other occupation, at home or outside, list that occupation, for example, *laundress, at home*		may be; state the kind of place where she works, as *private family, hotel*, or *boarding house*
1920	Same	Not mentioned	Same
1930	Designate as *homemaker* that woman member of the family who was responsible for the care of the home and family	Not mentioned	Same
1940	If the person did only housework, incidental work, or chores not directly connected with a family business enterprise, list as *not at work* rather than *unpaid family work*. List *at work* for a housewife keeping five or more boarders or lodgers	If the person did only housework, incidental work, or chores not directly connected with a family business enterprise, list as *not at work* rather than *unpaid family work*	*Housekeeper* mentioned as a person working in a hotel or for a private home
1950	Do not count doing housework as working, but chores for the family business, such as feeding chickens on a farm, do count	More than one person in a household may be engaged in keeping house	Mentioned as person who works in a hotel. A paid housekeeper in a private home has full responsibility for management of the household

(Continued)

Table 8.1   Continued

	Unpaid Wives	Grown Daughters	Housekeepers
1960	Not in labor force	Not mentioned	Under private household workers and under "housekeepers and stewards"
1970	Same	Not mentioned	Not mentioned
1980	Same	Not mentioned	Not mentioned
1990	Same	Not mentioned	Not mentioned
2000	Not mentioned	Not mentioned	Not mentioned
2010	Not mentioned	Not mentioned	Not mentioned

Sources: Social Explorer, *Census Questionnaires and Instructions: 1790 to 2000;* U.S. Commerce Department, Census Bureau, *200 Years of Census Taking;* U.S Commerce Department, Census Bureau, *Abstract of the Fifteenth Census: 1930;* U.S. Commerce Department, Census Bureau, *Urban Enumerators Reference Manual: 1950 Census;* and U.S. Commerce Department, Census Bureau, *U.S. Census: 1960. Employment Status and Work Experience.*

were instructed to count homemakers, housewives, grown daughters doing housework, and housekeepers over the decades. The wording has been standardized in some cases:

One of the complaints leveled against the 1870 Census was that homemakers were not counted as workers.[4] Officers of the Association for the Advancement of Women petitioned Congress, in part: "The home and woman as a home-keeper have no place in the report, only the occupations called 'gainful' being noted, and more than twelve millions of American women being overlooked as laborers or producers or left out, in common with those pursuing disreputable employments, and not even incidentally named as in any wise affecting the causes of increase or decrease of population or wealth."[5] They said that Francis Amasa Walker, superintendent of both the 1870 and 1880 Censuses, explained that the absence was because of "the reluctance of women to acknowledge that they did any work for a living; 'they lived at home!'"[6]

Susan B. Carter and Richard Sutch argued that in the 1880 Census many of the women who gave their occupation as "housekeeper" were removed from gainful occupation totals, presumably out of the suspicion that they were referring to unpaid work. If their calculations are correct, then 6.6 percent of married women did housekeeping in other people's homes for pay, at least part-time, in 1880.[7]

Robert W. Smuts, looking at the 1890 Census 70 years later, noted that it claimed only 2.5 percent of White married women did paid work. "In the light of what is known about sickness and accident rates," he wrote, "about the incidence of drunkenness and desertion, and about the paucity of public and private aid for the indigent, this is an unlikely number."[8] In part he blamed the census instructions whose "tone seems to imply that enumerators should use great caution in assigning an occupation to a woman."[9]

But Smuts also agreed with Francis Walker that one explanation for the low numbers might have been unwillingness of family members to admit that the woman of the house was employed:

> In 1890, as for generations before, many women worked for pay, but work ranked near the bottom of the status scale among women's activities. Most of the jobs open to them had little prestige. The overwhelming majority of women workers were domestics, farm laborers, or manufacturing operatives. Among the middle and upper classes paid work was generally regarded as an unfortunate necessity for widows, poor spinsters, and the wives and daughters of men who earned too little to support their families. Young women often worked before marriage, but the employment of a married woman outside her home was widely viewed as a danger to her own health, to her ability to bear children, to the welfare of her family, and to the jobs rightfully belonging to men. Whatever member of the family the census taker found at home had every reason to report the women in the family as housekeepers, students, or idle, rather than as workers.[10]

A special Census Bureau report on the 1900 results noted "a large but ill-defined body of persons, particularly young women, who live at home and do nothing that can be regarded as work." The author separated this group from the estimated several millions in the category of "wife, sister, or adult daughter who 'keeps house' for her family, [who] though she receives nominally no pecuniary return for her services and does not regard herself as having a gainful occupation, is helping to sustain the productive capacity of the community quite as truly as her male relatives who are earning money wages."

The author then goes on to suggest that inmates of prisons and charitable institutions who do labor belong in the same class as housewives: "not carrying their wares to market, but still producing economic utilities of recognized value, and therefore not to be regarded as a burden borne by the community."[11]

The 1910 Census was the first to specifically tie "gainfulness" to money. Specifically gainful employment was "the particular kind of work done by which the person enumerated earns money or a money equivalent."[12] Folbre and Abel observed that "one could argue that a housewife normally received a money equivalent—a share of her husband's market income—in return for her labor."[13]

The reports on the 1910 Census explained that the term "gainful workers," was intended to include "all workers, except women doing housework in their own homes, without salary or wages, and having no other employment, and children working at home, merely on general household work, on chores, or, at odd times, on other work." Unfortunately, "so many of the [census-takers] returned as *housekeepers* housewives doing housework in their own homes, without salaries or wages, and servants who were in no sense *housekeepers,* that, after a rigid exclusion of the most improbable cases, it is certain that so many housewives and servants are included under the head of *housekeepers* as to render the statistics very inaccurate."[14]

In 1920 the Census Bureau published an *Alphabetical Index to Occupations.* It advised census-takers that when a woman is listed as "housekeeper" she should be considered "not gainful, unless there is evidence that she is working out [that is, working for someone other than her family]."[15] This definition appeared in the 1930 edition as well.

At the end of the decade Joseph A. Hill wrote a monograph for the Census Bureau entitled *Women in Gainful Occupations, 1870 to 1920,* in which he complicated the terminology issue by using the term "home housekeeper."[16] Some earlier uses of that phrase are illustrative.

The first located publication of that term was by Mrs. E.R. Barlow in an 1880 magazine article: "Give me the honor of being a model home-housekeeper in preference to anything else. . . . Be true women. Home is your kingdom. You are its ruler."[17]

By contrast, the next recorded use was by Florence M. Adkinson in a speech to the State Board of Agriculture of Indiana in 1884:

> The woman who does housework away from home and is paid for it, has an occupation, and is classed as a worker, a housekeeper or domestic servant. If she does the same kind of work and much more of it for her family, she has no occupation, and is classed in the official record as a drone, a non-producer. That is specimen of masculine logic. . . . Suppose the work of the busy wife of the farmer or mechanic had to be hired . . . what would it

amount to in dollars and cents at the end of the year? And when the year is multiplied by forty, what think you is the value of the home housekeeper?[18]

The conflict between the views of Barlow and Adkinson outlines a debate that would continue for decades.

Returning to Hill's 1929 text, he observed that "while home house-keeping is technically a productive occupation, it is not a money earning occupation. The home housekeeper ordinarily receives no wages for her services and presumably is not engaged in that occupation primarily for the sake of getting a living. Her occupation lies outside the field of economic competition."[19]

One problem Hill found with trying to measure the worth of the housewife's labor was that

> the amount of housekeeping done by the individual home housekeeper and hence the economic value of the service she renders is a very elastic and indefinite unit. One woman's home housekeeping may be limited to dusting off the furniture once a day, while another works from early morn until late at night cooking, washing, ironing, sweeping, mending. Should each alike be enumerated as a home housekeeper or a home maker, or should a minimum amount of home housekeeping be prescribed as a qualification for inclusion in this class? Then there is the woman whose house-work is done through the employment of servants, but who supervises and directs the affairs of her household, and in that way performs an economic service which bears some analogy to that of the management of a business concern. These conditions make it impossible to obtain through a census any satisfactory statistical record of the work done by women not gainfully employed.

For Hill, women's work became economically important when they left the home for the factory and "their occupations took on the character of those in which men were engaged."[20] He estimated that the percentage of women working and those maintaining homes added up to the same percentage as gainfully occupied men, "and it should not be forgotten in this connection that very many of the women who are wage earners are likewise maintaining homes and mothering children."[21]

The 1930 Census took a special interest in people who were working at home versus those working elsewhere: "All professional workers are included in the class designated as employed away from home, even though in a few cases the professional work may be done in the workers' own home, it being very important to show in this group the whole number of home-makers doing professional work."[22] It distinguished between "gainfully employed homemakers" who worked at home and those whose occupations were followed somewhere else.[23] In the Census Abstract volume "Families with Home-maker" was followed on the next page by "Families Having Radio Set."[24]

The 1940 Census involved a major change since people were no longer recorded based on having "gainful employment" but rather on "being in the labor force." Under the old system a person who called himself a plumber, for example, would be listed with that occupation even if he hadn't worked in years, but in the new system only those who worked or looked for work the week before the census were considered to be in the labor force.

The bureau continued to report problems in tracking homemakers: "It is comparatively difficult to obtain a reliable employment-status classification for women because most of them are normally engaged at least to some extent in home housework though they may be working also for pay or profit or at unpaid family work. Women with part-time jobs may therefore have been reported in some cases as engaged in own home housework and not in the labor force, through oversight on the part of enumerators and respondents." The report noted that the problem is worst in rural areas because it is difficult to separate paid work or unpaid family work from "incidental farm chores and home housework."[25]

The 1940s had a huge effect on homemakers. First, World War II encouraged many of them to find work outside the home. In the years that followed technological changes made it more practical for a family to survive without a full-time person caring for the home. As Susan Hautaniemi noted, in 1940 78 percent of homes were heated by coal, coke, or wood, which required large amounts of equipment maintenance and house-cleaning. Daily trips to a grocer were a necessity for many families, since fewer than half the homes had mechanical refrigeration. This figure rose to 80 percent a decade later. These estimates do not include carrying water, sewing clothes, and many other chores that began to be relieved by technological advancements—which might be easier to pay for if two members of the family were earning salaries.[26]

In 1946, with World War II over, the Women's Bureau became interested especially in paid housekeepers, or people engaged in "household employment," which it said was the newly preferred term. In 1944 almost 10 percent of working women were engaged in this work and the Women's Bureau approved, saying that those who "perform innumerable little tasks that oil the daily routine of existence, are engaged in socially worthwhile services."[27]

However, the bureau noted that many women "dislike or desert household employment" in favor of work that is better standardized, protected by labor law, and more likely to offer advancement.[28] More than three-quarters of female war workers surveyed in 1945 wanted to keep their current employment in peacetime rather than to move to household employment.[29]

At the 1948 conference where President Truman praised homemakers, Hazel Kyrk, a professor at the University of Chicago, noted that there were no useful longitudinal figures on how many hours women spend on housekeeping. Workweeks in industry had shortened, but there was no way to know if the housewife had experienced the same change. Current records, she said, had housewives doing 46 hours of work per week, and if "the hours spent [on housework] by other family members and paid workers are added, the figure rises to the extraordinary total of 80 hours per week. It may be argued that these figures reflect the inefficiency and dawdling of these women, the amount of time spent in useless ways." She pointed out that it was difficult to speak of the average workload of the homemaker, since the presence of children, for example, made a huge difference.[30]

In 1950 the Census Bureau started emphasizing the term "unpaid family workers" for "those who participate in market production in a family enterprise without receiving an explicit wage or salary." While 1 hour of paid work during the week before the census qualified a person as a "labor force participant," unpaid family workers had to do 15 hours to be credited with the same status.[31]

Housewives were supposed to be banned from the unpaid family worker category, but the published report noted that enumerators sometimes coded "working" for people they had listed as "housewife" or "student." It concluded that "if an enumerator consistently made such entries, he evidently misunderstood the Census definition of work."[32]

The 1960s and 1970s saw a large movement of women into paid work, but a 1975 survey by the government found 49 percent of women listed "homemaker" as their principal occupation.[33] One-third of the women surveyed had no income of their own.[34]

Wendyce Brody, writing for the U.S. Social Security Administration in that same year, was concerned with measuring the cost of illness of housewives. She argued that "economists in general acknowledge the fact that our system of national accounting underestimates total economic output because it excludes production in the nonmarket sector." She quoted studies estimating unpaid labor's role in the gross national product as anywhere from 26 to 48 percent, and most of this came from the housewife.[35] When homemakers moved into paid employment and, in turn, paid someone else to do some of their previously unpaid household tasks, the result, said Brody, was "an unreal increase in output . . . in the national accounts."[36]

Brody's research was noted in an article in the *New York Times* entitled "How Do You Put a Price Tag on a Housewife's Work?" In it, Wellesley College economics professor Carolyn Shaw Bell asked, "What would happen to the level of wages now paid in the market to cooks and cleaners if all the unpaid housewives joined the ranks? There's no reason to think wages would stay as high as they are now. . . . Estimating the housewife's worth is a waste of time. You aren't improving her life unless you are fighting for equal rights and more daycare centers."[37]

In 1978 the Census Bureau held a conference entitled *Issues in Federal Statistical Needs Relating to Women.* One speaker, Nancy Smith Barrett, pointed out how stereotypes of family roles can inject bias into statistics. The Current Population Survey interviewers were told to ask, "What was . . . doing last week?" They were to offer as examples "working or something else" for adult males, "keeping house or something else" for "housewives," and "going to school or something else" for teens. "If such leading suggestions condition the response," Barrett noted, "it is possible that jobless women and teens will report themselves as keeping house or in school, even if they are looking for work and [therefore] in the labor force. Furthermore, if they have stopped looking for work because they think they can't find a job, they are less apt to show up in the official measure of 'discouraged workers' than adult males. Adult males, on the other hand, are led into reporting themselves in the labor force or discouraged."[38]

A year later a study published in the U.S. Public Health Service's journal *Public Health Reports* examined birth certificates and discovered that 64.7 percent of new mothers who listed themselves as "housewives" were actually gainfully employed by Census Bureau definitions. Roughly half of them had worked at some point during their pregnancy and the vast majority had worked in the three years before birth.[39]

This confusion over the roles of worker and mother was noted by Folbre and Abel in an article on gender bias in the census: "The very notion that individuals have only one occupation is androcentric—unlike men, women who work for pay normally perform the work of housewife as well. Further, traditional patriarchal norms attached some stigma to married women who relinquished their primary identity as housewife."[40]

A report from the National Center for Health Statistics demonstrated how the term "housewife" can muddy the waters so as to make the relationship between health and employment dangerously ambiguous. Diane K. Wagener et al. pointed out in a publication of the National Center for Health Statistics that "housewife" was listed as the longest-held occupation on more than half of the death certificates for women in 1980, but more than 90 percent of women at that time had worked for pay.

Ignoring the jobs these women held hides possible correlations between certain employments and health risks. For example, according to those 1980 figures, housewives had a greater-than-average risk of dying of heart disease. In effect, that artificially lowered the recorded risk of other occupations those women may have held.[41]

Marilyn Waring, the New Zealander politician who is sometimes called the founder of feminist economics, wrote: "Those who bring the fetus to term in the laboratory, or who care for the child in the orphanage or juvenile facility are seen as workers. They are economically active. But a mother, daily engaged unpaid in these activities, is 'just a housewife.' "[42]

Statistical Abstract

"Housekeepers and Stewards" show up in the list of occupations for the first time in the 1902 edition.[43]

"Housewives" are first mentioned in the *Statistical Abstract* in 1934. Under the table on "National Income" a note explained that it does not include, among other things, "the imputed value of services of housewives and other members of the family."[44]

"Homemakers" arrived in 1966. In the "Comparative International Statistics" section, a footnote said that the data for Indonesia "excludes large number of females classified as homemakers but also engaged in economic activity." Figures for several other countries exclude data for "unpaid family workers."[45]

The 1968 edition listed "homemakers and unpaid family members" under "vocational rehabilitation." They appeared in the "job or occupation" category rather than as a "disability."[46]

The last two volumes of the *Statistical Abstract* (2011 and 2012) contained an identical table reporting the "Average Hours per Week Spent Doing Unpaid Household Work and Paid Work by Sex and Age" from 2003 to 2007. The categories of unpaid household work were as follows:

Household activities

Food and drink preparation

Cleaning

Laundry and sewing

Household management

Lawn and garden care

Maintenance and repair

Caring for and helping household members

Purchasing goods and services

Travel related to unpaid household work

Men averaged 15.9 hours per week on unpaid household work and 31.4 hours of paid work. Women, on the other hand, averaged 26.7 hours of unpaid household work and 21 hours of paid work. Women aged 35–44 years did the most unpaid work of their sex (33.1 hours), while men 65–74 years of age led their sex with 19.9 hours.[47]

PART IV

Concepts of Employment

CHAPTER NINE

"Occupations Suitable for Women"

The 1940 Census recorded about 1,500 women working for the railroads as engineers, firemen, mechanics, repairmen, and car shop workers. In the published reports they were all counted as "tailors and tailoresses."[1]

Difficulties in recording female occupations in government statistics began a century earlier. One reason seems to be assumptions as to what types of jobs women could, should, or would want to do, and a willingness to make the data fit the theory.

The first census to ask about people's occupations was 1820, but it queried only the head of each household about the number of people engaged in commerce, agriculture, and manufacturing.[2]

The 1850 Census attempted to gather detailed occupational data for men and discovered that classifying the information into hundreds of categories was time consuming and expensive.[3] The next decennial census added occupational data about women; for example, 17 women were listed as working in coal mining.[4]

During the 1880 Census the statisticians began to sort the data about women's occupations in relation to marital status, but it was not until a decade later that useful data on that subject began to be published, and one could learn what percentage of married women held what types of occupations.[5]

Data from 1880 about the clerical field illustrates the difficulty the Office of the Census had in organizing occupation information. A total of 6,618 women were recorded in clerical jobs (not including salesclerks), but the data was not sufficiently detailed to distinguish clerks and copyists from bookkeepers, cashiers, and accountants. The published record arbitrarily assigned about 60 percent to the clerk category and lists the rest as bookkeepers, cashiers, and accountants. Stenographers and typists were hidden among those categories.[6]

The census of 1890 was the first to be tabulated mechanically, using punch cards. The published reports separated occupations into 50 male and 25 female categories. One purpose was to save pages: except for a few occupations with overlap (teachers, clerks, etc.), they needed to list only men or women, not both.[7]

In 1900 the occupations field on the punch cards used a 0 or 1 code to indicate jobs that could be done by either sex; 2–7 were reserved for male-only occupations and 8 and 9 for female-only.[8] By that point the managers were aware of the need to check these results for accuracy. One step was to automatically examine any cards that seemed to show unusual or contradictory data. That meant a manual recheck of the schedule (original census record) for anyone over the age of 90, women with more than 10 children, single women with more than one child, Blacks living in the North, and so on. Unusual occupations for a given sex also fell into that category.[9]

One modern scholar, Margo A. Conk, pointed out that this system was likely to create a subtle bias:

> The punching clerks were aware that their work would be rejected if they coded men into "female" occupations and women into "male" occupations, even if they were true to the schedules. Thus, from the clerk's point of view, it would perhaps be better to use a non-controversial occupation code in the first place and avoid having one's work scrutinized. . . . The Census therefore did not merely report the sexual division of labor, it also reinforced it by determining that certain answers on the schedules would be considered "wrong."[10]

Conk also noted that while records showing women, minorities, and children in important fields were double-checked for accuracy "it was never 'inconsistent' or 'unusual' for adult native white [sic] males to follow most and especially the high-status occupations."[11]

In 1907 the Census Bureau published its first volume on *Statistics of Women at Work,* based on otherwise unpublished data from the last decennial census. The book noted that women appeared in all but nine of the listed occupations:

> Naturally no women are reported as United States soldiers, sailors, or marines; nor were any reported as firemen (in fire department), as street

car drivers (though 2 were reported as motormen), as telegraph and tele-phone linemen, as apprentices or helpers to roofers or slaters, or as helpers to steam boiler makers or to brassworkers. But the reader may note with interest, and perhaps with some surprise, that 5 women were employed as [ship's] pilots, that on steam railroads 10 were employed as baggagemen, 31 as brakemen, 7 as conductors, 45 as engineers and firemen, and 26 as switchmen, yardmen, and flagmen; that 6 women were reported as ship carpenters, and 2 as roofers and slaters; that as many as 185 were returned as blacksmiths and 508 as machinists; that 8 were boilermakers, 31 were charcoal, coke and lime burners, and 11 were well borers. Such figures as these have little sociological significance beyond indicating that there are few kinds of work from which the female sex is absolutely debarred, either by nature or law or custom.[12]

The 10 occupations with the largest number of women contained at least three ambiguous ones that proved problematic for the statisticians for decades to come: farm laborers as opposed to farmers, paid house-keepers as opposed to unpaid homemakers, and nurses/midwives as opposed to servants caring for children.[13]

The struggle over the term "clerk" also continued. *Statistics of Women at Work* noted that in the 1900 Census the term included "such widely diverse pursuits as those of bank clerks, postal clerks, mail clerks, mail carriers, clerks in national, state, county, or city offices, and shipping clerks. Many of these occupations are not well adapted to the employ-ment of women, and consequently breadwinners of this sex are not espe-cially prominent among clerks and copyists."[14]

The 1910 Census began a newly critical examination of the occupa-tions in which women were reported. "Extra special agent"[15] Alba Edwards was in charge of occupation statistics for this census and the three that followed. He warned his own clerks that when "classifying an occupa-tional return, always consider in connection with it the other information given about the person, such as the relationship to the head of the family, sex, age, whether an employer or employee, ownership of home, etc."[16]

Edwards was interested in distinguishing between skilled, semiskilled, and unskilled occupations. Unfortunately, one of his criteria for the level of a particular job was the type of person who performed it. As Peter B. Meyer noted, Edwards promoted "the idea that a woman could have a skilled occupation but that an occupation made up mostly of women was not a skilled one."[17]

Edwards explained that "certain specific occupations which, techni-cally, are skilled occupations were classified as semi-skilled because the enumerators returned so many children, young persons, and women as pursuing these occupations as to render the occupations semiskilled, even though each of them did contain some skilled workers."[18]

To his credit, he made a note in the introductory text explaining part of the process:

> *Peculiar occupations for women*—The Thirteenth Census enumerators, like the enumerators at previous Censuses, returned women as following many occupations which are very peculiar and unusual for women.
>
> A careful examination of the schedules in such cases usually showed that errors had been made in the return, either of the sex or of the occupation. Most of these errors were found and corrected by the classifying clerks. Others were corrected during the work of final revision. Occasionally, however, no such errors were apparent on the schedules. These cases are reported, although it is probable that in most instances the women did not actually follow the occupations returned for them. The following are examples of such occupations:
>
> > Blacksmiths
> > Brick and stone masons
> > Elevator tenders
> > Furnacemen and smeltermen
> > Heaters (metal)
> > Longshoremen and stevedores
> > Machinists
> > Rollers and roll hands (metal)
> > Sailors and deck hands
> > Tinsmiths.[19]

Similar statements appear in the 1920 and 1930 volumes.

In preparation for the 1920 Census, the bureau published an *Index to Occupations* in two volumes, also the work of Alba Edwards. The purpose was to organize the occupations data and make the results easier to use. In it, Edwards warned his collators to "examine the schedule carefully" if women were listed in any "peculiar or unusual" occupations, such as these:

Auctioneer

Baggageman

Blacksmith

Boatman

Boiler maker

Boiler washer

Bootblack

Brakeman

Brass molder

Brickmason

Butcher

Cabinetmaker

Captain

Carpenter

Conductor, steam railroad

Constable

Cooper

Coppersmith

Deckhand

Deliveryman, bakery or laundry

Ditcher

Electrician

Engineer (any)

Engine hostler

Express messenger

Flagman, railroad

Foreman, livery stable

Foreman, lumber camp

Foreman, mine or quarry

Forester

Freight agent

Furnace man

Gas or steam fitter

Heater

Hostler

Inspector, mine or quarry

Inspector, street railroad

Laborer, charcoal or coke works

Laborer, coal yard

Laborer, gas works

Laborer, lumberyard

Laborer, road or street

Ladler or pourer (metal)

Lifesaver

Locomotive engineer

Locomotive fireman

Longshoreman

Lumberman

Manager, mine or quarry

Marine

Marshal

Master

Mate

Motorman

Oiler of machinery

Pilot

Plasterer

Plumber

Porter

Puddler

Raftsman

Railroad official

Railway mail clerk

Roller or roll hand (metal)

Roofer

Sailor

Sheriff

Slater

Smelterman

Soldier

Stevedore

Stonecutter

Stonemason

Structural iron worker

Switchman, railroad

Teamster

Tinsmith

Veterinary surgeon

Wheelwright

Woodchopper[20]

In all probability there were few women in these fields, but with each passing census a growing feedback loop made it harder to be sure. As Conk had noted, clerks were warned that "unusual occupations" would be double-checked, which might tend to decrease the number that they entered, which in its turn confirmed that those occupations were unusual and therefore suspicious.

In spite of these tactics, women were reported in all but 35 of the 572 occupations included in the 1920 Census. Joseph A. Hill, writing in a 1929 Census monograph entitled *Women in Gainful Occupations, 1870 to 1920,* cautioned:

> It is true that there is hardly any important branch of industry in which women are not employed in some capacity; but that does not mean that they are doing all or even nearly all the various kinds of work that men are doing. The variety of occupations in the field of modern industry is very great; and the census classification of occupations is necessarily a very summary one, in which many of the designations cover composite occupational or industrial groups, rather than single specific occupations. . . . For example, 2,198 women are classified as laborers in blast furnaces and steel rolling mills. But the term "laborer" as applied to this industry covers a great number of distinct employments, possibly more than a hundred. Just what these women laborers were doing in the rolling mills no one without an intimate knowledge of the industry could venture to say. It is quite probable that many of them were employed in some such occupation as that of "scrubber" or "sweeper. . . ."
>
> No serious significance should be attached to the fact that in successive censuses, a certain small number of women have been reported as carpenters, masons, blacksmiths, plumbers, and even as locomotive engineers. These are sporadic cases, and many of them probably represent errors occurring in the original schedules or in the tabulation of the returns. . . . The newspaper space writer or cartoonist may delight in featuring the woman blacksmith of the census as a village smithy in skirts or knickers working with hammer and anvil under the wide-spreading chestnut tree. But it is safe to say that it is a purely fanciful picture.[21]

The *Index to Occupations* Edwards prepared for the 1930 Census made some changes. It no longer listed the following occupations as peculiar for women: carpenter; deliveryman, bakery or laundry; laborer, charcoal or coke works; laborer, gas works; longshoreman; oiler of machinery; porter; roller or roll hand (metal); and sheriff.

It is odd to see "carpenter" vanish off the list since the 1930 instructions for enumerators (census-takers) continued to use it, along with "blacksmith," as prime examples of unusual occupations for women.[22]

It is impossible to tell at this point why Edwards dropped certain occupations from the list, or whether it made a significant difference. For example, the 1930 Census listed 274 female sheriffs.[23] Would there have been fewer if that job had stayed on the "Peculiar" list?

On the other hand, the following occupations were added to the "Peculiar" list in 1930:

Butler

Conductor, street railroad

Fireman, fire department

Foreman, road or street building

Garbage man or scavenger

Laborer, pipeline

Loom fixer

Molder (any metal)

Pressman, printing

Street cleaner

Toolmaker

Turfman or sportsman[24]

In the published census report Edwards detailed the process used to double-check unusual occupations and concluded: "Most of the cases in which the published statistics represent women, children, and colored [sic] persons as working at occupations very unusual for such persons probably represent such undetected errors on the schedules."[25]

Edwards also explained that "the decrease from 1920 to 1930 in the number of women shown as pursuing certain occupations unusual for women should be ascribed to the more rigid scrutiny of the returns in 1930."[26] Nevertheless, the 1930 Census found women in 504 of the 534 occupations listed.[27]

A possible explanation for the Census Bureau's thinking in this regard comes from the Women's Bureau of the Labor Department. In a bulletin titled *The Occupational Progress of Women, 1910–1930,* Mary V. Dempsey wrote:

> The widow who continues to run her husband's plumbing or carpenter
> shop after his death has a tendency to return her occupation as a plumber

or carpenter, though she may never have had the tools of the trade in her hands. Likewise, the girl who becomes expert in the operation of a certain machine, may, after long experience in a factory, decide to return her occupation as a machinist. Largely because of such returns, the error in the number of women reported in the building and hand trades is believed to be high, though every practicable means has been used to insure the accuracy of figures showing women in unusual occupations.[28]

A different government reflection on female occupations came in November 1930, when the U.S. Office of Education sponsored a symposium on "Home and Family Life in a Changing Civilization." The first of the four speakers (all men) was the commissioner of education, William J. Cooper, who noted: "A girl can now escape to almost any type of occupation she desires, and this is the real reason for the present breakdown of the family."[29]

The compilation and reporting of the 1940 Census took place as war industries were ramping up and accurate information on the labor force was a national priority. It was then that the errors and compromises of the past became impossible to ignore.

Only after the preliminary figures on occupation were released did it become clear that women had been recorded in occupations from which they had been excluded in earlier censuses. Edwards was left with three unpalatable choices: try to adjust the figures from previous decades; leave all the figures as is, creating the appearance of a sudden jump in female workers; or continue to artificially depress the numbers in the current census. He chose the third option.[30]

Because of the urgent need for the data, Edwards explained, the bureau decided to

> forego, for the most part, the process of checking the questionable cards back to the schedules and to make no attempt to check occasional returns of unusual occupations for females, except in those extreme cases where the occupation seemed to be quite impossible, as, for example, women returned as locomotive engineers. Returns of this latter case were adjusted, and all cases where the questionable item represented considerable numbers were looked up and corrected; but small numbers of border-line cases, such as women returned as blacksmiths, were allowed to remain. In particular, these nominal increases should not be interpreted as indicating an expansion of the field of female activities.[31]

Edwards could not simply convert, say, women machinists to machine tenders, because the published preliminary reports had already revealed the numbers of skilled and semiskilled workers. Thus, women recorded in the fields he found most suspicious were transferred to occupations

Edwards found more believable but that were at the same skill level. Approximately 400 female railroad conductors appeared as "officials, lodge, society, union, etc." An estimated 800 women firefighters were recorded as "guards, watchmen, and doorkeepers." That same category was augmented with an estimated 2,200 females who had actually been reported as "soldiers, sailors, marines, and coast guards." As Conk observed, "The notable point about such a procedure is that it is obviously wrong."[32]

One unexpected result of the manipulation of the occupation figures is that when women responded to the call for workers in war-related industry, the increase seemed even more dramatic than it was.

Of course, not all oddities of occupational categories occurred on one side. The 1940 Census recorded more than 3,600 men who washed clothes for private families. They were duly listed as "laundresses."[33]

The United States Employment Service (USES) was an agency assigned to develop a system of employment offices nationwide.[34] In 1942 it published *Occupations Suitable for Women*. The impetus was the fact that the nation's entry into war was increasing demand for production while it removed men from the civilian labor force.[35]

The book's viewpoint was more enthusiastic about its subject than Alba Edwards's had been: "It can hardly be said that *any* occupation is absolutely unsuitable for the employment of women. Women have shown that they can do, or learn to do, almost any kind of work. To say that a given occupation is suitable for the employment of women, however, is not to say that any woman could perform it. A woman with suitable physical strength and other characteristics and abilities must be chosen."[36] In spite of this, the book included only about 20 percent of the 17,452 occupations listed in the same agency's *Dictionary of Occupational Titles*.[37]

USES offered three categories: women now employed, apparently suitable, and partially suitable.[38]

Here are some examples from the approximately 2,100 occupations included in war industries:

Upholstery seamstress (now employed)
Locomotive crane operator (apparently suitable)
Floor machinist (partially suitable)[39]

Examples from the approximately 1,600 nonwar-industries occupations:

Chief steward (now employed)
Pretzel-cooker (apparently suitable)
Seed analyst (partially suitable)[40]

The 1950 Census broke occupations down into 445 items and found women employed in all of them except "millers, grain, flour, feed, etc."[41] In the 1960 Census there were 297 occupation codes, resulting in a large number of "not elsewhere classified." For that reason the Occupational Classification System, as it was called, was expanded to 441 occupations in the 1970 Census.[42]

What appeared in the front of most 1970 volumes, however, was an abbreviated version called the Intermediate Occupation Classification (IOC), which contained only 129 categories for males and 90 for females.[43]

Table 9.1   Occupations of the 1970 *Intermediate Occupation Classification* list for only one sex.

Occupations Listed Only for Women	Occupations Listed Only for Men
Cutlery, hand tools, and other hardware manufacturing	Automobile mechanics
	Blacksmiths
Household appliances manufacturing	Bakers
Retail trade	Bulldozer operators
Secretaries, legal	Cabinetmakers
Secretaries, medical	Carpenters
Teachers, college and university	Compositors and typesetters
Agriculture	Electricians
Art, drama, and music	Firemen
Atmospheric, earth, marine, and space	Former members of the armed forces
	Furriers
Business and commerce	Garbage collectors
Coaches and physical education	Locomotive engineers
Home economics	Loom fixers
Law	Motion picture projectionists
Psychology	Policemen and detectives
Sociology	Shoe repairmen
Theology	Teachers, college and university
	Miscellaneous social sciences
	Telephone installers and repairmen
	Transportation managers
	Tailors

Source: U.S. Commerce Department, Social and Economic Statistics Bureau, Census Bureau, *Census of Population: 1970, Occupational Characteristics,* xiii–xix.

What makes this doubly confusing is that (1) the IOC listed some surprising occupations as being suitable for both sexes, such as midwives and sailors, and (2) people of both sexes actually appeared in the data tables for some supposedly sex-specific occupations.[44]

Table 9.1 shows some of the occupations the IOC identified with only one sex.

The Census Bureau was still seeking consistency and correcting apparent mistakes. The occupational data written in by almost 8 percent of the census recipients was considered inadequate and was therefore supplemented by machine. As Conk explained: "For example, if an individual with a blank occupation code reported working in a jewelry store but was not the owner or manager, the bureau coded the person as a jeweler or watchmaker if a male, but a jewelry salesclerk if a female."[45]

The struggle to identify civilian occupations by sex seems to have been given up by 1977 when the Commerce Department's Office of Federal Statistical Policy and Standards published its *Standard Occupational Classification Manual*. The terms "women," "sex," and "female" do not appear in it.[46]

Statistical Abstract

The first appearance of occupations data in the *Statistical Abstract* was in the 1895 edition. It gave only five categories: agriculture, fisheries, and mining; professional service; domestic and personal service; trade and transportation; and manufacturing and mechanical industries. Each of these categories was broken down by sex.[47]

The 1902 volume split the employed into 140 occupations, everything from clergymen to butter and cheese makers to photographers. Women appeared in every class except two: soldiers, sailors, and marines; and telegraph and telephone linemen.[48] From that year on the number of occupations continued to increase.

CHAPTER TEN

"Gainful Employment"

To make sense of the history of statistics about American working women, one has to consider the concept of "gainful employment" or "gainful occupation." This concept first appeared in the reports on the 1870 Census, the same one that first noted the number of women at work. (Data about occupations of individuals was gathered in 1850, but only for free males. In 1860 it was collected for both sexes, but only the information about males was published.)[1]

The 1870 Census reports explained that the "tables of occupations embrace gainful and reputable occupations only." Neither the instructions to the census-takers nor the published reports defined exactly what "gainful" meant. The book hinted at it by saying that it would not include those "who have no recognized occupation for which they receive compensation in the shape of wages or salary, or from which they derive products of a merchantable character."[2]

It will become clear that this terminology prevented many women from being counted as employed. The degree to which that happened is still argued by economists.

Francis Amasa Walker, the superintendent of the 1870 Census, reported that 91 percent of men aged 16 to 59 were in the workforce, but only 16 percent of women.[3] This left him with the need to explain how other millions of women were spending their time.

"It would not seem to be difficult to account for the females of each [age] class who are not represented,"[4] he assured his readers. Briefly, Walker subtracted the number of females he estimated were in school and then assumed that another 100,000 girls of that age belonged to the "pauper, vagrant, or criminal class."[5]

Finally, Walker calculated that "a clear deduction should be made of one person on account of each family returned in the census, in all, 7,579,863." In other words, for every family there had to be one woman "keeping house" (the quotation marks are his), and he then estimated that 180,000 of those at the same time had gainful occupations.[6] Modern researcher Margo Anderson explained: "He simply assumed each family had to have a female 'keeping house' and apparently did not cross-check his assumption to see if there was one woman age 16 or over in each family reported in the census."[7]

That left one and a half million women still unaccounted for. Walker concluded that they were "grown daughters living at home, widowed mothers supported by their children, ladies living upon the income of accumulated property, as well as women of the pauper, vagrant, and criminal classes."[8]

Walker also made a list of all the categories that adults could occupy. Men could be workers, students, vagrants, paupers, criminals, disabled, retired, or living on acquired or inherited wealth. Women, on the other hand, could not belong to the categories of the disabled or retired.[9]

One of the oddities of all these calculations is that in a separate volume of the same census Walker noted that the occupation figures for women were much less accurate than those for men and explained why:

> It is taken for granted that every man has an occupation, and . . . only in rare cases, too inconsiderable to be taken into account in such a discussion, have assistant marshals [i.e. census takers] failed to ask and obtain the occupation of men, or boys old enough to work with effect. It is precisely the other way with women and young children. The assumption is, as the fact generally is, that they are not engaged in remunerative employments. Those who are so engaged constitute the exception, and it follows, from a plain principle of human nature, that assistant marshals will not unfrequently forget or neglect to ask the question.[10]

Anderson offers a different explanation for the contradiction: "Ideally men worked outside the home while their women were supposed to maintain the domestic world within. Implicitly, therefore, if women were found working outside the domestic sphere, they were 'out of place' in a double sense. . . . Walker's conception of the labor force had effectively made 'gainful work' a deviant social status for women."[11]

Writing in the 1980s, Penelope Ciancanelli suggested that standard definitions of labor undercounted or ignored four categories of women's work: (1) the labor of "unpaid family workers," such as women who kept the books for their husbands or toiled on the home farm; (2) independent commodity production such as food products or housewares; (3) piece-work done at home; and (4) the "production of goods and services for direct consumption . . . usually called housework."[12]

Concerning Ciancanelli's first category, Lisa Geib-Gunderson wrote: "Surprisingly, fully 57.2 percent of all married women had husbands who were self-employed in 1880 but were *not* recorded as gainfully occupied and an additional 3.3 percent of married women were living in house-holds with boarders, but not counted as employed. In 1900, the percent-ages are 44.8 for self-employed and 5.6 for boarder households, and for 1910, the percentages are 25.6 and 6.7, respectively."[13]

The reason for mentioning "boarders" is that taking in lodgers or boarders (lodgers who also ate in) was for many years the main "infor-mal" business women could engage in.[14] For example, in Philadelphia in 1880 one household in six had unrelated individuals boarding. Nonethe-less, according to the census, less than 1 percent of homes in that city had a person employed as a boardinghouse keeper.[15]

The instructions to enumerators for the 1910 Census, for example, make it clear that a person's occupation should be listed as "keeper—boarding house" only if it is "his (or her) principal means of support or principal source of income. . . . If, however, a family keeps a few boarders or roomers merely as a means of supplementing or eking out the earn-ings or income obtained from other occupations or from other sources, no one in the family should be turned as a boarding or lodging house keeper."[16]

The Women's Bureau discussed the problem in a publication that used 1920 Census data to study "nearly 40,000 gainfully employed women."[17]

> If a woman is concerned chiefly in running her home, into which she takes boarders or lodgers to supplement the family income, the principal source of income originating elsewhere, she is not listed by the Bureau of the Cen-sus as gainfully employed even though the boarders may materially increase the labor involved in running her home. . . . [I]n two of the three cities for which the information was tabulated there was no substantial difference between the average number of boarders and lodgers taken by women who engaged in the work as a main source of income and by those who took in boarders and lodgers as a means of supplementing the family earnings.[18]

Returning to the 1900 Census, a special "Supplementary Analysis" noted that only one-third of the population had gainful occupations.

While the report then said that "of the remaining two-thirds no notice is taken," it went on to say that

> the Census distinction between gainful and nongainful occupations is by no means identical with the economic distinction between productive and unproductive laborers. On the one hand, the nongainful class includes . . . several million productive laborers, and on the other hand, some of the persons credited with gainful occupations would not be recognized by all economists as productive laborers—e.g., professional athletes and clairvoyants. . . .
>
> A man and his wife may both be productive laborers, but their positions are nevertheless very unlike. The quality of a man's living depends in general upon his economic efficacy. But in the case of a housewife such a direct relation can hardly be said to exist. On the contrary, the manner in which a wife lives generally varies inversely as [*sic*] the amount of work she does. If her husband is successful in his business, she enjoys a comfortable or luxurious style of living, and, at the same time, is relieved in large measure of the burden of domestic labor. But if her husband does not prosper, the wife is likely to work hard and fare ill. In short, the wife, though a productive laborer, is a dependent, in the sense that her position in society is determined by her husband's and not by her own economic efficiency.

The census report goes on to say that the wife does not "influence market conditions, nor on the other hand is she influenced by them. She does not experience the cultural discipline of direct economic competition."

The report uses the term "breadwinner" for the "self-supporting" people who "earn their own living" through gainful employment. All other people are said to make up the "residual class," including most unpaid homemakers and "a large but ill-defined body of persons, particularly young women, who live at home and do nothing that can be regarded as work."[19]The Supplementary Analysis also stated that "on marriage the woman, if she has a money-making occupation, in the great majority of cases exchanges it for domestic duties." They calculated that perhaps 5 or 6 percent of wives had gainful occupations and that was "probably to be accounted for by the inability of the husband to work. There are, however, no data to show in how many cases both husband and wife act as breadwinners." Noting that most divorced women have jobs, they speculated that "the increase in the number of divorces is in large measure a result of the more independent economic position of women."[20]

As Penelope Ciancanelli wrote in the 1980s:

> The chief weakness of the 1900 Census of Occupations is the absence of any objective criteria for determining gainful occupation. The core of the

modern labor force definition—employment for pay—was not made explicit until the Census of 1910. This apparently led enumerators to fall back on the standards and definitions of "occupation" that were customary or normative. Since neither unpaid family labor nor taking in boarders was considered an occupation, these were not counted as such. The result was a large undercount of gainfully occupied married women.[21]

In 1907 Congress authorized the Bureau of Labor Statistics to conduct a massive study on how the workplace affected women and children. This was eventually published as the 19-volume series *Report on Condition of Woman and Child Wage-Earners in the United States.* The Census Bureau supplemented that research with *Statistics of Women at Work,* a book based on unpublished data from the most recent census.

This census report noted that about 20 percent of women had gainful employment compared to 90 percent of men, explaining that with women "the adoption of an occupation, although by no means unusual, is far from being customary . . . and with this sex, moreover, the pursuit of an occupation is probably more often temporary than permanent."[22]

It is possible that the interest Congress was taking in working women and children was a partial cause for one of the most controversial milestones in federal data gathering. Up to this point the number and percentage of women in gainful employment had moved upward in a modest trend over the decades.

Things changed dramatically with the 1910 Census. The figures that year showed that between 1900 and 1910 the number of females aged 10 and up doing gainful work rose by 51.4 percent. If the numbers are limited to those above the age of 15, the rise is almost 100 percent. The figure in agriculture rose by almost 130 percent, despite the actual number of women living on farms declining.[23] These boosts were particularly open to challenge because the 1920 figures returned to the more modest levels.

Alba Edwards, then the superintendent of the Census Bureau, offered the popular explanation for the change when he noted that "a part of the great increase reported for the decade 1900 to 1910 was apparent only and was due to a difference in the instructions to enumerators at the two censuses, rather than to so marked an increase in the proportion of women actually engaged in gainful labor."[24]

These sections of the instructions were the suspected culprits:

144. Column 18. *Trade or profession.*—An entry should be made in this column for *every* person enumerated. The occupation, if any, followed by a child, of any age, or by a woman is just as important, for census purposes,

as the occupation followed by a man. Therefore, it must never be taken for granted, without inquiry, that a woman, or child, has no occupation.

154. *Women doing farm work.*—A woman working regularly at outdoor farm work, even though she works on the home farm for her husband, son, or other relative and does not receive money wages, should be returned in column 18 as a *farm laborer*. Distinguish, however, such women who work on the home farm from those who work away from home, by writing in column 19 either *home farm* or *working out,* as the case may require. Of course, a woman who herself operates or runs a farm should be reported as a *farmer,* and not as a *farm laborer.*[25]

As decades passed and the perception of women's roles changed, different statisticians offered alternative explanations for the 1910 shift. Writing in the 1940s, John D. Durand pointed out that "the major purpose of the gainful worker statistics in the censuses prior to 1940 was the enumeration of occupations. Analyses of labor supply, employment, etc. were secondary considerations."[26] That is, the type of work you claimed as your own was more important than where or even whether you were currently doing it. This tended to depress figures about married women's gainful work, Durand theorized, because most of them would tend to list their main occupation as housewife.[27] The problem with that theory is that it would tend to affect all the censuses equally.

A.J. Jaffe, writing in 1956, argued that the 1910 figures on women's gainful employment, far from being distorted upward, were the only accurate ones: "This writer believes that the 1910 census constituted the first attempt to include almost everyone who could conceivably be classified as being in the working force. Hence, it is the earliest census which provides data almost comparable in coverage with labor force data for 1940 and later years."[28] His article was published in the Labor Department's journal, *Monthly Labor Review,* but in a most unusual move, the editors gave over the next page to two articles by federal statisticians challenging his conclusions.

Robert W. Smuts, writing in 1960, argued that the long series of data was not coherent; that is, the data on women's gainful employment could not be usefully compared over the decades. Some argued that procedural changes had not greatly affected the data because the census-takers had been "too inexperienced and poorly trained to pay much attention to their instructions." Smuts replied: "The results of the 1910 census indicate, however, that this is a dubious assumption."[29] He also felt that married women's labor participation changed little in the 1890–1930 period.[30]

It is no surprise that for the 1920 Census the census-takers' instructions were rewritten in a way that would discourage a startling increase in the count of employed women: "The term 'gainful workers,' therefore, includes all workers except women doing housework in their own homes and children working at home merely on general housework, on chores, or at odd times on other work."[31] While "gainful" was still not defined, the census-takers were told to report only work that "earns money or a money equivalent."[32]

No longer would the enumerators be urged to consider the occupation of a woman just as important as that of a man. The reported number of women in gainful occupations dropped from 25.5 percent to 24 percent in that decade, which is particularly surprising since a considerable number of men had been removed from the workforce by World War I.[33]

As early as the 1940s the Census Bureau recognized that the 1920 drop in female farm workers was an artifact of the process used to collect the data. This was part of the explanation Alba Edwards offered in a book called *Comparative Occupation Statistics:*

> The emphasis, in 1910, was upon *returning* as a farm laborer every woman working regularly at outdoor farm work, while, in 1920, the emphasis was upon *not returning* as a farm laborer any woman who worked at outdoor work *"only occasionally"* or *"only a short time each day."*[34]

In that same book Edwards removed 630,985 females from the 1910 agricultural estimate and added 75,000 to the same count for 1920.[35] This creates a smoother curve over time, although Smuts noted that "why a smooth curve is more reliable than a bumpy one is not self-evident."[36]

The 1930 Census, taken just months after the crash that started the Great Depression, faced particular challenges in counting working women. By that time, as Edwards explained, "in Census usage, the terms 'gainful workers' and 'gainfully occupied' include all persons who usually earn money or a money equivalent, or who assist in the production of marketable goods, whether or not they were employed at the time of the enumeration."[37] Nevertheless, as modern scholars Nancy Folbre and Marjorie Abel noted: "Even in that year many women who assisted in the production of marketable goods were clearly not enumerated."[38]

The year 1940 saw the end of the gainful employment era and the rise of the "labor force" concept. While gainful employment focused on anyone who claimed a legitimate money-making occupation, whether they were actually working or not, at the time labor force data was intended to include only those who, during a specific week, were either working or seeking employment.[39] These changes made it difficult to compare pre- and post-1940 figures, but are generally agreed to lead to more accurate data.

It seems clear that the decades of gainful employment numbers distorted the facts of women's lives in ways that cannot be known for certain. However, as Ciancanelli observed: "The identification by labor force surveys of *no* married men as unpaid family workers and of very few 'wives' as self-employed proprietors suggests that the sex division of labor structures this occupation in ways that are not completely understood."[40]

Statistical Abstract

The 1902 edition of the *Statistical Abstract* reported the number of people at least 10 years old engaged in gainful occupations, broken down both by sex and by detailed occupations. For example, there were 27,772 female bookkeepers and accountants in 1890, and 75,153 of them in 1900, but neither of these figures would likely have included wives of professionals who kept their husband's books.[41]

The 1944–1945 volume contained a two-page introduction to its Labor Force chapter explaining the change from what it called the "gainful worker" approach. Statistics of both kinds follow, with both sexes being represented.[42] This explanation continued to appear through the 1960 edition.[43]

The term "gainfully employed" continued to appear through the 2003 edition in reference to people with disabilities and vocational rehabilitation.[44]

CHAPTER ELEVEN

Income

In 1853 the New York State Teachers Association held its annual meeting in Rochester with more than 500 people in attendance. When the question was raised about why the profession received such little respect, one young female teacher rose to be recognized.

This caused a shock because, although most attendees were women, women were not permitted to speak, vote, or hold office in the organization. For at least 10 minutes debate raced through the hall as to whether this woman should be allowed to speak. She stayed on her feet, knowing that if she sat down the battle would be lost. Eventually it was agreed that she could address the meeting and Susan B. Anthony began her public career.

> It seems to me, gentlemen, that none of you quite comprehend the cause of the disrespect of which you complain. Do you not see that so long as society says a woman is incompetent to be a lawyer, minister or doctor, but has ample ability to be a teacher, that every man of you who chooses this profession tacitly acknowledges that he has no more brains than a woman? And this, too, is the reason that teaching is a less lucrative profession, as here men must compete with the cheap labor of woman. Would you exalt your profession, exalt those who labor with you. Would you make it more lucrative, increase the salaries of the women engaged in the noble work of educating our future Presidents, Senators, and Congressmen.[1]

The issue Anthony raised at the end has never gone away. Sharon Tof-fee Shepela and Ann T. Viviano wrote more than 130 years later: "Women are paid less because they are in women's jobs, and women's jobs are paid less because they are done by women."[2]

In 1869, Francis Amasa Walker, about to take on the position of census superintendent, wrote an article in *Atlantic Monthly* describing the faults of the previous census, and some of his reflections concerned the employment of women. He argued that the woman who "works at home," by which he meant doing piecework, is generally

> not wholly dependent on her labor for support; but having a father, son, brother, or husband with whom she lives, takes this means of adding something to the family income, or of securing perhaps a little convenient pocket-money.
>
> Now it is this competition of women having a partial subsistence secured that tells most speedily and heavily upon the wages of women. A class of competitors of this kind will do more to bring down and keep down the price of work than the accession of five times their number strictly and solely dependent on their labor.

In other words, women who don't need to support themselves can accept lower wages.

> The women of our cities, although the sex is not apt to be very severely logical on the subject of its grievances, already recognize this competition as one of the chief causes which keep the price of their labor so far below that of men. The census would, therefore, make a valuable contribution to the industrial and social knowledge of the country if it would show what proportion of the half-million women employed in mechanical pursuits work in shop, and what proportion take their work home.[3]

Twenty years later Carroll D. Wright, the nation's first commissioner of Labor, pondered the issue in his report *Working Women in Large Cities:*

> Much is heard at the present time of the very low wages paid working women. It must be clear that they do not rise, on the average, above $5 per week, or $5.24 as indicated by this report. . . . The figures tell a sad story, and one is forced to ask how women can live on such earnings.[4]

Wright had an explanation for women living on earnings that "seem not only ridiculously low, but dangerously so." Women "could only displace men because they were willing to work for less wages."[5] Like Walker, he assumed that "many girls, living with their fathers and mothers," were working only for "pin money."[6]

In 1897 Commissioner Wright published *Work and Wages of Men, Women, and Children,* which reported on a study intended to determine whether women and children were taking factory jobs from men.

More than 1,000 establishments were visited and data was collected about almost 150,000 people. This report found that factory women were earning, on average, less than half as much as men.[7]

The study also asked whether women and children were as efficient as men at doing the same work. In hundreds of establishments employers were asked to rate their workers with a letter grade in terms of efficiency. Carroll D. Wright noted in his introduction that in some cases there is no mention that men may be doing heavier work and women lighter.[8]

To pick one example from hundreds: At a coffin maker in Minnesota, there were nine male cloth gluers and three female cloth gluers. Three of the men were rated lower in efficiency than all the other workers, but the lowest paid among them was paid about 25 percent more than the highest paid women.[9]

In cases where workers of the same efficiency level could be contrasted, there were 129 instances in which women, on average, were earning more than men (10.4 percent more), 595 instances in which men, on average, were earning more than women (32.3 percent more), and 57 in which their earnings were the same.[10]

In 1903 Commissioner Wright wrote a magazine article entitled "Why Women Are Paid Less Than Men." He argued that women were paid less because they were new to industry and its demands, had not unionized, and had not yet become politically active. Women also received financial "assistance from family and friends" and did inferior work because they expected to quit soon in favor of marriage.[11]

But all of this, he predicted, would be a temporary thing:

> As woman has the power given her to support herself, she will be less inclined to seek marriage relations simply for the purpose of securing what may seem to be a home and protection. The necessity under which many young women live, of looking to marriage as a freedom from the bondage of some kinds of labor, tends, in my mind, to be the worst form of prostitution that exists. I cannot see much difference between a woman who sells her whole freedom and her soul to a man for life because he furnishes her with certain conveniences and one who sells her temporary freedom and her soul for a temporary remuneration, except this, that the former may be worse than the latter.[12]

In *Statistics of Income 1916*, the Internal Revenue Service made an attempt to determine what percentage of the nation's income was earned by women. It was essentially foiled by the fact that majority of income tax returns were joint returns filed by "heads of family" on behalf of both husband and wife. However, 1.75 percent of the returns were filed by married women making separate returns, and they accounted for 3.07 percent of total net income; 6.14 percent of all returns were filed by other females, and they brought home 6.58 percent of the total net.[13]

In that same year of 1916 the Bureau of Labor Statistics (BLS) published a 1,000-page summary of its 19-volume *Report on Condition of Woman and Child Wage Earners*. The BLS took note of the difference of income between the sexes and pondered the reasons:

> In general the lower earnings of women seem due to a variety of causes, such as their lack of training which keeps them out of the better-paid work, a lack of self-assertion which makes them willing to accept low wages, and a lack of experience and organization which makes it impossible for them to secure the wages which men would probably insist upon having.[14]

The *Summary* also suggested that women were paid less because of the categories of work they did, because of their lesser strength, speed, or skill, and "in a very few instances, so few as to be negligible, it seemed due to no cause but that the women were willing to do the work for less and therefore were employed."[15]

The same book also noted that in one of the industries they studied almost 90 percent of women contributed all of their earnings to their family.[16] This gave the lie to what Mary Anderson, who became the first head of the Women's Bureau in 1920, later called "the most familiar and exasperating problem" of the "pin money theory." It was widely believed that working women did not really need their earnings.

> One of the first things we did in the Women's Bureau was to make a thorough investigation of the share of wage-earning women in family support. . . . It showed how many times it took more than the husband's or father's wages to support the family. It showed how many girls were sending money home or turning over their whole pay envelopes to their families. It showed how married women carried the double job of homemaker and wage earner.[17]

Anderson was probably referring to *What the Wage Earning Woman Contributes to Family Support,* written by Agnes L. Peterson and published by the Women's Bureau in 1929. Peterson argued that

> the data suggest that in many homes in the United States women form the last line of economic defense. . . . If this service to the family were evaluated in relation to the earnings and to the personal need of the woman

concerned, it would represent a spirit of devotion that is, to say the least, heroic.[18]

Peterson complained that "the general custom of paying wages on the basis of sex not only is unjust but complicates home problems for women. It is a relic of the dark ages when even many women failed to place an economic value on productive labor done in the home."[19]

The 1920 Census did not offer statistics on the marital status of working women, so the Women's Bureau made its own estimates: "In 10 studies single women form less than 50 per cent of the group and in 3 the proportion drops below 35 per cent. This is most remarkable, in view of the fact that one-fifth of all employed women are under 20 years of age."[20]

Peterson noted: "One of the greatest differences between the old and the new order for wage-earning women lies in the fact that in many cases marriage fails to bring to women the economic security considered formerly to be one of its chief advantages. Nowadays, marriage may bring new financial responsibilities for wife as well as for husband."[21] More than half of the working women surveyed contributed all their earnings to their families.[22]

In 1927 the first edition of the *Handbook of Labor Statistics* (*HLS*) made the following observation:

Under the present social order the father is the natural provider for all members of the family. It follows that whenever the wage earner lacks the means to provide for the becoming maintenance of his wife and children marriage and home life are discouraged, women and children are obliged to labor, and there is brought about a steady deterioration and lowering of standards in the families affected. Therefore a living wage means a family living wage.[23]

The *HLS* also proposed that women were paid less because the industries that were open to them paid less. Also, some of these industries such as sewing and candy-making were more subject to seasonal unemployment.[24]

The same edition of the *HLS* reported on the strike benefits offered by unions to their members. Bookbinders, for example, paid married men $15 a week, single men $10, and women $8. In some industries, the unions grouped women with the apprentices.[25]

In 1938 the Women's Bureau published *Differences in the Earnings of Women and Men*. To make its point the page before the first page announced: "WOMEN RECEIVE MUCH LOWER PAY THAN MEN. This is generally true regardless of date, industry, type of occupation, method of pay, or other qualifying factor."[26] The author, Mary Elizabeth Pidgeon, pointed out that women's low wages tended to depress men's as well.[27]

Pidgeon asked "WHY ARE WOMEN'S WAGES LOWER?" and supplied four pages of answers, including this one: "One argument that has been used to justify depressed wages for women is that men have families to support. However, the unmarried man, who is likely to assume less responsibility than his sister for their parents' obligations, is not paid less than the family man because of his lack of dependents."[28]

The 1940 Census was the first to ask respondents their income.[29] Rather startlingly, a greater percentage of women than men reported having a wage or salary income in 1939: 79.5 to 71.3. This might be explained in part by the lower salaries women continued to receive: the median income of men was $800 to $999, while that of women was $600 to $799.[30]

In January 1947 President Truman made his first Economic Report to Congress. Among his policy proposals was this: "We must end discrimination in employment or wages against certain classes of workers regardless of their individual abilities. Discrimination against certain racial and religious groups, against workers in late middle age, and against women, not only is repugnant to the principles of our democracy, but often creates artificial 'labor shortages' in the midst of labor surplus."[31]

Sixteen years later President Kennedy signed the Equal Pay Act, which said that an employer could not pay men and women different amounts for the same job.[32] Exceptions were possible, such as seniority or merit.[33]

Title VII of the Civil Rights Act of 1964, as amended in 1972, prohibited employers from discriminating against minorities and women in any aspect of employment, including pay.[34]

The laws requiring equal pay for the same job did not solve the dilemma of women's low pay. Another concept that arrived in the mid-1970s was "comparable worth." Here is how the General Accounting Office defined it:

> Some individuals and groups assert that, because men and women usually work in different occupations, the Equal Pay Act is unable to end wage discrimination against women. The concept of comparable worth thus goes beyond equal pay for equal work and suggests that there should be equal pay for work of equal "value" to an employer, even though the jobs are not the same. The value of a job, in this context, is commonly measured in terms of skill, effort, responsibility, and working conditions.
>
> The term "pay equity" is sometimes used interchangeably with the term comparable worth. Nonetheless, pay equity encompasses a broader

concept than does comparable worth in that it refers to any efforts designed to assure that fair and objective means are used to set wages.[35]

One example of the problem was given in 1977 by the National Commission on the Observance of International Women's Year, which found that 20 percent of the employed women they surveyed were unable to compare their pay and promotion to those of men because "no men work in my job type." The same survey found that one-third of women had no income of their own.[36]

Consider an example from the 1980 Census. Pharmacy was a male-dominated field, nursing a female one. The median wage for male pharmacists was $23,000 and for females $18,000. But in nursing the median wage for male nurses was also higher than that for women, by 1,000 dollars.[37]

During 1985 the Labor Department published a series of presentations that had been made at the Annual Meetings of the American Statistical Association. One of them was by the economist Carolyn Shaw Bell whose subject was "Comparative Worth: How Do We Know It Will Work?" She responded: "We don't. We are completely unable to predict the outcomes of an effective comparative worth policy, whether mandated by law or adopted by private decisionmakers."[38]

Further on she noted:

> There are then two ways by which to conclude that discrimination exists. One is to assume that women are being confined to the lower-wage jobs. The other is to hold that women tend to enter certain occupations, and that those jobs pay less because they are "female jobs. . . ."
>
> Indeed, evidence exists that as formerly male jobs (stenographers at the turn of the century and bank tellers during the postwar years) have become almost exclusively female, relative pay levels for those occupations have fallen. It follows, according to this line of reasoning, that it will do no good to admit women to men's jobs, that what is needed is to raise the prevailing low levels of pay for female jobs. Hence the need for comparative worth.[39]

The biggest victory for pay equity was the AFSCME Decision, a 1983 case in which a federal judge ruled that Washington State had discriminated against workers in predominantly female jobs. Plaintiffs were awarded $400 million. However, in 1985 the Ninth Circuit overturned this decision. Judge (now Supreme Court justice) Anthony Kennedy wrote that Washington State was not obligated "to eliminate an economic inequality it did not create."[40]

In that same year the General Accounting Office prepared a list of answers for members of Congress concerning *Comparable Worth and Sex-Based Wage Discrimination*. It concluded:

(1) There is no current statute which uses gender to differentiate between employees; (2) Congress rejected language requiring equal pay for comparable work in favor of the equal work standard currently contained in the act; (3) consideration is not given to the gender of private sector employees in federal pay surveys; (4) individual characteristics are not considered in job evaluations, but rather, job characteristics are evaluated; and (5) since evaluation systems are subjective, it is possible for two evaluation experts to arrive at different conclusions.[41]

Federal figures over the years continued to show sex differences in incomes. After the 2000 Census a special report was produced on the subject. Some of the points it made follow:

The highest-paid occupation for men and for women is *Physicians and surgeons,* but the female median ($88,000) is only 63 percent of the male median ($140,000). Different degrees of specialization within an occupation and different choices of industry or business organization may affect the ratio. For example, women might choose more frequently than men to practice in lower-paid medical specialties.[42]

The report does not address the question that opened this chapter: are women drawn to lower-paying specialties, or are those specialties paid less because women are drawn to them?

Fifteen of the 20 highest-paid occupations for men were among the highest for women as well, but in all cases the female median salary was lower than that of men. "In fact, the occupation third on the list for women makes the same as the occupation last on the list for men."[43] Education and experience did not account for the difference. In the lowest-paid occupation, dishwashers, women's median income was 74 percent of that of men.[44]

It seems unnecessary to repeat the many reports by government agencies on the gap between the incomes of men and women. Among those who have made the point in the last few decades are the BLS, the Civil Rights Commission, the Women's Bureau, the Census Bureau, and the President's Council of Economic Advisors.[45]

In 2016 the Democratic staff of the Joint Economic Committee published *Gender Pay Inequality: Consequences for Women, Families and the*

Economy. This background report offered a list of factors contributing to the gap in pay:

- Women are more likely than men to interrupt their careers to care for children.
- Working mothers often pay a "Mommy Penalty."
- Women are more likely than men to be primary caregivers of other family members.
- Women who are forced to work part-time earn less.
- Women often work in occupations that pay less.
- Women are underrepresented in leadership.

When all of these factors were taken into consideration, 40 percent of the income gap remained unaccounted for. This leaves the possibility that more than one-third of the difference in income is the result of sex discrimination.[46]

Statistical Abstract

"Median money income of families" appeared in the 1964 volume of the *Statistical Abstract*.[47] Three years later data on the income of unrelated individuals was added, and both tables were then broken down by sex. In data for the most recent year (1965), families headed by a man averaged $7,235 but reached $8,597 if the wife was in the paid labor force. Families headed by a woman had a median income of $3,582.[48]

The preface of that same 1967 edition announced the inclusion of almost 80 new tables, one of which it described as "Median Earnings." In fact the actual title was "Median Earnings of Male Civilians by Occupation of Longest Job."[49] No explanation was offered for leaving out data on female civilians.

Income numbers organized by sex arrived two years later. The median figure for men was $5,571 and for women $1,819.[50]

The year 1970 introduced a table on "Top Wealthholders." Between 1953 and 1962 the percentage of women in that category rose from 32.7 percent to 38.6 percent. There were 28,369 female millionaires in 1962, compared to 31,202 men. Women millionaires were almost five times as likely as their male counterparts to be widowed.[51]

More income data appeared in 1973, including "Wife's Contribution to Family Income."[52]

CHAPTER TWELVE

Unemployment during the Great Depression

In January 1930, a few months after the Great Depression started, President Hoover declared that things were improving. He based his statement in part on numbers from the U.S. Employment Service, which forecast future growth based on the hiring plans of employers. The industrial commissioner of New York State, Frances Perkins, used data from the U.S. Bureau of Labor Statistics to prove him wrong.[1] Two years later Perkins's boss, Governor Franklin Delano Roosevelt, defeated Hoover for the presidency, and she became secretary of Labor. She was the first woman to serve in the cabinet.

Figures on unemployment have always been subject to political use and political debate. One of many points of confusion is that in the world of federal statistics to be "unemployed" does not mean merely that one is not working, nor even that one does not have a paid job.

In the 1980s A.J. Jaffe and Herbert F. Spirer explained how this came to be. During the Great Depression "lawmakers and the executive branch alike were faced with the question: How many people are unemployed and need jobs? Only with this information could the government decide how much money and effort to allocate to job creation programs. No one had any answers, for no one knew with any reasonable degree of certainty the number of unemployed."[2] The Works Progress Administration (WPA) had the job of defining employment and unemployment. The result was the concept of the "labor force," which included only people working for money, or trying to do so.

It was felt that there was no point counting housewives or voluntary workers (such as people who voluntarily assist a religious institution without pay) since Congress was not considering appropriating aid for such people. . . . Thus, the labor market is defined as those people who are employed plus those among the civilian, noninstitutional population who are actively seeking jobs.[3]

This meant that only those looking for work are considered unemployed. But assumptions about sex can shape conclusions about who is and is not seeking a job.

A monograph by Mary V. Dempsey, published in 1933 by the Women's Bureau, explained some of the difficulties. In *The Occupational Progress of Women, 1910 to 1930,* Dempsey pointed out that the 1930 Census recorded a 25.8 percent increase over 1920 in women who worked for money, including those temporarily unemployed.

> However the census enumerator was left to decide what constituted temporary unemployment, and there is no positive assurance that he took time to explain to each person interviewed that the usual occupation was what he wanted to know.
>
> Many women whose factory or mercantile employment had ceased around Christmas 1929, and who saw no chance of reemployment in the immediate future, undoubtedly stated that they had no occupation when interviewed in April. Presumably the enumerator accepted this statement without question, in some instances at least. Especially would this be true when the enumerator found the temporarily unemployed married woman busily engaged as a housewife at the time she was interviewed. In certain cases he no doubt assumed, without giving the matter serious thought, that she had always been so engaged, but the number of such instances is problematical. In other words, the enumerator may have obtained neither the usual occupation nor the fact of unemployment in the case of certain women who had been out of work for some time and who said off-hand that they had no occupation.
>
> It is not improbable that more unemployed women than men may have thus been entirely omitted from the number of gainful workers as listed by the census, and these omissions may include more married women than single women. If this be true, than the number of working women enumerated in 1930, large as it is, may even be a slight understatement of those usually engaged in gainful occupations, and the figure may reflect to a slight degree the extent of lessened industrial activity, though the bureau's instructions ruled otherwise.[4]

The 1930 Census showed women having a lower unemployment rate than men, which is typical of economic downturns. They also typically have a slower recovery, as occurred during the recent Great Recession.[5]

Of course, careless assumptions by census-takers are not the only reason why women's unemployment rate could be lower than men's in an economic downturn. Women were paid less, which made them a bargain. The Census Bureau also suggested that "women are more likely to retire from the labor force on losing their jobs than are men."[6]

There was also the matter of "sex-segregation of occupations." As Paula Rayman pointed out: "During the depression female occupations contracted less than male occupations; unemployment rates for women thus were deeply affected by linking gender and occupational factors. . . . In addition to clerical work, nurses, laundresses, and domestic servants enjoyed more than average stability."[7]

Unemployment figures also ignored the fact that many people were engaged in temporary or part-time work when they would have preferred or needed full-time work. As Winifred D. Wandersee noted, "Many working women . . . although listed as employed, were actually underemployed. Saleswomen were typical in this respect. Many of them worked part-time during the peak hours of business. For some women, particularly married women, this was a convenient arrangement. But for others who needed full-time employment, the job was taken simply because there was no full-time work to be had."[8]

Mary Elizabeth Pidgeon of the Women's Bureau wrote a book-length report detailing the "continual, often extreme, fluctuation in the employment of women from month to month and year to year," which occurred during the early part of the Great Depression.[9]

An example of those fluctuations can be seen by comparing the 1930 Census with the special Census of Unemployment taken the next January, which covered 18 cities and 3 boroughs of New York City.[10] The 1930 Census found 668,661 women unemployed. Less than a year later the national estimate rose to 2,000,000.[11] The percentage of women unemployed in 1931 ranged from 9.4 percent in San Francisco to 26.0 percent in Houston. In most cities the figures for men were worse.[12]

The same special Census of Unemployment found that one-half of unemployed men were heads of families, while almost 10 percent of unemployed women were as well.[13] Since women were not listed as heads if an adult male was present, it is likely that nobody in those homes had a job.

The Bureau of Labor Statistics published a new edition of the *Handbook of Labor Statistics (HLS)* in 1936, featuring a 20-page section on "Women in Industry." The *HLS* noted that early in the Great Depression there had been "a distinct effort to develop a drive against married women in industry, which in this country met with only limited success."[14]

At first, the *Handbook* reported, the problems of women were ignored in the larger emergency. Recognition of the female predicament started outside the government:

> Private agencies realized clearly the acuteness of the situation for the unattached women living in large cities who found their jobs gone and their savings exhausted, and the public was shocked when later it became known that women and girls, as well as men and boys, had taken to the road; but there was a rather widespread, tacit acceptance of the idea that such things were exceptional; that in general, women's responsibilities were not as heavy as men's; and that on the whole they were probably getting along not too badly.[15]

In that regard it is worth noting that some of the earliest major nongovernment studies that claimed to give a complete overview of the types of unemployed people ignored women entirely.[16]

The 1940 Census adopted the labor force definitions, which the WPA had created. The instructions for the census-takers told them to list as unemployed "each person seeking work or assigned to public emergency work who has had previous work experience on a private job or a non-emergency Government job lasting 1 month or more full time."[17]

The census-taker would write down the number of weeks the worker had been out of work. But an example of an exception would be

> the case of a housewife who worked as a stenographer before her marriage and began to seek work after her husband lost his job on October 1, 1939; for this housewife enter "26," the number of weeks elapsed between October 1, 1939, and March 30, 1940. This is the proper entry because, while she may not have had a job for pay or profit for several years, she did not begin to seek work until her husband became unemployed and has been seeking work for only 26 weeks.[18]

The Census Bureau lamented the difficulty of getting a clear analysis of the female situation: "some women who had lost their jobs and were keeping house while looking for another employment opportunity may have been classified as engaged in home housework instead of seeking work."[19]

Another difficulty concerned seasonal workers, mostly farm labor. Whether such a person would be defined as unemployed differed according to the 1930 and 1940 definitions. It could also differ depending on the worker's sex. According to a 1940 Census report:

> Practically all of the male seasonal workers, other than students, between the ages of 20 and 64 years were probably enumerated as gainful workers

in 1930, since enumerators who found such men idle at the time of enu-meration were almost certain to inquire whether they did not follow a gainful occupation at other times of the year. On the other hand, some of the male seasonal workers in this age range were included by error in the 1940 labor force, since enumerators were likely to regard them as unem-ployed, or as "having a job" and to report them as in the labor force in spite of their inactivity during the census week. . . .

In the case of females, the proportion of seasonal workers, other than students, who were classified as gainful workers in 1930 was probably much smaller than in the case of males. Enumerators undoubtedly tended to neglect the occupational questions for women who were obviously engaged in housekeeping at the time of the census. Even if such women were asked to state their occupations, they were likely to report themselves as housewives if the season during which they followed a gainful occupa-tion was limited to a few months of the year.[20]

The same report looked at the people who had been identified by census-takers as unemployed during the 1930 Census but were removed from the final calculations. For example, 6,000 people were rejected from "unemployment status" because "the persons had been working for mem-bers of their own families without money compensation." It is reasonable to assume that the majority of them were female. The 1940 Census rejected the unemployment status of a total of 12,000 females over the age of 13 for various reasons. Four times that many men suffered the same fate.[21]

Statistical Abstract

The 1931 volume of the *Statistical Abstract* broke unemployment down into seven categories, some of which, it acknowledged, "would not, even under the most elastic definition, be considered 'unemployed.'" Only the two largest categories were divided by sex: "persons out of a job, able to work, and looking for a job" and "persons having jobs but on lay off with-out pay, excluding those sick or voluntarily idle." Among the categories not divided by sex were "persons out of a job and not looking for work" and "persons having jobs but voluntarily idle without pay."[22]

This table disappeared in 1933. Two years later data arrived on "Unem-ployment Relief," counting families and single persons receiving pay-ments from public funds. These were not distinguished by sex.[23]

PART V

Women at Work

CHAPTER THIRTEEN

The Bureau of Labor Statistics and the Women's Bureau

To discuss government statistics about the employment of women, it is necessary to start with these two agencies in the Department of Labor. Most of the data comes from them.

Technically, the Bureau of Labor Statistics (BLS) is older than the department in which it dwells. It began with the name Bureau of Labor, as part of the Interior Department, in 1885.[1]

The first commissioner of the BLS was Carroll D. Wright, who had previously held a similar position in Massachusetts and promised to operate the agency as "a scientific office, not as a Bureau of agitation or propaganda."[2]

In 1903, Commissioner Wright wrote a magazine article entitled "Why Women Are Paid Less Than Men." He explained that he had once felt that women entering the factory system would cause harm to both them and to the American family, but his investigations changed his mind.[3] "Until within a comparatively recent period, woman's subjection to man has been well-nigh complete in all respects," he noted. "Should industrial equality [for women] be secured political equality must surely follow."[4] Before a woman was permitted to work in factories

she played little or no part in material production. She was used to home duties, to field drudgeries, and to the work necessary for the assistance of her husband or father in the hand labor which he performed; but under that system she lived a narrow, contracted, unwholesome life in the lower walks of industry, and she was not known or recognized in the higher. . . . [T]here are but few lines of remunerative employment not now open to women.[5]

Wright left the agency in 1905, two years after it became part of the newly created Commerce and Labor Department.[6] The bureau took on its present name in 1913 when it became part of the new Labor Department.[7]

In 1907 Congress authorized a study of the working conditions of women and children. The Bureau of Labor conducted a massive, two-year research campaign that resulted in the *Report on Condition of Woman and Child Wage Earners in the United States,* 19 volumes covering everything from juvenile delinquency to infant mortality in a mill town to trade unionism among women. The results contained much that shocked America's conscience. For example, the studies showed that many cotton-mill families were getting by on less food money than federal prisoners.[8] The publications led to more surveys being done by state governments and to changes in labor laws.

Starting in 1960 the BLS began a series of statistical publications called Special Labor Force Reports. The second volume was "Marital Status of Workers, 1959," and, like most of the publications on that subject, it concentrated almost entirely on the marital status of women workers, because the BLS saw the growth of women working outside the home as one of the "outstanding developments affecting the labor force."[9]

In 2004 the BLS became involved in a controversy related to what some interpreted as a deliberate attempt by George W. Bush's administration to conceal information of which it disapproved. Specifically, the bureau announced its plan to make major changes in the Current Employment Statistics (CES) survey.

The CES is a monthly survey based on the payroll records of thousands of businesses. The bureau had been collecting separate data by sex in major industries since 1937,[10] but it announced that it would no longer report that information in the CES. It gave three reasons: the requirement provided too much of a burden on the cooperating businesses, the *Current Population Reports* (CPR) provided similar information, and the information was not used very much.[11]

Among those responding to this change was the Institute for Women's Policy Research (IWPR), a nongovernment organization. The IWPR said, in part:

> While we certainly are sympathetic with the desire of the BLS to reduce respondent burden, it is important to realize that these data on women workers are unique and extremely useful for research on women's employment. Since the proposed revisions to the survey include expanding reporting in other areas, it seems especially unreasonable to discontinue reporting on these important data on women workers.

As we all know, women and men generally work in very different places in the labor market; occupational segregation by sex is a persistent feature of U.S. employment. Job losses and job gains over the course of a recession and recovery vary tremendously by industry, leading to unpredictable differences between women's and men's experiences over the business cycle and in response to structural economic change. Without accurate, timely data, we may develop misleading pictures of employment changes for both men and women and institute ineffective policy solutions.[12]

The IWPR also pointed out that the CPR data was organized by household and was therefore useless in tracking, for example, women's employment by industry. It also gave examples of how it was currently using the data to analyze how the 2001 recession had affected women's jobs.[13]

In 2006 Congress forced the BLS to start collecting data by sex again, which meant the bureau also had to reconstruct the months of missing statistics.[14]

The BLS currently has a website filled with data, including these pages:

- *Educational Attainment of Women in the Labor Force, 1970–2010*
- *Highlights of Women's Earnings.* 1998–2014 editions
- *The Labor Force Experience of Women from "Generation X"* (2002)
- *Labor Force Participation Rates among Mothers, 1975–2008*
- *Wives Who Earn More Than Their Husbands, 1987–2014*
- *Women in the Labor Force: A Databook.* 2004–2015 editions[15]

Another result of the 19-volume study on the working conditions of children and women was the creation in 1912 of a Children's Bureau within the Department of Commerce and Labor.[16] Technically a woman's division had been created the year before, but Congress appropriated no funds for it.[17]

More important, the BLS had stayed true to Carroll Wright's promise at its founding to be "scientific" and not an advocate for a position or group. Women were beginning to demand that an agency be created that would not only gather statistics about them but speak up for their sex as well.

In 1913 Flora McDonald Thompson, president of the Housekeepers Alliance, wrote a letter to the secretary of Labor, which read in part:

A Bureau of Woman Labor is necessary to reclaim the home makers of the country from the status of the economic submerged. . . . The Bureau of Labor Statistics has . . . [not] done more than estimate cost and prices with respect to the raw materials consumed in living; it has ignored the medium through which those materials are converted into the elements of life—women working for the family in the home. It has counted no cost in connection with the unpaid labor of wives. . . . A Bureau of Woman Labor would have for one of its chief functions to develop exact notions of value with respect to the unpaid labor of wives and to the exercise of the office of maternity.[18]

Although bills were introduced in Congress to create such an agency, nothing was achieved until 1918 when Women in Industry Service (WIS) was created as a war measure. The duty of WIS was to determine policies related to the working hours, conditions, and wages of women in war-related industries.[19] The agency noted in its first annual report: "The small appropriation of the Woman in Industry Service made it impossible to carry on any extensive statistical inquiry, although the data would have been vital in appraising the status of women workers during this period."[20]

One of WIS's accomplishments was the publication of *Standards for the Employment of Women in Industry* in 1918. The *Standards* continued to be revised as recently as 1965.[21] The introduction of the first edition explained:

> The greater necessity for control of the standards of women's employment is due to the fact that women have been in a weaker position economically than men. Reconstruction [after the war] will give an opportunity for a new upbuilding of safeguards to conserve alike the industrial efficiency and the health of women, and to make it impossible for selfish interests to exploit them as unwilling competitors in lowering standards of wages, hours, working conditions, and industrial relations which are for the best interest of the workers, the industries, and the citizenship of the country.[22]

The 1918 standards limited women to 8 hours of work per day and no more than 48 hours a week. It called for women to receive the same wages as men for the same work. There were rules for comfort and sanitation, posture, and safety among others. Home work was forbidden, and women were supposed to be supervised by female executives.[23] Clearly, these goals were never achieved.

A permanent Women's Bureau was finally created in the Labor Department in 1920, the same year women won the right to vote. The bureau was given the duty to "formulate standards and policies which shall promote the welfare of wage-earning women, improve their working conditions, increase their efficiency, and advance their opportunities for profitable employment." It was also authorized to investigate all issues related to women in industry.[24]

The Women's Bureau is headed by a director, apparently the only position in the federal government still required, by law, to be filled by a woman.[25] The first director was Mary Anderson, a Swedish immigrant who had entered the job market as a domestic servant at $1.50 a week. She served until 1944. The bureau began with a staff of 20 and a yearly budget of $30,000.[26]

In its first decade the bureau published more than 80 studies filled with statistics as well as anecdotal data. Over the past century the bureau has published material on a wide variety of topics.

There was, however, a continual struggle for funding. For example, after the 1920 Census the Women's Bureau wanted to do a special study of the data collected about working women but had enough money only to examine the information about one city, Passaic, New Jersey.[27]

In its first decades the Women's Bureau favored protective legislation for women—that is, laws that limited the maximum number of hours females could work, banned night work, and so on. This allied the bureau with women's trade unions but led to conflict with organizations working for the Equal Rights Amendment (first proposed in 1921).[28]

In 1929 the American Statistical Association (a nongovernmental organization) asked the Women's Bureau "to provide some basis for guiding policies as to whether employment figures should be collected and presented separately for each sex." In order to comply, the bureau studied employment trends in Ohio by sex for the years 1914–1924. The results showed that figures for the sexes were usually similar, but when the economy took a large rise or fall the results for men and women varied widely, and "trends indicated by the total are representative of neither women's nor men's employment, but illustrate the neutralizing effect of combining the figures for the two sexes when the trends of their employment are in opposite directions."[29]

During World War II the Women's Bureau studied the "Rosie the Riveter" phenomenon, as millions of women moved into employment, especially in the war industries. The bureau published 13 reports on women in wartime industries, as well as "Equal Pay for Women in War Industries."[30]

Starting in 1952 the Women's Bureau began publishing an important digest of statistical data called the *Handbook on Women Workers*. It continued until 1993. Table 13.1, while somewhat simplified (e.g., ignoring changes in terminology), shows how the topics considered worthy of discussion changed over time.

Table 13.1   *Handbook on Women Workers:* Subjects covered in different editions.

	1952	1958	1965	1975	1983	1993
Demographic data						
Age	*	*	*	*	*	*
Race	*	*	*	*	*	*
Hispanic/Spanish origin				*	*	*
Education	*	*	*	*	*	*
Family						
Marital status	*	*	*	*	*	*
Women head/maintain families	*	*	*	*	*	*
Working mothers	*	*	*	*	*	*
Working wives	*	*	*	*	*	*
Family status		*	*	*	*	*
Child care			*	*	*	*
Money						
Earnings/income	*	*	*	*	*	*
Retirement income		*				
Investment income		*	*			
Women in poverty				*	*	*
Working/nonworking						
Employment and unemployment			*	*	*	*
Nonworking women			*	*	*	
Homemakers			*			
Displaced homemakers					*	*
How women find jobs				*	*	
Occupations						
Occupation and industry	*	*	*	*	*	*
Part-time work	*	*	*	*	*	*
Apprenticeship		*	*			
Dual/multiple jobs			*	*	*	*
Armed services			*	*	*	*
Elective office				*		

(Continued)

	1952	1958	1965	1975	1983	1993
Farm workers/farmers			*	*	*	
Nontraditional occupations					*	
Diversity in workstyle						*
Contingent and home-based employment						*
Women business owners						*
Work issues						
Legal issues	*	*	*	*	*	*
Unions	*	*	*	*	*	*
Injuries	*					
Labor turnover or tenure			*	*	*	
Absenteeism			*	*		
Sexual harassment					*	*
Occupational safety and health					*	*
Glass ceiling						*

Sources: U.S. Labor Department, Women's Bureau, *1952 Handbook of Facts;* U.S. Labor Department, Women's Bureau, *1958 Handbook;* U.S. Labor Department, Women's Bureau, *Handbook 1965;* U.S. Labor Department, Women's Bureau, *1975 Handbook;* U.S. Labor Department, Women's Bureau, *Time of Change;* U.S. Labor Department, Women's Bureau, *1993 Handbook.*

The year 1953 saw an important change when President Eisenhower appointed Alice K. Leopold as assistant to the secretary of Labor for women's affairs. Her background was in business rather than labor and she oriented the Women's Bureau with commerce rather than the unions.[31]

By 1971, the Women's Bureau was noting how changes in society had altered its own duties:

Fifty years ago, when the Women's Bureau was founded, our primary concern was the exploitation of women workers. No longer is this true. No longer do we need to place primary emphasis on the establishment of safety standards or the elimination of long working hours and appalling working conditions.

But there are still serious inequalities in the labor market which result in the underutilization of women workers. There are still barriers which deny women the freedom to prepare for and enter employment suitable to their individual interests and abilities.[32]

Changes, of course, continued apace. In 1985, the bureau noted: "Most adult working age women are employed. Most women with preschool or school-age children are in the labor force. Less than a decade ago, neither of those statements was true."[33]

In 1999 President Bill Clinton created the Equal Pay Matters Initiative, which, according to Barbara Finlay, provided extra funds to the Women's Bureau to "educate employers about equal pay issues, to improve the enforcement of Title VII pay-discrimination laws, and to provide women workers with relevant information and resources." The program recovered over $15 million in back pay for women and minorities. That initiative was eliminated during the first term of George W. Bush, as part of what some people called his "War on Women."[34]

Under Clinton the Women's Bureau's mission statement had included such responsibilities as "to advocate and inform women directly and the public as well, of women's rights and employment issues. . . . [The Bureau researches] and analyzes information about women and work." Under Bush, these points were replaced with: "To promote profitable employment opportunities for women, to empower them by enhancing their skills and improving their working conditions, and to provide employers with more alternatives to meet their labor needs."[35]

In 2004 the National Council for Research on Women (NCRW) (a nonprofit group) issued a report called *Missing: Information about Women's Lives*, which criticized the actions of the Bush administration:

> Does it matter that a major resource for working women, the Department of Labor's Women's Bureau, an agency charged by Congress with providing information on women's economic status and rights, is now nearly silent on those issues? Yes! Women lose the tools they need to know their rights in the workplace, advance their careers, and help support their families when helpful publications focused specifically on job rights are no longer available. A look at various public websites indicates that information accumulated over decades under both Republican and Democratic administrations, including a wide variety of helpful factsheets that analyze women's status and rights, is no longer available.[36]

The NCRW noted that many Women's Bureau publications had disappeared from its website. These included the following:

- *1993 Handbook on Women Workers* (statistical report)
- *Black Women in the Labor Force*

- *Domestic Violence: A Workplace Issue*
- *Don't Work in the Dark—Know Your Rights*
- *Median Annual Earnings for Year-Round Full-Time Workers by Sex in Current and Real Dollars, 1951–1997* (statistical report)
- *Outlook on Women Veterans*
- *Women Who Maintain Families*
- *Women's Earnings as Percent of Men's 1979–1997* (statistical report)
- *Women's Jobs 1964–1996: More Than 30 Years of Progress* (statistical report)
- *Worth More Than We Earn: Fair Pay for Working Women*

Among the few new titles that had replaced the preceding ones on the website were the following:

- *Hot Jobs for the 21st Century*
- *Women Business Owners*
- *Women in High Tech Jobs*[37]

The researcher who compiled this list of changes, Gwendolyn Beetham, asked: "Why doesn't a Bureau set up to deal with working women's issues prioritize the same issues as women workers themselves?"[38]

During the Obama administration the mission statement of the bureau changed again. In part, it said:

Our Goals
- Reduce barriers that inhibit or prevent women's access to—and retention in—better jobs
- Ensure women's fair treatment in the workplace

Our Strategies
- Improve workplace practices and supports
- Promote greater access to and preparation for better jobs for women
- Promote fair compensation and equal pay[39]

Statistical Abstract

The Bureau of Labor first appeared in the 1904 edition of the *Statistical Abstract,* but only as a budget item.[40] It was recognized as a producer of data the next year, credited with a single table about buildings and loan associations.[41] The BLS appeared for the first time under its new name in the 1913 edition.[42]

In the same way, the Women's Bureau made its first appearance in *Statistical Abstract 1923* as a spender of money[43] but did not appear as a source of data until 33 years later, when the *1954 Handbook on Women Workers* was mentioned.[44]

CHAPTER FOURTEEN

Employment

In 1910 Helen L. Sumner wrote *History of Women in Industry in the United States,* a book that was published as a congressional document. In her introduction she made an important point:

> Women have always worked, and their work has probably always been quite as important a factor in the total economy of society as it is today. But during the nineteenth century a transformation occurred in their economic position and in the character and conditions of their work. Their unpaid services have been transformed into paid services, their work has been removed from the home to the factory and workshop, their range of possible employment has been increased and at the same time their monopoly of their traditional occupations has been destroyed. The individuality of their work has been lost in a standardized product.[1]

This chapter cannot attempt to capture the entire history of the transformation of women's paid employment but will examine highlights of how it has been reflected in federal statistics.

The 1820 Census gathered information on the number of people of both sexes employed by industry but didn't publish the results. In 1840 some types of businesses were queried about how many people they employed, while others were asked only for the "number of men." Silk manufacturers were also asked how many women and children were employed.[2]

However, it might be unwise to rely too much on that census. In 1843 the American Statistical Association (ASA) complained of its many errors. According to Carroll D. Wright's history of the census, published in 1900, the ASA said that the census-takers, in judging occupations,

> seem to have included the whole population, men, women and children, in these classes, arranging them, probably, according to the employment of

the head of the family, and some seem to have noticed only the males over 21 years of age; others seem to have noticed all who were sufficiently able to perform any service; and, lastly, some seem to have entirely neglected this duty, and have recorded none in some of the employments; and in many counties none are reported to have any employment whatever.[3]

The next census asked only "free males" over the age of 14 about their occupations. As statistician William C. Hunt noted in a 1909 history, the question did not apply to "females or slaves."[4] In 1860 all free people over the age of 14 were asked their occupation, but the data was published "without distinction of sex."[5]

Starting in 1870 the Census was managed by Francis Amasa Walker, a distinguished statistician. He argued that the occupation figures were relatively correct for men's jobs but not for women's because census-takers tended to assume women and children didn't work and therefore forgot to ask.[6]

In 1880 Walker noticed that women accounted for one-quarter of the rise in the number of people with occupations in the last decade, a higher percentage than in the past.[7] Nonetheless, 11 million women had no occupation listed, compared to 1 million men. He suggested the discrepancy was made up of "the greater classes of women—wives, mothers, or grown daughters, keeping house for their families or living at home without any special avocation."[8]

Modern scholars Susan B. Carter and Richard Sutch offered a different explanation for the women without occupations. They studied the Public Use Microdata Sample (PUMS), a 1 percent sample of the original census records, and concluded that the 1880 Census figures were "heavily edited to reduce the number of individuals with occupations. For youthful and older males and all women, the editing was so substantial as to qualitatively affect the apparent trend in labor-force participation." Walker, they claimed, "knowingly, willfully, and secretly" changed the figures.[9]

The PUMS data showed 35 percent more younger women employed than the published figures recognized. Women in the prime employment age showed a 44 percent increase over the official data, and the PUMS figures for older women were almost 150 percent higher than the numbers Walker had approved. No rate was published for the employment rate of married women in 1880, but using the PUMS records Carter and Sutch estimated it at 12.3 percent.[10] They concluded that Walker had removed from the tables anyone he suspected of working only part-time.[11] Lisa Geib-Gunderson also used PUMS data to conclude that the Census Bureau's underreporting of women with paid occupations continued, though at a decreasing level, through 1910.[12]

In 1889 Carroll D. Wright, then the first commissioner of Labor, wrote *Working Women in Large Cities,* based on interviews with 17,000 women doing manual labor in 22 cities.[13] He reported this about the mostly female operatives who conducted the interviews:

> The agents of the Department have carried their work into the lowest and worst places in the cities named, because in such places are to be found women who are struggling for a livelihood in most respectable callings, living in such places as a matter of necessity, since they can not afford to live otherwise; the women, however, who prefer the slums, but who are not legitimately to be classed with the working women, are not included in this investigation.[14]

The average age of the women was 22 years, 7 months.[15] The average time in their current occupation was almost 4 years, 10 months.[16]

Only 745 of the women were married and 1,038 were widowed. Divorced women were not mentioned. "The working women, then," Wright concluded, "as a rule, are single women, fighting their industrial fight until other conditions shall release them from it."[17]

Almost 15,000 of the working women lived at home, and two-thirds of those "not only work at their regular occupations but assist in the housework at home." Wright noted that "a very large percentage, and one that is to be regretted, comprehending 2,309, do not attend church at all."[18] With a surprising note of ambivalence, Wright concluded that most of "the working women in our great cities are under home influences. Whatever those influences are, the women are under them."[19]

Modern scholars have been able to examine only the city averages that served as the basis for Wright's report, because the original surveys have never been found.[20]

The next Census, that of 1890, was the first to use automation: records were entered onto punch cards that were tabulated by machines. This was the first appearance of the punch cards, which ran computers for most of the latter half of the 20th century.[21]

It was also the first census to report occupational data by marital status. Wright, who had taken charge of the Census Office in 1893, noted that this information was most important "relative to married females engaged in remunerative work." He found that the fields in which married women made up the largest percentage of female workers were laundresses, farm workers, unspecified laborers, and boarding and lodging housekeepers. Widows made up more than three-quarters of the female farmers, planters, and overseers, as well as three-fifths of the female boarding and lodging housekeepers.[22]

Finally, the 1890 Census saw the production of the first *Statistical Atlas,* an attempt to convey the highlights of the data in a graphic manner. Among the facts the authors thought of interest was that among

> the females, we find the highest proportion of female wage earners among the negroes [sic]. This is accounted for by the fact that this race is largely employed as domestic servants, and in the cotton region the women work very generally in the field. The proportion of female wage earners among the foreign whites [sic] and the native whites [sic] of foreign parentage is very nearly equal, and is much larger than among the native whites [sic] of native parentage.[23]

Modern scholar Claudia Goldin argued that the 1890 Census was relatively accurate in measuring women's labor outside the home but miscounted the work they did at home and on the farm. She calculated that the productivity of women overall was 14 percent higher than the official figures.[24]

Penelope Ciancanelli noted that the census-takers of 1900 were accused of racism (although that word was not used) by no less than the authors of the reports on the census that followed 10 years later.[25] The 1910 Census report complained that "the inefficiency and carelessness of the enumerators" as well as the "greater amount of ignorance in the negro [sic] population" led to inaccurate descriptions of African American's occupations, and this was especially true of the female population.

> In general, there was too great a tendency among the enumerators to return a gainful occupation for every negro [sic], especially for every negro [sic] woman and child. While it is well known that the negro [sic] women and children in the South work in the fields much more commonly than do white [sic] women and children in any section of the country, still the returns showed that frequently "gainful" occupations were returned for negro [sic] women and children in the South who, elsewhere, would not have been considered gainfully employed.[26]

It was also becoming clear to some scholars that it was difficult to compare the figures for women and children across the decades because each census had approached the question so differently. As Edith Abbott wrote in *Women in Industry,* a book commercially published in 1910:

> To summarize briefly this information as to available statistics: for 1850 and 1860 we have the number of women reported only from the manufactures schedules, and the age of women is not given; for 1870–1900 we have the number of women reported both from the population (occupations) schedules and from the manufactures schedules, the former giving

the number of men and women over ten and the manufactures returns having been changed in 1870 to give the number of men and women over sixteen and the number of children, boys and girls not distinguished, under sixteen.[27]

The next census brought a new set of controversies. The 1910 figures showed a large increase in employed women. At the time this was mostly credited to (or blamed on) a change in the instructions to census-takers that emphasized that "it must never be taken for granted, without inquiry, that a woman, or child, has no occupation."[28]

Some of the interesting points from the occupation data from the 1910 Census are as follows:

- Four percent of the people working in transportation were women, but 80 percent of those women were telephone operators, then considered part of the transportation industry.

- Almost 13 percent of the people in trade were females, more than half of whom were saleswomen in stores.

- More than two-fifths of people in professional services were women; 85 percent of those were musicians, teachers, or nurses.

- The number of household servants had almost doubled in 40 years. This was due to "a steadily growing supply of labor and an ever-increasing demand." In most cases these servants were new immigrants, living in their employer's home.

- Less than 1 percent of aviators—who were categorized with showmen—were women. "The figures do not of course represent numbers of women with pilot's licenses. Rather they reflect the small demand for women to enter aviation as paid pilots."[29]

One of the most important events related to working women that took place in 1910 was the first fruits of a project that had begun a few years earlier. In 1907 Congress ordered the secretary of the Commerce and Labor Department to "investigate and report on the industrial, social, moral, educational, and physical condition of woman and child workers in the United States wherever employed, with special reference to their age, hours of labor, term of employment, health, illiteracy, sanitary and other conditions surrounding their occupation, and the means employed for the protection of their health, person, and morals."[30] Some members of Congress argued that the government had no right to investigate the matter, but the Bureau of Labor was authorized to go ahead.[31] The result was a 19-volume series entitled *Report on Condition of Woman and Child Wage-Earners in the United States.*[32]

Various aspects of this series are found in many chapters of this book, but the following sample of volume titles gives some idea of the range that was covered.[33]

1. *Cotton Textile Industry*
2. *Men's Ready-Made Clothing*
3. *Glass Industry*
4. *Silk Industry*
5. *Wage-Earning Women in Stores and Factories*
9. *History of Women in Industry in the United States*
10. *History of Women in Trade-Unions*
11. *Employment of Women in the Metal Trades*
12. *Employment of Women in Laundries*
13. *Infant Mortality and Its Relation to the Employment of Mothers*
14. *Causes of Death among Woman and Child Cotton-Mill Operatives*
15. *Relation between Occupation and Criminality of Workers*
16. *Family Budgets of Typical Cotton-Mill Workers*
17. *Hookworm Disease among Cotton-Mill Operatives*
18. *Employment of Women and Children in Selected Industries*
19. *Labor Laws and Factory Conditions*

One of the more interesting elements in the series was the Bureau of Labor's attempt to coin a new phrase, "women adrift." This referred to women who were "practically without homes," which did not mean homeless in the modern sense. Instead, it referred to a female (and only a female) lacking adult relatives who "in time of need or temptation could give her financial aid or moral support."[34]

> Is a girl wage-earner without a home when she has lost her mother? She may have a father keeping a watchful eye upon her and well able to care for her in time of need; or if her father is in needy circumstances there may still be sufficient solidarity in the family group. . . .
>
> Is she without a home when she has lost her father? The income of the family may be such (even though that income is confined solely to the earnings of the working member) as to permit the mother to remain in the home and perform the duties of a mother—look after the comfort, health, and moral welfare of her children.[35]

Married women were also considered adrift if they had to "earn a living for themselves and their children . . . because they are without homes that are in any sense an asset as is usually meant when reference is made to 'the wage-earning women living at home.' All of these 'homes' were supported and presided over by women wage-earners."[36]

One reason for the concern over these women without support systems was the low salaries they were paid. The *Report* noted that, at least among department store managers, there "seemed a general recognition" that many of their saleswomen were not paid enough to "live on honestly," and therefore they required their employees to live at home, or at least to claim that they did.[37]

Modern scholars Nancy Folbre and Marjorie Abel reported that according to the "adrift" measure "an estimated 14 percent of working women lacked proper moorings."[38] The new phrase did not catch on.

In response to Congress's request for information, in 1907 the Census Bureau published *Statistics of Women at Work,* based on unpublished data from the most recent decennial event. The object was to provide information about "who and how many are the women engaged in gainful occupations rather than the question of the influence and conditions of their employment."[39]

It reported that 125 occupations employed more than 1,000 females each. Sixty-three occupations supported more than 5,000 women.[40] But many women still listed no occupation, and the authors of the report had a theory about this:

> With women the adoption of an occupation, although by no means unusual, is far from being customary, and in the well-to-do classes of society is exceptional; and with this sex, moreover, the pursuit of an occupation is probably more often temporary than permanent. . . .
>
> Probably few women take up a remunerative occupation who are so situated that they can live comfortably without it. . . . Doubtless a considerable number of the women who engage in such pursuits as teaching, literary work, or some other of the so-called liberal professions, are not constrained thereto by any necessity of earning a living, but are actuated by the motives that do not differ materially from those which appeal to men in similar circumstances, such as some form of ambition, a love of activity, or a desire for social usefulness. But it is safe to say that while women of this class may be increasing in numbers, they make up only a very small fraction of the total number of women returned by the census as breadwinners.[41]

The study noted that female breadwinners were largely young, with more than two-thirds under the age of 35.[42] It offered an explanation for this:

> This decline reflects the fact that a large proportion of the women who take up an occupation in early life abandon it later when they marry.

Indeed, from an economic standpoint, marriage for a woman is in some respects analogous to an occupation for a man; and it has been said with some truth that marriage is woman's occupation or profession. The resemblance is twofold. Through marriage, as from an occupation, a woman usually secures at least a livelihood and perhaps the enjoyment of wealth and luxury and again marriage, like an occupation, normally and usually imposes upon a woman certain duties and responsibilities, namely those arising from the care of home and family, involving in the majority of cases more or less labor in the form of housework. Thus, under ordinary conditions the married woman lacks the incentive as well as the time or opportunity to engage in a breadwinning occupation. Moreover, there are natural and obvious barriers to the employment of married women in pursuits which take them from their homes, especially in cases where there are children in the home.

Usually, therefore, a woman who may have taken up a breadwinning occupation in early life gives up that occupation when she marries, or soon thereafter, and devotes herself to the duties of domestic life.[43]

The 19-volume report proved so popular that a single-volume summary of more than 1,000 pages was published in 1916.[44] In the years immediately following the report, several states conducted similar studies of their own. As a result six states banned night work for women. Minimum wage for women and mothers' pensions laws were enacted for the first time in many states.[45]

Modern readers may be surprised to learn that the first examination of sex discrimination within the federal government dates from 1917. Specifically, in answer to a query from the Interior Department, George Otis Smith, director of the U.S. Geological Survey (USGS), explained that much of the USGS's work "requires field ability for which it is necessary to employ men rather than women. In the field branches, therefore, women necessarily are unable to meet the strain attendant upon constant exposure in all kinds of weather, and in the strenuous physical exertions that are required of the geologists, topographers, and hydrographic engineers." Meanwhile, in the Division of Engraving and Printing "the work is necessarily of a man's type, requiring the handling of machinery, heavy lifting, dirty work and various trades to which men are especially adapted." The laborers, messengers, mechanics, and holders of similar jobs consisted of 130 men and 1 woman. On the other hand, almost two-thirds of the clerical employees were women.[46]

In 1920 the newly formed Women's Bureau of the Labor Department published a summary of state legislation regulating night work by women. Six states limited their hours.[47] Twelve states forbid women from working at night in certain occupations, such as street car lines, textile manufactures, laundries, and as messengers.[48] "These laws," said the bureau, "constitute the legal expression in the United States of the belief that night work is injurious to workers."[49] Oddly enough, it didn't say injurious to *women* workers.

The Women's Bureau supported such legislation, as opposed to organizations, such as the National Women's Party, that were calling for an Equal Rights Amendment and saw protectionist laws as an obstacle. That side won a victory in 1923 when the Supreme Court decided *Adkins v. Children's Hospital of Washington D.C.*, the first of several cases in which they overturned laws providing a minimum wage for women. Their argument was that because "contractual, political, and civil" sex differences "had come almost, if not quite, to the vanishing point," women had the same freedom of contract as men.[50]

In 1927 the Bureau of Labor Statistics (BLS) published the first *Handbook of Labor Statistics (HLS)*. The early versions contained many pages of narrative, and that first volume had a long chapter on women workers. For example:

> For a long time the employment of a woman in factory, mill, or store was looked upon as a temporary phase; her serious business in life was in the home, and her work outside was either an unfortunate accident or a means of passing the time until she had the home in which to carry on her normal activities. Because of this belief, comparatively little interest was manifested in the conditions under which she worked, the wages she got, or the work she did. Industry was looked upon as predominantly a masculine affair, into which from time to time individual women might enter, stay a short time, and pass on, but their presence there was too temporary a matter to demand any serious consideration.[51]

Table 14.1 shows some of the subjects covered in the "Women in Industry" section of the first *Handbook*.

While women received their own section in the first *HLS*, they sometimes received short shrift in other parts of the book. For example, a study of 61,193 saw mill employees found that "38 were women found working in a common-labor capacity in 5 mills in 4 States." However, it was noted with no explanation that the females "were not included in the following tables."[52]

The date of the 1930 Census was less than six months after the stock market crash, which is considered the start of the Great Depression.[53] Clearly it was taking a snapshot of an unusual moment in American

Table 14.1   Selected tables from the 1924 to 1926 and 1941 editions of the
            Handbook of Labor Statistics.

1924–1926	1941
Age distribution	Chief occupations of gainfully employed women
Effects of new inventions on women's employment	Company policies in event of childbirth
Family status of working women	Comparison of women's and men's wages
Hours and whether defined by law	Earnings of office workers
Nativity and race	Employment of women
Number employed	Employment of women after marriage
Occupational division (e.g., agriculture)	Employment of women in the federal government
Protective legislation for women	In selected industries and states
States	Labor laws applying to women only
Trends of employment of women and men	Occupational diseases among women
Wages and earnings	Proportions of women in the labor force of various manufacturing industries
	Responsibility of women for support of others
	Trends in employment of women, 1938–1940
	Woman workers and family finances
	Women in labor unions
	Women in the labor force, 1940
	Women's wages

Sources: U.S. Labor Department, Bureau of Labor Statistics, *Handbook of Labor Statistics 1924–26,* 637–64; U.S. Labor Department, Bureau of Labor Statistics, *Handbook of Labor Statistics 1941 Volume 1,* 946–92.

history. Yet the 1920 Census was taken a little more than a year after World War I ended, when many veterans were still seeking jobs. As Mary V. Dempsey wrote in a Women's Bureau publication, this created difficulties "when one attempts to compare 1930 census occupation statistics with those for 1920."[54]

But there are also systemic problems involved in counting women's jobs in the early 20th century. Ciancanelli argued that "the structural basis for the undercount of married women in the United States from 1900 to 1930 is their concentration in patriarchal production units." By this she meant such arrangements as family farms and businesses, and industrial homework supervised by a husband or other male relative.[55] She maintained, based on Women's Bureau studies, that married women's participation in the labor force from 1900 to 1930 was 10 times higher than the census estimates.[56] She also points out that during this period a man's claim to be self-employed was taken at face value by the Census Bureau, but in order to be recorded with the same status a woman had to work regularly and for a certain number of hours.[57]

The year 1937 saw the creation of a new product from the BLS, namely Current Employment Statistics (CES). The CES is a monthly survey of business payrolls. From the beginning it has always provided data divided by sexes. It currently covers 900 industries.[58]

In 1938 Alba M. Edwards, who was responsible for the occupation statistics of the census, authored a government book categorizing "social-economic grouping of the gainful workers." He was less interested in occupations or divisions of industry than in the sets of skilled, semi-skilled, and unskilled workers. He situated a large proportion of female workers in his professional, clerical, semiskilled, and servant groups. Fewer women appeared in the proprietary, official and management, and skilled worker divisions. He noted that the proportion of women in clerical occupations had doubled between 1910 and 1930 to almost 30 percent.[59]

Most of the publications of the 1940 Census came out during World War II, which naturally affected their viewpoint and focus. For example, the volume on *Characteristics of Persons Not in the Labor Force* was concerned with people who could step into jobs in the war industries or openings left by departing soldiers:

Any large addition to the labor force will therefore have to be taken chiefly from the large groups of women occupied with home duties. The ones who can most easily take jobs are presumably married daughters, daughters-in-law, etc. living with their parents or other relatives, but there were only about 900,000 potential workers of this type between the ages of 18 and 44. Most of the additional workers will therefore have to be drawn from the great reservoir of 21,400,000 wives of heads [of households].[60]

Another volume of the census, *Comparative Occupation Statistics 1870 to 1940,* noted the changes related to female workers:

As previously stated, there has been a marked change since 1870 in the popular sentiment regarding women working outside their homes. In addition, there has been a particularly great increase in the demand for workers in some of the occupations for which women appear to be especially well adapted—clerical and kindred pursuits, some of the professional pursuits, and some of the semiskilled pursuits.

This movement of women into gainful occupations cannot be viewed as a mere makeshift to bridge over temporary economic conditions, nor as the result of a transient feminine whim. It is a basic movement, to which society must adjust itself, and with the social and economic effects of which society must reckon.[61]

The 1941 edition of the *Handbook of Labor Statistics* was the last to feature narrative as opposed to only tables of data. It was also the last to have a separate section on "Women in Industry," provided by the Women's Bureau. In later editions information on female workers was integrated into the rest of the volume. Table 14.1 shows some of the subjects covered by this volume, compared to those included in the first edition of the *HLS.*

One subject of special interest and controversy in this volume was "employment of women after marriage." It reported that a survey of 484 firms in 1939 showed that 111 had a policy of forbidding female office workers to remain in their jobs if they married, and 38 had the same policy for factory workers.[62] Some companies permitted the laid-off bride to reapply "if the woman became a widow or her husband became disabled and could not support her. Divorce or unemployment of the husband was considered by a smaller number of companies as a reason for such permission." Some businesses were willing to consider their now-married ex-employees for temporary work in rush periods.[63]

At 143 of the surveyed companies, married office employees who become pregnant were fired. In the other 135 with policies, they were permitted to apply for leave of absences. In the case of pregnant factory workers, two-thirds of the companies insisted on termination of employment.[64]

In this edition of the *HLS* the Women's Bureau continued to fight the idea that women were only working for "pin money," although that phrase was not used. It pointed out that "probably more than one-tenth" of employed women in the United States were the entire support of their families. At least one-tenth of families were headed by women, and that was probably an underestimate "since the census enumerators normally report a man as the family head wherever possible to do so."[65]

During that same year, the Women's Bureau reinforced its argument in *Women Workers in Their Family Environment:*

> Today the public recognizes the widow's need to support herself and her children. It recognizes the adult single woman's need for self-support but does not acknowledge, in the scale of wages paid, her contributions to family support. The public still has to be convinced that married women have the right to work, that they may face an inescapable need to supplement and often supply the entire income, and that they can work without harm being done to the home and to the working standards of men and women wage earners.[66]

Most working women, said the report, came from "the broken and the composite family. . . . The family without a father, the family without a mother, the family with neither father nor mother, the family with relatives living with them."[67] Three-fifths of families with a working woman were, therefore, not the "normal American family."[68]

In 1950 the BLS published *Tables of Working Life: Length of Working Life for Men.* In 1956 it did the same for women. The bureau noted that this subject was of special interest "because of the recent rapid increase in the number of working women, [and] provides a basis for the analysis of factors that affect the work careers of women—marriage, the birth of children, and widowhood and divorce."[69]

The report found "(1) that marriage and the presence of children are the most important factors tending to keep women out of the work force; and (2) that women are apt to seek reemployment when their children reach school age and their family responsibilities are somewhat diminished."[70] It concluded that women's "work life potential" was about "one-fourth of their life expectancy."[71]

During the 1970 Census, for the first time, people in urban areas who did not work and were not looking for work were asked why. The questions assumed a male responder, except for the section on "Family Responsibilities," which were written with a woman in mind. For example, "if she says that she doesn't know anybody to 'baby-sit,' mark 'Other,'" "(Ask for married women with husband a household member): How does your husband feel about you going to work?"[72]

During this time period one million women gave "home responsibilities" as their reason for not seeking work. By 1983 it was almost one and a half million. In the same survey, such a "small number" of men offered that explanation that it was included under "other reasons."[73]

In 1972 President Nixon set up the Advisory Committee on the Economic Role of Women, which was to meet periodically with the chairman of the Council of Economic Advisers.[74] The next year his *Economic Report of the President* contained a chapter on "The Economic Role of Women."[75]

The report called the percentage of women working outside the home "one of the most important changes in the American economy in this century."[76] It noted that "by entering the labor force women did not leave a life of leisure for work, but rather changed from one kind of work, work at home, to another kind of work, work in the market." The changes that made this possible included longer lives, fewer children, and birth control.[77]

In 1978 the Labor Department published *Women in Traditionally Male Jobs: The Experiences of Ten Public Utility Companies*. It found that a great majority of the female employees were judged by peers and managers to be working at least as well as the males. "Significantly, however, there was evidence that the target women had to be performing better than most men in order to earn a rating of 'good' or 'excellent.'"[78]

This was also the period when "pink collar" began to appear in federal publications.[79] The term, coined by Louise Kapp Howe, referred to jobs that were held mostly by women, especially in the service industry.[80] In 1979 the National Advisory Council on Women's Educational Programs began to speak of the "eighty percent," meaning women with blue- or pink-collar jobs.[81]

Concern about this problem was not new. Valerie Kincade Oppenheimer had pointed out a decade earlier that census data tended to underestimate the "balkanization" of the labor market because of the inevitably limited number of categories available. "For example, according to the 1950 classification system, barbers, beauticians, and manicurists were all lumped together. Women constituted 50 percent of the workers of this group." But 92 percent of hairdressers and cosmetologists were women.[82]

Also in 1978, the Census Bureau held a conference on *Issues in Federal Statistical Needs Relating to Women*. Among the speakers was Nancy Smith Barrett, who argued that women's behavior in the labor market needed to be measured differently from men's because

> for men, once school is completed, life-cycle events usually have very little impact on the decision to participate in the paid labor force. Further, since participation is usually continuous, age minus years in school can be accepted as a proxy for work experience. For women, on the other hand, a longer run view is required both to assess the relation between life-cycle

transitions (such as marriage, childbirth, and divorce) and labor force participation as well as to obtain a profile of work experience. These factors are important not only in explaining participation behavior but also for understanding differences in wages, occupation, and other measures of labor market status between men and women.[83]

Barrett also pointed out that the BLS used "establishment surveys" to gather data on "wage and salary employment, hours, earnings, and labor turnover in nonagricultural firms, by industry and geographic location." However, only the data on employment was broken down by sex.[84]

In 1979 the BLS published the first of a new series, *Women in the Labor Force*. The agency explained that

> with the dramatic increase in women's labor force participation and its continuation even during the deep recession of 1974–75, new and more timely approaches to statistics on the family became necessary. We could not wait for a whole year to find out how much of the increase in the number of working wives was related to their husband's unemployment; or whether women without young children were more likely than others to enter the work force; or how concentrated unemployment was within different types of families.[85]

Among the most important findings was that "wives with unemployed husbands have considerably more difficulty in finding jobs than wives with employed husbands."[86]

The BLS also found that the "so-called typical family . . . a husband who works, a wife who is not in the labor force, and two children" made up only 7 percent of the total. More than half the families had at least two earners.[87]

In 1992 the Merit Systems Protection Board published a report on women in federal government jobs. *A Question of Equity: Women and the Glass Ceiling* found that barriers to success still existed. "Almost as many women as men are now employed in white-collar jobs in the Federal executive branch, yet only about 1 out of every 4 supervisors and 1 out of every 10 executives are women."[88]

The report also found that child care responsibilities limited women's careers. The surveys found that women without children dedicated as much time to their jobs on average as men without children, but women with young children devoted less time to work than did any men.[89]

In 2012 the White House Council on Women and Girls, which had been created by President Obama, published *Keeping America's Women*

Moving Forward, a report on the administration's progress on that subject:

> Today, more than ever before, women are playing a central role in the American economy. Women now make up nearly 50% of our workforce, are a growing number of breadwinners in their families, and are the majority of students in our colleges and graduate schools. American women own 30% of small businesses, which generate $1.2 trillion a year in sales. Since 1962, women's participation in the labor market has risen by 20 percentage points while the United States' Gross Domestic Product (GDP) has more than quadrupled. And according to a report by McKinsey [& Company], if the United States raised female labor participation rates to the average participation rate of the top 10 states, our economy would add 5.1 million women workers, the equivalent of a 3–4% increase in GDP.
>
> Consequently, when women still face barriers to participation in the workplace and marketplace, that is not just a "women's issue." When women still make just 77 cents for every dollar men make, or have to pay more for their health care than men, that hurts entire families who cannot afford to lose part of their income each month. When a job does not offer adequate family leave or sick leave, that also hurts men who need to help care for a new baby or an ailing parent. When women entrepreneurs continue to have a harder time accessing the capital they need to start and sustain their businesses, create new jobs, and sell new products, that hurts our entire economy. And when approximately two million women fall victim to domestic violence each year, that costs our nation $8 billion annually in lost productivity and health care expenses and results in the loss of 8 million paid days of work a year.[90]

Statistical Abstract

The 1895 edition of the *Statistical Abstract* was the first to offer occupational data. It covered 1870, 1880, and 1890, with breakdowns by occupation and sex. "Domestic and personal services" was the largest field for women in all three decades.[91]

The year 1907 brought a table on females over the age of 15 "employed as breadwinners." The percentage rose from 16 percent to 20.6 percent between 1880 and 1900.[92]

The 1960 volume introduced data on mothers with children under the age of 12 who were employed full-time. It provided the marital status as well as the number of young children.[93]

The 1972 edition boasted of adding 16 tables to provide new data about women and minorities. These included husband–wife work experience, married women by occupation, and wife's contribution to family income.[94] It also expanded the information on labor force participation by marital status to cover both sexes, after a decade of only covering women.[95]

CHAPTER FIFTEEN

Women Factory Workers

While this country has always had conflicted feelings about working women, perhaps no group of them has come in for more scrutiny than women working in manufacturing industries, especially factories. Government studies have worried about the health of these women, the effect their employment has on their children, and whether they take jobs away from men, to name just a few issues.

This chapter will cover some of the early statistics about women in factories, concentrating on several large reports on the subject.

The 1820 Census of Manufacturers collected information on the number of male and female adults and children employed, but didn't publish the results. However, according to a study of that data made a century later, women were found to be employed in at least 75 types of manufacturing.[1] Women made up roughly 10 percent of manufacturing employees, while children were more than double that percentage.[2]

For the 1840 Census some industries were asked the "number of persons employed," while for others (e.g., cannon and small arms, precious metals) it was strictly the "number of men." Only the silk industry was asked about "women and children employed" separately from the number of men.[3]

The 1870 Census volume noted that, while the figures on manufacturing jobs were generally accurate, "women and children employed in factories are omitted in large numbers."[4]

The 1880 Census *Compendium* delved into the matter of workers, especially factory workers, in detail. Why, it asked, do some cities have a larger percentage of people working than others? There were more workers per capita in a "far western city like Kansas City," because men had "recently gone thither to seek their fortunes," leaving behind women and those too young or old to work. On the other hand, in eastern mill towns "where females and children are largely in excess, we find an even higher percentage of bread-winners." This is because the textile plants employed women "who in a western city would be living at home keeping the house," and children, who would otherwise be in school.[5]

The authors of the *Compendium* also noticed that the tables on manufacturing recorded more people working in factories than did the tables on occupations. They repeated the note from 1870 about women and children being omitted and then added:

> Thus omissions may take place either through the failure of the enumerators to ask questions relating to occupation concerning such persons, assuming that they have no avocation outside their homes, or from the indisposition of the persons themselves or the heads of their families to speak of them as in employment.

The authors also noted that such omissions were not found in occupations inhabited "almost exclusively by adult males, like the trades of carpenter, blacksmith, mason, or printer, or the professions of lawyer, physician, or clergyman."[6]

The number of women whose work was recognized by the census increased by almost 280,000 between 1870 and 1880. Two-thirds of this increase was in "manufacturing, mechanical, and mining industries," which is, to say, mostly factory work.[7] Industries employing the largest percentage of women and young children included women's clothing (88.33 percent women), shirts (86.37 percent women), men's furnishing goods (85.6 percent women), millinery and lace goods (80.66 percent women), and umbrellas and canes (51.52 percent women).[8]

Perhaps the most interesting element of the 1880 Census was a 70-page essay by Special Agent Carroll D. Wright. His "Report on the Factory System of the United States" was tucked within the *Report on the Manufactures* for the decennial census.

Wright examined the "apparent evils" of the factory system. He concluded that the worst of those was that

> the factory system necessitates the employment of women and children to an injurious extent, and consequently its tendency is to destroy family ties and domestic habits and ultimately the home.
>
> In one sense this is true; in another it is not true. . . . The majority of human beings are born to the lot of toiling with their hands for their daily bread. This decree necessitates employment, and until all classes can be

employed at fairly remunerative rates poverty, even to pauperism, must be a large factor in society. This was the case at the birth of the factory system.

Wright argued that the factories did not make things worse than they had been in the era of farm labor and work done in the home; it simply made the conditions more visible: "The factory brought these evils to the light, and the employment of women and children became an offense in the eyes of the public."

Wright said that paid employment in factories permitted the women and children to move "from the ranks of degrading dependence and pauperism to the ranks of comparative comfort and the dignity which comes from self support."[9]

At this point Wright's argument became a bit self-contradictory. He theorized that the employment of married women was "the very worst feature of factory employment."[10] However, it should not be blamed for "the very high percentage of deaths [of children] under five years in factory towns." Rather, he pinned the death of young children on crowding and bad sanitation in the towns, arguing that "the factory is better for married and even pregnant women than unwholesome houses."[11]

Wright felt that

the conditions of the homes of these women are as deleterious to their health, and to infants born to them, as the work of the factories. I am also satisfied that to exclude such women from the factory would be an act of great injustice to those concerned. . . .

Does the employment of women and children tend to destroy the home? To the extent that women who are mothers and have care of a household, and who become careless of maternal ties through hard work and maternal duties combines, it does; for the factory mother who has buried several children learns sooner or later to speak of her losses in a careless and unfeeling manner. Domestic felicity does not and cannot reach a very high place when a mother must arise before the rest of the family to prepare hastily the breakfast for all, then hasten to the mill and make her time good till the noon hour, when the dinner must be prepared as hastily as was the breakfast; while at night, after a day of constant labor, she must see that supper is served and then take up the thousand and one duties of the household, which keep her busy till the hour has long passed when she should be asleep. No ten-hour law has been able to reach the factory woman with a family.[12]

Wright was appointed the nation's first commissioner of Labor in 1885.[13] Four years later he penned *Working Women in Large Cities*, based on interviews conducted with more than 17,000 women. In most cases the interviews were performed by women who, Wright noted, "have stood on an equality in all respects with the male force of the Department, and have been compensated equally with them."[14]

The study covers only women doing manual labor, not "the professional and semi-professional callings, like those of teaching, stenography, typewriting, telegraphy, etc.," nor "women employed in textile factories," because most such mills were not located in the 22 large cities examined.[15] For each city Wright covers general conditions, housing, associations for working women, church attendance, conjugal status, earnings, and much more.

As was typical of the time, there is a thorough detailing of "native-born" and "foreign-born" parents. On the other hand, race is almost never mentioned, presumably because only White women were interviewed. One typical exception appears in his report on Richmond, Virginia: "In the tobacco factories, where races are mixed, immorality is much more noticeable than elsewhere."[16]

There is a section summarizing "condition of health, by industries." From a modern point of view, the data is unsatisfactory, limited to good, fair, and bad health, and not indicating how long the women worked in the factories. However, certain industries seemed to have the most dramatic effects on the health of the workers interviewed: hosiery factory (from 2 workers out of 246 who were in bad health when they started work to 10 when they were interviewed), paper bag factory (from 8 out of 718 to 18), and shirt factory (from 5 out of 677 to 21). The total of female workers in bad health went from 185 out of 16,427 to 485.[17]

Congress authorized another study, published in 1897, specifically to determine whether women and children were taking factory jobs away from men. Surveyors visited more than 1,000 establishments, mostly factories, in 30 states and collected data for close to 150,000 men and women. This report found that the number of gainfully employed women had doubled since 1870 but that, on average, they earned less than half as much as men.[18]

The study also reported that 90 percent of female employees were single. It did not reveal the marital status of male employees.[19]

The agents conducting this study also asked employers why they chose women over men:

> The reasons for the preference for women are variously given, the most common being their greater adaptability for the work for which they are employed. It is also stated that they are more reliable, more easily

controlled, cheaper, more temperate, more easily procured, neater, more rapid, more industrious, more careful, more polite, less liable to strike, learn more rapidly, etc.[20]

The employers were then asked why more women were not hired:

Machinery is gradually displacing them in many industries, as more automatic work is done by machines than formerly; very often women who are better adapted and cheaper are unreliable; their physical strength is inadequate for heavy work; females have always been employed in certain occupations, men not being fitted for them and never engaging in them; women can be employed only in certain occupations; very scarce, and hard to find suitable women; men do better work than women, and if they were fitted for and understood certain work they would be preferred; women in many instances can not be depended upon; some industries largely employing women are gradually being forced out of business by the changes in fashion . . . the Cigar Makers' Union opposes the employment of women.[21]

In 1907 Congress ordered the secretary of Commerce and Labor to investigate the conditions of women and child workers throughout the country. The result was a 19-volume series entitled *Report on Condition of Woman and Child Wage-Earners in the United States*.

The *Summary* volume addressed the common complaint that women were pushing men out of their jobs by suggesting that the reverse was true:

[A] process of substitution has been going on by which men have been gradually taking the leading roles in industries formerly carried on in the home and considered distinctly feminine, such as spinning and weaving and garment making and knitting. As the women have been more or less dispossessed in their specialties, they have either gone into work formerly considered men's, such as the printing trade, or entered newly established industries which had not been definitely taken over by either sex. In both cases they are usually found doing the least skilled or poorest paid work.

The individual woman entered the industrial world under the pressure of necessity. The employer invited their entrance en masse because they were cheap, and above all because they were docile and easily managed. They were cheap and easily managed partly because they were in the main young, partly because they were unorganized, and partly because, as they expected to stay in the industrial world only a short time, they considered it better to accept conditions as they found them than to fight for improvements.[22]

The first volume of the *Report on Condition* series was one of many concerned with factory work, in this case, cotton mills. Labor commissioner

Charles P. Neill deliberately chose a man who was "southern in every respect"[23] to lead the investigation of cotton mills, hoping to avoid charges of prejudice against the mills where so many children were employed. This immediately led advocates of children to complain that the investigation was rigged. Nevertheless, when the report came out Neill was accused of slandering the South with sensationalism. He replied: "If the results were sensational, it was due to the facts and not to any desire on the part of the Bureau to make them sensational."[24]

The government agents interviewed women who worked night shifts in factories and found that "on one day at least the mother went from 18 to 24 hours without sleeping. One woman, who gave as her reason for working at night that she could take care of her home, garden, cow, and boy during the day, was found at 11 in the morning hanging up her clothes. She had had no sleep during the preceding 24 hours."[25]

The report investigated how many hours of housework were being done by women who worked in cotton mills and concluded that "the standard of housekeeping . . . was very low." Some mothers brought their children into the mills, either to work or simply to play.[26]

The chapter on "Hygienic Conditions" had sections on lighting, ventilation and humidity, dust and lint, and spitting on the floor. Spitting was found to be customary in 183 of the almost 200 mills visited, 75 of which provided cuspidors.[27]

On the brighter side, the report found that the moral standards in the mills were generally high. It credited this in part to the fact that there was no opportunity for managers to bribe women into bad behavior because "there are no promotions so far as female employees are concerned. Women never become section hands, second hands, or overseers."[28]

The government was so concerned with the morality of women workers that there is an entire volume in the series on the effect of occupations on the female character. The author of that book, Mary Conyngton, noted how factories were changing women's lives:

> The tailoress in 1870 might be and often was the village garment maker, going her rounds from house to house, a recognized and important figure in the community, an independent and respected personality. The tailoress of to-day is far more apt to be employed within a garment-making factory, an automaton during work hours, an indistinguishable atom of the crowded city life outside of them. . . . The home industries are disappearing or giving place to the sweated trades.[29]

The year 1927 saw a new publication from the Labor Department: the *Handbook of Labor Statistics* (*HLS*). This book had a chapter on women workers, which recognized the special attention being paid to women in industry but also offered a note of caution in regard to the terminology: "Although there are over 8,000,000 women gainfully employed, public interest, as manifested in studies, investigations, and legislation, is mainly concerned with those who are frequently but not very accurately referred to as being industrially employed." This group included workers in factories, as one might expect, but also those employed in "laundries, hotels, and restaurants, in mercantile establishments, in transportation as represented by the telephone and telegraph, and to some extent in clerical occupations."[30]

In a chapter on labor turnover, that first *HLS* included statistics from Cheney Bros., a silk company, revealing that employee turnover was lowest among married men and highest among married women. Single women stayed on the job longer than single men, however.[31]

The 1941 *Handbook* was concerned with issues of work-sharing and layoff policies in factories. It summarized an article surveying workers in a unionized plant:

> On lay-off decisions involving a choice between a single girl and a married woman with a husband working, there was a considerable opinion in favor of laying off the married woman, more or less regardless of seniority. Even among the men and women whose families would have been affected by such a decision there was a definite sentiment in favor of laying off the married women. . . .
>
> In one X company case a woman (threatened with lay-off because her husband was working, [sic] continued to deny categorically that she was married even when confronted with a copy of her marriage certificate obtained from city hall. . . .
>
> There was a strong social feeling in the factory that the married women whose husbands were working belonged at home. Whether logical or not, this feeling existed and had to be faced.[32]

Later editions of the *HLS* did away with narrative, confining themselves to data tables. There have been no more significant executive branch reports on women factory workers.

Statistical Abstract

The 1895 edition of the *Statistical Abstract* had a table on "SEX and CLASSES of Occupations." It offered only five categories, one of which was "manufacturing and mechanical industries." This field contained just over four million males and one million females.[33]

The 1902 edition of the *Statistical Abstract* was the first to include a table on "Population at Least 10 Years of Age Engaged in Gainful Occupations

Classified by Sex, etc." It is not always obvious which employees are factory workers. Dressmakers could have been working in factories or doing piecework at home. The fact that there were almost 350,000 of them suggests massive industrialization, but the fact that all but 2,090 were women seems to hint at some home work as well. On the other hand, there can be no doubt that "cotton mill operatives" worked in factories and 120,216 of the more than 246,000 operatives were women.[34]

After 1902 figures about occupations were a constant in the series.

CHAPTER SIXTEEN

"Farm Females"

In 1912 the Statistics Bureau of the U.S. Agriculture Department (USDA) published a report on the wages of farm laborers. It ended rather unexpectedly with an angry denial of charges that life on the farm was driving women insane:

A PERSISTENT CALUMNY WITHOUT THE LEAST FOUNDATION

For many years the published statement has been current that farm life has made the women of the farm especially prone to insanity. It has been represented that the solitude of the life, the drudgery, the want of variety, and what not, have created a greater percentage of insanity among farm women than among the women of any other life or occupation.

Assertions of this sort were made 15 or 20 years ago, and were accompanied with no precise statement of facts and no references to authorities or the results of investigations. Notwithstanding the loose character of these early statements, all evidently based upon a solitary origin, they have been repeated so generally and persistently that they have come to be accepted as representative of a well-known fact, and are at this day repeated by persons who ordinarily are careful and accurate in their statements, as well as by the multitude of writers and speakers who are not careful.

The author, George K. Holmes, identified the original source of this rumor as "a woman who was a prolific writer for the press upon domestic subjects."[1] He contacted the (unnamed) superintendent of the state asylum in Iowa, who said that in that rural state men were more likely to be institutionalized than women, although that might be "because insane women can more easily be controlled by their husbands and cared for at home than insane men can be controlled by wives and other persons and be properly cared for at home. Notwithstanding this fact, I am of the opinion that a farmer's wife is no more likely to become insane, even in pioneer days, in an agricultural State than he is."[2]

Holmes concludes:

> A farmer's wife who is in a good physical condition and who has her husband at home with her for most of his meals and to lodge there every night, and a farmer's wife who has several healthy loving, independent, industrious, and well-behaved children, is less likely to become insane than the average club woman in town who has few children, probably none, who is giving much of her time to literary work, spending many of her evenings to a late hour in the discharge of social functions, whose husband is absent from home a good share of the time, and who perhaps is making her home in a double house, or in an apartment house, or in a large family hotel.
>
> The more natural and healthy a life a woman leads the less likely she is to become deranged. The condition of a farmer's wife who in company with her children lives out of doors much of the time, caring for chickens and working in the garden a little with flowers and vegetables and fruits, is most favorable to her, and in such a life she is not likely to develop a mental attitude, [*sic*] an environment which tends toward insanity.[3]

Leaving aside the question of how accurately Holmes was describing the lives of rural or urban women, his insertion of the subject into a report on wages demonstrates that the well-being of farm women was much on the government's mind, as it had been for some time.

The 1871 *Report of the Commissioner of Agriculture* included a special section on women, beginning with a lament on the state of female education in this country: "To learn to pen gracefully a note of invitation, to sing a few staves of music, to finger mechanically piano-keys, to dance, and to simper affectedly, are chief accomplishments to which even the beginnings of solid culture are subordinate." The author suggests that a broad curriculum of industrial education would be inappropriate for women due to "the differing mental and physical constitutions of the sexes, and their different vocations in life," but if the education were "limited to agriculture, girls should not be excluded from participation. . . . Not that women should hold the plow, or dig ditches, or build fences; there are occupations pertaining to agriculture essentially feminine, and rural and household arts in which women are qualified by nature to excel but for which only scientific and general culture and specific technical training can thoroughly fit them."[4]

What follows are some sample notes from the 10 pages of data on women in agriculture in that 1871 report:

- "In Missouri . . . it is said that 'one woman in a garden or at the sorghum kettle is considered equal to two men.'"

- "Girls are almost exclusively employed in hop-picking, wherever hops are grown, their nimble fingers rendering them superior to men or boys; but they usually receive but one-fourth the wages of men in the hop-yard."

- In Wisconsin a "muscular maiden" aged 21, "delights in chopping wood, splitting rails, breaking colts, and holding the 'breaking-up plow,' and is an excellent marksman with a rifle, doing all these things with masculine skill. Of course, her example is not to be commended, though a better one for the race than that of some gossamer embodiments of an effete civilization."

- "Throughout the Southern States a large portion of the females among the negroes [sic] were accustomed to general farm labor, most of whom now decline it, appearing to regard it as a relic of slavery, and not 'suited to ladies.'"

- Women who manage farms (usually widows) succeed at about the same rate as men, but the report suggests this is because those who are not confident in the task sell their farms.

- In Nelson County [Virginia] some women "are expert at cradling [reaping grain], and seem pleased with it, regarding it as more or less of a frolic."

- "An aged couple in Washington County, New York, owned a farm of 250 acres. As they became incapacitated for its management, one of the boys assumed control, but soon made a failure, and was followed in succession by several brothers, until the homestead became almost hopelessly incumbered [sic, i.e. by debt]. Then a maiden sister accepted the trust, and in eight years, without other capital for its improvement, removed all incumbrances [sic], and placed the paternal acres in a flourishing and productive condition."

- One correspondent states that "the day is past in progressive Nebraska for the 'weaker vessel' to get less pay than men for the same work."

- In certain cases, such as Cherokee, Georgia, "a few widows manage their farms without any adult males to help; and they plow, hoe, harvest, bind, and gather their crops, shear sheep, and carry on all farming operations."

- Canadian and Irish women work on farm shares in sections of New England: "Many of them are as smart as the men; but as a rule they are less efficient and receive proportionately less pay."

- "In Lincoln County, in Maine, a correspondent writes that 'female out-door labor is unknown—incompatible with New England institutions.'"

- "A crusty bachelor maliciously hints that the agricultural occupation preferred by women in his section is 'raising Cain.' "[5]

In 1907 the Census Bureau published *Statistics of Women at Work,* the first government report on that subject. It noted that more than 5 percent of the people reported by the census as "farmers, planters, and overseers" were women, which might seem "somewhat surprising" since farming was "an occupation which is naturally regarded as one followed almost exclusively by men."[6] Almost three-quarters of the women farmers were widows.[7]

A year later President Theodore Roosevelt created the Country Life Commission (CLC) to examine the factors that were causing people to leave rural areas for the cities. The commission surveyed 100,000 families and held 30 hearings for "farmers and farmers' wives."[8]

It was quickly noted that while "farmers' wives" were a target of the commission's interest, that sex was not invited to participate in the high-level work. The famous author Charlotte Perkins Gilman asked, in an article in *Good Housekeeping Magazine:*

Why are there no women on the commission?

It needs men to study the economics of the farmer's trade, the buying of machinery and selling of crops, but all the rest of the matter in hand lies in the woman's long-defined province—the affairs of the home. . . .

We may appoint experts to tell the farmer what to do with his cows and pigs, and even enforce right conditions by law, but when it comes to the "mothers, wives and daughters"—they are the ones to be consulted. . . .

Presently we should find out that the women of our country who work on farms are the hardest worked and least paid of any class we have. There is no sweatshop that fails to pay something to its hard-driven slaves; but the sweatshop called a kitchen gives no wages. The work of the farmer's wife begins earlier than his, for she gets his breakfast; lasts longer than his, for she has the supper dishes to clean up, and mending to do in the evening; is more wearing than his because it is carried on together with the cares and labors of child-rearing; and it is far more dangerous than his, as is shown by the death rate.[9]

As modern scholar Jane B. Knowles noted, rural women seized on the CLC "as a means of making their voices heard. The message they delivered to the commission was one of isolation, endless hard work, lack of any household help, poor health and sanitation, schools that did not provide a useful education for rural children, lack of women's organizations, and the declining significance of rural churches."[10]

The commission recognized this in its reports: "Whatever general hardships, such as poverty, isolation, lack of labor-saving devices, may exist on any given farm, the burden of these hardships falls more heavily on the farmer's wife than on the farmer himself."

The CLC concluded that only "a general elevation of country living" would improve the life of farm women. They needed less work, more mechanical assistance, and better organizations.[11]

In 1910, while the commission was still engaged in its work, the decennial census produced results that astonished everyone. The number of women engaged in agricultural pursuits rose by 85 percent from 1900, during a decade in which the actual number of farms dropped.[12] In some parts of the country, the rise was closer to 300 percent.[13]

Had the dramatic increase really occurred, or were the new figures simply more accurate than the previous ones? The Census Bureau's preferred explanation was that the rise was an anomaly caused by a change in the instructions to the census-takers. "It is hardly probable," according to the report on population, "that in the United States, in 1910, more than one farm laborer in every four was a woman."[14]

In 1900 the relevant instructions had read: "In farming sections, where a farm is found that is under the management or supervision of a woman as owner or tenant, return the occupation of such woman as 'farmer' in all cases."[15] The suspect instructions in 1910 said that any woman "working regularly at outdoor farm work, even though she works on the home farm for her husband, son, or other relative and does not receive money wages, should be returned in column 18 as a *farm laborer*."[16]

It is worth emphasizing that this increase happened even though women had to be "working regularly" on the farm to be counted, while men did not.[17] Also, providing food, laundry, and cleaning services for hired help was not counted as labor.[18]

In 1911, the same year the CLC released its report worrying that farm women were working too hard, George K. Holmes, a year before he defended the farm women's sanity, published another report complaining, without any offer of evidence, that farm women were forgetting how to work at all. This appeared in the *Yearbook of the U.S. Department of Agriculture 1910*, which ignored the work of Roosevelt's commission entirely.

The outdoor work of white [sic] women on farms of medium or better sorts has greatly declined from early days, and the decline has been rapid during the last generation. Farmers' wives and daughters no longer milk the cows and work in the field and care for the live stock as of yore; they do not work in the kitchen and garden as before; nor assist in the fruit and berry harvest. They are making less butter, and cheese making on the farm has become a lost art. They may care for the poultry and the bees, do house-work and gather vegetables for the table, and cook and keep the dwelling in order. This is substantially the limit.[19]

The next year Holmes wrote the first comprehensive study of the farm labor supply. In a section on "Women and Negroes in Agriculture," he concluded that dating back to the earliest figures, 1870, it seemed that one farm laborer in seven was a woman.[20]

In another report that same year Holmes offered a litany of complaints about farm women sacrificing their duties in favor of "social obligations" such as

the Grange, the woman's clubs, the [Ladies of the] Maccabees, the Wom-en's Christian Temperance Union, the local church, the farmers' clubs, and a list that might be much extended. . . .

The old-time domestic industries are all but forgotten. The women of the farm make no more soap, candles, or lye, and so on with a long list of the domestic products of former days; it is rare that one of the younger of the women knows how to knit. Throughout large areas the pride of the housewife in great store of preserved, dried, and pickled fruits, berries, and vegetables exists chiefly in history, and dependence is placed mostly upon the local store for the products of the cannery and the evaporator.[21]

Despite Holmes's repeated assertion that farm women were under-worked and overly fond of socializing, his bosses at the USDA continued to be concerned about them. In 1913 Secretary of Agriculture David Franklin Houston received a letter from North Carolina newspaper pub-lisher Clarence Poe, which read in part: "Have some bulletins for the farmer's wife as well as for the farmer himself. The farm woman has been the most neglected factor in the rural problem, and she has been espe-cially neglected by the National Department of Agriculture. Of course, a few such bulletins are printed, but not enough."[22]

In response Secretary Houston sent a letter to the "housewives" of 55,000 farmers, asking how the department "could render more direct service to the farm women of the United States." He encouraged his cor-respondents to share the letter with friends and organization, and received more than 2,200 replies.[23] The results, arranged by subjects and then geo-graphically, filled four reports with laments of "loneliness, isolation, and lack of social and educational opportunity," alternating with reports of "complete contentment with farm life."[24]

Some of the letters were written by the husbands rather than the women who had been addressed. The reports observed that "the vast majority of them seemed to recognize that the women on the farms do not always receive their full due and that improvements are needed." Negative letters from men were "entirely exceptional."[25]

The wives (and occasional husbands) complained about bad roads and expensive telephones that increased their isolation, and the need for more social engagements and churches. They also complained, as Poe had suggested in his original letter, that the department was not providing them with useful information.[26]

Jane B. Knowles noted that "USDA's leadership was clearly nonplussed by some of this outpouring because the department had for several years been attempting to provide at least some of the help these women sought. In each of the four volumes of the survey report, appendices prepared by USDA provided lists of appropriate Bulletins women could consult."[27] These requests led to the creation of the Cooperative Extension Service in 1914, in the first federal law to mention home economics.[28] Through the service the Agriculture Department worked with land grant universities to provide training and information directly to farmers and their families.[29]

In 1920, Florence E. Ward, who was in charge of extension work with women in the north and west, wrote a pamphlet for the Agriculture Department entitled *The Farm Woman's Problems*. It was based on surveys of more than 10,000 farm women.[30] Ward makes it clear that the motivation for this research is "the economic importance of a contented rural population willing to stay on the land and help to build it up." People were leaving the country for the cities, and daughters were exiting at a higher rate than sons.[31]

She noted that "in industries, where love and service are not the ruling motives, a walkout might be foreshadowed by [the fact] that the average working day, summer and winter, for over 9,000 farm women is 11.3 hours, and that 87 per cent of 8,772 women report no regular vacation during the year, although a large per cent tell of scattered 'days off' in the family automobile."[32]

Ward pointed out that much of the labor could be eased if the farmhouse were equipped as well as "even the up-to-date barn." Women were spending their time caring for kerosene lamps, heating with stoves, fetching water, and doing other tasks for which technological replacements already existed.[33]

Were women engaged in real farm work or merely doing chores around the house? Ward's survey found that 25 percent helped with the livestock, 24 percent worked in the fields, and 32 percent did the farm accounting.[34]

The difficulty of measuring a housewife's contribution to the farm can be examined through a simple example of dairy products. Ward noted that

- one-third of the farms report selling butter;
- 36 percent of the women on those farms help with the milking;
- 88 percent wash the milk pails;
- 65 percent wash the separator;
- 60 percent make butter;
- 29 percent keep the records;
- 33 percent sell butter;
- 11 percent "have butter money."[35]

In their comments most women expressed satisfaction with country life but had complaints about the lack of money and conveniences: "Does the farmer lack business sagacity who invests in the sulky plow, used only during one season of the year, and puts off the purchase of a washing machine?"[36]

The year 1920 also brought the decennial census, and the statisticians did not want to repeat what they saw as the exaggerated numbers for women farm workers. The relevant instructions to census-takers began: "For a woman who works *only occasionally,* or *only a short time each day* at outdoor farm or garden work, or in the dairy, or in caring for live stock or poultry, the return should be *none* [that is, no occupation]."[37] As Joseph A. Hill wrote in a Census Bureau monograph: "In 1910 the emphasis was upon *returning* as a farm laborer every woman working regularly at outdoor farm *not returning* as work; in 1920 the emphasis was upon a farm laborer any woman who worked at outdoor work only occasionally or only a short time each day." This was at least one reason that the percentage of women recorded as gainfully employed dropped in 1920, from 25.5 to 24 percent, reversing the trend of half a century.[38]

Looking back from the 1980s, Penelope Ciancanelli argued that from 1900 to 1930 the instructions to census-takers "were ones that assumed a sex division of labor rather than documenting it."[39]

In 1931 the *Yearbook of Agriculture* reported that the USDA's Bureau of Home Economics had studied the use of time by 1,041 homemakers throughout the country.[40] "Farm homemakers" spent an average of four hours a day, seven days a week, on leisure activities (reading, meetings, church, transportation, etc.). Other rural homemakers averaged a half hour more and urban homemakers a half hour beyond that. The three groups spent an almost identical amount of time on housework, but on top of that, farm women averaged 1 hour and 19 minutes per day on farm work.[41]

The 1940 Census changed the focus for occupational statistics from "gainful employment" to the broader "labor force," which was based on whether someone had worked in a certain week. If a farmer had been unable to work during that week because of bad weather or illness, he was still counted as a farmer, but "the wife of the farmer, or other members of the farmer's family," were only counted if they actually performed farm work in the relevant week.[42] This was the apparent cause for a decrease of 19 percent in "farm laborers, unpaid family workers" between 1930 and 1940.[43]

Most scholars agreed that the inaccuracy of early censuses of women workers was mostly corrected by the 1940 Census, but a 1944 survey conducted jointly by the Census Bureau and the Agricultural Economics Bureau found that more than three million people previously recorded as nonworkers had done at least one hour of unpaid work around the farm during the survey week.[44] A total of 1,380,000 farm women reported doing at least 19 hours of unpaid farm work a week, and 620,000 reported at least 30 hours. That was three times the number recorded by the 1940 Census.[45]

Louis Ducoff and Gertrude Bancroft, writing in 1945, offered several reasons for the difference, including

> the tendency of enumerators to classify women and school-age children as non-workers rather than to ask a sufficient number of questions to disclose that they did in fact do some work. Experience shows that a direct question such as "did you do any work?" will always produce more affirmative replies than one which approaches the problem indirectly. The understatement is probably accentuated when the work question is phrased in terms of "at work on a job" since "job" has paid connotations to farm correspondents.[46]

While the rules for what constituted farm labor changed with each Census of Agriculture, they continued to make it difficult for anyone except adult men to be counted. For example, an unpaid member of the operator's family was tallied in 1945 only if he or she worked at least two days in the first week of January, not a season much known for farming. Rules for hired hands and the operators themselves were always different.[47]

As for the "farm operator," only one could be listed for each farm. In the case of a partnership—or a marriage—someone must be excluded.[48] In fact, it was not until 1978 that the Census decided that, if both husband

and wife worked on the farm, they themselves could decide who would be reported as the sole operator.[49]

It was during this period that the USDA contracted with a nonprofit organization, the National Opinion Research Center (NORC) to conduct the first Survey of Farm Women. In 1980 NORC interviewed 2,509 farm women and 569 farm men (mostly their husbands) by phone.[50]

Some of the highlights of the findings included the following:

- Almost 60 percent of the women had grown up on a farm or ranch.
- 96 percent of the women were married.
- 31 percent were working off the farm.
- Most of the women participated in bookkeeping, running errands, and preparing meals for the family.
- About two-thirds of the women whose farms involved livestock engaged in animal care.[51]

The interviewers were interested in women's involvement in management:

Very few farm women make final decisions entirely on their own. On the other hand, about half of the women indicated that they shared final decisions with their husbands about such matters as purchasing or selling land or acquiring farm equipment. In addition, about one-third of the women were involved in final decisions about renting land, the timing of the product sales, producing something new or trying new production practices. About 90 percent of the women were satisfied with their level of responsibility for decision making on their operations.[52]

Sixty percent of the married women "felt that they could continue to run their operations alone if something should happen to their husbands." In spite of this, only 1 in 12 described herself on income tax forms as "a farmer or rancher—or as a farm wife." The majority labeled themselves as housewives.[53] There were tax advantages to women not being listed as farm operators or employees, but the NORC report also noted that "most farm women do not think of themselves as farmers, with some saying explicitly that only men can be farmers—and they themselves are not like men."[54]

Interestingly, most of the comments by men agreed with the women about their abilities and participation.[55] On the other hand, according to one USDA statistician, "farm men often are unaware of the degree of involvement of women in tractor and mechanical operation."[56]

According to the USDA the Farm Women's Survey showed that "farm women are quite satisfied with farming as a way of life and with the communities where they live. The women are not satisfied with farming as a way to make a living."[57]

Vocabulary continued to evolve. A 1989 USDA report acknowledged that one farm could have more than one operator, and "seventy percent of female operators were married to another operator."[58]

A Census Bureau report on *Residents of Farms and Rural Areas, 1991,* dropped the word "farmer" entirely. Its subjects were simply "farm females" and "farm males."[59]

Starting the next year, the Census of Agriculture was taken over by the USDA, and it does not hesitate to use the word "farmer." For example, the webpage giving highlights of the 2012 Census reports that the number of female farmers who were principal operators dropped by almost 6 percent since 2007, a much larger percentage drop than male farmers, but the total number of female farm operators fell by only half as much as their male counterparts.[60]

Statistical Abstract

Agriculture is a major focus of the early volumes of *Statistical Abstracts,* starting with the first book in 1878.[61] At the start the major interest was crops and acreage.

The 1895 edition of the *Statistical Abstract* had a table on "SEX and CLASSES of Occupations." It offered only five categories. "Agriculture, fisheries, and mining" provided work for 9 million people, and almost 700,000 of them were female.[62]

The 1902 edition of the *Statistical Abstract* provided data, broken down by sex, on people over the age of nine with occupations. "Agricultural pursuits" contained eight subcategories. The largest category of women workers was "agricultural laborers" (663,209), while the smallest was "lumbermen and raftsman" (exactly 100 females).[63]

It wasn't until the 20th edition, in 1902, that a section on "Occupations, Labor, and Wages" appeared, which featured tables on both male and female "breadwinners." It reported, for example, that in 1890, 447,104 females over the age of nine were engaged as "agricultural laborers." This was about 15 percent of that occupational group.[64]

Tables with characteristics of farm operators appeared in the 1970s, but sex was not added to the list of characteristics until 1985. The earliest figures in that volume, covering 1978, indicate that women constituted about 5 percent of farm operators.[65]

CHAPTER SEVENTEEN

Women Business Owners, Women-Owned Businesses

In a bulletin published in 1939, the Women's Bureau of the U.S. Department of Labor took note of Miss Josephine Roche, who became the president of the Rocky Mountain Fuel Company in 1927 and decided to manage it "along lines of cooperation with the mine operatives."

In 1928 the company had offered a bold and even defiant mission statement:

> To promote and establish industrial justice, to substitute reason for violence, confidence for misunderstanding, integrity and good faith for dishonest practices, and a union of effort for the chaos of the present economic warfare; to avoid needless and wasteful strikes and lockouts through the investigation and correction of their underlying causes; to establish genuine collective bargaining between mine workers and operators through free and independent organization; to stabilize employment, production, and markets through cooperative endeavor and the aid of science; to assure mine workers and operators continuing mutual benefit and consumers a dependable supply of coal at reasonable and uniform prices; to defend our joint undertaking against every conspiracy or vicious practice which seeks to destroy it; and in all other respects to enlist public confidence and support by safeguarding the public interest.

The year after this policy was announced, the company reported an increase in profits, productivity, and miners' wages.[1]

Although the bulletin doesn't mention it, Roche's father—from whom she inherited the company—had been involved in breaking up the miners' unions during the Colorado Labor War in which more than 50 people were slain.[2] In this light her decision to cooperate with the miners seems a radical step.

Roche is an extreme example of one type of early woman business owner: the inheritor of a husband's or father's firm. The other end of the spectrum are the self-employed. Both groups are hard to identify in early statistical publications.

One problem is that the compilers were interested in *occupations,* not business ownership. And so a 1933 report by the Women's Bureau noted, "Healthy increases occurred among women engaged in proprietary, official, and supervisory pursuits in nearly every field of employment," but did not attempt to separate proprietors from managers.[3]

Table 17.1 shows some cases in which the report identifies owners.

Other occupations are harder to categorize. Is a "billiards room keeper" an owner or a manager?

Complicating the matter is what the statisticians saw as a tendency of women who inherited a small business to list themselves as being engaged in the occupation when they might actually be a supervisor. As a 1947 bulletin put it: "Census experts have stated that while there undoubtedly have been women in certain of these occupations investigation might have shown that the woman reported as a 'blacksmith' was an owner of a blacksmith shop left her by her husband rather than a worker actively on the job."[4] It is not possible now to determine how accurate that assumption was. Neither can we tell how many male shop owners also claimed a skill they did not possess.

By 1950 the Women's Bureau was reporting specifically on self-employed women—at least those listed in management. It said that about 60 percent of the women in management were self-employed, the same rate as that for men.

Table 17.1   Selected occupations from a 1933 Women's Bureau report.

Occupation	Male	Female
Owners and proprietors of log and timber camps	5,641	9
Garage owners and proprietors	50,383	335
Owners and proprietors, truck, transfer, and cab companies	30,326	426
Owners and proprietors, cleaning, dyeing, and pressing shops	15,207	1,068
Laundry owners and proprietors	14,474	966

Source: U.S. Labor Department, Women's Bureau, *Occupational Progress,* 65 and 72.

Generally, the more capital a type of business required, the less likely it was to be owned by a woman—a situation that continues today. From the same 1950 report:

> Types of industry that have seemed especially promising to women who run their own business include retail trade and the various personal services, in each of which about two-thirds or more of the women proprietors or managers are self-employed. Other occupations with considerably smaller numbers of women in management, but with half or more of these self-employed, are business services, construction, miscellaneous repair services, and auto repair services or garages. At the other end of the scale, only very small proportions of the women in management in banking and finance or utilities are self-employed.[5]

The 1958 *Handbook on Women Workers* reported that the number of women listed as proprietors, officials, and managers (except farms) had doubled since 1940 to over one million. "The classification is a very broad one and ranges from a large number of women proprietors running their own businesses to a relatively few high-level corporate officials. Most of the women proprietors were engaged in retail trade, operating such establishments as restaurants, food stores, or apparel shops."[6]

The various *Handbooks* took notice of the legal hurdles for married women in owning a business. For example, from the 1958 edition: "Five states have statutes under which court sanction, and in some cases the husband's consent, is required for a wife's legal venture into an independent business, if she is to keep the profits for her own account."[7]

It is important to note that counting the number of women who own businesses is not the same thing as counting the number of businesses owned by women. An individual might own 10 companies, while 1 company might be jointly owned by 10 women.

The first official attempt to count the establishments rather than the people came in 1972, when two agencies of the Commerce Department, the Census Bureau and the Office of Minority Business Enterprise, joined forces on the first comprehensive report on women-owned businesses. The men who headed those agencies noted in their introduction: "It is significant that this report was generated during International Women's Year, inasmuch as the data presented here will provide a benchmark to those interested both in measuring the progress of businesses owned by women and in pursuing more equitable treatment for these ventures."

The report noted that most women-owned firms were "sole proprietorships and concentrated in industries which normally do not generate a large volume of receipts per firm." Only 13 percent of them had employees. Most firms were in services and retail.[8]

The 1975 *Handbook on Women Workers* finally gave figures on the self-employed, with a total of 1,545,000 (4.6 percent).[9] This didn't count women who worked for corporations but considered themselves self-employed because they owned or were part owners of the corporation.[10]

A year later Louis F. Laun, the deputy Small Business Administration (SBA) administrator, spoke at a Senate hearing on his agency's relationship with women. He explained that "there has been no recordkeeping on the sex of the recipients of SBA's loans, management assistance or technical assistance," because the law governing the program did not mention sex nor marital status.[11]

To receive grants, Laun said, women must prove that they are disadvantaged. "If women as a class are declared a minority, it will be virtually impossible to accomplish the goals and objectives for which our special emphasis programs were created." It would mean "diluting existing programs." He added that women qualified if, for example, they "were denied credit because of their sex" or are in what is considered a "male-type" business. In fiscal year 1975 9 percent of SBA loans went to women-owned businesses, 6 percent of money loaned.[12]

Senator Jacob Javits (R-NY) noted the recent change in regulations forbidding discrimination because of marital status and asked, "What has taken so long about recognizing that women are people?" Laun replied that the rules always prohibited discrimination: "We have not just discovered this; in a sense, we are just keeping statistics on it."[13]

Senator Bob Packwood (R-OR) observed at the same hearing, "Every business we have ever talked with since 1964 onwards does not discriminate on the basis of sex. They have 45 secretaries. This is the answer, we have as many women as men."[14] (Twenty years later Packwood was forced to resign from the Senate due to charges of sexual assault and harassment.)[15]

In 1980 the Census Bureau put out two reports on the subject, based on different sources of evidence. *Women-Owned Businesses 1977* used data from tax returns, supplied by the Internal Revenue Service, and from the Social Security Administration.[16] *Selected Characteristics of Women-Owned Businesses 1977*, on the other hand, included information from the first attempt to collect data on the subject through a sample survey conducted by mail. This survey gathered information on receipts size, employment size, legal form of organization, and so on. Some of the highlights follow.

- 7.1 percent of businesses were women-owned, accounting for 6.6 percent of receipts.

- The median net income for women-owned businesses was $6,481.

- Fewer than a third of the companies had paid employees.

- The majority were financed with the owner's savings, and 80 percent started with capital of less than $10,000.

- Oddly enough women who owned very small firms and very large firms had something in common: they averaged (median) fewer than 23 hours a week managing their businesses, while owners in the $50,000–$99,999 receipt range averaged 42 hours.

- Almost three-quarters of the owners were unmarried, but married women owned more firms in the more profitable industries.[17]

In a (nongovernmental) study of female entrepreneurship published in 1989, Kathleen C. Brannen noted that the Commerce Department's 1977 *Women-Owned Businesses* report showed a drop of these businesses by two-thirds in five years. "The explanation: the base was changed in 1977 to exclude 1120 corporation data, although table headings continued to refer to 'all United States firms.'" In fact, there were enough problems with the 1972 "benchmark" data that the 1977 report had to include corrected numbers for comparison's sake.[18]

The 1980 Census of Population identified the self-employed, but only in some fields. There were 560,000 self-employed "managers and administrators," and 160,000 of them were women.[19] In sales, there were 440,000 self-employed "supervisors and proprietors," and 134,000 were female.[20] A separate volume on *Place of Work* gave much more detail about the self-employed but did not break it down by sex.[21]

The 1983 *Handbook on Women Workers* was entitled *Time of Change* (and published a year late). It reported that "only 6 percent (2.4 million) of women workers were self-employed in 1981."[22] The median income for self-employed nonfarm women workers was $5,310, about one-quarter of the figure for men.[23]

In 1990 the SBA issued *A Status Report to Congress: Statistical Information on Women in Business.* In spite of its name, the book is entirely about women who *own* businesses. Ironically, the federal book with a misleading title complained about a "lack of current federal data." It stated that "series on women-owned businesses are generally limited in coverage, timeliness, and comparability. No single source of data on women-owned businesses covers all of these businesses, and combining data from different sources obtains only an imperfect picture of the overall women-owned business population."

The SBA was concerned that the *Survey of Women-Owned Businesses* did not include regular corporations owned by women. Therefore, the Federal Reserve Board (with SBA's help) started the National Survey of Small

Business Finances (now called the SSBF), which reported that in 1987 there were almost 200,000 corporations owned by women, with receipts of close to $200,000 billion. It concluded that more than one-quarter of businesses are women-owned but account for less than 5 percent of receipts.[24]

SSBF data was incorporated in the 1998 edition of *Women in Business,* which remained interested only in business owners. Once again, the SBA urged that "more quality data" was needed, but this time it had no examples more specific than "research on the economic implications of this booming business sector" and "identifying barriers."[25]

In 1988 Congress authorized the creation of the National Women's Business Council (NWBC), "to review the status of women-owned businesses nationwide and to develop detailed multiyear plans in connection with both private and public sector actions to assist and promote such businesses."[26] The council published its first statistical compendium on women-owned businesses in 1994.[27]

The figures for 1997 delivered a shock: women-owned businesses dropped from 6.4 million to 5.4 million. Once again, the reason was a change in definition: the Census Bureau had decided to count only private companies with at least 51 percent ownership by women. That eliminated all public companies as well as firms owned equally by male and female partners, such as husband and wife (or "mom and pop") businesses, which the Census estimated at around two million.[28]

The reason for this switch was not malicious; the intention was to align the figures with federal procurement rules, which required 51 percent ownership for a firm to benefit from set-asides for women and minorities, but Cynthia E. Griffin, writing in *Entrepreneur,* worried about how this drop might be perceived: "Will bankers be less likely to lend to you if they think women-owned businesses are a dying breed? Will a smaller pool of women entrepreneurs be seen as deserving a smaller piece of the government pie?"[29]

The NWBC was still trying to deal with this issue in its second compendium, dated 2001. Beside 5.4 million women-owned businesses, it noted, there are "also 3.6 million jointly-owned firms within the U.S., accounting for 17% of all firms; two million of these 3.6 million firms would have been classified as women-owned under the 1992 definition of a woman-owned business, bringing the total number of privately-held women-owned firms to 7.4 million, or approximately 36% of all firms."[30]

The same report noted continuing gaps in the data:

- The Census Bureau count did not include publicly traded firms. "Without these firms, which account for the highest revenues and largest employment among women-owned firms, the true impact of women-owned firms is not being captured. Further, because publicly-traded firms are included in statistics for all firms, the share of number, revenues and employment contributed by women-owned businesses are being under-reported."

- "Information about access to capital issues continued to be sparse and was often anecdotal only. Due in part to the large amounts of financing coming from informal sources, full information is difficult to obtain."

- "Statistical information on Federal procurement from women-owned businesses is available, but it is not directly comparable across the multiple data sources."[31]

In 2010 the Commerce Department's Economics and Statistics Administration (ESA) looked into the future "at the request of the White House Council on Women and Girls." The result was *Women-Owned Businesses in the 21st Century*. (Why this was done separately from the NWBC's continuing work is not explained. The book mentions NWBC's surveys only once, in an appendix.)[32]

The ESA report noted that during the difficult economic times after 9/11 women-owned businesses did better than the average, largely because they were centered in economic sectors that were growing, such as health care and education.[33] It would be interesting to know if this pattern held true in the recent recession.

Another interesting aspect of the ESA report is its attempt to determine why men-owned businesses fare differently from those owned by women, and the different characteristics of their owners. For example:

- "Men are more likely than women to start a business for financial considerations, whereas women state they are more interested in careers that help them achieve a work-life balance and that can provide personal satisfaction and recognition."

- Self-employed women average spending more time on child care and household activities than self-employed men and—perhaps counterintuitively—non-self-employed women.[34]

Two years later the NWBC published *Women-Owned Firms in the U.S.*, based on the Census Bureau's 2007 Survey of Business Owners (and turnabout being fair play, it mentions the ESA's 2010 study exactly once). This book focuses on the business cycle of women-owned companies:

- More than three-quarters of the firms are founded by their owners, and more than half start with $5,000 or less in capital.

- The biggest three sectors are as follows:
  - Professional, scientific, and technical services (14.1 percent), primary sector for firms owned by White women.
  - Health care and social assistance (15.8 percent), primary sector for African American, Hispanic, and American Indian and Alaska Native women-owned firms.
  - "Other services" (including such diverse elements as machinery repair and promoting religious activities) (16.1 percent) was the primary sector for Asian and Native Hawaiian and Other Pacific Islander women-owned firms.[35]

Statistical Abstract

Self-employed persons first appeared in the *Statistical Abstract* in 1949. Only subsets of two categories were counted: professional workers and "proprietors, managers, and officials." In both cases, men and women were listed separately.[36]

In 1952 a table was added for all self-employed persons, broken down by race and sex.[37] In years that followed, tables that broke the group down by state, income, and color appeared and disappeared; sometimes sexes were listed, sometimes not.

In 1961 all the tables in this field mysteriously went unisex.[38] Starting in 1963 sex was identified again.[39]

"Women-owned businesses" first makes an appearance in the 1976 volume of the *Statistical Abstract,* with data taken from the 1972 study.[40]

The last government-produced volume of the *Statistical Abstract* (2012) listed women-owned firms by kind of business[41] and included a separate table with ownership by sex, ethnicity, race, and veteran's status. All the figures are for 2007.[42]

PART VI

Women and Health

CHAPTER EIGHTEEN

Nonreproductive Health Issues

In her two-volume bibliography of women in government publications, Mary Ellen Huls stated: "Government documents on women's health have dealt mainly with substance abuse and cancer of the female reproductive system."[1] This terse summary was perhaps an exaggeration.

One way of measuring the federal government's focus on women's health is through *Vital and Health Statistics,* more than 20 series of publications that have been produced by the National Center for Health Statistics (NCHS) since 1963. Figure 18.1 divides those reports whose titles include either "women" (but not "men and women") or "mothers" according to their main subjects. More than three-quarters of those reports are about motherhood or methods of preventing motherhood. Those subjects are covered in different chapters of this book; this one centers on other aspects of female wellness and disease.

In 2002 the Office on Women's Health published *A Century of Women's Health* to celebrate 100 years of federal progress on the subject, as well as the office's own tenth anniversary. The book offered this summary:

In the early 20th century, women's health was primarily equated with maternal health and the role of women as mothers. With the birth control movement of the 1920s, the definition of women's health began to include issues of reproductive health and control over the spacing (or timing) of each child's birth. By the 1960s and 1970s, reproductive health issues were at the center of a new wave of women's health activism. These issues included the controversial legalization of abortion and the de-medicalization of pregnancy and childbirth. By the last decades of the century, the definition of women's health had expanded to include many other social, legal, medical, and economic issues. Topics such as stress, violence, poverty and

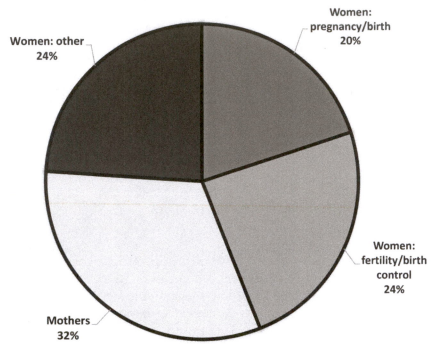

Figure 18.1 *Vital and Health Statistics* series. Percentage of titles mentioning "women" or "mothers" in specific contexts.

Source: U.S. Health and Human Services Department, Centers for Disease Control and Prevention, National Center for Health Statistics, *Vital and Health Statistics Series.*

discrimination began to find their places within debates and discussions of women's health. Women were also more likely than men to be victims of child abuse, domestic violence, and gender discrimination, problems that were increasingly recognized as public health issues.[2]

The 1850 Census was the first to cover health issues, and it was interested only in lifelong conditions such as blindness, deafness, and the "insane and idiotic." The figures indicated that White men and women were about equally likely to be insane, which was also true of "Free colored [sic]," but female slaves were almost 50 percent more likely to be counted as insane as their male counterparts. In all three classes men were more likely to be registered as "idiotic."[3]

The first data to appear in census reports about physical health concerned death. In 1855 Census superintendent J.D.B. De Bow authored a book on mortality statistics. The largest cause of death for both sexes was zymotic illnesses (i.e., acute infectious diseases).[4]

A report on the results of the next census urged special attention to statistics about violent death because the causes are "less shrouded in mystery than those of disease." Women were less likely than men to die from "drowning, fall, fire-arms, freezing" and railroad accidents, but they were more susceptible to death by fire "naturally following from domestic avocations and differences in attire." The overall conclusion was that "the male class are fully twice as much exposed to dangers as the female class in their usual habits of life."[5]

Some of the first non-census publications from the executive branch to consider women's health came from the Treasury Department because that is where the Public Health Service (PHS) was first located. A good example is *Healthy Happy Womanhood,* a pamphlet published by the PHS in 1920. It begins by invoking Joan of Arc: "She has come to stand for the woman with a vision, the woman who is seeking to do her part for the betterment of the world."[6] It then goes on to discuss the secrets of health—exercise, posture, nutrition, and so on—before getting to its main subject: venereal disease and how to prevent it: "Girls and women have a special work to do, therefore, in helping to build up a high standard of sex con duct. They must demand clean living from the men with whom they associate."[7]

The National Health Survey was created in 1957 to monitor the health of the nation. Now called the National Health Interview Survey, or NHIS, it collects data on a broad range of health topics through personal household interviews conducted by the Census Bureau.[8] The questionnaires and data, broken down by sex, are available on the web from 1962 forward.[9]

The year 1964 saw the release of one of the most influential medical reports in federal history: *Smoking and Health,* published by Surgeon General Luther Terry, the head of the PHS. The Surgeon General's Report, as it came to be known, made the correlations between tobacco use and illness clear.

The report found that less data was available about women's smoking habits than those of men. There was less evidence that smoking caused lung cancer in women, but the numbers "point in the same direction."[10] Also, women who smoke while pregnant tended to have babies of lighter birth weight.[11]

Surgeons general have continued to publish annual reports on smoking, usually with a theme. The 1980 volume was entitled *Health Consequences of Smoking for Women.* It found that women were catching up with men on initiating smoking but were less successful at quitting.[12] Starting in 1974 more 12- to 14-year-old girls were smoking than boys (in 1979,

4.3 percent to 3.2 percent). The same was true with ages 12 to 18.[13] The mortality ratio for all women who smoked was 26 percent higher than for women who did not.[14]

The next surgeon general report on *Women and Smoking* appeared in 2001. It warned that smoking-related disease among women had become a "full-blown epidemic." It stated that "more women are estimated to have died of lung cancer in the year 2000 than of cancers of the breast, uterus, and ovary combined."[15]

Returning to the NHIS, mentioned earlier, it is also the main source of data for *Health, United States,* a report that the NCHS has published regularly since 1975.

At a Census Bureau conference on *Issues in Federal Statistical Needs Relating to Women,* held in 1978, Charlotte Muller critiqued the "Data on the Nation's Health" section of the 1976–1977 edition of *Health, United States.*

Muller noted that figures by sex were not always listed or were not combined with other data such as race or income. "Age at completion of projected fertility" was not estimated. Some of her suggestions for data that should be collected are paraphrased:

- Do women use sick leave to take care of other family members' illnesses or medical appointments?
- Should "privacy concerns" be listed as a barrier to care?
- How do the sexes vary on health care finance?
- Do male and female physicians differ in how they assess the seriousness of male and female conditions?
- Do treatments for the same diagnosis vary with sex?
- How do different medical appointment systems affect each sex?[16]

While most of Muller's questions are not answered in later editions of *Health, United States,* the data offered did change over time. Table 18.1 shows the topics listed under the heading "Women's Health" at 10-year intervals.

Returning to 1975, a crucial conference on the subject was held that year. The published proceedings, *Women and Their Health: Research Implications for a New Era,* was the first federal publication to examine whether women were being neglected in the field of medical research.[17]

In response to that conference the NCHS conducted a study of women's visits to doctor's offices, published in 1980. Because almost 80 percent "of women in the civilian noninstitutionalized population of the

Table 18.1　*Health, United States*—Women's Health topics.

	1975	1985	1995	2005	2015
Abortion	*	*	*	*	*
Acute conditions	*				
Age	*				
Alcohol consumption	*	*	*	*	*
Asthma	*			*	
Blood pressure	*				
Cancer relationship to alcohol/tobacco use	*				
Children with defective vision	*				
Chronic conditions, selected	*				
Death rates, all causes	*	*	*	*	*
Death rates, educational attainment	*		*	*	
Dental caries (cavities), untreated	*			*	*
Dental visits	*	*	*	*	*
Dependency ratio	*				
Diabetes	*			*	*
Disabilities	*				
Doctor visits	*	*			*
Exercise	*				
Health insurance	*		*		*
Health occupations	*				
Hospital utilization, inpatient	*	*	*	*	*
Infant deaths	*				
Infants with congenital malformations	*				
Life expectancy	*	*	*	*	*
Mental health facilities	*	*			
Mentally handicapped	*				
Nurses	*				
Nursing home utilization	*	*	*	*	
Overweight and obesity	*	*	*	*	*
Pap smear (Pap test)	*			*	
Population, resident	*	*	*		*
Postpartum sterilization	*				

(*Continued*)

Table 18.1   Continued

	1975	1985	1995	2005	2015
Pregnancy complications	*				
Preventive care exam	*				
Restricted mobility	*				
Self-assessment of health	*	*			
Smoking	*		*		
Breast cancer		*		*	*
Cholesterol		*	*	*	*
Cigarette smoking		*	*	*	*
Contraception		*	*	*	*
Death rates, selected causes		*		*	*
Deaths, complications of pregnancy		*			
Deaths, cancer		*			
Deaths, homicide		*			
Deaths, suicide		*			
Expected births		*	*		
Fertility rates		*	*	*	*
Heart disease, respondent-reported		*			*
Hypertension		*	*	*	*
Limitation of activity		*			
Marijuana use		*	*	*	*
Medical students		*	*		
AIDS cases			*	*	
Birth rates			*	*	*
Births, number			*	*	*
Breast-feeding			*		*
Cancer incidence rates			*	*	*
Cancer survival, five-year relative			*	*	*
Cocaine use			*	*	
Deaths, leading causes			*	*	*
Dental students			*		
Education of mother			*		
Emergency department visits			*	*	*

(Continued)

	1975	1985	1995	2005	2015
Health status, respondent-assessed			*	*	*
Home health care patients			*	*	
Hospice patients			*	*	
Hospital utilization, outpatient department			*	*	*
Inhalants			*	*	
Mammography			*	*	*
Medicare			*		
Nursing students			*		
Optometry students			*		
Poverty			*	*	*
Prenatal care			*	*	
Teenage childbearing			*	*	*
Unmarried mothers			*	*	*
Years of potential life lost			*	*	*
Access to care				*	
Back pain, low				*	*
Cesarean delivery, low-risk				*	*
Death rates, urbanization				*	
Drugs prescribed during medical visits				*	
Drugs, prescription, use in past 30 days				*	*
Energy and macronutrient intake				*	*
Hay fever				*	
Headache, severe or migraine				*	*
Hearing trouble				*	*
Illicit drug use				*	*
Neck pain				*	*
Occupational injury deaths				*	*
Physical activity				*	*
Prescription medicine expense				*	
Serious psychological distress				*	*
Sinusitis				*	
Vaccinations				*	*
Vision trouble				*	*

(Continued)

Table 18.1   Continued

	1975	1985	1995	2005	2015
Basic actions difficulty					*
Births, preterm					*
Cancer, respondent-reported					*
Colorectal tests or procedures					*
Complex activity limitation					*
Disability measures, selected					*
Drug poisoning					*
Expenses, health care					*
Glycemic control					*
HIV diagnoses					*
Injury					*
Normal weight					*
Stroke, respondent-reported					*
Unmet need					*

Sources: U.S. Health, Education, and Welfare Department, Human Resources Administration, National Center for Health Statistics, *Health, United States 1975;* U.S. Health and Human Services Department, Public Health Service, National Center for Health Statistics, *Health, United States 1985;* U.S. Health and Human Services Department, Public Health Service, National Center for Health Statistics, *Health, United States 1995;* U.S. Health and Human Services Department, Centers for Disease Control and Prevention, National Center for Health Statistics, *Health, United States 2005;* U.S. Health and Human Services Department, Centers for Disease Control and Prevention, National Center for Health Statistics, *Health, United States 2015.*

United States saw a physician at least once during 1977, therefore, basic data concerning physician services used by women are fundamental to research designed to address many of these concerns."[18]

The study found that women averaged 3.5 visits to physicians' offices per year, with 90 percent of the visits made by White women. Seniors visited the most.[19]

The report listed 57 reasons for doctor's appointments, together accounting for two-thirds of the visits. The five most common diagnosis codes were prenatal care, medical or specialist care, essential benign hypertension, medical and surgical aftercare, and neuroses. These accounted for almost one-quarter of the visits.[20] Women were more likely than men to visit the doctor for "slightly serious or not serious" problems.[21]

The year 1980 was halfway through the United Nations Decade for Women, and a conference was held in Copenhagen to discuss women's progress in health, education, and employment. The United States filed a "country report" entitled *Woman and Health 1980,* written by Emily C. Moore, the first comprehensive report of its kind.[22] In preparing this study, Moore consulted with more than 50 women's groups.[23] There were more than 80 pages of data on women's health and related issues. It was apparently the first PHS report to discuss the issues of "lesbian women."[24]

In 1983, the assistant secretary for health, Dr. Edward N. Brandt, established the U.S. Public Health Service Task Force on Women's Health Issues in recognition of the paucity of data related to women's health. The task force produced a publication in 1985, *Women's Health,* which delineated a series of criteria for "differentiating a health problem, condition, or disease as a woman's issue." The criteria included the following:

- Diseases or conditions unique to women or some subgroup of women
- Diseases or conditions more prevalent in women or some subgroup of women
- Diseases or conditions more serious in women or some subgroup of women
- Diseases or conditions for which risk factors are different for women or some subgroup of women
- Diseases or conditions for which interventions are different in women or some subgroup of women

The report also recommended that "biomedical and behavioral research should be expanded to ensure emphasis on conditions and diseases unique to, or more prevalent in, women in all age groups."[25] One result of this report was the creation within the PHS of the Coordinating Committee on Women's Health Issues.[26]

The earliest statistical report located with "breast cancer" in its title appeared in 1989. Congress's Office of Technology Assessment published a staff paper discussing whether Medicare should begin to cover breast screening. The staff concluded that screening would probably not save money over the cost of cancer treatment but that "it seems somewhat unfair to require a relatively low-cost program like breast cancer screening to demonstrate that it is cost-effective."[27]

The next year saw the production of another report requested by Congress, one that proved crucial to the government's relationship with female health care. The General Accounting Office (GAO) published *Problems in Implementing Policy on Women in Study Populations,* which made it clear that medical research was not regularly including women.

While the National Institutes of Health (NIH) had changed its policies to promote inclusion, that change was not reflected in its grant applications. What is more, the policy only affected external research and did not apply to work by federal scientists.[28]

One example mentioned in this report involved the National Heart, Lung, and Blood Institute, which, in 1981, studied 22,000 men and found that a single aspirin every other day reduced the incidence of heart attacks. "However," said the GAO, "we now have the dilemma of not knowing whether this preventive strategy would help women, harm them, or have no effect."[29] As Congresswoman Louise M. Slaughter reflected in 1993 at a conference on *Women in Clinical Studies,* "perhaps the 1990 GAO report started it all."[30]

That same year the NIH created the Office of Research on Women's Health (ORWH) to be the focal point for women's health research. Its responsibilities included supporting research related to conditions affecting women, ensuring that women were included in research studies, and making sure that NIH research addresses women's health issues.[31] In 2011 ORWH said its main interests were the following:

- Female-specific research (primarily reproductive)
- Differences or similarities between males and females (sex differences research)
- Differences within populations of women and men (health disparities), especially those populations that traditionally have been excluded or understudied in clinical research[32]

Returning to 1981, a major health crisis was first announced in the PHS's *Morbidity and Mortality Weekly Report,* dated June 5. The article stated that "5 young men, all active homosexuals," had been treated in Los Angeles hospitals for *Pneumocystis carinii* pneumonia and two of them had died. This was the first government report on what became known as AIDS.[33] In the first year of what became a huge epidemic, 13 (4 percent) of the cases reported to the Centers for Disease Control were heterosexual women.[34]

In 1991 the Health and Human Services Department created the Office on Women's Health (ORWH), which "coordinates women's health efforts across HHS and addresses critical women's health issues by informing and advancing policies, educating health care professionals and consumers, and supporting model programs."[35]

In 1997 the NCHS published *Women: Work and Health.* This report combined data from more than 10 series produced by several different federal agencies. It attempted to describe "the sociodynamics, household characteristics, and health of women according to workforce status and job conditions."[36] It contained more than 60 pages of tables on workforce status, workplace characteristics, work injuries, illnesses, fatalities and health conditions attributed to work, comparisons of health of employed workers and those not in labor force, knowledge of health risks, and employee benefits.[37]

In 2010 the ORWH published *Highlights of NIH Women's Health and Sex Differences Research 1990–2010*. While it is nonstatistical, it contains more than 100 pages summarizing studies concerning women's health and sex differences. One example showed that heart attacks in women are not preceded by the symptoms familiar in men.[38]

The federal government currently has many websites dedicated to female wellness issues. For example, the NCHS has *Women's Health*.[39] There is also one for men.

As of this writing the website of the GAO, which assesses how well federal programs are working, has 16 publications with "breast cancer" in the abstract. The most recent of these (October 2016) is about initiatives in breast cancer education created by the Health and Human Services Department.[40]

Statistical Abstract

The 1925 edition of the *Statistical Abstract* was the first to mention health. Specifically it had several tables about the patients in mental hospitals. The only table broken down by sex listed the patients by types of psychosis. For both sexes the largest category was "dementia praecox (schizophrenia)."[41]

All the tables mentioned here are categorized by sex, unless otherwise specified.

A table on "Days of Disability" began to appear in 1960. Women had more "Restricted-Activity Days" and "Bed-Disability Days" but fewer "Work-Loss Days." The latter might have been because only people who listed "working" as their main activity were counted in that category. There were also tables of the average weights of men and women and the number of people, by sex, injured by types of accidents.[42]

The next year's edition added tables on physician and dental visits.[43]

Statistics on smoking habits appeared in 1963, but under the category "manufactures." The few women who smoked only pipes or cigars were counted with the 72.7 percent of women whose smoking of cigarettes was listed as "none or occasional."[44] Cigarette smoking showed up in 1968 paired with "Health Characteristics" and "Death Rates," just after a table on "Narcotic Addiction."[45]

The 1967 edition saw the introduction of data on the incidence of heart disease, arthritis, and hypertension.[46] There were also tables on hospital utilization for older persons, which broadened to include all persons the next year. The year 1967 also included a table on the medical costs for married couples, non-married men, and non-married women.[47]

In 1970 the health section of the *Statistical Abstract* added data about physicians by sex.[48] Two years later it gained a table on activity limitations caused by various chronic conditions. Men were slightly more susceptible to these than women.[49]

Data on nursing home residents arrived in 1974. In 1969 2.8 percent of the female population were in such residences, compared to 1.3 percent of men.[50]

The 1975 edition delivered a table on "Estimated Alcoholism, by Sex, by States." It offered a definition of alcoholism that referred to the person in question as "he."[51]

The next year offered new data on employed people in selected health occupations, long-term care institutions, and the legally blind.[52] There was also a table on "Preventive Care Procedures," covering both sexes, and including breast examination and Pap smears for women.[53]

The 1977 edition introduced data on surgical operations and physical exercise;[54] 1979 brought a single table on the use of coffee, aspirin, and sleeping pills.[55]

The 1980 edition included new data on acute medical conditions and elevated blood pressure.[56] The edition two years later brought "known cases of diabetes."[57]

The 1984 edition introduced a table on "Hospital Discharges." The most common "diagnosis" (that is the word used) for women discharged was "delivery." This was followed by "diseases of the heart," which was number one for men.[58]

Statistics about insurance became more prominent in the *Statistical Abstract* during this decade. "Health Insurance Coverage" appeared in 1986.[59]

"New cases of cancer" was first covered in 1987.[60] The next year presented data on "AIDS cases reported" and "functional limitations" of people over the age of 65.[61]

The 1989 edition introduced a table on patients discharged from hospitals, sorted by the source of their expected payment. There was also, for the first time, a table on nursing home discharges.[62]

That same year first provided data on "Women Who Knew How to Do Breast Self-Examination and Women Who Had a Breast Examination or PAP Smear—Selected Characteristics."[63] In 1990 that changed to "Women Who Have Had a Mammogram, Breast Physical Exam or Who Perform Breast Self-Exams (BSE)."[64]

The 1990 edition also saw the introduction of tables on hospice care, overweight and obesity, and visits to hospital emergency departments.[65]

The 1997 edition introduced a table on "Self-Perception of Being Overweight." More than 90 percent of women who actually were overweight believed themselves to be so, while almost half of women who were not overweight thought they were. Figures were significantly lower for men in both cases.[66]

In the same year use of mammography by women over 40 began to be singled out for study, along with figures for ambulatory surgery.[67]

The 1998 edition introduced tables on the percentage of adults who engage in leisure-time physical activities, and the same for high school students.[68]

The 2007 edition introduced new data on a number of health topics. These included selected diseases and asthma in children. A table on Medicaid beneficiaries provided information on "BCCA women," referring to "Breast and Cervical Cancer Assistance."[69]

The next year brought tables on selected cosmetic procedures. The most common surgical procedures among women were breast augmentation, liposuction, eyelid surgery, tummy tuck, and breast reduction. The most common male surgical procedures were liposuction, nose reshaping, eyelid surgery, male breast reduction, and face lifts. Botox injection was the most common nonsurgical procedure for both sexes.[70]

The 2011 volume introduced data on "Insufficient Rest or Sleep." Women reported this problem more often than men.[71]

The final volume of the *Statistical Abstract* produced by the federal government, in 2012, added a table on "Living with an AIDS Diagnosis"; 114,000 women fell into that category, less than one-third the number of men. The largest number of transmissions for women had been through heterosexual contact.[72]

CHAPTER NINETEEN

Contraception

The first congressional hearings on birth control were held in 1931, to consider a bill that would have permitted information on contraceptives to be sent through the U.S. mail—but only if sent from or to a physician. Among the witnesses was Margaret Sanger, the national leader of the cause of contraception. She said: "We want to make it possible for motherhood to be conscious and controlled. We want to make it possible for mothers to have safe, scientific information to prevent conception so that they may regulate the size of their families, so that they may space out the number of children in the family in consideration of the mother's health, of the father's earning capacity, and of the welfare of each child."[1]

Three more decades passed before the Supreme Court ruled, in 1965, that states could not forbid married couples from using birth control.[2] Only in 1972 did the court extend that right to all individuals.[3]

Some members of Franklin Delano Roosevelt's administration tried to get the federal government to take an interest in family planning in the 1930s, but Katharine Lenroot, the head of the Children's Bureau, refused to take a position on the subject, fearing that pushback might threaten her other programs.[4] The first real federal involvement came in 1942 when the Public Health Service began urging that women involved in war industries should practice child spacing.[5]

Family size in the United States peaked at 3.7 children in 1957. Reliable birth control in the form of the pill and intrauterine device arrived around 1960.[6]

The Supreme Court decision in 1965 finally spurred the federal government to offer grants to family planning clinics.[7] The following January,

John W. Gardner, the secretary of Health, Education, and Welfare announced:

> The policy of this Department is to conduct and support programs of basic and applied research on the above topics [population dynamics, fertility, sterility, and family planning], to conduct and support training programs; to collect and make available such data as may be necessary, to support, on request, health programs making family planning information and services available, and to provide family planning information and services, on request, to individuals who receive health services from operating agencies of the Department.
>
> The objectives of the departmental policy are to improve the health of the people, to strengthen the integrity of the family, and to provide families the freedom of choice to determine the spacing of their children and the size of their families.

Gardner added that the programs "shall guarantee freedom from coercion or pressure of mind or conscience."[8]

A report from the same department a few years later focused on those in need of subsidized family planning services:

> The great majority of families in this country have long had freedom of choice about the size of their families and the spacing of their children. It is the very poor who have been denied this freedom, partly because they did not understand that scientific methods make family planning possible, but mainly because there were no convenient services available and they had no means of paying for the necessary services and supplies.

The authors of that report thought five million women were unable to afford the services on their own. Half a million received federally subsidized programs in 1967; 300,000 more received access through private funds. "Available data are not adequate to indicate how many more of the 5 million women desire services but have been unable to get them."[9]

Anyone familiar with government processes would recognize that all this interest and activity would result in a desire for statistical data. The next few years saw the department trying to cope with gathering the information. As one writer said, "The number of women being served was becoming so large that it was almost impossible to keep records on them."[10]

The Provisional Reporting System for Family Planning Services (PRS) began in 1969. It attempted to keep track of all the federally subsidized family planning clinics, and whatever private clinics volunteered to participate. The first published data covered 1971, during which almost

730,000 women made their first visits to public family planning clinics; 798,129 women overall made 1,267,973 visits to the reporting clinics.[11]

In 1972 the Bureau of Community Health Services began publication of *Family Planning Digest,* a bimonthly journal, which ended its run in 1975.[12]

But more important, on the first day of 1972 the PRS was replaced by the National Reporting System for Family Planning Services (NRSFPS).[13] The system was run by the National Center for Health Statistics, but things did not go smoothly. As Joy G. Dryfoos explained a few years later: "The NCHS was assigned the responsibility for operating the NRS-FPS, although it had no mandate or precedent for operating a patient-record system, nor did it control the funding for either the services or the data system. . . . The early years of the NRSFPS were chaotic. . . . It seemed as if the provider agencies would never stop complaining."[14]

The year 1973 saw the launch of the National Survey of Family Growth (NSFG), which

> gathers information on family life, marriage and divorce, pregnancy, infertility, use of contraception, and general and reproductive health. . . .
>
> The NSFG was first designed to be nationally representative of women 15–44 years of age in the civilian, noninstitutionalized population of the United States (household population). The survey sample is designed to produce national data, not estimates for individual states. Later changes to the NSFG include adding an independent sample of men (2002) and expanding the age range to 15–49 (2015). NSFG is conducted through in-person interview, with a portion of the more sensitive questions answered privately by self-administration. The interviews are voluntary and confidential. The response rate for recent data releases is around 73%.[15]

The National Center for Health Statistics started publishing *Data from the National Survey of Family Growth* in 1977 as *Series 23* in its Vital and Health Statistics reports. The first volume was *Utilization of Family Planning Services by Currently Married Women 15–44 Years of Age: United States, 1973.* The most recent publication, dated 2011, was *Teenagers in the United States: Sexual Activity, Contraceptive Use, and Childbearing, 2006–2010.*[16]

The NSFG website currently lists data on condom use and contraception among its "key statistics."[17]

In 1975 the NCHS published the first edition of *Health, United States,* a continuing series of data compilations. It reported that more than two-thirds of married women aged 15 to 44 or their husbands were using contraception.[18] The most popular methods were the pill (24.7 percent of those married women using contraception), condom (9.3 percent), and wife sterilized (8.5 percent).[19]

By comparison, the 2013 data, found in the 2015 edition, stated that the percentage of married women using contraception had dropped to 61.7.[20] The most popular methods were the pill (26.7 percent of all "contracepting women," married or not), female sterilization (25.1 percent), and condom (22.8 percent). (More than one method could be listed in that year's survey.) Methods that vanished over the 40-year period included diaphragm, foam, and douche. Methods that appeared after 1975 include implant, injectable, and others that were used too infrequently to measure.[21]

Returning to the 1970s, the NRSFPS continued to experience difficulties. In 1977 it was changed from 100 percent survey to a sample for budgetary reasons.[22]

The same period saw the creation of the National Inventory of Family Planning Services (NIFPS), which gathered data about the places where the services were offered rather than the people receiving them. It surveyed 9,077 sites in 1978 and received data from 77 percent of them;[23] 5,033 of them were medical sites, and 1,999 were nonmedical (i.e., they performed record keeping, information provision, contraceptive education).[24] Like so many series in this field, the NIFPS seems to have stopped almost as soon as it started.

In 2007 the National Center for Health Statistics started a new series called *Data Briefs*. The most recent relevant publication, dated 2015, is *Sexual Activity, Contraceptive Use, and Childbearing of Teenagers Aged 15–19 in the United States*. The study found that almost 80 percent of female teenagers and 84 percent of male teenagers used contraception during their first sexual intercourse.[25]

What has the federal government's involvement in contraception accomplished? In 2014 the Census Bureau's Center for Economic Studies published *Fifty Years of Family Planning: New Evidence on the Long-Run Effects of Increasing Access to Contraception*, written by Martha J. Bailey. It does not represent the agency's viewpoint and explicitly excludes data on abortion. Among the highlights of the findings:

> The results suggest that increasing access to family planning reduced mothers' reports of child "unwantedness" but had no measurable effects on infants' weight at birth, infant mortality, or maternal mortality in the 1960s and 1970s. In the long run, increasing access to family planning is associated with 2 percent higher family incomes among the affected

cohorts as adults, largely due to increases in men's wage earnings and weeks and hours worked. Federal grants for family planning also increased children's educational attainment. College completion (proxied by 16 or more years of education attained) increased by 2 to 7 percent for children whose mothers had access to family planning, relative to children who were born in the same location just before family planning programs began.[26]

Statistical Abstract

"Contraception" first appeared in the *Statistical Abstract* in 1976, one year after "abortion." The data was only for married women aged 15 to 44 and found that almost 70 percent of them were using some form of contraception.[27]

In 1986 that table was expanded to all women rather than just married ones.[28] The same year introduced data on the use of family planning clinics and the ability to bear children, including contraceptive sterilization.[29]

CHAPTER TWENTY

Abortion

On April 8, 2011, Senator Jon Kyl (R-AZ) spoke on the floor of the Senate, protesting the $363 million that the federal government was paying to Planned Parenthood annually. "Everybody goes to clinics, to hospitals, to doctors, and so on," Kyl said. "Some people go to Planned Parenthood. But you don't have to go to Planned Parenthood to get your cholesterol or your blood pressure checked. If you want an abortion, you go to Planned Parenthood, and that's well over 90 percent of what Planned Parenthood does."

The organization in question quickly responded that only 3 percent of the services it performed were abortion-related.[1]

Kyl used his congressional privilege to change the official transcript. The *Congressional Record* therefore reports that what he said was: "If you want an abortion you go to Planned Parenthood and that is what Planned Parenthood does."[2] This is arguably less accurate than what he actually said, but it is no longer a statistical claim.

Abortion has been controversial in this country at least since state laws on the subject began to be liberalized in the 1950s. The U.S. Supreme Court decided in the 1973 case *Roe v. Wade* that the Fourteenth Amendment of the Constitution protected, in some circumstances, a woman's decision on carrying a pregnancy to term, but this has by no means settled the public issue.[3]

Not surprisingly, the government has had difficulties in collecting statistics on abortion, and even in deciding exactly what it wanted to measure. It has even resorted to using third-party data, in part because some state governments refuse to participate in the national system.

Early common law in the United States did not treat abortion as a criminal offense before "quickening" (the first time movement of the fetus is sensed), but starting in the mid-19th century, each state passed laws on the subject. One major motive was to protect the life of the pregnant woman, since at that time the death rate from abortions was significantly higher than that related to childbirth.[4] Typically, the laws permitted abortions only to save the woman's life.[5]

Because abortions were essentially illegal during this period, it is impossible to know how many occurred. Speculation on the number varied widely in government publications.

For example, at a 1931 Senate hearing on birth control, Reverend Charles Francis Potter argued in favor of legalizing contraception as a method of decreasing abortions. He said that "estimates by social observers" put the number of illegal abortions as high as 2,000,000 per year.[6]

However, a year later a presentation at another Senate hearing on the same subject included Dr. Fred J. Taussig's estimation of 700,000 abortions per year.[7]

One of the earliest mentions of abortion in a publication of government statistics appeared in the volume of the 1880 Census entitled *Report on the Defective, Dependent and Delinquent Classes*. In his introduction the author, Frederick Howard Wines, having discussed the numbers of "idiots" (i.e., mentally retarded people) in the United States, pondered the cause of that condition:

> I am indebted to the superintendent of a training-school for idiots for the additional suggestion that among the causes of idiocy there is little reason to doubt that abortions and attempts at abortion must be included. Where abortion does not occur, the child upon whose life an assault has been made *in utero* comes into the world a wreck. And investigation would perhaps show that an attack upon the life of one child affects the development of every child subsequently born of the same mother. This is a field of investigation which has not, I believe, been explored, and which some physician interested in the subject may find it worth while [sic] to study. If there should prove to be any substantial basis for this theory it would afford a fresh illustration of the revenges of nature.[8]

The same volume included a table detailing offenses for which people were in prison. Approximately 11,000 were listed for "offenses against the person," and 55 of them had been convicted for procuring or attempting to procure an abortion; 15 of those were women.[9]

In regard to abortion as a criminal activity, it is worth noting that it does not appear in the standard statistical collection on the subject, *Uniform Crime Reports*, which the FBI began publishing in the 1930s.

One figure that has appeared in federal statistics from early times is the number of women recorded as dying due to abortions. For example, the first *Report on Vital Statistics,* in 1890, listed five classes of deaths under "affections connected with pregnancy." Abortion was the fourth largest of these, causing 838 deaths.[10]

In the Census Bureau's *Mortality Statistics: 1910,* deaths due to abortion are no longer mentioned, although "accidents of labor" and "accidents of pregnancy" are counted.[11] In the 1931–1932 volume, abortion reappeared with two categories: with septic conditions and without. Both were broken down by White and Colored.[12]

Starting in 1931 the Census Bureau reports on stillbirths (i.e., deaths of babies, not mothers) included the following:

Abortion, miscarriage, premature birth, induced, criminal

Abortion, miscarriage, premature birth, induced, therapeutic

Abortion, miscarriage, premature birth, induced, self-induced

Abortion, miscarriage, premature birth, induced, unspecified

Abortion, miscarriage, premature birth, spontaneous

Other abortions and miscarriages

Other premature births

Of these, the smallest category was criminal (3 deaths) and the largest was "other premature" (730).[13] In all cases, the sex of the stillborn was given if known. The book also reported on the birth order; two of the stillbirths in 1931 were their mothers' 26th babies.[14] Similar tables appeared for several years.

In the 1940s government reports on maternal deaths distinguished many categories of abortion: spontaneous, therapeutic, self-induced, and nontherapeutic induced by others.[15]

In 1950, however, the World Health Organization recommended the use of the term "fetal death" to avoid confusion over different uses of abortion, miscarriage, stillbirth, and associated terms.[16] Starting with the 1950 volume *Vital Statistics* dropped the categorization of types of abortion and concentrated instead on symptoms involved, namely sepsis and toxemia.[17]

In 1960 and 1970 *Vital Statistics* again distinguished women's deaths caused by abortions "induced for medical or legal reasons" from those induced for all other reasons.[18] By 1980 the series was specifying "illegally induced abortions."[19]

A report from the National Center for Health Statistics noted in 1966 that deaths from "maternal causes" had dropped by more than 50 percent in the previous decade, but "the rate for abortion remains virtually unchanged." It did not distinguish legal from illegal abortions.[20]

Studies estimated that about 8,000 legal abortions were taking place in hospitals per year in the mid-1960s. Forty percent of these were granted because of psychiatric reasons and 25 percent due to maternal rubella.[21]

But the atmosphere was ripe for a change in the statutes. In 1957 the American Law Institute (a nongovernment organization) had modified its model penal code to recommend that abortions be permitted in cases of rape, incest, risk of birth with grave physical or mental deficits, and risks to the mental health of the woman. It was not until a decade later that Colorado became the first state to adopt these changes into law.[22]

By 1969 nine states had similar statutes.[23] In that year the Center for Disease Control (CDC) began its abortion surveillance program "to document the number and characteristics of women obtaining legal induced abortions."[24]

These CDC annual reports are based on data provided voluntarily by the states and are therefore incomplete. For example, in that first year only four of the nine states with revised laws provided statistics.

In 1970, 19 states and the District of Columbia reported to the CDC.[25] Five of these states took their data from "fetal death certificates," which were actually designed for miscarriages, and failed to include some of the desired information.[26] While 180,000 abortions were reported that year, one study estimated that another 20,000 legal abortions went unreported.[27]

By 1970 four states permitted abortion "on the decision of a pregnant woman and her physician." Of the states with less restrictive laws, only New York allowed nonresidents to have abortions. Not surprisingly, it had the highest abortion to live birth ratio: 534 to 1,000.[28]

How did the new laws affect female mortality? The law in New York changed halfway through 1970. New York City reported 11 deaths from illegal abortions in the first six months of the year and 6 in the last half. On the other hand, there were eight deaths from legal abortions during the first six months and five in the last six. According to one study, "The health care delivery system in New York City was inexperienced in the provision of abortion services, and was, in many ways, unprepared to cope with the vast number of local and non-resident women requesting abortions."[29] Therefore, the high number was no surprise.

In 1971, almost 40 percent of reported abortions nationwide were performed to out-of-state residents.[30] No doubt one reason for this was that

31 states had "more restrictive" laws permitting abortion only to protect the life of the pregnant woman. The oldest of those laws dated from 1835 (Missouri) and the most recent from 1943 (North Dakota).[31]

Was the number of abortions actually rising as laws became less restrictive? A study by Edward A. Duffy, published in 1971 by the U.S. Health Services and Mental Health Administration, noted: "This may or may not be the case. The total number of legal abortions is rising significantly. The underlying population of abortions is rising above the surface because of the improved legal climate, but, like an iceberg, it is entirely possible that the major part is still underneath. Its real size, whether constant or changing, is not known."[32] Duffy cited one study that estimated more than 800,000 illegal abortions were performed in 1967.[33]

. . . *To Form a More Perfect Union,* the report of the National Commission on the Observance of International Women's Year 1975, stated that "four percent of American women admit to having had an abortion. Divorced or separated women report this slightly more frequently (9 percent)."[34]

Interestingly, two very different groups were complaining at this time that abortions were overburdening medical facilities: those who were against abortion and those who said current conditions created hardship for the poor.[35] "Restrictive abortion laws are de facto discriminatory," Duffy wrote, "as the affluent can much more easily obtain a safe abortion than a poor person. Abortions can be obtained by a non-resident in California, Kansas, New York, England, Japan, and other areas if the woman has sufficient resources."[36]

Roe v. Wade forced many states to change their laws, starting in 1973. The CDC urged that any abortion legislation should require that at a minimum the following data be recorded: hospital or other facility, woman's place of residence, date of birth, race, marital status, number of living children, number of previous abortions, first day of last normal menstrual period, physician's estimated length of gestation, date of abortion, and type of procedure.[37]

In that same year the National Center for Health Statistics began to publish *Health, United States,* an annual collection of data required for various reports to Congress. The timeline in Table 20.1 shows how the information published changed, generally decreasing, over the decades. For example, "maternal deaths during abortions" is not published after the late 1990s, and "method used" disappeared a few years later. In the most recent years the only figures on the subject that still appeared in *Health, United States* were the number of legal abortions, the ratio per 1,000 women aged 15 to 44, the ratio per 1,000 live

Table 20.1   Data about abortions appearing in *Health, United States,* over five-year intervals.

	1975	1980	1985	1990	1995	2000	2005	2010	2015
Legal abortions reported: CDC	*	*	*	*	*	*	*	*	*
Legal abortions reported: AGI		*	*	*	*	*	*	*	*
Percentage of legal abortions reported to the CDC									*
Legal abortions per 1,000 women aged 15 to 44									*
Legal abortions per 100 live births			*	*	*	*	*	*	
Legal abortions per 1,000 live births									*
Age	*	*	*	*	*	*	*	*	
Marital status	*	*	*	*	*	*	*	*	
Region	*								
Location: in/out state of residence		*	*	*	*	*			
Race: White/all other		*	*	*	*	*			
Race: White/Black or African American							*	*	
Race and Hispanic origin						*	*	*	
Hispanic origin						*	*	*	
Number of living children		*							
Previous live births				*	*	*	*	*	
Previous induced abortions			*	*	*	*	*	*	
Period of gestation	*	*	*	*	*	*	*	*	
Maternal deaths	*	*	*	*	*				

(*Continued*)

	1975	1980	1985	1990	1995	2000	2005	2010	2015
Maternal death rate per 100,000 abortions	*	*	*	*	*				
Relative risk of death		*	*						
Method	*	*	*	*	*	*			

Sources: U.S. Health, Education, and Welfare Department, Human Resources Administration, National Center for Health Statistics, *Health, United States 1975,* 215–17; U.S. Health, Education, and Welfare Department, Public Health Service, Office of Health Research, Statistics and Technology, National Center for Health Statistics, National Center for Health Services Research, *Health, United States, 1980,* 123–24; U.S. Health and Human Services Department, Public Health Service, National Center for Health Statistics, *Health, United States 1985,* 33–35; U.S. Health and Human Services Department, Public Health Service, Centers for Disease Control and Prevention, National Center for Health Statistics, *Health, United States 1990,* 61–63; U.S. Health and Human Services Department, Public Health Service, National Center for Health Statistics, *Health, United States 1995,* 94–96; U.S. Health and Human Services Department, Centers for Disease Control and Prevention, National Center for Health Statistics, *Health, United States 2000,* 144–45; U.S. Health and Human Services Department, Centers for Disease Control and Prevention, National Center for Health Statistics, *Health, United States 2005,* 149; U.S. Health and Human Services Department, Centers for Disease Control and Prevention, National Center for Health Statistics, *Health, United States 2010,* 116–17; U.S. Health and Human Services Department, Centers for Disease Control and Prevention, National Center for Health Statistics, *Health, United States 2015,* 78.

births, and one new addition: the percentage of legal abortions reported to the CDC.

In 1977 Congress passed the Hyde Amendment, restricting the use of federal funding for abortions. In the 1980s several states went further by restricting the use of Medicaid funds for the procedure. At this point the percentage of pregnancies resulting in live births began to rise.[38]

The Government Accountability Office, formerly the General Accounting Office, is the independent agency that investigates government programs on behalf of Congress. Its website lists almost 500 reports that include the term "abortion." Some of the topics it has been asked to examine include the following:

- Abortion Clinics: Information on the Effectiveness of the Freedom of Access to Clinic Entrances Act
- Foreign Assistance: Clearer Guidance Needed on Compliance Overseas with Legislation Prohibiting Abortion-Related Lobbying

- Health Insurance Exchanges: Coverage of Non-Excepted Abortion Services by Qualified Health Plans

The states are still not legally obligated to provide abortion statistics to the federal government. States that have chosen not to do so follow:

Alaska: 1998–2002

California 1998–

Delaware 2009

Louisiana 2005–2006

Maryland 2007–2010

New Hampshire 1998–

Oklahoma 1998–1999

West Virginia 2003–2004[39]

Since California has the largest population of any state, it would be particularly useful to know how many abortions occur there, but state law forbids its Department of Public Health from collecting or reporting this data.[40] When California stopped reporting, CDC's count of abortions dropped by 25 percent.[41]

When the government cannot or chooses not to gather statistics, it sometimes publishes data from other sources it considers reliable. Various federal series such as the CDC's *Vital and Health Statistics*[42] and the Census Bureau's *Statistical Abstract* rely in part on the Guttmacher Institute (AGI) for abortion data.

The Guttmacher Institute was founded in 1968 by the Planned Parenthood Foundation of America (PPFA). It became a separate institution in 1977, dedicated to research, policy analysis, and education concerning reproductive health, and is named in honor of Dr. Alan Guttmacher, former president of PPFA.[43]

The AGI gathers data by surveying all known abortion providers every three to four years.[44] These surveys cover all states, unlike the official data acquired by the CDC. While the CDC provides statistics about the women who receive abortions, the AGI only counts the abortions themselves.[45]

In a 2014 publication the National Center for Health Statistics noted that "the total annual number of abortions recorded by CDC was consistently approximately 70 percent of the number recorded by the Guttmacher Institute, which uses numerous active follow-up techniques to increase the completeness of the data obtained through its periodic national census of abortion providers."[46] Follow-up techniques include questionnaires sent to all clinics, physicians, and hospitals identified as potential providers of abortions, with mailings and telephone contact for nonresponders.[47]

The beginning of this chapter discussed abortion through the lens of early crime statistics. For comparison, consider the *Sourcebook of Criminal Justice Statistics,* which has been prepared since 1973 by the University of Albany.[48] Until 2012 it was funded by the U.S. Department of Justice and considered a government publication.[49]

An appendix in the 1973 edition listed all the offenses the book attempted to cover, some of which were no longer considered crimes by then. The last category in the list, which seems to be a catch-all, included abortion, as well as bastardy, displaying red or black flags, miscegenation, and many other offenses.[50] Under "Definition of Terms," the 1995 edition includes abortion-related crime with "other public-order offenses," such as bigamy, civil disorder, and hunting on Indian lands.[51]

The *Sourcebook* for 1975 reported 12 federal prosecutions for abortion in 1973, all in the District of Columbia. Four resulted in guilty verdicts.[52] The 1994 edition was the first to register the bombing of an abortion clinic.[53]

The *Sourcebook* also includes surveys on "Public Attitudes toward Crime and Criminal-Justice Related Topics." Questions about abortion first appeared in 1978.[54] The topic still appears in the *Sourcebook* besides survey questions on such topics as homosexual relations, legalization of marijuana, and torture.[55]

A final oddity of the government's attitude toward statistics on abortion can be found in the National Survey of Family Growth (NSFG), which was created in 1973 to gather, through interviews with women, details on births, marriage, and contraception, among other things. The NSFG's "Key Statistics" page covers condom use, and contraception, but does not mention abortion. The topic does appear in one table on "Teenage Pregnancy."[56]

Statistical Abstract

Abortion first appeared in the *Statistical Abstract* in 1975, with data from 1973, the year that the Supreme Court rewrote national law on the subject in *Roe v. Wade.* There were two tables:

"Table 80. Number of legal abortions, abortion rates per 1,000 women, 15–44, and abortion ratios per 1,000 live births, by state of occurrence: 1973." The data came from a survey of hospitals, clinics, and physicians conducted by the Alan Guttmacher Institute, originally published in AGI's journal, *Family Planning Perspectives*.[57] By the next year additional data was also coming from the U.S. Center for Disease Control, then part of the U.S. Department of Health, Education, and Welfare.[58]

"Table 81. Characteristics of women obtaining reported legal abortions by length of gestation, marital status, and number of living children— selected states, by state of occurrence: 1973." This data came from the state health agencies. The *Statistical Abstract* noted: "After the 1973 Supreme Court decision, abortions were performed in many states long before reporting systems were established. States shown are those for which this type of data was available." Twenty-three states plus the District of Columbia were included.[59] By 1976 the number had risen to thirty.[60]

The 1990 *Statistical Abstract* demonstrated how carefully one has to interpret statistics in this kind of compendium. Table 100 says that in 1980 the "abortion ratio per 1,000 live births" for non-Whites was 642. Table 101 on the same page says that the "abortion ratio" for non-Whites was 392. What explains the difference? The numbers in Table 100 "are computed as the number of abortions per 1,000 live births from July 1 of year shown to June 30 of following year."[61] The figures in Table 101 are based on the "number of abortions per 1,000 abortions *and* live births"[62] (emphasis added).

By 1995 two new tables appeared: "Pregnancies, Number and Outcome" and "Pregnancies by Outcome, Age of Woman, and Race." Each had four categories: total, live births, induced abortions, and fetal losses.[63]

In 2012, the final year that the *Statistical Abstract* was published by the government, only the following data appeared:

- Abortions—number and rate by race
- Abortions by selected characteristics (age, race, and ethnicity; marital status; number of prior live births; number of prior induced abortions; weeks of gestation)
- Abortions—number and rate by states[64]

PART VII

Women and the Law

CHAPTER TWENTY-ONE

Women as Criminals

The first significant statistical report on crime produced by the federal government appeared in the *Compendium* of the 1850 Census, in the section titled "Moral and Social Condition." It shared those pages with data on religious worship, education, and the press, among other activities.[1]

The data is not actually about crimes, but prisoners. The figures provided are spotty, but the most complete table is a count of the occupants of every prison in each state. There were 4,643 White men and 115 White women. Among the "Colored, including slaves" there were 801 men and 87 women. The highest number of White women was in Sing Sing Prison in New York. There were 21 Colored women in Sing Sing and an equal number in Baltimore Prison.[2]

A footnote mentioned that "female felons, of whom there are a large number, are not sent to the state prison in Massachusetts." Presumably they were kept in local jails, and therefore not counted in this report.[3]

The 1880 Census provided a more detailed look, in a volume entitled *Report on the Defective, Dependent and Delinquent Classes.* Among other tables, it included figures for inmates, organized by the type of crime. Table 21.1 shows all the crimes for which women were in prison.

Table 21.2 is a list of crimes particularly relevant to women for which only men were in prison.

The author of that report was Frederick Howard Wines, and in 1888 he gave a speech to the National Prison Association, which provided an interesting insight into what he thought but presumably felt he could not say in a federal publication. He pointed out with disapproval that more than 30 children under the age of 10 were in prisons, including a few under the age of one year: "Some of them were no doubt born in prison."

Table 21.1   Number of women in U.S. prisons in 1880, by offense.

Abandonment of children	2
Administering narcotic drugs with felonious intent	16
Adultery	48
Aiding or effecting escape of prisoner	4
Arson	49
Assault	159
Bigamy or polygamy	15
Burglary	115
Carrying deadly weapon, concealed	5
Common prostitute	127
Common thief	3
Concealing abducted child*	1
Conspiracy to commit crime	2
Contempt of court	2
Contracting marriage between White person and person not of the same race (synonym: miscegenation)	2
Crime against nature (synonym: sodomy, buggery, bestiality)	1
Cruelty to child	3
Cruelty to persons	1
Disobedience (insubordination, incorrigibility, and stubbornness)	5
Disorderly conduct	717
Disturbing religious meeting	2
Drunk and disorderly	1,048
Embezzlement	5
Erecting or maintaining nuisance	11
Extortion	1
Failure of physician or midwife to make return of births or death*	2
Forgery and counterfeiting	16
Fornication	14
Fraud	7
Gambling	1
Homicide: murder	251
Illicit cohabitation	6

(Continued)

Incest	2
Indecent exposure	1
Keeping disorderly house	72
Kidnaping	3
Larceny	881
Malicious mischief	14
Malpractice	1
Mayhem	1
Obscenity	3
Open lewdness	50
Perjury	28
Poisoning reservoir, well, or spring	1
Procuring abortion	15
Profanity	7
Provoking breach of the peace	87
Rape, accessory*	4
Receiving stolen goods	25
Resistance to officer	2
Robbery	32
Suspicion	3
Threats	3
Trespass	3
Unlawful sale of liquor	9
Unlawfully exhibit a deadly weapon	1
Vagrancy	414
Violating liquor law	1
Violating postal or revenue laws	3
Violating lottery law*	1
Other+	530

Some categories (such as types of assaults) have been combined.

All parentheses are in the original table.

* Only women were in prison for this offense.

+ Includes many vague and technical terms.

Source: U.S. Interior Department, Census Office, *Report on the Defective,* 504–11.

Table 21.2   Relevant crimes for which only men were in prison, 1880.

Abandonment of family

Assault with intent to commit crime against nature

Attempting to procure abortion

Bastardy

Circulating obscene literature

Contracting marriage without license

Insulting female

Keeping house for exhibition of obscene prints, pictures, or literature

Rape

Rape of child

Assault with intent to rape

Attempt to commit rape by means other than assault

Seduction

Seduction of ward by guardian

Attempt to seduce

Source: U.S. Interior Department, Census Office, *Report on the Defective,* 504–11.

Wines also took note of elderly prisoners:

> Think of 168 women in prison, all of whom are over sixty years of age, and three of them over eighty! It may be proper to hold them, where they have no home and no friends, as an act of humanity. But imprisonment must have wrought its full effect upon them, and in them; they cannot be, in view of their infirmity of body and mind, any longer a menace to the security of society; and one would think that they might be allowed to close their eyes upon the scenes of earth, outside of prison walls.[4]

Wines noted that there were 12 men in prison for every woman. He offered several explanations:

> This is partly because women are better than men, and partly because they are more timorous and less aggressive: if a wicked woman wants a crime committed, it is easy for her to get a man to do it for her. Partly, too, the smaller proportion of women who are prisoners is due to the leniency of the officers of the law in dealing with them. Most of the offenses committed by women are not of a serious character.[5]

As decades passed the census included more details about prisoners, but other data about crime and criminals remained difficult to find. In

1900, for example, the Census explained how it chose to deal with people who honestly reported their dishonest labor:

> Finally, persons reported on the population schedules as engaged in disreputable callings are not credited with having gainful occupations. Ordinarily a professional thief, gambler, or keeper of a house of ill fame [i.e. a brothel] makes a false return, telling the enumerator, for example, that he is a night watchman, a speculator, or a boarding-house keeper. Such persons, of course, are classified by the Census Bureau according to the occupation which they claim. But in the comparatively few cases where the truth is told the return is entirely disregarded and the person treated as having no occupation.[6]

In 1904 the Census Bureau published its first volume specifically on the prison population. As a much-later publication of the Bureau of Justice Statistics noted, the report was concerned with sentencing variations between sexes and regions. "Females had shorter sentences for homicide and for offenses against society than males. This fact was attributed to the assumption that crimes within the categories might have been less serious."[7]

In 1911, as part of its 19-volume report on the effects wage earning had on women and children, the Bureau of Labor Statistics published a book by Mary Conyngton entitled *Relation between Occupation and Criminality of Women*. She explained the reason for the book as follows:

> There has been a rather widespread impression, not confined to popular discussion but reflected in some of the more serious studies of criminological and social questions, that [women's new role in industry] not only might be but is harmful, and that the widening of their sphere of industrial activity is accompanied by a marked increase of criminality among women.[8]

In order to search for a connection between occupations and crime, Conyngton attempted to discover what jobs women prisoners had held before their convictions. This turned out to be difficult because many states did not ask for that data, and even where it was required,

> the law is frequently nullified by the indifference of the officials who should execute it. "What's the use of asking these women what their occupation is?" said one warden in a State where the law required that this fact be ascertained for every prisoner received. "They won't tell the truth about it, anyway, so I just put it down as housework. Maybe some of them do something else, but then others don't do anything at all, so it probably averages up all right."[9]

Conyngton found that many prison officials assumed that female offenders were coming to them from the new areas of employment—factories, department stores, and so on—but the actual statistics proved otherwise.[10]

The occupations that provided the largest per capita percentage of prisoners (i.e., based on how many women in the general population held a given occupation) turned out to be the traditional women's work of servants and waitresses. In fact, these groups produced four times per capita as many convicted women as the manufacturing industries.[11]

Did educational attainment correlate to crime? Again, that was difficult to tell because all that was usually measured in the prisons was literacy, and "if a woman can produce some hieroglyphics which bear a distant resemblance to her name, and can spell out a few words, she is put down as able to read and write." However, Conyngton found no college graduates behind bars.[12] She also located no example "of a woman [prisoner] trying to hide some past downfall by assigning herself to a lower grade than the highest she had ever held."[13]

Conyngton noted that "the better class of workers" were rare among the prisoners and probationers:

One manufacturing center was visited which lay within the sphere of influence of a large and notoriously demoralizing city which had a large foreign population, and in which there were innumerable openings for women as operatives in the mills and factories and as clerks, stenographers, and bookkeepers in the offices; yet the inquiry for women of these vocations met the usual negative.

"No; we don't have that kind of woman," said the warden; "ours are all women of a lower class, who couldn't hold such positions."

"But how about mill operatives? Don't you get some of them?"

"No; I've been here five years and we haven't had any yet."

"Oh, hold on, Cap.; you're forgetting," broke in the clerk. "Don't you remember three years ago, when there was a strike at the X_____ mill, two of the girls were brought in for calling the strike breakers names?"

"That's so," admitted the warden, "I'd forgotten that."[14]

The experts Conyngton spoke to noted that the number of women criminals seemed to be dropping. She proposed that the new economic opportunities were actually causing women to move away from crime, not, as some people feared, to be corrupted into it.[15]

As for the women in prison, Conyngton said that some were "moral imbeciles," and others of low intelligence and therefore unlikely to find work in the new industries.[16]

Differing definitions of crimes also made her work harder. For example,

> in one locality if a woman is convicted of keeping a disorderly house it may mean only that a considerable amount of loud talking, singing, and quarreling goes on there which makes it a nuisance to the neighbors. In another it invariably means that she maintains a house of ill fame. A charge of vagrancy brought against a woman in one place means that she is a tramp; in another it indicates that she is living by illicit means, but that the police lack evidence to convict her of the specific offense.[17]

Almost 200 women under the age of 25 were in prison for "incorrigibility," which could mean a minor who wanted to marry a man her family disapproved of, or "a moral pervert of the worst kind, of inconceivably depraved tastes and practices."[18] More than 600 women were in prison for serious or minor "offenses against chastity."[19]

Conyngton also looked into "immorality" as opposed to crime. While the term is not defined, it seems to refer to premarital sex, illegitimate births, and prostitution. She argued that the causes of women turning to sexual misconduct were not new occupations in factories and department stores, and added that no social workers contacted "assigned poverty or low wages as a direct and immediate cause of immorality."[20] Instead, the causes were perceived to be bad homes, "mental deficiency," cultural differences, and a lack of sex education.[21]

Conyngton also laid blame on a "lack of innocent amusement." She pointed to the saloon, dance hall, "cheap theater with its highly miscolored picture of life," vaudeville, moving pictures, and similar places where a woman was "liable to find abnormal excitement, dangerous companionship, and every incitement to begin the course which leads so many to harm."[22]

The problem of accurately measuring crime and criminals has never gone away. The nation's first attempt to study the matter comprehensively was the National Commission on Law Observance and Enforcement, better known as the Wickersham Commission. It was actually created by President Hoover in 1929 to determine the positive and negative effects of prohibition, but the commission took a very broad approach.[23]

Most of the data about women is mixed into the general text of the Wickersham reports, but there are a few exceptions. For example, in a volume called *Report on Cost of Crime,* an author named Sidney O. Simpson tried to calculate the private losses due to crime, but he threw in the towel in regard to sex crimes:

> In the first place, it may fairly be doubted whether many of these offenses (rape, adultery, fornication, incest, prostitution, etc.) can be regarded as

involving any direct economic loss at all. The injury to the individuals involved and to the community is of quite a different character. The fact is that in dealing with offenses of this class, we are no longer in a field where the law is seeking to protect economic interests, and hence economic measures of loss are basically impossible of application.[24]

The commission advocated separate prisons for women, finding that "women's institutions are on the whole better staffed and better administered than institutions for men, that their purposes are less punitive, and that they have a higher degree of success with those who experience incarceration in them. Men's institutions, we think, have much to learn from women's institutions."[25]

A year before the Wickersham reports were published, the Federal Bureau of Investigation (FBI) took a major step forward by creating the *Uniform Crime Reports* (*UCR*), still published today. The *UCR* consists of data on certain categories of major crime as voluntarily reported by police forces around the country.

While it provides the data most commonly relied on for this subject, the *UCR* has obvious weaknesses. Different police forces will differ as to how they enforce laws, interpret their own data, and decide what information to submit. Also, as one critic noted "arrest statistics do not represent the universe of all those who commit crimes, but rather the nonrandomly distributed chance of being caught from criminal activity."[26] Another said: "Because of police discretion, [*Uniform Crime Reports*] may be a more accurate indicator of police behavior than anything else. Officers make the decision to arrest or not, and the *UCR* is based on crimes known to the police and reported." Some estimates say *UCR* underestimates crime by 50 percent.[27]

Women first appeared in *UCR* in the data for 1932; 7.4 percent of those arrested in the fourth quarter of that year were female. Among those arrested, a smaller percentage of women than men were arrested for robbery or burglary, but a larger share of women were arrested for larceny and narcotics use.[28]

The biggest categories for women were larceny-theft (16.76 percent of women arrested), sex offenses (except rape) (12.12 percent), disorderly conduct and vagrancy (12.0 percent), and "suspicion and investigation" (17.43 percent). In each of these categories, a larger percentage of women were arrested than men. This was also true of some less-populated categories: felonious homicide, assault, forgery and counterfeiting, and liquor laws (but not drunkenness); 1.41 percent of arrested men were charged with rape; no women were.[29]

In 1942, just after the United States entered World War II, the *UCR* took note of arrests of females increasing, while those of men decreased, and the FBI expressed concern:

> The number of young men less than voting age arrested for larceny decreased 11.5 percent, while girls under 21 arrested for such offenses increased 27.5 percent. . . .
> The alarming upswing in crime among women and girls points to the need for renewed efforts to keep the home front clean, wholesome, and strong. Boom conditions and "easy money" in the hands of youthful persons, together with a possible let-down in the influence of the home, are factors which must be offset in designing programs to combat the general upswinging crime curve among women and girls, and the increases in certain types of crimes committed by boys.[30]

In the mid-1970s the Justice Department's Law Enforcement Assistance Administration (LEAA) created a Task Force on Women to examine the treatment of females by the justice system. The task force's report, published in 1975, has sections on women as offenders, juvenile offenders, victims, and grant recipients. (Female police officers are confined to a section on "Women as Employees and Volunteers.")[31] Just as the Wickersham Commission had 40 years earlier, the LEAA task force studied women in prisons, but it found more cause for concern:

> Women in prison are the forgotten offenders. Because of their small numbers, the female offender's needs and problems have been largely overlooked by the criminal justice system. In 1971, approximately 18 out of every 100 persons arrested for a serious crime were women. Of those convicted of a serious crime, 9 out of 100 were women, but only 3 out of every 100 persons sentenced to a State or Federal prison were women. Recent National Prisoner Statistics show that of the 204,349 inmates in State and Federal institutions in 1973, 6,684 were women. In addition, approximately 7,000 women were locked up in more than 3,900 local jails scattered across the country.[32]

But if the problems women faced in prison were connected to being such a small percentage of that population, the task force also worried that that might soon be changing. They noted that between 1960 and 1973 the number of women arrested for major crimes increased at more than triple the rate of men.[33]

The task force report's recommendations included examining alternatives to incarceration, vocational training, the study of laws that punished women more severely than men for the same crime, and reconsidering victimless crimes.[34]

Two years later the LEAA published a *National Study of Women's Correctional Programs*. It determined that approximately two-thirds of incarcerated women were under the age of 30. Half were African American. Fewer than half had dependent children; 43 percent had been convicted of violent crimes.[35]

In the 1990s the Justice Department's National Institute of Corrections (NIC) created a new classification system for women prisoners because by that time there were too many to continue to treat them as an afterthought. The number of women in prison had nearly tripled between 1985 and 1996.[36] The NIC found that women prisoners had less violence in their records, had generally been convicted of minor, nonviolent crimes, and had fewer convictions. Their behavior in prison was better than that of men. The majority had children and "most have primary responsibility for child rearing, and most have legal custody."[37]

The FBI developed another method of collecting voluntary data from local police in the 1980s. The National Incident-Based Reporting System (NIBRS) gathered data on a larger spread of serious crimes and with greater detail. More details are provided about each incident, the demographics of the offenders and victims, and the outcome of the case.[38]

A recent example of research based on the NIBRS system is a 2016 article by Lisa L. Holleran and Donna M. Vandiver, the first to study how the presence of a female offender changes the characteristics of homicides. They found that when women offenders were present (with or without male offenders), it was less likely that firearms would be used and more likely that victims would be male and younger.[39]

Statistical Abstract

Prisoners made their first appearance in the 1926 volume of the *Statistical Abstract*. That book reported that as of January 1, 1923, there were almost 104,000 men in prisons and just over 5,000 women.[40] There were five more crime-related tables, including a list of offenses, but none were broken down by sex.

The 1944–1945 volume was the first to have a chapter on "Crime and Criminals." It contained 12 tables, 4 of which were arranged by sex. The most important of these included a breakdown by color and age as well as sex, and a listing of prisoners by "commitments," meaning what offenses they were imprisoned for, in 1942. The largest category for females was "disorderly conduct and vagrancy." Their most frequent felony conviction was "larceny, other than auto theft."[41]

The year 1965 saw the inclusion of a table, broken down by sex, of juvenile delinquents in custody. In 1960 there had been 11,930 females in training schools and almost three times as many males. There were 3,141 females in detention homes and 2.5 times as many males.[42]

The 1990 volume added a table on "Drug Use among Persons Arrested" in 20 selected cities. In early 1989 the highest percentage of arrested women who tested positive for drugs was 87 percent in Washington, D.C.; 75 percent of men there also did.[43]

CHAPTER TWENTY-TWO

Prostitution

In the Bureau of Labor Statistics' 1911 report *Relation between Occupation and Criminality of Women,* author Mary Conyngton reached page 82 out of 119 before mentioning the word "prostitute" or "prostitution." Instead, she spoke of "what is technically known as immorality," or "professionally immoral women," and it is not always clear when she was referring to what she finally refers to as "occasional prostitutes," "professional prostitutes," "kept women," or simply to women who had sex outside of marriage.[1] She even noted one department store manager whose definition of immorality included any woman speaking to "men in a free and easy manner."[2]

One of the difficulties in tracing statistics about prostitution is the many euphemisms for what has been nicknamed "the oldest profession," and is more recently sometimes called "sex work." The latter term has not been generally embraced by the federal government, although the Centers for Disease Control and Prevention does use it in discussing HIV prevention.[3]

Another difficulty was illustrated by Census superintendent Francis Amasa Walker in his report on the 1870 Census:

The following tables embrace gainful and reputable occupations only. . . . All persons, moreover, whose means of livelihood are criminal, or, in the general judgment of mankind, shameful, are excluded.

The reasons for excluding gamblers, prostitutes, keepers of brothels, and such persons from the Tables of Occupations, has not been found in any sensitiveness at the mention or recognition of these classes as actually existing in the community, but in the consideration that, from the necessity of the case, the numbers thus reported must be wholly inadequate to the fact, and that a seeming count of them in the census would have the effect to mislead rather than to instruct. Here and there, at the enumeration of the Ninth Census, such persons had the assurance to report themselves by their true designations, or assistant marshals took the responsibility (and in some cases the risk) of writing down the real occupation of members of these classes who had sought to misstate their avocations, or to disguise them under ambiguous terms; but an analysis of the schedules soon made it evident that this had not been done, as indeed was not to be expected, with such uniformity as to secure even approximately correct results. All such titles were therefore dropped. . . . There are no means known to the Superintendent for accurately calculating the number thus excluded or excluding themselves.[4]

The published reports on the next census, as usual, listed no prostitutes. Nonetheless, their existence in the records can be detected. In the *Report on the Defective, Dependent, and Delinquent Classes in the 1880 Census*, Frederick Howard Wines noted that

houses of prostitution to the number of 4,067 are reported in 183 towns; in 94 other towns there are said to be none. From 215 towns we have no information. If any value is to be attached to the statements made by the heads of police departments (and I do not see how it is possible to refuse to them a certain amount of credence), the number of such houses cannot exceed 5,000 or 6,000, and, on the supposition that, in the large and small places taken together, the number of inmates averages five, there are not in the United States (at least in towns of more than 5,000 inhabitants) more than 30,000 prostitutes of this open description.

Wines noted that certain cities claim to be "free from this curse," with the largest being "the city of Brooklyn, where the chief of police insists that his statement must be accepted as literally and absolutely correct. . . . If these towns are as virtuous as they claim to be they are indeed fortunate; if not, the police are blind."[5]

But if there were, as Wines deduced, 30,000 prostitutes in the United States, where are they hiding in the census reports? The Integrated Public Use Microdata Series (IPUMSusa) is a project of the University of Minnesota that examines a sample of the complete records for individuals from the older censuses. The IPUMSusa sample from the 1880 Census discovered 74 women who had listed their profession as prostitute. It is, however, impossible to tell where these women were buried in the published occupation reports.[6]

In 1889 Carroll D. Wright, the first commissioner of Labor and a future superintendent of the Census, wrote a government report on *Working Women in Large Cities*. The data was gathered by interviews conducted with more than 17,000 women. All of the interviews were performed by women census agents except those that filled the section on "The Character of Working Women."[7] Male agents spoke with almost 4,000 prostitutes to determine their previous occupations.

Wright wrote that "it is often flippantly asserted that the shop girls, those comprising the class under investigation, recruit the ranks of prostitution." He warned that his data was only about "what may be called professional prostitutes. . . . [Q]uiet, unobtrusive, and unobserved prostitution, which exists in all communities, has no place in the present consideration."[8]

Wright noted a "fact which strikes one sadly is the large number who enter prostitution directly from their homes." That was almost one-third percent of the total. Nearly 30 percent of the prostitutes had previously done "house work, hotel work, and cooking." A mere 13 percent had been "dressmakers, employés of cloak and shirt factories, etc." Wright concluded that "one need not hesitate in asserting that the working women of the country are as honest and as virtuous as any class of citizens."[9]

The subject shows up in a different way in the Census Bureau report *Marriage and Divorce 1867–1906*. "Prostitution before marriage" was one of the more than 400 causes or combinations of causes given for divorce, with 36 granted to men for that reason.[10]

In 1907 Congress responded to concerns over foreigners arriving in the country by creating the U.S. Commission on Immigration, better known as the Dillingham Commission.[11] It was particularly interested in determining the ethnic background of the newcomers—even creating a *Dictionary of Races or Peoples*[12]—but 1 of its 41 reports was *Importing Women for Immoral Purposes* (1909).

The book was based in part on investigations by undercover agents, which involved danger: "One woman agent was attacked and beaten, escaping serious injury, if not murder, only with the greatest difficulty, and yet the next day she went cheerfully back to her work, though of course in another locality, where she was not known."[13]

The commission stated that "the importation and harboring of alien women and girls for immoral purposes and the practice of prostitution by them—the so-called 'white-slave traffic'—is the most pitiful and the most revolting phase of the immigration question."[14] It also distinguished between the recruitment of "immoral women" and that of "innocent girls."[15]

The Dillingham Commission noted that in 1907–1908, 93 women were deported through Ellis Island for prostitution. Of those convicted of prostitution in night courts in New York City in a five-month period, 1,512 were native born and 581 were foreigners.[16]

As for the phrase, "white-slave traffic," mentioned by the Dillingham Commission, a modern writer noted, "Progressive era reformers used the catchwords 'white slavery' to promote the vision of women held in bondage against their will, of mysterious druggings and abductions of helpless young girls, and of unexplained disappearances of innocent and naïve immigrants forced into lives of prostitution and vice."[17]

A year after that report was published Congress took action in the form of the White Slave Traffic Act, better known as the Mann Act. This law, which is still in effect today, made it a federal crime to transport in interstate or foreign commerce "any woman or girl for the purpose of prostitution or debauchery, or for any other immoral purpose."[18]

The act assumed that all female prostitutes were helpless victims, with no agency of their own. Nonetheless, the Supreme Court quickly concluded that women who willingly crossed state lines could be tried for "conspiring" to transport themselves.[19]

Marlene D. Beckman studied all the female violators of the Mann Act who were sent to Alderson, the first federal prison exclusively for women, during the first decade after it opened in 1927. Twenty-three percent of the women had not been traveling for any financial reason, but at least one of the partners was married to someone else. Sixteen percent had been paid to have sex with someone other than the man she was traveling with (typically at her husband or partner's insistence). Fifteen percent were prostitutes who had crossed borders to reach customers. Almost half of the convicts were women working as madams or procurers.[20]

The year after the Mann Act passed, 1911, saw the release of Conyngton's report on *Relation between Occupation and Criminality of Women*. She argued that the alleged relationship between immorality and women in modern jobs was a myth, or at least more complicated than it appeared. She offered the following example from an unnamed "worker specially qualified to speak on the subject."

The belief you mention in the general immorality of saleswomen is certainly widespread, but I have found nothing to prove it well grounded. In the course of some investigations into the methods by which department stores seek to secure and retain the trade of the professionally immoral women, a trade which, as you probably know, is considered exceptionally valuable, I came on something which may throw some light on the existence of the belief. Mr. _____, who was first a department manager in several large stores, and then himself established a millinery business, said he had found the best way of gaining and holding this trade was by having a forewoman who was "in" with such women, which of course meant that she herself led an immoral life, thus being able to meet them in the way of friendship, and to gain their trade as a natural matter.

"Didn't you find such a forewoman had a bad effect on your other employees?" I asked.

"Yes," he replied, "she certainly did get some of the others into her habits. But as soon as I found out they were going that way, I discharged them."[21]

During World War I Congress created the Interdepartmental Social Hygiene Board (ISHB) to prevent and treat venereal diseases. The major concern was the increase in such illnesses among the armed forces.[22] The federal government created a "five-mile sanitized zone" around military reservations. Suspected prostitutes could be forcibly examined and, if venereal diseases were found, sent to a facility.[23]

The program "restricting the activities" of such women lasted 27 months and boasted of preventing 260,000 infections.[24] More than 15,000 women—and no men—were arrested in this way and, according to a modern writer, "incarcerated in detention houses for an average stay of ten weeks or in reformatories for an average stay of a year."[25] The institutions included hospitals, an "Industrial Farm," a "Girls' Detention Ward," an "Industrial School for Colored Girls," and a "Welfare Home for Women."[26] Seventeen of these federally supported institutions had "guards or watchmen, barbed-wire fences, or both."[27]

Modern scholar Kimberley A. Reilly argued that this period marked a change in the American view of the sexes. In Victorian times the assumption was that wicked men were seducing innocent girls. Now the girls were seen as sullying virtuous soldiers.[28]

In 1920 the ISHB produced a "Study of 6,000 Case Records of Delinquent Women and Girls." This contained much data on the females who were considered "the greatest problems" faced by the board. Seventy percent of them had gonorrhea, syphilis, or both.[29]

The average age of these females varied from age 18 to 22, depending on the state. One "delinquent" in New York was seven years old; another in Georgia was 80.[30]

As Reilly noted, "Policymakers legally and discursively conflated young women who participated in casual sex with prostitutes."[31] In fact, the section of the 1920 report entitled "Sex History" stated that 10.8 percent of the 6,000 worse cases had no convictions of any kind.

Almost 80 percent had been convicted of sex offenses. Almost half were "either irregular or professional prostitutes." More than 20 percent were "promiscuous, though not for money."

When asked the reason for their first sexual experience, the most common answers were, in order of frequency:

1. "Love"
2. "Promise to marry"
3. "Rape"
4. "Needed money"
5. "Influence of bad company"[32]

Forty-two percent of the women were married, including common-law marriages. Almost 30 percent were living with their husbands. Almost 15 percent were in the category of "divorced, deserted, separated, widowed, bigamous marriages."[33]

The FBI's *Uniform Crime Reports* (*UCR*) first singled out "prostitution and commercialized vice" from other sex crimes in 1933, its third year. Oddly, it doesn't give the number of arrests or convictions, but only the number of arrested persons with previous convictions of various types, and percentages by race.[34] The following year it reported 42,111 charged and held for prosecution for that crime.[35]

"Prostitution and commercialized vice" is still being reported in the digital version of *UCR*. In 2014 the number of arrests was estimated at 47,598.[36]

During World War II, the battle against prostitution and venereal disease was headed by the Social Protection Division in the Office of Community War Services (OCWS) and was overseen by Eliot Ness of *The Untouchables* fame.[37]

While the ISHB in World War I emphasized confining infected women, the OCWS showed more interest in treating them and improving their social condition. One of its publications noted, "If the promiscuous girls go back to promiscuity, if the prostitutes go back to their trade, if the low-paid workers and stranded girls leave the rapid treatment centers only to face again the same problems and difficulties which contributed toward their contracting a venereal disease, medical treatment will be only a momentary pause in a vicious and inevitable circle."[38]

In the last few decades federal attention has focused more on juvenile prostitution and on human trafficking, also called trafficking in persons. The Women's Bureau described this crime thus in a 2002 publication:

> 1) Sex trafficking in which a commercial sex act is induced by force, fraud, or coercion or in which the person induced to perform such an act is under 18; or 2) the recruitment, harboring, transportation, provision, or obtaining of a person for labor or services, through the use of force, fraud, or coercion, for the purpose of subjecting that person to involuntary servitude, peonage, debt bondage, or slavery.[39]

Of course, this can be seen as a more recent, less racist, variation of "white slave trafficking," with an additional recognition that not all prostitution is involuntary.

Statistical Abstract

The word "prostitution" does not appear in the *Statistical Abstract*. However, starting with the 1921 edition, "white slavery" is identified as a crime the FBI is authorized to investigate.[40]

In 1943 "Mann Act (White Slave Traffic)" arrived under "Criminal Proceedings in District Courts" and "Number of Offenses."[41] "White Slave Traffic" makes its last appearance in the 1991 edition, in a table that gave the convictions of federal prisoners who were released in 1986.[42]

CHAPTER TWENTY-THREE

Women as Crime Victims

In 1978 U.S. Representative Barbara A. Mikulski (D-MD) spoke at a Census Bureau conference on *Issues in Federal Statistical Needs Relating to Women*. She explained what had happened a year earlier when she and two colleagues began drafting a law related to family violence.

Immediately I was besieged, both by press and other members of Congress and their committees, for data. How many women are victims of battering? What are the statistics? On and on went the questions.

So we turned to Federal agencies and people whom we thought could help, so that we could begin to rally support. Number one, we found that there was no way, at this point, or at least a year ago, of knowing how many women were battered. Number two, that there was no reporting to police. Number three, that it wasn't required in crime statistics. LEAA [Law Enforcement Assistance Administration] didn't include it. The FBI didn't include it. The Justice Department didn't necessarily take a look at it in any kind of systematic way that we could use.

I could only conclude that one of the reasons that those questions have not been asked in the 200 years of our Republic was that people simply did not consider them important. . . .

During the course of the hearings on family violence, the National Institute of Mental Health told me that they had been studying family violence since 1968. That's already a decade. During that testimony, they told me, "We've been studying it for 10 years and it's in epidemic proportion." So I said, "Can you tell me how many women have been killed?" "No." "Can you tell me anything about battering? Can you tell me about the women who have been bloodied and burned and beaten?" "No." Then I said, "Even if you can't give me the exact numbers, you're sitting there telling me it reached epidemic proportion." They said, "Yes." I said, "What the hell did you do with those numbers? Did you even tell anybody? Have you told [Secretary of Health, Education, and Welfare Joseph A.] Califano?" "No, he's new."

"Did you tell anybody in the past 10 years who's been a Secretary, Assistant Secretary? Did you even tell your liaison or your coordinator? You know, the new chair of your inter-agency task force on coordination."

The answer was "No," so that, though they have studied the problem for 10 years, there was no initiative to do anything with those particular data to generate action. . . .

Well, this isn't a butterfly collection, ladies and gentlemen, that people gather for their own private enjoyment. This is public dollars to get public information to help the American people.[1]

Mikulski's complaint about inadequate data concerning domestic violence has been repeated by others through the decades. As will become clear, different federal agencies have tried many different systems for collecting information on this sensitive subject.

Federal collection of data about the victims of crime (as opposed to about criminals or the crimes themselves) began to come into its own in the 1970s. The National Crime Panel (which has evolved into the National Crime Victimization Survey) started in 1972. It is based on randomized nationwide surveys of households, collecting characteristics about people and the crimes they have experienced.[2]

These studies have served as the basis for the *Criminal Victimization in the United States* series. Among the findings reported in the first volume, in 1973, was the fact that men were twice as likely as women to be victims of violent crime.[3] However, women were more likely to be injured in a robbery or assault than men.[4]

Much of the statistical data about women and crime has to do with domestic violence, and, as is so often the case, part of the problem in tracing the subject over time is change in vocabulary. As Table 23.1 demonstrates, new terminology has been adopted, sometimes in an effort to be more sensitive to victims, sometimes to be inclusive of both sexes.

Domestic violence began to appear regularly in federal data in 1977. Most of these early publications came, not from the Justice Department, but from the U.S. Civil Rights Commission (CRC), which held a series of hearings on women and abuse around the country.[5]

In 1982 these hearings served as the basis for a CRC report, *Under the Rule of Thumb,* which began with the Middle Ages and followed the subject through current U.S. laws. It estimated the number of battered wives in this country at over a million.[6]

Table 23.1 Domestic violence terminology: Earliest uses found in federal reports.

1891	Wife beating
1975	Family violence
1976	Battered wives
	Spouse abuse
	Wife abuse
1977	Abused women
	Battered women
1978	Domestic abuse
1996	Intimate partner violence
	Survivor (as opposed to "victim")

The term "domestic violence" is too ambiguous to date (i.e., it could mean a civil uprising).

Sources: Examples for the given dates include Robbins, "Report of Nez Percé Agency," 233; U.S. Congress, Senate, Judiciary Committee, Constitutional Rights Subcommittee, *Individual Rights,* 342; U.S. Civil Rights Commission, *Legal Status of Homemakers in Colorado,* 62; U.S. National Commission on the Observance of International Woman's Year, Homemaker's Committee, *Legal Status of Women in Missouri,* 3; U.S. American Indian Policy Review Commission, Alcohol and Drug Abuse Task Force, *Report on Alcohol,* 17; U.S. Civil Rights Commission, *Unfinished Business,* 31; U.S. Civil Rights Commission, *Silent Victims;* U.S. Civil Rights Commission, *Battered Women,* 291; U.S. Health and Human Services Department, Public Health Service, *Progress Report,* no page number; U.S. Justice Department, *A Community Checklist.*

Two years later the Bureau of Justice Statistics (BJS) first addressed the subject with a five-page report on *Family Violence,* calling it "a serious problem about which little is known with any certainty." It pointed out that neither the *Uniform Crime Reports* nor the National Crime Survey was well designed to estimate family violence and yet "it is striking, though, that the National Crime Survey uncovers about 450,000 cases of family violence each year through a technique originally designed to measure such crimes as burglary, robbery, larceny and aggravated assault."

The BJS made it clear that the figures in its report were an undercount because they were only "estimates of the amount of family violence that people considered to be criminal in nature and that the victims chose to and were able to relate to survey interviewers." Family violence might not be reported because the victim did not consider it a crime, or was ashamed, or because the perpetrator was present during the interview.[7]

The year 1984 also saw the completion of the Attorney General's Task Force on Family Violence. A *New York Times* interview described assistant attorney general Lois Haight Herrington as the chairman of the task force, although the *Final Report* gave that honor to a male police chief. In the interview Herrington complained about the lack of reliable statistics on the subject: "The only family relationship in crime that we can presently validate is murder."[8]

The task force recommended a series of changes to the *Uniform Crime Reports* and the National Crime Survey "to more accurately measure the extent of family violence in America, especially the physical and sexual abuse of children and abuse of the elderly." It estimated that only one-third of all crime incidents were reported to the police.[9]

In 1986 the BJS published a five-page pamphlet that challenged a long-held myth. Specifically, the numbers showed that women who called the police after being assaulted by their husbands were less, rather than more, likely to be assaulted again.[10]

The late 1980s saw the FBI introduce the National Incident-Based Reporting System (NIBRS), which provided more information about certain violent crimes. NIBRS has no specific category for domestic violence, but it does list victim–offender relationships. Unfortunately, the relationship categories do not include many categories of intimate partners.[11] More regrettably, states that participate in NIBRS don't use the data to count domestic violence incidents; instead, they rely only on the number of cases reported to the police.[12]

The next census demonstrated another change in the culture. Since 1970 the Census Bureau had attempted to count the number of "transients," people living in hotels, missions, and the like.[13] The 1990 Census was the first to specifically include "Shelters for Abused Women."[14]

These shelters were "self-enumerated," meaning that, for the residents' privacy and protection, shelter staff were trained by Census personnel to fill out the forms and no government agents entered the shelters. In order to protect the residents, the local census office was used as the address.[15]

By contrast, in the next census, shelters for abused women were not counted in the shelter list at all "because of the extremely confidential nature of these facilities' locations. Their residents are, however, included in the total census counts."[16] The 2010 Census combined these shelters with "religious group quarters."[17]

The 1992 issue of *Criminal Victimization in the United States* had a special section on "Family Violence," the first volume to address that issue. No explanation was offered as to why this data was separated from the rest. The report indicated that men and women had comparable rates of victimization from well-known offenders, but women were more than three times as likely to be attacked by relatives.[18]

In 1994 Congress passed the Violence Against Women Act (VAWA), which according to one group of researchers "changed laws and promoted legal interventions at the same time that it called for research to inform policy and to evaluate practices meant to prevent violence against women."[19] It authorized the creation of agencies to study the issue, money for prosecutions, and civil redress for victims.[20]

That same year saw the first fruits of the redesign of the National Crime Victimization Survey (NCVS), which had been a decade in the making. Following the recommendations of earlier commissions, one goal of the NCVS was "to produce more accurate reporting of incidents of rape and sexual assault and of any kind of crimes committed by intimates or family members." Questions were added to the survey to show that "the interviewer was interested in a broad spectrum of incidents, not just those involving weapons, severe violence, or violence perpetrated by strangers." Jargon of the police and legal system was replaced with specific behavior wording.[21] Interviewees were told "Please mention it even if you are not certain it was a crime" and invited to reschedule for a more "convenient" time, when an abuser might not be present.[22]

The survey results estimated that women aged 12 and over suffered almost five million violent victimizations in 1992 and 1993; 75 percent of lone-offender violence and 45 percent of multiple-offender attacks were perpetrated by people women knew. In almost 30 percent the lone offender was an intimate (husband, ex-husband, boyfriend, or ex-boyfriend). Women were about six times more likely than men to experience violence committed by an intimate.[23]

In 2001, the BJS published a report on intimate partner violence (IPV), based on the NCVS. Once again there was a warning about its limited reliability:

> Caution is warranted in interpreting intimate partner violence and marital status in the NCVS because marital status may be related to a respondent's willingness or ability to disclose violence by an intimate partner. For example, a married woman may not view, may not wish to view, or may be unable to report the behavior of her partner as violent or criminal. That same woman, if separated or divorced, may view or may be able to report the same behavior as violent.
>
> Also, because the NCVS samples households, it does not capture the experiences of homeless individuals or those living in institutional settings

such as shelters for homeless or battered persons. Nor can it capture the experiences of an individual who has left a household to escape violence.[24]

Congress decided to examine IPV as a public health issue and authorized the Centers for Disease Control and Prevention (CDC) to make estimates of the number of IPV-related injuries, and to calculate their costs to the health care system. In 2003 the CDC published the results. It had sponsored a one-time National Violence Against Women Survey (NVAWS), consisting of phone interviews with 8,000 women and 8,000 men.[25]

NVAWS resulted in an estimate that 5.3 million IPV victimizations happened to U.S. women over the age of 17 each year, resulting in two million injuries. More than half a million of those injuries required medical attention. IPV victims lost nearly eight million days of work, equivalent to 32,000 full-time jobs.[26]

Yet again, the report took note of the difficulty of gathering accurate data:

> Because no national system exists for ongoing collection of data about IPV against women, estimates are often drawn from data gathered for other purposes. For example, hospitals collect information about victims to provide patient care and for billing purposes; they may record few details about the violence itself or about the perpetrator and his or her relationship to the victim. In contrast, police collect data that will aid in apprehending the perpetrator, and thus may collect little information about the victim.[27]

The year 2010 saw the start of a new operation from the CDC, the National Intimate Partner and Sexual Violence Survey. The survey, which is ongoing, found that intimate violence is a public health problem, resulting in "physical injury; depression, anxiety, low self-esteem, and suicide attempts; and other health conditions such as gastro-intestinal disorders, substance abuse, sexually transmitted diseases, and gynecological or pregnancy complications. . . . [V]ictims of IPV are more likely to smoke, engage in heavy/binge drinking, engage in behaviors that increase the risk of HIV, and endorse other unhealthy behaviors."[28]

The National Institute of Justice's (NIJ) 1996 report to Congress provided the first federal statistics on a newly recognized problem: stalking. Using the results of studies funded by the VAWA, NIJ concluded that "stalking is a much larger problem than previously assumed, affecting an estimated 2 million victims annually. The vast majority of victims are female (78 percent) and the vast majority of perpetrators are male (87 percent)."[29]

Two years later the NIJ and the CDC issued the first of a series of reports on violence against women. *Stalking in America* was based on the "first-ever national survey" on the subject. Eight percent of women and 2 percent of men had experienced stalking at some point in their lives.[30]

In 2001 the Violence Against Women Office, created in the Justice Department as a result of the VAWA, issued a report to Congress on *Stalking and Domestic Violence*. It began with a warning about cyberstalking, a danger so new that no statistics were yet available.[31]

The office also reported on a survey of law enforcement agencies and prosecution offices about regular (non-cyber) stalking. Only one of 222 police forces had an anti-stalking unit. In most cases that offense was investigated by general detectives or a domestic violence squad. Thirteen percent of police agencies provided stalking training independent of domestic violence training; 82 percent of prosecutors' offices had training on stalking.[32]

In 2006 the Census Bureau conducted the Supplemental Victimization Survey on behalf of the BJS. More than 65,000 people participated. The actual subject was stalking and the title was deliberately ambiguous in order to "avoid biasing the responses of individuals and the subsequent estimates."[33]

The survey was searching for anyone who had experienced people doing any of the following:

- Making unwanted phone calls
- Sending unsolicited or unwanted letters or e-mails
- Following or spying on victim
- Showing up at places without a legitimate reason
- Waiting at places for the victim
- Leaving unwanted items, presents, or flowers
- Posting information or spreading rumors about the victim on the Internet, in a public place, or by word of mouth.[34]

The survey found that 14 out of every 1,000 persons over the age of 17 were victims of stalking. About half of these victims experienced at least one unwanted contact per week. Eleven percent said they had been stalked for five years or more. Women were at greater risk of stalking, but both sexes were equally likely to experience harassment. One victim in four reported some form of cyberstalking.[35]

The results of this survey were published in 2009 but had to be revised in 2012 after it was discovered that the earlier figures accidentally included reports of spam e-mail, Internet scams, and contacts from bill collectors as stalking or harassment. The corrected figures estimated that 3.3 million people over the age of 17 were stalked during a year; 3.1 percent of women and 1.6 percent of men had been stalked or harassed.[36]

In 2016 the Government Accountability office (GAO) determined that

> four federal agencies—the Departments of Defense, Education, Health and Human Services (HHS), and Justice—manage at least 10 efforts to collect data on sexual violence, which differ in target population, terminology, measurements, and methodology. . . . [T]he same act of sexual violence could be categorized by one data collection effort as "rape," whereas it could be categorized by other efforts as "assault-sexual" or "nonconsensual sexual acts," among other terms.

The GAO recommended three of the departments "make information that is included in their measurements of sexual violence publicly available" and asked the Office of Management and Budget (OMB), which has responsibility for coordinating federal statistics, to create a forum for interagency cooperation. According to the GAO, the OMB responded "that convening a forum may not be the most effective use of resources at this time, in part because the data collection efforts are not far enough along in their research."[37]

Statistical Abstract

"Victims of Crime" first appeared as a table in the 1967 edition, 24 years after "Number of Arrests" found a place in the *Statistical Abstract*.[38] The data, which describes events in 1965, comes from a study conducted by a nongovernment agency, the National Opinion Research Center. It covers forcible rape, robbery, aggravated assault, burglary, larceny, and motor vehicle theft. More men than women were victims in all categories except rape.[39]

"Homicides and Suicides" shows up as a table occasionally starting in the 1920s but were not broken down by sex until 1958.[40] "Victimization Rates" appear for the first time in 1975, estimating how many violent crimes take place per 1,000 people.[41]

"Intimate Partner Violence" gained a table in the 2001 edition. About 1.2 million cases were estimated, with approximately 90 percent of the victims being women.[42] "Stalking and Harassment" made its first appearance in 2010.[43]

CHAPTER TWENTY-FOUR

Rape

The verse of Victorian poet George Meredith does not find its way into U.S. federal documents often, but an influential staff report of the National Commission on the Causes and Prevention of Violence (1970) found room for these lines:

No villain need be! Passions spin the plot:
We are betrayed by what is false within.[1]

The report was discussing a new concept in criminology: "victim precipitation." This is the theory that "the victim at times contributes to the commission of the offense." Alongside examples related to robbery and assault by strangers, the report included these: "By unconsciously inviting the offense through an emotional pathology (e.g. a wife has masochistic needs that are satisfied by her assaultive husband), [or] by direct invitation or incitation (e.g., a female engages in heavy petting and, at the last moment, begins to resist the man's advances)."[2] The latter the commission staff defined as "victim precipitated forcible rape." They concluded that about 4 percent of rapes fell into that category.[3]

Rape data has long been controversial due to disagreements over definitions, reluctance to discuss such a personal topic, and the recognition that it is one of the most underreported crimes.

The first federal statistics on rape appeared in the 1880 Census and, as would continue for many years, focused only on the offender, not the victim. A total of 479 men were in prison for assault with intent to rape, 1,012 for rape, 4 for rape of a child, and 1 for "attempt to commit rape by means other than assault."[4]

Historical Corrections Statistics in the United States, published by the Bureau of Justice Statistics (BJS) in 1986, reported that there were 259 lynchings for the crime of rape between 1880 and 1889; 44 percent of all lynchings during that period were of Blacks, but the figures don't indicate how many of those were for rape. The last lynching of a Black man listed was in 1962 and was not for rape. Oddly enough, the BJS borrowed its data on this subject from a commercially published book, *The Negro Almanac.*[5]

The FBI started *Uniform Crime Reports* (*UCR*) in the 1930s, and while it remains the standard report on its subject, it has never been free of controversy. One group of modern scholars said that it "is probably not an exaggeration to say that the *UCR* is the most frequently and strongly criticized set of criminological data."[6] Among the key problems are that *UCR* covers only crimes reported to the police and that the data is collected by many local police forces, whose standards and definitions vary. Both of these issues are relevant to rape, which is notoriously underreported, and often open to interpretation by authorities.

Rape appeared in the first issue of *UCR*, with a count of incidents known to the police that took place in August 1930. Fifteen of the 48 states reported no occurrences that month.[7]

In the early years statutory rape cases were counted in *UCR*. This changed starting in 1958 when only forcible rapes began to be included.[8]

In 2013, the *UCR* program changed its definition of rape. Among other changes, the new definition does not specify the sex of the victim:

> Previously, offense data for forcible rape were collected under the legacy UCR definition: the carnal knowledge of a female forcibly and against her will. . . . The revised UCR definition of rape is: penetration, no matter how slight, of the vagina or anus with any body part or object, or oral penetration by a sex organ of another person, without the consent of the victim. Attempts or assaults to commit rape are also included; however, statutory rape and incest are excluded.[9]

The same 1970 report that introduced the concept of victim precipitation studied 1967 police figures on rape for 17 cities. The authors were concerned with the personal dynamics involved because

> from a legal perspective, the kind of personal relationship between victim and offender is probably more important in forcible rape than in any of the other major violent acts. The law and informal ethical codes recognize degrees of moral weakness and culpability which partly depend on the

relationship. A young girl is considered an innocent victim in an incest relationship, for example. But the victim is thought to be less innocent if mutual drinking was involved or a close relationship existed prior to the offense.[10]

The report found that 53 percent of rape victims were total strangers to the attackers. In 29 percent of the cases there was an acquaintance relationship. Ten percent of the cases involved "primary group relationships." The authors decided that "if a woman is attacked, then, considerable justification does appear to exist for the fear that the offender will be a stranger."[11]

After indulging what a modern reader might interpret as victim-blaming, the report went on to what might be considered classism. The authors suggested that many reported cases of acquaintance rape could involve

someone not yet established as a boyfriend or paramour [who] presses for sexual favors. Although the woman can initially encourage the advance, she may then resist. If the male is not dissuaded and forcefully succeeds in his physical quest, the result may be a report of rape . . . this pattern may be especially true to life experience among the lower classes, where a disproportionate amount of forcible rape and other major violence occurs. The attitude that women are objects of exploitation is common among lower-class male society. . . . When added to the relative dearth of articulate verbal communication and techniques for deflating aggression among lower class individuals, these behavior patterns and attitudes describe how the male may often attempt to elevate an acquaintanceship physically to a more intimate relationship, despite the protests of the woman.[12]

The commission's reference to the lower classes apparently did not imply race: the report found no correlation between races and acquaintance rape. It did find that 10 percent of rapes were committed by Blacks against Whites. Less than 1 percent were committed by whites [sic] against Negroes, but "because white [sic] males have long had nearly institutionalized access to Negro women with relatively little fear of being reported, it is likely that the true proportion of Negroes raped by whites [sic] is larger."[13]

The National Crime Panel began in 1972, conducted by the Law Enforcement Assistance Administration and the Census Bureau. The panel interviewed 250,000 people in large cities and came up with an estimate of 315 rapes for every 100,000 females 12 and up. It also recorded the victim's race, age, major activity, and marital status, as well as many details about the event.[14]

The estimate was almost certainly low because, according to a later BJS report, in the early years of these studies "it was deemed inappropriate for a government-sponsored survey to ask respondents directly about rape. Reports of rape and attempted rape were obtained only if the respondent volunteered this information in response to questions about assault and attacks."[15]

By 1993 the newly redesigned panel, now known as the National Crime Victimization Survey, had changed its approach:

> The new survey asks directly about rape and attempted rape. It also distinguishes among sex crimes by asking directly about sexual attack, coerced and unwanted sexual activity (with and without force), and verbal threats of rape or sexual attack. These new questions elicit more reports of rape and attempted rape, and the new questionnaire yields estimates for related sexual crimes not previously measured.

In the new system, an action was counted as a rape if the description merited it, even if the victim did not consider it as such, for example, "if the rape is committed by a woman's husband, and she does not consider this a rape." Most of these surveys were conducted by telephone, and most questions were designed for "yes" or "no" answers, to make it difficult for anyone overhearing to recognize what was being discussed.[16]

One of the factors that led to the change in thought about rape and the increase in discussion of the topic was the publication in 1975 of Susan Brownmiller's *Against Our Will: Men, Women, and Rape*. She argued that rape was not an act of passion but "nothing more or less than a conscious process of intimidation by which *all men* keep *all women* in a state of fear."[17]

Brownmiller's best-selling book was not a government publication, but it made use of federal statistics. For example, her chapter on the "police-blotter rapist" relies on the *Uniform Crime Reports* to build a portrait of the supposedly average offender.[18]

Brownmiller also discussed the Army Courts Martial for rape during and after World War II, finding that most of these assaults happened during the occupation, not during the stress of combat.[19] In addition, she made note of the National Commission on the Causes and Prevention of Violence's use of the concept of victim precipitation.

Two years after *Against Our Will* was published, the National Institute of Law Enforcement and Criminal Justice (NILECJ) conducted the first surveys on the attitudes of police and prosecutors to forcible rape. The foreword pointed out that "public attitudes toward the crime of rape are changing, due in large part to the influence of the women's rights movement of the past decade. Increasingly, rape is recognized as a violent crime against the person, rather than a sexual act."[20]

The response from police departments showed a lack of uniformity as to what constituted rape. (Is attempted rape included? What constituted "threat of force?")[21] Also, some agencies dedicated special units to the crime, while others lumped it with homicide, juvenile offenses, or robbery.[22]

As for the response from prosecutors' offices, the NILECJ summarized the data this way:

> Most agencies confront a rape event involving a victim and a suspect who were total strangers. The event was likely to have occurred in a motor vehicle or out-of-doors. The use of physical force and/or the presence of a weapon (firearm) were probable. The victim was likely to have resisted her attacker and received physical injury. The more her resistance, the more serious the injury. More than one form of sexual penetration occurred. Although she did not know her assailant beforehand, she will be able to identify him if he is seen again. The alleged assailant was an individual known by police since he was involved in previous crimes or sex offenses. The victim reported the event directly to the police within one hour of its occurrence.

The report concluded that prosecutors would not file charges unless there was (1) proof of penetration provided by a medical facility, (2) evidence of lack of consent, and (3) threat or use of force.[23] NILECJ found that "prosecutors have been slower to respond than law enforcement officials to community and victim concerns for the development of improved methods for handling forcible rape cases."[24]

In 1979 the National Criminal Justice Information and Statistics Service published *Rape Victimization in 26 Cities*. Besides the geographical limitation, it dealt only with female rape because "the small number of cases in which the victim was a male severely limits what can be said about these incidents. In addition, the crime of rape is generally, both legally and socially, considered a crime against women." The report also chose to provide only data about "stranger-to-stranger" rapes on the ground that the surveys involved had probably undercounted "nonstranger rapes."[25]

Another way to study how the federal government's interest in rape data changed over the years is through the *Sourcebook of Criminal Justice Statistics*. It was first published in 1973 but gained an index only 10 years later. Table 24.1 shows the subtopics that appeared under "Forcible Rape" in the index during each decade.

Table 24.1   "Forcible Rape" subcategories in the index of the *Sourcebook of Criminal Justice Statistics.*

	1983	1993	2003	2016
Arrests	*	*	*	*
Clearance by arrest	*	*	*	*
Death penalty	*			
Federal defendants/court cases	*	*	*	*
Federal parks	*			
Offenses known to police	*	*	*	*
Prisoners	*	*	*	*
Public opinion	*			
Victimization	*	*	*	*
Bail		*		
Declined for prosecution		*		
Hate crimes		*	*	*
Number		*		
Parole		*	*	*
Pretrial release/detention		*	*	*
Probation		*	*	*
Rate		*	*	*
Sentences		*	*	*
Basis for wiretap			*	*
Community supervision			*	*
Convictions			*	*
Jail inmates			*	*
Number in large cities			*	*
State court cases			*	*
Urban county court cases			*	*
Method of conviction				*
Offender characteristics				*
Self-protective measures taken				*
Some slight variations in terminology have been blended together				
Some categories became more detailed over time				

Sources: U.S. Justice Department, Bureau of Justice Statistics, *Sourcebook of Criminal Justice Statistics 1983,* 691; U.S. Justice Department, Justice Programs Office, Bureau of Justice Statistics, *Sourcebook of Criminal Justice Statistics 1993,* 779–80; U.S. Justice Department, Justice Programs Office, Bureau of Justice Statistics, *Sourcebook of Criminal Justice Statistics 2003,* 629; University at Albany, School of Criminal Justice, Hindelang Criminal Justice Research Center, *Sourcebook of Criminal Justice Statistics.*

By 2003 the *Sourcebook* was pointing out that while its figures still assumed that rape was exclusively a crime against women "some States have enacted gender-neutral rape or sexual assault statutes that prohibit forced sexual penetration of either sex." Therefore, the data from those states actually included both sexes.[26]

Returning to the 1980s, the BJS entered the picture in 1985 with *The Crime of Rape,* a five-page pamphlet that it described as the "first in-depth study" of the 1.5 million rapes/attempted rapes in the United States from 1973 to 1982. This data, taken from the National Crime Survey, included the setting, the sex of the victim, injuries, weapons, and methods of self-defense. It also covered the relationship between offender and victim, saying that "the most frightening form of rape, an assault by a total stranger," was the most common.[27]

In an illustration of the contradictions of data collected from different sources, the National Crime Survey, based on random household interviews, gave the rate of rape as double that of *Uniform Crime Reports,* which depended on police data. Nonetheless, about one-third of rapes reported to the police were not counted by the National Crime Survey.[28]

In 2000 the National Institute of Justice published *Extent, Nature, and Consequences of Intimate Partner Violence,* a book that examined crimes committed by current or past partners of the victims. The data came from the National Violence Against Women Survey (NVAWS), a nationwide phone interview project, and it was the first national survey to estimate lifetime figures for intimate partner violence rape. It found that, of those surveyed, 7.7 percent of women and 0.3 percent of men had been raped by a current or past intimate partner at some time.[29] The NVAWS estimation of rapes committed in 1995 was almost four times as high as the National Criminal Victimization Survey estimate for the same year.[30]

Also in 2000 the NIJ produced its first report on *The Sexual Victimization of College Women,* based on telephone surveys conducted in 1996;[31] 1.7 percent of the respondents had experienced a completed rape, while another 1.1 percent had been the victim of attempted rape.[32] Just over half of the attacks took place after midnight.[33] Most of the attacks took place off campus, although the authors caution that they might have been related to college life.[34]

The National Survey of Family Growth has been conducted by the Health and Human Services Department since 1973. It is primarily a study of fertility and family planning, but in 2002 the survey began asking people between the age of 18 and 24 "who had first sex before age 20 by how much first sexual intercourse was wanted"; 13.4 percent of females agreed that "I really didn't want it to happen at the time." In 2011–2013 that percentage dropped to 10.7 percent. The figures for male respondents were 9.8 percent and 7.9 percent.[35] During the latter period 6.2 percent of women in the same age group said that their first vaginal intercourse was not voluntary.[36]

In 2007 the National Institute of Justice published its first study of intoxication-facilitated rape. A total of 3,001 women were asked during phone interviews: "Has anyone ever had sex with you when you didn't want to after they gave you, or you had taken enough drugs to make you very high, intoxicated, or passed out?" Eighteen percent of women had had at least one experience of rape, and an estimated 3.1 million women had experienced rape while in an incapacitated condition, with 2.6 million of those involving drugs and/or alcohol.[37]

It is worth noting that neither the revised definition of rape in the *Uniform Crime Reports* nor the statistical categories in *Criminal Victimization in the United States* identify rapes in which the victim is under the influence of drugs or alcohol. (The mention of drugs/alcohol in Table 24.2 is a reference to the offender's condition, not that of the victim.)

Table 24.2   Characteristics of rape analyzed at the *Criminal Victimization in the United States* website, 2016.

Agency type providing assistance to victim

Loss

Economic

Time from work

Number of incidents

Offender

Age

Alcohol/drug use

Gender

Multiple victimizations

Number of

Race

Single victimizations

Victim–offender relationship

Weapons used

Physical force, who used first

(Continued)

Place of occurrence

Police response to reported incident

Reporting to police

Age

Ethnicity

Gender

Race

Reasons for

Reasons for not

Self-protective measures

Series victimizations

Time of occurrence

Victim–offender relationship

Nonstrangers

Strangers

Victims

Activity at time of incident

Age

Characteristics of household

Distance from home

Ethnicity

Family income

Gender

Marital status

Medical care

Number of

Race

Residence

Number of years lived at

Region of

Urban, suburban, rural

Source: U.S. Justice Department, Justice Programs Office, Bureau of Justice Statistics, *Criminal Victimization—Rape/Sexual Assault.*

The federal government continues to seek new ways of collecting, processing, and publicizing data about rape. In 2013, the BJS published *Female Victims of Sexual Violence, 1994–2010*, based on the National Crime Victimization Survey. It noted trends in rape and sexual assault, finding that the rate of rape or sexual assault dropped by two-thirds during that period, while the rate for attempted or threatened rape was mostly stable.[38]

Table 24.2 demonstrates the complexity of current statistics on rape and the amount of detail that the government is willing to include. It shows all the categories under the topic "Rape/Sexual Assault" on the website for *Criminal Victimization in the United States* as of 2016.

Statistical Abstract

The subject of crime first appears in the 1943 edition of the *Statistical Abstract*. There were 6,081 arrests for rape in 1942.[39]

In 1950 the volumes started to show trends in crime. Rape dropped 2.3 percent between 1947 and 1948.[40]

"Victims of Crime" began to appear in 1967.[41] More men than women were victims in all categories except rape, which was "not applicable" to men, according to the *Abstract*.[42]

Victimization rates for crimes against persons began to appear in 1977. No figures were given for male victims because the "estimated number of victimizations [is] too small to be statistically reliable."[43]

In 1979, for the first time, statistics were offered about women arrested for committing "forcible rape." Approximately 200 arrests were listed for 1974 and for 1978.[44] Before that, the category was considered "not applicable."[45]

The year 1990 introduced a table recording "Crime Incidents by Place and Time." It lists the number of rapes occurring inside own home, near own home, on public transportation, and so on.[46]

PART VIII

Women at War

CHAPTER TWENTY-FIVE

Rosie the Riveter: Civilian Women during the World Wars

At the end of World War I working women were encouraged to go home and make their jobs available to the men returning from battle. Some of the one and a half million women who had entered war industries had no desire to leave.[1]

In certain cities women had been hired as conductors for street cars, elevated railroads, and subways. As the war wound down authorities proclaimed that these jobs were too difficult for women and night shifts too dangerous. The newly formed Women's Bureau in the Labor Department quoted a woman who had been working in that industry:

> Lightest work I ever did and best pay. Have worked at housework, checking orders in a drug factory, done clerical work, and as a telephone operator. Had to do heavy lifting when I checked orders in the drug company; filled a man's place at $15 a week, while men beside me got twice that. Do you wonder I appreciate being treated as well and paid just the same as a man? Then they fuss about our late runs; why I worked at the telephone exchange from 11 p.m. to 7 a.m. night after night, but no one got excited over that.[2]

In both world wars women were encouraged to run their homes thriftily, to mend and reuse, and to grow as much food as possible, all tasks that fit well within traditional feminine roles. But they were also encouraged to get jobs outside the home, to free a man for the firing line. As the street car operator noted, there was an inherent conflict there. One example of this issue is the different approaches taken by two federal agencies that were born in 1918.

During World War I federal officials consulted with the Women's Trade Union League (WTUL) on "how best to meet the needs of working women." This led to the Department of Labor creating the Women in Industry Service (WIS) to monitor the conditions of women working in factories with government contracts. The director was Mary Van Kleeck, a longtime WTUL member. WIS set standards and conducted national surveys on safety, wage, and hours for women war workers. After the war President Wilson replaced the WIS with a permanent agency, the Women's Bureau.[3]

The other agency was the National War Labor Board (NWLB), which, in the words of one modern scholar, "administered America's first comprehensive experiment in labor-government-management relations."[4] The board's union and management membership were assigned to keep the labor peace.

The cochairs of the board, including former president William Howard Taft, were astonished by the low wages women were receiving—including those paid by the federal government—and the board awarded equal pay to women in 48 cases.[5] The board also created a team of female investigators to study women's working conditions, separate from the team that studied men's issues.[6]

But the board's decisions did not always favor women. The NWLB sometimes set wages for businesses in defense industries and frequently arranged those of women at three-quarters of the rate for men.[7] Often, as in the case of the street car operators, unions pushed against women employees. For example, with the encouragement of organized labor, the board decided that the Cleveland railroads could fire its women workers, even though it was "true the company will have to lower its standards somewhat" to find men for the jobs.[8] The board dissolved itself in 1919, a year after the war ended.[9]

One change that became increasingly noticeable during World War I was what the Civil Service Commission later called "the infiltration of women into the Government in times of national stress."[10] This was pointed out in the Commission's Annual Report of 1918:

The most notable change in Government personnel brought about by the war is in the employment of women. They are everywhere, and offices which formerly insisted on men employees are now acceding to the Commission's recommendation that their examinations be open to women applicants.

Between fiscal years 1910 and 1918 the number of women who were examined for federal jobs rose by 441 percent, compared to only 122 percent for men.[11]

Most of the data available about women in industry during World War I was collected and published by the Women's Bureau after the conflict was over. While these pamphlets contain some statistics, they are richer in anecdotal evidence. For example, these appeared in *The New Position of Women in American Industry:*

- "At the time-honored work of sweeping and cleaning a large group of women were employed."
- A veneer manufacturer: "We are keeping women [because] they do their work nicer, and while it takes more of them to do it, it is a little more satisfactory."
- A lumber manufacturer: "For the most part the work in and around our plant is too heavy for women to perform. There were some places, however, where we could use negro [sic] women to fairly good advantage where the work was light and a minimum of danger."
- An automobile body factory superintendent: "[The work the girls] did was on a par with the work as made by men."
- A sawmill operator: "Women were enthusiastic at first but when the novelty wore off and the weather got bad they were ready to quit. None have applied for work since."
- A sled manufacturer: "The great objection to employing women is the fact of the nine-hour [a day] limit."
- "Two women handle the lumber together. Men always carry one board no matter what its weight; while women carry two if they can make it."
- "We have gotten some [women] back, but they have been spoiled by war wages."[12]

This report pointed out that when women workers failed it was often because of "deficiencies in equipment and accommodations." However, it also admitted that "the incompetent, the indifferent, and the incorrigible" were bound to be among those attracted to the new opportunities: "The world's wastrels beget girls as well as boys and both make their intermittent trails through industry in war time as well as in peace time."[13]

Mary Anderson, the first head of the Women's Bureau, noted of the women working in war plants that "they were doing good work, but they did not get much recognition, and because there were no statistics, no one knew how many were employed."[14]

If a lack of statistics was a problem for women workers in World War I, it was not one in World War II. That struggle was, as one modern scholar put it, "a massively informed war."[15] The government collected, analyzed, publicized—and in some cases, concealed—data on many topics.

In September 1939, a week after war was declared in Europe, President Roosevelt declared a limited national emergency. During the next spring emergency management measures were set in place that designated certain businesses as "defense industries."[16]

At that point there were 13 million women in the labor force (i.e., either working or looking for work).[17] On the other hand, there were 37 million women at least 14 years old who were not in the labor force.[18]

The Women's Bureau launched into action. In 1940 its magazine *The Woman Worker* estimated that two million women were immediately available for defense work and "almost a sixth of these already have the necessary skills or at least some experience, enabling them to adapt themselves easily."[19] It published a guide to "Effective Use of Women in the Defense Program," which said that women "excel at work requiring manipulative dexterity and speed, but which permits the individual to set her own tempo and to work in a sitting position," work that called for "little physical exertion."[20]

In the first issue of 1941 *The Woman Worker* warned that many defense jobs were open only to men, "for example, marine surveyor, welding inspector, boiler inspector, glass blower," but women could find opportunities as "stenographers, typists, bilingual stenographers, medical technicians, and punchcard operators."

The first job statistic published in *The Woman Worker* that year was that 10,000 women had applied for the job of "camp hostess," working in service clubs at military bases, but only 100 such jobs were available.[21]

Women were quickly moving beyond work as stenographers and hostesses. The Civil Service Commission (CSC), chaired by Lucille Foster McMillin,[22] published annual reports on *A Study of Women's Participation in Federal Defense Activities:* "Great events have always carried women forward in their quest to find a secure place in the fields of labor. Nevertheless, their primary instinct has been, and still is, to cherish their greater interest in the protection of the home, the family, and the community."[23]

The first CSC report noted that by the fall of 1941 more than 400 women were working with explosives at the Picatinny Arsenal in New Jersey. In Maryland, 2,000 women worked three shifts six days a week, making gas masks. And in Philadelphia: "Tiny delicate parts, cumbersome to the heavy hands of men, are handled easily and efficiently by the quick fingers of women. Here, women are munition inspectors."[24]

The second annual report featured many photos illustrating "PICTUR-ESQUE JOBS OF WOMEN IN DEFENSE."[25] Throughout these publications the CSC tried to have it both ways, emphasizing women's hard work while insisting they were still lady-like:

- "Here, their quality of patience, their temperament, their dexterity, their devotion to duty, are vitally essential as their deft hands turn out the missiles of defense."[26]

- A woman who had studied biology and chemistry in college was doing "a man's job" at an ordinance plant.[27]

- Women were "more eager to learn; consistent; and more 'durable' (they tire out less easily when engaged continually on one operation)." They have "a deadlier shooting eye than men."

- Women were "(a) inferior at bench work; (b) slower at using a hammer and chisel, at least skillfully; (c) unable to fill positions requiring the physical strength of a man; (d) unwilling to accept appointment in some instances because of the absence or the inadequacy of sanitary facilities, and (e) not so competent as men in analyzing situations."[28]

- "With compacts and lipsticks in their pockets, they are making records in the operation of turret lathes and gear-cutting machines. They are putting planes in the air with a skill equal to that of many men." They handle heavy machinery "with calm indifference and high efficiency."[29]

Other agencies were taking note of the new workers as well. The 1941 *Handbook of Labor Statistics* was the first to cover "Women in Defense Industries," with data borrowed from *The Woman Worker*. It reported that between the end of 1940 and the early months of 1941 the number of women working in defense went up by one-half to two-thirds, depending on the industry.[30]

During 1942 the United States Employment Service published *Occupations Suitable for Women*, which included only about one-fifth of the jobs listed in the *Dictionary of Occupational Titles*. However, the book noted, in periods such as a war, "the employment of women usually makes deeper and deeper inroads into the groups of 'less suitable' jobs."[31]

The Commerce Department magazine *Domestic Commerce* celebrated in its August 1943 issue that working women were good news for the makeup industry: "The average girl in war industry is spending about $2.37 a month for self-beautification compared with $1.82 before entering war plants."[32]

The 1941–1942 report of the Selective Service, the agency charged with managing the draft of young men, included a 25-page supplement on "womanpower," a word that was finding its way into the national vocabulary. Womanpower, the report said, was "the greatest source of reserve both in providing additional manpower needed in the extension of war production and replacement of men needed or destined for the armed forces."[33]

The Selective Service declared that it was ready to register women if Congress authorized it. (This was discussed but never happened.)[34] Among those the service quoted on this subject was Mary Anderson, director of the Women's Bureau, although, in what some might consider a Freudian slip, she was identified as the head of a different Labor Department office, the Children's Bureau.[35] A few years later Anderson commented that "there was a great tendency among government officials, particularly during World War II, to speak about 'the people' as a whole, but when they spoke of 'the people' they meant the men."[36]

Women's Bureau publications emphasized two types of statistics: the vital work women were doing for the war effort and the problems they faced in doing it.

Some examples of the former follow:

- In 1942 women mechanics were hired at Brooklyn Navy Yard, for the first time in its 140-year history. Twelve of the 125 women were African Americans, including a "negro [sic] girl," who received the highest civil service exam score among of the 6,000 female applicants.[37]

- One major aircraft company moved from 2 percent women in its workforce in 1941 to 50 percent a year later. "Women are particularly good at fine processes requiring painstaking application. They have patience and finger dexterity and soon learn to make careful adjustments at high speed with great accuracy."[38]

- "From the attack on Pearl Harbor in December 1941 to March 1944 some 6 ½ million women newly entered the labor force. . . . At the war peak in July 1944 women in the labor force totaled 20.8 million, compared with 13.8 million in March 1940."[39]

- In July 1941 one major shipbuilder wouldn't even hire women as secretaries. Two years later women held nearly 200 different jobs in navy yards and commercial shipyards.[40]

- "Almost half of the women employed in the war period in most of the 10 areas had not wanted jobs the week before Pearl Harbor."[41]

Among the problems the Women's Bureau pointed out were the following:

- "Mrs. Stay-At-Home was buying up all the bargains; Mrs. War Worker found the stocks depleted."[42]

- "It is important to the placement staff looking for workers to be employed on board ship that the frame of a woman is such that it is more difficult for her than for a man to maintain her balance; that a woman's blood has a higher water content than a man's and contains up to 20 percent fewer red corpuscles; that her heart beats about 8 times more a minute; and her muscles, proportionately longer and thinner, allow her a squeeze only about three fifths, and muscular strength only about one-half, that of the average man . . . she tends to tire more quickly than a man."[43]

- An aircraft company found that absenteeism among women "was caused not by hangovers but by a lack of such community services as laundries and restaurants. Bomber production was being affected because workers in these plants could not get their washing done nor buy their meals in restaurants."[44]

- "The housing that had been used by migratory workers was not satisfactory for women, nor were there sanitary or bathing facilities, and the growers frankly preferred Mexicans if they could get them, who would accept the housing they had."[45]

Anderson's bureau continued to push, as it had since its creation, for equal wages for women.[46] It pointed out that "Women Support Families Too!" with more than 12 percent of working women providing the only income in their families.[47]

However, the equal wage principle wasn't always carried out, even when commanded by federal decree. In 1942 the assistant secretary of the Navy required that employees in navy yards of both sexes should receive equal pay, but in one yard men without experience were hired at 74 cents an hour while all new female hires received 58 cents.[48]

Starting in 1943, the housewife, or what the Women's Bureau had called "Mrs. Stay-At-Home," became a target or at least a convenient cat's paw, in a battle of numbers between organized labor and the Bureau of Labor Statistics (BLS). The BLS's data showed that the cost of living had risen by about 20 percent during the war.[49] This was crucial because the NWLB had begun pegging wage increases to that index.

The Congress of Industrial Organizations and the American Federation of Labor, together representing the majority of trade unions, complained that the BLS's estimates were far too low. Labor's figures, based on interviewing housewives, set the rise in the cost of living from 1941 to 1944 at 43.5 percent.[50]

According to Thomas A. Stapleford, both sides used the "rhetorical housewife" in their arguments, treating her as "wise when she agreed with the social and political experts—whether home economists, New Deal politicians, or labor leaders—and ignorant (or ignored) when she did not."[51] The BLS even created a scripted radio program called "House-wife Versus Economist," in which the acting head of the agency convinced his wife that his figures on prices were more accurate than her "intuition."[52]

One irony of this battle is that the section of BLS that studied the cost of living was known within the bureau as a "matriarchy," because most of the workers, from the chief down, were women. But of course, they were not housewives.[53]

After the war ended, the Women's Bureau conducted a survey of more than 13,000 women who had worked in "10 war-congested [geographic] manufacturing areas."[54] The most important findings follow:

> First, the war brought about great increases in the number of women employed in each of the 10 areas and in the number of women who planned to remain in the labor force in the respective areas.
>
> Second, there were tremendous increases in the proportions of women employed in industries producing directly for war purposes, and the take-home earnings of those women considerably exceeded the take-home earnings of women employed in other industries.
>
> Third, a high proportion of the women employed during the war period reported that they carried heavy economic responsibilities at home, and a high proportion of those who planned to continue working after the war gave economic reasons for their decisions.[55]

A year later, in 1947, the Women's Bureau published a survey of women's hours in wartime plants, with the goal of determining "what scheduled hours are best to maintain a stable, healthy staff of women workers." Most of the occupations were "man-paced," a term the report did not define. The conclusion is that a 40-hour week, 8 hours a day, gave the best results in attendance.[56]

While the woman war worker is the female icon of the period, it is important to remember that she did not represent the majority. As Karen Anderson put it: "Because most American women remained homemakers during the war, Rosie was not the typical wartime woman."[57]

Statistical Abstract

The 1917 *Statistical Abstract* contained some information about the United States entering World War I in April. There were 11 pages about the draft but, not surprisingly, no mention of women.[58]

The 1918 volume contains a larger section of the war, but the only mention of women is in the section on the American National Red Cross.

Table 25.1   Women's war work during World War I.

Women in war work	2,250,000 (4.4%)
Women in nonwar work	25,750,000 (50.5%)
Total women of producing age	28,000,000 (54.9%)
Old women and girls	23,000,000 (45.1%)
Total females	51,000,000

Source: U.S. Commerce Department, Foreign and Domestic Commerce Bureau, *Statistical Abstract 1919*, 728. Percentages have been inserted.

Specifically, the Women's Volunteer Motor Corps had about 3,000 members.[59]

That figure rose to 12,000 in the 1919 volume, which added that 5,753 men and women sailed overseas on various Red Cross duties.[60] More than 24,000 nurses had enrolled in the Red Cross as well.[61] Another table reported on the American population's occupations during the war. Besides saying how many men are in the military, it reported on certain figures for each sex. Similar figures appeared in the 1920 and 1921 volumes. Table 25.1 records women's activities in the war.

Most of the relevant figures in *Statistical Abstracts* that cover the years of World War II were from the 1940 Census, before the United States entered the war. However, the 1946 edition has quarterly figures on the estimated civilian labor force by age and sex throughout the war. The highest figure for employed women was 18,830,000 in the third quarter of 1945.[62]

CHAPTER TWENTY-SIX

Women in the Military

In her two-volume bibliography of women in government publications, Mary Ellen Huls noted that "government publications on the role of women in the armed forces in non-medical capacities begin with World War II."[1] Until that event, women other than nurses were a rare and exceptional occurrence in the military.

One such example was Deborah Sampson Gannett, who not only served in the army during the American Revolution disguised as a man but also received a pension from Congress for her service.[2] During the Civil War an "amazingly large number of women" managed to serve in disguise. One government publication estimates that at least 400 women fought in the Union army alone.[3]

During World War I undisguised women wore military uniforms for the first time. Almost 50,000 served, three-quarters of them in the Army or Navy Nurse Corps.[4] While the law did not permit women to otherwise join the army, 12,500 became "Yeomen (F)" in the navy, mostly serving in clerical positions.[5] The Marines also accepted women for similar posts, although it assumed, incorrectly as it turned out, that it would need three females to replace two males.[6]

In 1941, as the nation prepared for the possibility that World War II might reach us, Congresswoman Edith Nourse Rogers proposed that a women's unit be created in the army. She had served as a Red Cross volunteer in France during the first war and said: "I was resolved that our women would not again serve with the Army without the protection men got."[7] Unfortunately, the compromise that was reached, the Women's Army Auxiliary Corps (WAACs), did not achieve her goals. It was, as an army history book put it, "a military organization, but without Army rank, officer status, equal pay, or Army benefits such as retirement and veteran's rights."[8]

As the war continued, the WAACs gave way to the WACs (Women's Army Corps) whose more than 100,000 members had the same ranks and privileges as male servicemen and could serve overseas.[9] The official history of the WACs, published in 1954, is more than 800 pages long, which is more remarkable because some army commands forbid the collection of statistics by sex, and others failed to do so. At the time that book was published, the history of the other forces' women's reserves was still classified.[10]

The navy's equivalent of the WACs was the Women Accepted for Volunteer Emergency Service (WAVES). The Coast Guard had the SPARS (from the Guard's motto: "Semper Paratus—Always Ready"). The Coast Guard recruiting posters urged women to "Make a Date with Uncle Sam."[11]

Marine commandant Major General Thomas Holcomb was reluctant to create a Marine Corps Women's Reserve, but personnel needs forced him to agree. When asked if they would have a name like WACs or WAVES he replied: "They are Marines. They don't have a nickname and they don't need one." This response made him very popular with his female troops.[12]

By the high point of enlistment in summer 1944, there were 18,000 women Marines.[13] During World War II nearly 350,000 women served in uniform.[14]

When peace arrived women were no longer welcome in the armed forces. By 1948 there were fewer than 15,000 women in military uniform, and they were all nurses.[15]

During that year Congress passed the Women's Armed Services Integration Act, which permitted females into the military again, but gave the secretaries of each branch the authority to determine what types of assignments they could be given. Certain combat duties were forbidden by law, and all of them were banned in practice.[16]

Three years later Secretary of Defense George C. Marshall established a civilian group, the Defense Advisory Committee on Women in the Services (DACOWITS), to advise his office on issues related to enlisting, retaining, and making better use of women in the armed forces.[17]

The 1948 law restricted the number of women who could serve, but that section was repealed in 1967.[18] In the early 1970s, as the draft was ending and Congress passed the Equal Rights Amendment (which was never ratified by the states), the Defense Department began looking for ways to fill the ranks with more women. Between 1972 and 1974 the number of females in uniform rose from 31,000 to approximately 73,000.[19]

One result of this increase was the realization that more information was needed about women who were serving or had served in uniform. The 1980 Census was the first to ask women about their veteran status and their period of service.[20] This data allowed the Veterans Administration (VA) to calculate that 4 percent of the veteran population was female. A total of 740,000 of them, more than 40 percent, had served in war.[21]

In 1984 the VA published a survey on aging women vets. It found that 8 percent of veterans over 65 were female. Among the many facts discovered were that women vets were half as likely as their male counterparts to use VA hospitals, although the reasons they gave for their choices were similar to their male counterparts. Three times as many female vets (13 percent versus 4 percent) never married.[22]

The following year the VA published a 284-page book, which it described as the "first systematic survey of the current status, need and experiences of women veterans of the United States Armed Forces." It was based on interviews with more than 3,000 women.[23] One highlight was the discovery that only 5 percent of female veterans had served in a combat situation, and only 1 percent of the veterans had served a full 20 years, completing a career. The report explained:

> Although many women veterans report that they left the service because the war ended or their obligation was completed, a substantial minority (15%) report that they were forced to leave *by the military* because of pregnancy or children. This is distinct from those who left because *they* wanted to get married or have a family. Despite the discontinuation of the policy in the 1970s of separating women for pregnancy, nearly one out of six women veterans who entered in the post-Vietnam era (14%) say that they were forced to leave by the military because of pregnancy or children.[24]

The most recent edition of *Profile of Women Veterans* was published by the VA in 2014. It compared women vets to men vets and also to women who had not served. It found that 9 percent of veterans were women, and more women vets than men were minorities. The median age for female vets was 49, while that for male vets was 15 years higher.[25]

In 1984 DACOWITS asked the Office of the Secretary of Defense to assess how women in the military are "progressing (over time and compared to men)." The result was an annual publication, *Military Women in the Department of Defense,* with data selected from 60 million individual records.[26] It ceased publication six years later.

By 1996 the Defense Department was the nation's largest employer of women, with more than half a million women in uniformed and civilian jobs. It also boasted of operating the "nation's largest affordable employee sponsored child care program."[27]

But none of this progress happened without conflict. The Pentagon recognized that there were problems and conducted its first survey on sexual harassment in 1988. Almost one-quarter of respondents reported experiencing sexual harassment at work at least once in the prior year. Women were almost four times as likely to report sexual harassment as men. Fifteen percent of women and 2 percent of men said they had been pressured for sexual favors. Rape or attempted rape was reported by 5 percent of female and 1 percent of male respondents.[28] This research continues as part of the Workplace and Gender Relations Survey of Active Duty Members (WGRA).[29]

Occasional events have focused national and government attention on dangers women have faced from their comrades. One of the first dramatic examples was Tailhook '91. Tailhook was an annual symposium for naval aviators; it was not official but received considerable support from the navy. Tailhook had a reputation for being the scene of wild partying, and during the 35th annual event, held in 1991, 83 women and seven men were assaulted.[30]

The year 2004 saw the first report from the Office of the Secretary of Defense to Congress on sexual assault in armed forces. It contained 1,700 reports of this crime. The same year saw the first survey on sexual harassment in the military reserves; 19 percent of women and 3 percent of men said they had experienced sexual harassment; 46 percent of women and 60 of men said it was declining in the military.[31]

A year later the Defense Department began to set up policies against sexual harassment and violence at the service academies. The first annual report on the subject came out two years later. Students at the academies reported 40 cases of sexual assault. Half of these were "restricted," meaning that they could not be investigated without the victims' permission, so data was necessarily limited.[32]

The year 2005 also saw the Defense Department set up the Sexual Assault Prevention and Response Office "to promote prevention, encourage increased reporting of the crime, and improve response capabilities for victims."[33] The year 2014 showed the highest number of sexual assault cases ever reported: 6,131.[34] The next year showed a small drop.[35]

As of June 2016, the website of the Office of the Inspector General (OIG) for the U.S. Defense Department lists 14 reports it has published related to sexual assault in the military.[36] The earliest was a 2003 report on a survey on sexual assault conducted with female cadets by the U.S. Air Force Academy; 7.4 percent of respondents reported being the victim of at least one rape or attempted rape at the academy; 18.8 percent had suffered at least one incident of sexual assault, a total of 177 cases; 68.8 percent had experienced sexual harassment.[37] Other reports on the OIG page include investigations of specific assaults, studies of policy development, and an examination of defense response to sexual assaults in Iraq.[38]

The Government Accountability Office (formerly the General Accounting Office), whose job is to assess how well federal programs are running, included on its website in June 2016 more than 40 reports related to sexual harassment and the military.[39] The earliest with that phrase in the title was from 1994 and, again, was about the service academies. The most recent report, from 2015, was about the failure of procedures to deal with sexual assaults on men, who were found to be less likely than women to report such attacks.[40]

As stated earlier, the agency that is supposed to advise the Pentagon on all issues related to women is DACOWITS. George W. Bush was often accused of decreasing the information publically available about government actions, and about women in particular, but his record in this case is somewhat mixed; specifically, he allowed DACOWITS to do less but provided more data about what it was doing.

In 2002, under Bush, the DACOWITS charter was changed for the first time since 1951; it now included military families as opposed to just military women.[41] The administration decreased the committee's size and budget, while putting its agenda under the Pentagon's control.[42] On the other hand, the DACOWITS Annual Reports, under the new charter, were available to the public for the first time.[43]

The office of Congresswoman Carolyn B. Mahoney prepared a report in 2004, which argued:

> The president's actions are problematic not only because they are unjust to women, but also because they threaten our nation's military readiness. In the words of Deputy Secretary of Defense Paul Wolfowitz: "As we consider the issue of womanpower in the service today it's not just a matter of women being entitled to serve this country. It is a simple fact that we could not operate our military services without women. And as skill levels essential to our missions continue to increase, it will be even more essential that we draw from all our citizens, that we draw from the largest pool of talent available." As Deputy Secretary Wolfowitz says, servicewomen are essential to our military readiness. Military women need to be able to focus on the job of defending our country without internal hindrances. By purposely rolling back efforts to address the obstacles that remain for women in the armed forces, President Bush's actions do not support our women in uniform and thereby put our nation's military preparedness at risk.[44]

Table 26.1 Subjects researched by DACOWITS.

	Bush Appointees							Obama Appointees					
	2003	2004	2005	2006	2007	2008	2009	2010	2011	2012	2013	2014	2015
Military action													
Combat and closed positions							*	*	*	*	*	*	*
Deployment		*											
Equipment and uniforms								*		*	*		*
Weapons training									*				
Family													
Education for military children						*							
Families of wounded warriors							*						
Family well-being			*										
Military spouse careers					*								
Health and safety													
Health care	*				*					*	*	*	
Protected health care information													*

246

PTSD treatment											*
Sexual assault/harassment	*		*	*	*	*		*	*	*	*
Career											
Accession								*	*	*	*
Career progression and mentoring									*		
Career–life balance	*										
Guard and reserve issues	*										
Lawyers, clergy, and doctors		*							*		
Marine performance evaluation							*				
Retention	*	*									
Other											
Social media											*
Success strategies			*								

PTSD: post-traumatic stress disorder.

Sources: U.S. Defense Department, Defense Advisory Committee on Women in the Services, *2003 Report* through *2015 Report*.

The Obama administration changed the charter again, eliminating the study of military families from the committee's duties and focusing more on women's combat-related duties.[45]

Table 26.1 shows the subjects researched in each year since DACOW-ITS' reports have been available to the public. They have been organized into categories for ease of comprehension here.

Statistical Abstract

The first hint in the *Statistical Abstract* that women might be serving in the armed forces appeared in the 1921 edition. Specifically, a table on expenditures of the American National Red Cross included "Relief of Military Service Men and Women."[46] This would have referred to nurses.

The 1943 edition, published during World War II, reported 4,917 officers and 55,326 enlisted persons in the WACs. Figures also appeared for the Navy, Marine Corps and Coast Guard Women's Reserves. There were tables for nurses and related health occupations, with no sex specified.[47] Figures for women in the military appear regularly from that point on.

"Veterans in civil life" were broken down by race and sex for the first time in the 1962 volume.[48] The next year characteristics of male veterans became more detailed (urban/rural, education, and age), but female veterans disappeared entirely.[49] Starting in 1967 sex was ignored, and all veterans were listed together.[50] Women veterans did not receive a separate count again in the *Statistical Abstract* for 33 years.[51]

PART IX

Conclusion

CHAPTER TWENTY-SEVEN

Conclusion

Sybilla (or Sybille) Masters of Pennsylvania was responsible for the first patent ever granted to a North American. She had invented a device for processing Indian corn, or maize. However, the patent was actually granted to her husband Thomas, because in 1715 the British government had no precedent or procedure for giving one to a woman.[1]

Masters's case is interesting because she was first and because she was not able to receive the patent herself, but it also raises some larger questions. We know about her because her name appeared in the patent papers, but how many women's inventions were assigned to male relatives without their being mentioned at all? And does it matter if women's accomplishments are buried in the historical record?

There are those who argue that the government has no business collecting statistics about women as opposed to men. Some of them are ready to "declare victory" and say there is no need to keep track of a battle that has already been won. All the way back in 1923 the Supreme Court declared that it was not appropriate to give women protection on the job that was not available to men because public differences between the sexes "had come almost, if not quite, to the vanishing point."[2] In 2002 a conservative group, the Center for Military Readiness, argued that it was time to eliminate the Defense Advisory Committee on Women in the Services: "A decision to drop the DACOWITS would demonstrate that women in uniform have truly 'arrived' as valued members of the national defense team."[3]

Some people have argued against the government collecting statistics at all. Before the first census President Washington lamented that the results were bound to be misleadingly low because "the religious scruples of some, would not allow them to give in their lists; [and] the fears of others that it was intended as the foundation of a tax induced them to conceal or diminish theirs."[4] In the run-up to the most recent census, Congresswoman Michele Bachmann (R-MN) worried about the "very intricate, very personal" questions she incorrectly thought would be on the census form and at first said her family would provide no information except for the number of persons.[5]

Even those who express no other concerns about statistics may consider their collection and publication expendable in times of shrinking budgets. The Obama administration killed the *Statistical Abstract* series after more than 130 years as a cost-saving measure.

At that time the editor of one commercial industry journal that had regularly contributed data to the *Statistical Abstract* lamented: "The government of a free country that would readily reduce its people's access to information leaves itself susceptible to doubt regarding how much information it really wants the people to have. . . . Apparently the job now lies entirely in the private sector."[6]

If gathering statistics in general and about women in particular is expensive, sometimes unwelcome, and, as this book demonstrates, can result in inaccurate results, are there convincing reasons to keep doing it?

Governments and businesses need accurate data to make feasible plans. Federal agencies started collecting unemployment data during the Great Depression in order to determine how much money should be spent on job creation.[7] If assumptions about women, or any other group, prejudice the data, then government programs, or for that matter sales campaigns, are less likely to be effective. This book contains multiple examples, over many decades, of government authors expressing their astonishment that so many women were working for a living.

If no data is bad, bad data can be worse. In the early decades of the 20th century Alba Edwards warned the census clerks collating occupational data to be suspicious of women recorded as holding unusual jobs.[8] Some scholars argue that this created a vicious circle, with each deflated census report "proving" the original assumption and thus making it even harder for female pioneers to be included in the next census.

Federal statistics become part of the conventional wisdom, affecting not only government programs but also decisions people make in everyday life. If the census claims there are no women in a given profession, it seems likely that many women would decide that that occupation is not open to them. When a technical change in definition caused the reported number of women-owned businesses to drop by 15 percent, there was reasonable fear that this would make financing for such businesses harder to find.[9]

Flawed and missing data can even affect people's health. The National Institute of Mental Health collected data about domestic violence for a decade without sharing the results or telling anyone that this crime was a problem of "epidemic proportion."[10] Obviously this slowed down the possibility of a government response that might have saved lives.

Another example was the tendency, before the 1980s, to conduct medical research only on men. This led to false assumptions about the best methods of treating and preventing illnesses in half the population.[11]

If preserving the dreams and health of women is not a sufficient reason to want adequate statistics, there is a strictly practical one as well. In 2012 the White House Council on Women and Girls warned that, since women were now a major force in the economy, "when women still face barriers to participation in the workplace and marketplace, that is not just a 'women's issue.'"[12] It could affect the financial well-being of the entire nation.

Juanita M. Kreps was an economist as well as the first woman to hold the post of secretary of Commerce. At a 1979 conference on women, she argued: "A vague sense of injustice is not adequate to attract attention and action. It takes statistics to influence Government's decisions. It takes statistics to determine the flow of dollars. Individual cases of discrimination can be ignored, rationalized, hushed up, or settled with little fanfare. It is much more difficult to ignore persistent and shocking statistics."[13]

This chapter began with Sybilla Masters, the first woman in America known to be responsible for a patent, although it was granted to her husband. Things have, of course, changed in the 300 years since her achievement. In a document on women inventors called *Buttons to Biotech,* the Patent and Trademark Office reported that the number of granted patents including at least one female inventor increased by 45 percent in a two-year period.[14] That impressive increase occurred between 1996 and 1998. As to what has happened since, unfortunately, there are no published statistics to tell us.

Notes

Chronology

1. U.S. Commerce Department, Census Bureau, *Census '80: Continuing the Factfinder Tradition,* 34.

2. Ibid., 34.

3. U.S. Commerce and Labor Department, Census Bureau, *Statistics of Women at Work.*

4. U.S. Labor Department, Bureau of Labor Statistics, *Summary of the Report.*

5. U.S. Labor Department, Bureau of Labor Statistics, *Handbook of Labor Statistics 1924-26,* 391.

6. U.S. Labor Department, Women in Industry Service, *First Annual Report,* 6.

7. U.S. Labor Department, Women's Bureau, *Our History.*

8. U.S. Labor Department, Bureau of Labor Statistics, *Handbook of Labor Statistics 1924-26,* 391.

9. U.S. Labor Department, Women's Bureau, *Milestones,* 30.

10. U.S. Defense Department, Defense Advisory Committee on Women in the Services, *Defense Advisory Committee on Women in the Armed Services.*

11. U.S. President's Commission on the Status of Women, *Report of the Committee on Civil and Political Rights.*

12. *Equal Pay Act,* U.S. Code 29 (2012), §§206 et seq.

13. *Civil Rights Act of 1964,* as amended in 1972, Title VII, U.S. Code 42 (2012), §§2000e et seq.

14. *Griswold v. Connecticut,* 381 U.S. 479 (1965).

15. U.S. Defense Department, *Military Women in the Department of Defense,* 1.

16. U.S. General Accounting Office, *Job Opportunities for Women,* 1.

17. U.S. Labor Department, Employment and Training Administration, *Women in Traditionally Male Jobs,* 1.

18. *Roe v. Wade,* 410 U.S. 113 (1973).

19. U.S. Labor Department, Women's Bureau, *Facts about Women Heads,* 1.
20. Slaughter, "Remarks," viii.
21. U.S. Defense Department, Inspector General's Office, *Tailhook '91.*
22. U.S. Justice Programs Office, National Institute of Justice, *Stalking in America,* 1.
23. Finlay, *George W. Bush and the War on Women,* 15.
24. National Council for Research on Women, *Missing: Information about Women's Lives,* 4.
25. U.S. Defense Department, Defense Advisory Committee on Women in the Services, *2009 Report,* i.
26. U.S. Commerce Department, Economics and Statistics Administration, and U.S. Executive Office of the President, Office of Management and Budget, *Women in America.*
27. U.S. Defense Department, Defense Advisory Committee on Women in the Services, *2010 Report,* i and 20.

Chapter 1 Introduction

1. U.S. Commerce Department, Census Bureau, *Thirteenth Census: Volume IV,* 22–23.
2. Frankel, "Why the CDC Still."
3. Jacobson, "Jon Kyl Says."

Chapter 2 Statistical System of the United States

1. U.S. Const. Art. I, § 2.
2. Scott, *Census, U.S.A.,* 15.
3. Ibid., 14–15.
4. Ibid., 20–21.
5. Ibid., 20.
6. Ibid., 28–31.
7. U.S. Census Office, *Statistical View,* 18.
8. Eckler, *Bureau of the Census,* 9–10.
9. Ibid., 15–16.
10. Snow, "Census Pop Culture"; U.S. Commerce Department, Census Bureau, *Census '80: Continuing the Factfinder Tradition,* 276; U.S. Commerce Department, Office of Public affairs, *Uncle Sam Counts,* 8.
11. U.S. Commerce Department, Census Bureau, *Census of Population: 1970. Volume 1. Characteristics of the Population. Part 1. United States Summary—Section 1,* v.
12. Dinan, "EXCLUSIVE: Minn. Lawmaker Vows."
13. National Academies of Science, Engineering and Medicine, *Coordinating and Sustaining Federal Statistics.*
14. Eckler, *Bureau of the Census,* 15–16.

15. Statistics Canada, *Statistics Canada.*

16. Some sources add the Environmental Protection Agency's Office of Environmental Information. For example, see FedStats, "Showcase."

17. U.S. White House, *Structure of the Federal Statistical System.*

18. Cortada, *All the Facts,* 141.

19. U.S. Education Department, Institute of Education Sciences, National Center for Educational Statistics, *Education Statistics and Education Policy.*

20. U.S. Labor Department, Bureau of Labor Statistics, *BLS History.*

21. Anderson, "Census and the Federal Statistical System," 157–58.

22. Cortada, *All the Facts,* 142.

23. U.S. National Science Foundation, *Minor Miracle,* 29.

24. Smith, "NCHS Dataline," 136.

25. U.S. Agriculture Department, National Agricultural Statistics Service, *About NASS: History of Agricultural Statistics.*

26. U.S. National Archives and Records Administration, *Records of the Economic Research Service.*

27. U.S. National Archives and Records Administration, *Records of the Bureau of Economic Analysis.*

28. U.S. Energy Department, Energy Information Administration, *About EIA: Legislative Timeline.*

29. U.S. Justice Department, Justice Programs Office, Bureau of Justice Statistics, *About the Bureau of Justice Statistics.*

30. U.S. Transportation Department, Bureau of Transportation Statistics, *About BTS.*

31. U.S. Labor Department, Bureau of Labor Statistics, *BLS History.*

32. FedStats, "Agencies."

33. U.S. Labor Department, Women's Bureau, *Milestones.*

34. U.S. Treasury Department, *Statistical Abstract 1878,* 134.

35. U.S. Treasury Department, *Statistical Abstract 1879,* 153–54.

36. U.S. Treasury Department, Statistics Bureau, *Statistical Abstract 1885,* 176.

37. U.S. Treasury Department, Statistics Bureau, *Statistical Abstract 1888,* 231.

38. U.S. Treasury Department, Statistics Bureau, *Statistical Abstract 1889,* 257.

39. U.S. Commerce and Labor Department, Statistics Bureau, *Statistical Abstract 1910,* 642.

40. U.S. Commerce Department, Foreign and Domestic Commerce Bureau, *Statistical Abstract 1922,* 81.

41. U.S. Commerce Department, Census Bureau, *Statistical Abstract 1944/5,* 499.

42. U.S. Commerce Department, Census Bureau, *Statistical Abstract 1965,* 175.

43. U.S. Commerce Department, Census Bureau, *Statistical Abstract 1978,* 653.

44. U.S. Commerce Department, Economics and Statistics Administration, Census Bureau, *Statistical Abstract 1992,* 90.

45. U.S. Commerce Department, Economics and Statistics Administration, Census Bureau, *Statistical Abstract 1995,* 170.

46. U.S. Commerce Department, Economics and Statistics Administration, Census Bureau, *Statistical Abstract 2008,* 712.

Chapter 3 Population and Age

1. U.S. Commerce and Labor Department, Census Bureau, *Special Reports: Supplementary Analysis: 1900,* 88.

2. U.S. Commerce Department, Census Bureau, *Thirteenth Census: Volume I, 1910, General Report,* 248.

3. Kohlhell, "Calif. Students Now."

4. U.S. Commerce Department, Economics and Statistics Administration, Census Bureau, *1790 Overview.*

5. U.S. Interior Department, *Statistics: 1860,* vi–vii.

6. U.S. Census Office, *Statistical View,* 49.

7. Ibid., 56.

8. Ibid., 63 and 66.

9. U.S. Interior Department, Census Superintendent, *Population 1860,* 281. Quotation marks in the original.

10. U.S. Interior Department, Census Office, *Ninth Census Volume I. 1870,* xxxviii.

11. Ibid., xxxviii.

12. U.S. Interior Department, *Statistical Atlas 1870,* 2.

13. U.S. Commerce and Labor Department, Census Bureau, *Special Reports: Supplementary Analysis: 1900,* 88.

14. Ibid., 88.

15. U.S. Commerce Department, Economics and Statistics Administration, Census Bureau, *Age and Sex Composition 2010,* 13.

16. U.S. Commerce and Labor Department, Census Bureau, *Special Reports: Supplementary Analysis: 1900,* 101.

17. U.S. Commerce Department, Census Bureau, *Thirteenth Census: Volume I,* 247.

18. Ibid., 248.

19. Ibid., 249.

20. Ibid., 249.

21. Ibid., 1033.

22. U.S. Commerce Department, Economics and Statistics Administration, Census Bureau, *Age and Sex Composition 2010,* 4.

23. U.S. Treasury Department, *Statistical Abstract 1878,* 143–45.

24. U.S. Commerce and Labor Department, Statistics Bureau, *Statistical Abstract 1905,* 34.

25. U.S. Treasury Department, *Statistical Abstract 1898,* 18.

26. U.S. Commerce Department, Foreign and Domestic Commerce Bureau, *Statistical Abstract 1922,* 38.

27. U.S. Commerce Department, Foreign and Domestic Commerce Bureau, *Statistical Abstract 1923,* 13 and 16.

28. U.S. Commerce Department, Census Bureau, *Statistical Abstract 1976,* 25, and U.S. Commerce Department, Economics and Statistics Administration, Census Bureau, *Statistical Abstract 1999,* 938.

Chapter 4 Marriage, Divorce, and Cohabitation

1. U.S. Commerce Department, Census Bureau, *Perspectives on American Husbands and Wives,* 3.

2. U.S. Commerce Department, Census Bureau, *Sixteenth Census: 1940. Population Volume IV, Part 1,* 3.

3. U.S. Health and Human Services Department, Public Health Service, Health Resources Administration, National Center for Health Statistics, *100 Years of Marriage,* 1.

4. U.S. Labor Commissioner, *Report on Marriage,* 29.

5. Ibid., 129.

6. Ibid., 55.

7. Ibid., 150.

8. Ibid., 170.

9. S., "Record of Broken Vows," 16.

10. U.S. Interior Department, Census Office, *Report on Population, 1890, Part 1,* clxxix.

11. U.S. Commerce and Labor Department, Census Bureau, *Special Reports: Supplementary Analysis: 1900,* 385.

12. Ibid., 385.

13. Ibid., 443.

14. Ibid., 385.

15. U.S. Commerce Department, Census Bureau, *U.S. Census 1960: Subject Reports: Marital Status.*

16. U.S. Commerce and Labor Department, Census Bureau, *Special Reports: Supplementary Analysis: 1900,* 385.

17. Hacker, "When Saying 'I Do,'" 56–57.

18. Schmeckebier, *Statistical Work,* 64.

19. Hacker, "When Saying 'I Do,'" 58.

20. U.S. Labor Department, Naturalization Bureau, *Annual Report of the Commissioner of Naturalization,* 13.

21. U.S. Commerce and Labor Department, Census Bureau, *Marriage and Divorce 1887–1906,* 41.

22. Ibid., 34.

23. Ibid., 37.

24. Ibid., 47.

25. U.S. Commerce Department, Census Bureau, *200 Years of Census Taking,* 57.

26. U.S. Commerce and Labor Department, Census Bureau, *Census 1910. Volume III,* 1196.

27. U.S. Commerce Department, Census Bureau, *U.S. Census 1950. Volume IV, Part 2. Chapter E,* vii.

28. U.S. Commerce Department, Social and Economic Statistics Administration, Census Bureau, *Census of Population: 1970. Procedural History,* 15–22.

29. U.S. Commerce Department, Census Bureau, *Marriage, Divorce, Widowhood,* 2 and throughout.

30. Mosher, "Fertility and Family Planning," 317.

31. U.S. Health and Human Services Department, Centers for Disease Control and Prevention, National Center for Health Statistics, *About the National Survey of Family Growth.*

32. U.S. Health and Human Services Department, Centers for Disease Control and Prevention, National Center for Health Statistics, *Key Statistics.*

33. U.S. Health and Human Services Department, Public Health Service, Centers for Disease Control, National Center for Health Statistics, *Remarriages and Subsequent Divorces,* 2.

34. U.S. Commerce Department, Census Bureau, "Remarriage among Women," 1.

35. U.S. Commerce Department, Economics and Statistics Administration, Census Bureau, *Frequently Asked Questions,* 1.

36. U.S. Health and Human Services Department, Centers for Disease Control and Prevention, National Center for Health Statistics, *Cohabitation, Marriage, Divorce,* 5.

37. U.S. Commerce Department, Economics and Statistics Administration, Census Bureau, *Marital Events of Americans,* 1.

38. Ibid., 2.

39. U.S. Health and Human Services Department, Centers for Disease Control and Prevention, *First Premarital Cohabitation,* 1.

40. Ibid., 4.

41. Ibid., 5.

42. Ibid., 1.

43. U.S. Commerce Department, Economics and Statistics Administration, Census Bureau, *Same-Sex Couple Households,* 1.

44. Lewis et al., *Measuring Same-Sex Couples,* 2.

45. Ibid., 11–13.

46. U.S. Commerce Department, Economics and Statistics Administration, Census Bureau, *Same Sex Couples Main.*

47. U.S. Commerce Department, Economics and Statistics Administration, Census Bureau, *Changes to the American Community Survey,* 4.

48. U.S. Commerce Department, Economics and Statistics Administration, Census Bureau, *Characteristics of Same Sex Couple Households: Historic Tables,* 1.

49. U.S. Treasury Department, Tax Analysis Office, *Joint Filing by Same-Sex Couples,* 1.

50. Ibid., 11.

51. U.S. Commerce and Labor Department, Statistics Bureau, *Statistical Abstract 1907,* 186.

52. U.S. Commerce and Labor Department, Statistics Bureau, *Statistical Abstract 1908,* 92.

53. U.S. Commerce and Labor Department, Foreign and Domestic Commerce Bureau, *Statistical Abstract 1912,* 92.

54. U.S. Commerce Department, Census Bureau, *Statistical Abstract 1953,* 81.

55. U.S. Commerce Department, Census Bureau, *Statistical Abstract 1955,* 194–95.

56. U.S. Commerce Department, Census Bureau, *Statistical Abstract 1979,* 42.

57. U.S. Commerce Department, Census Bureau, *Statistical Abstract 1977,* 40.

58. U.S. Commerce Department, Economics and Statistics Administration, Census Bureau, *Statistical Abstract 1992,* 93.

59. U.S. Commerce Department, Economics and Statistics Administration, Census Bureau, *Statistical Abstract 2001,* 812.

60. U.S. Commerce Department, Economics and Statistics Administration, Census Bureau, *Statistical Abstract 2002,* 43.

61. U.S. Commerce Department, Economics and Statistics Administration, Census Bureau, *Statistical Abstract 2012,* 74.

Chapter 5 Motherhood

1. U.S. Commerce Department, Census Bureau, *Trends in Child Care Arrangements,* 1.

2. U.S. Interior Department, *Statistics of the United States in 1860,* 247.

3. Wright, *History and Growth,* 94.

4. U.S. Interior Department, Census Office, *Compendium of the Census: 1890. Part III,* 73.

5. U.S. Commerce Department, Census Bureau, *Population: Fertility by Duration,* vii.

6. Ibid., iii.

7. Ibid., vii.

8. U.S. Commerce Department, Census Bureau, *1950 Census: Fertility,* 6.

9. Ibid., 7.

10. Ibid., 11.

11. U.S. Commerce Department, Census Bureau, *U.S. Census 1960: Women by Children,* x.

12. Ibid., 90–99.

13. U.S. Labor Department, Children's Bureau, *Maternal Mortality,* 7.

14. U.S. Labor Department, Children's Bureau, *Mothers' Aid,* 1.

15. Ibid., 8.

16. Waldman and Whitmore, "Children of Working Mothers," 50.

17. U.S. Health, Education, and Welfare Department, Public Health Service, Health Resources Administration, National Center for Health Statistics, *Wanted and Unwanted Births,* 1.

18. U.S. Health, Education, and Welfare Department, Public Health Service, Health, Statistics, and Technology Office, National Center for Health Statistics, *Trends in Breast Feeding,* 2–3.

19. U.S. Health and Human Services Department, Public Health Service, National Center for Health Statistics, *Midwife and Out-of-Hospital Deliveries,* 1.

20. U.S. Health and Human Services Department, Centers for Disease Control and Prevention, *PRAMS.*

21. U.S. Health and Human Services Department, Public Health Service, Centers for Disease Control and Prevention, National Center for Health Statistics, *Health Aspects of Pregnancy,* 1.

22. U.S. Education Department, National Center for Education Statistics, *Fathers' and Mothers' Involvement,* vi.

23. U.S. National Archives and Records Administration, Federal Register Office, *U.S. Government Manual 1988/89,* 303.

24. U.S. Health and Human Services Department, Health Resources and Services Administration, Maternal and Child Health Bureau, *Title V: A Snapshot of Maternal and Child Health 2000,* 5.

25. Aughinbaugh, *Maternal Employment,* abstract page.

26. U.S. Health and Human Services Department, Centers for Disease Control and Prevention, National Center for Health Statistics, *Mean Age of Mothers,* 1.

27. U.S. Commerce Department, Census Bureau, *Statistical Abstract 1940,* 89.

28. U.S. Commerce Department, Census Bureau, *Statistical Abstract 1943,* 89.

29. U.S. Commerce Department, Census Bureau, *Statistical Abstract 1954,* 269.

30. Ibid., 66.

31. U.S. Commerce Department, Census Bureau, *Statistical Abstract 1957,* 397.

32. U.S. Commerce Department, Census Bureau, *Statistical Abstract 1958,* 41.

33. U.S. Commerce Department, Census Bureau, *Statistical Abstract 1960,* 215.

34. U.S. Commerce Department, Social and Economic Statistics Administration, Census Bureau, *Statistical Abstracts 1973,* 55.

35. U.S. Commerce Department, Census Bureau, *Statistical Abstract 1978,* 142.

36. U.S. Commerce Department, Census Bureau, *Statistical Abstract 1980,* 51 and 259.

37. Ibid., 52.

38. U.S. Commerce Department, Census Bureau, *Statistical Abstract 1986,* 60–61.

39. U.S. Commerce Department, Economics and Statistics Administration, Census Bureau, *Statistical Abstract 1995,* 83.

40. U.S. Commerce Department, Economics and Statistics Administration, Census Bureau, *Statistical Abstract 1996,* 78.

41. U.S. Commerce Department, Economics and Statistics Administration, Census Bureau, *Statistical Abstract 2012,* 70–72.

Chapter 6   Single Mothers

1. U.S. USAGov, *USA.gov,* and U.S. Health and Human Services Department, Centers for Disease Control and Prevention, National Center for Health Statistics, *Unmarried Childbearing.*

2. U.S Commerce Department, Census Bureau, *200 Years of Census Taking,* various pages.

3. U.S. Interior Department, Census Office, *Report on Crime, Pauperism, and Benevolence, Part 2,* 859–60 and 1012–13.

4. U.S. Labor Department, Children's Bureau, *Children of Illegitimate Birth and Measures,* 1.

5. U.S. Labor Department, Children's Bureau, *Children of Illegitimate Birth Whose Mothers Have Kept Their Custody,* 1.

6. U.S. Commerce Department, Census Bureau, *Differential Fertility 1940 and 1910: Women by Number of Children Ever Born,* 2.

7. U.S. Commerce Department, Census Bureau, *Census 1960: Women by Number of Children Ever Born,* x.

8. U.S. Commerce Department, Census Bureau, *200 Years of Census Taking,* 83.

9. U.S. Commerce Department, Census Bureau, *1970 Census of Population: Subject Reports: Childspacing,* xiii–iv.

10. Cutright, "Illegitimacy and Income Supplements," 90.

11. Ibid., 91.

12. Krause, "Child Welfare, Parental Responsibility," 256.

13. U.S. Health, Education, and Welfare Department, Public Health Service, Health Resources Administration, National Center for Health Statistics, *Trends in Illegitimacy,* 16.

14. U.S. Commerce Department, Census Bureau, *Premarital Fertility,* 1.

15. Ibid., 5.

16. U.S. Commerce Department, Census Bureau, *1980 Census, Users' Guide,* 1.

17. U.S. Health and Human Services Department, Public Health Service, National Center for Health Statistics, *Trends in Teenage Childbearing,* 6.

18. U.S. Commerce Department, Economics and Statistics Administration, Census Bureau, *Households, Families, and Children,* 10.

19. U.S. Health and Human Services Department, Centers for Disease Control and Prevention, National Center for Health Statistics, *Report to Congress.*

20. Moore, "Nonmarital Childbearing in the United States," viii.

21. U.S. Commerce Department, Economics and Statistics Administration, Census Bureau, *Trends in Marital Status,* Abstract.

22. U.S. Congress, House, Ways and Means Committee, *2004 Green Book,* M-9.

23. Kreider, "Differences in Statistics."

24. U.S. Commerce Department, Foreign and Domestic Commerce Bureau, *Statistical Abstract 1935,* 79.

25. U.S. Commerce Department, Census Bureau, *Statistical Abstract 1957,* iv.

26. U.S. Commerce Department, Census Bureau, *Statistical Abstract 1976,* 58.

27. U.S. Commerce Department, Census Bureau, *Statistical Abstract 1968*, 40.

28. U.S. Commerce Department, Economics and Statistics Administration, Census Bureau, *Statistical Abstract 1991*, 55.

29. U.S. Commerce Department, Census Bureau, *Statistical Abstract 1977*, 61.

30. U.S. Commerce Department, Census Bureau, *Statistical Abstract 1990*, 67.

31. U.S. Commerce Department, Census Bureau, *Statistical Abstract 1979*, 65.

32. U.S. Commerce Department, Economics and Statistics Administration, Census Bureau, *Statistical Abstract 1996*, 303.

Chapter 7   Heads of Household, Heads of Family

1. "Why—and How—We Should Queer the Census," 10.

2. See, for example, U.S. Commerce Department, Economics and Statistics Administration, Census Bureau, *Households and Families: 2010*, 7.

3. Presser, "Decapitating the U.S. Census," 145.

4. Goldin, "Household and Market Production," 113.

5. Folbre and Abel, "Women's Work and Women's Households," 565.

6. U.S. Commerce and Labor Department, Census Bureau, *Statistics of Women at Work*, 25.

7. Ibid., 28.

8. U.S. Commerce Department, Census Bureau, *Abstract of the Fifteenth Census*, 402.

9. Ibid., 38.

10. U.S. Commerce Department, Census Bureau, *Sixteenth Census: Population Volume IV, Part 1*, 5.

11. U.S. Commerce Department, Census Bureau, *U.S. Census of Population 1950. Volume IV, Part 2. Chapter A*, xi.

12. Ibid., 2A-44.

13. Presser, "Decapitating the U.S. Census," 148.

14. U.S. Commerce Department, Census Bureau, *Female Family Heads*, 1.

15. Presser, "Decapitating the U.S. Census," 146.

16. Ibid., 148.

17. Ibid., 148–49.

18. Ibid., 152.

19. Ibid., 149.

20. Barrett, "Data Needs For Evaluating," 13.

21. Norwood, "New Approaches to Statistics," 32.

22. U.S. Labor Department, Women's Bureau, *Facts about Women Heads*, 1.

23. U.S. Commerce Department, Census Bureau, *Families Maintained by Female Householders 1970–79*, 1.

24. Johnson and Waldman, "Most Women Who Maintain Families," 33.

25. U.S. Justice Department, Justice Programs Office, Bureau of Justice Statistics, *Criminal Victimization 2003*, 26.

26. Bricker et al., "Changes in U.S. Family," 32.

27. U.S. Federal Reserve System. *Janet L. Yellen.*

28. U.S. Treasury Department, Internal Revenue Service, *Publication 501,* 8.

29. U.S. Commerce Department, Census Bureau, *Statistical Abstract 1944/5,* 2.

30. U.S. Commerce Department, Economics and Statistics Administration, Census Bureau, *Statistical Abstract 2012,* 469, etc.

31. U.S. Commerce Department, Census Bureau, *Statistical Abstract 1947,* 35.

32. See, for example, U.S. Commerce Department, Census Bureau, *Statistical Abstract 1948,* 248; U.S. Commerce Department, Census Bureau, *Statistical Abstract 1951,* 269; and U.S. Commerce Department, Census Bureau, *Statistical Abstract 1954,* 263.

33. U.S. Commerce Department, Census Bureau, *Statistical Abstract 1980,* 3.

34. Ibid., 51.

35. U.S. Commerce Department, Economics and Statistics Administration, Census Bureau, *Statistical Abstract 2003,* 64.

Chapter 8 Housewives, Homemakers, and Housekeepers

1. U.S. Labor Department, Women's Bureau, *Report on 1948 Women's Bureau Conference,* 1.

2. U.S. Health, Education, and Welfare Department, Education Office, *Management Problems of Homemakers Employed outside the Home.*

3. Folbre and Abel, "Women's Work and Women's Households," 564.

4. U.S. Labor Department, Women's Bureau, *Women's Occupations through Seven Decades,* 53.

5. U.S. Congress, Senate, *Memorial of Mary F. Eastman,* 1.

6. Association for the Advancement of Women, *Historical Account of the Association,* 9. It is not clear whether those last four words are a quotation from Walker.

7. Carter and Sutch, "Fixing the Facts," no page numbers.

8. Smuts, "Female Labor Force," 76.

9. Ibid., 73.

10. Ibid., 74–75.

11. U.S. Commerce and Labor Department, Census Bureau, *Special Reports: Supplementary Analysis and Derivative Tables: 1900,* 439–40.

12. U.S. Commerce Department, Census Bureau, *200 Years of Census Taking,* 52.

13. Folbre and Abel, "Women's Work and Women's Households," 549.

14. U.S. Commerce Department, Census Bureau, *Thirteenth Census: 1910,* 15.

15. U.S. Commerce Department, Census Bureau, *Alphabetical Index to Occupations 1920,* 11.

16. U.S. Commerce Department, Census Bureau, *Women in Gainful Occupations,* 2.

17. Barlow, "She Looketh Well," 621.

18. Adkinson, "Industrial Progress of Woman," 224.

19. U.S. Commerce Department, Census Bureau, *Women in Gainful Occupations*, 2.

20. Ibid., 4.

21. Ibid., 5–6.

22. U.S. Commerce Department, Census Bureau, *Abstract of the Fifteenth Census: 1930*, 402.

23. Ibid., 402.

24. Ibid., 413–14.

25. U.S. Commerce Department, Census Bureau, *Sixteenth Census: Usual Occupation*, 2.

26. Hautaniemi, "Technology, Women's Labor," 111.

27. U.S. Labor Department, Women's Bureau, *Domestic Employment*, 1.

28. Ibid., 2.

29. Ibid., 55.

30. Kyrk, "Family Responsibilities of Earning Women," 65.

31. Folbre and Abel, "Women's Work and Women's Households," 557.

32. U.S. Commerce Department, Census Bureau, *1950 Censuses: How They Were Taken*, 58.

33. U.S. National Commission on the Observance of International Women's Year, *American Women Today and Tomorrow*, 12.

34. Ibid., 14.

35. U.S. Social Security Administration, *Economic Value of a Housewife*, 1.

36. Ibid., 2.

37. Love, "How Do You Put a Price Tag," 40.

38. Barrett, "Data Needs for Evaluating," 13.

39. Carucci and Prasad, "Comparison of Mothers' Occupations," 435.

40. Folbre and Abel, "Women's Work and Women's Households," 548.

41. U.S. Health and Human Services Department, Centers for Disease Control and Prevention, National Center for Health Statistics, *Women: Work and Health*, 10–11.

42. Waring, *If Women Counted*, 41.

43. U.S. Treasury Department, Statistics Bureau, *Statistical Abstract 1902*, 496.

44. U.S. Commerce Department, Foreign and Domestic Commerce Bureau, *Statistical Abstract 1934*, 263.

45. U.S. Commerce Department, Census Bureau, *Statistical Abstract 1966*, 915–16.

46. U.S. Commerce Department, Census Bureau, *Statistical Abstract 1968*, 304.

47. U.S. Commerce Department, Economics and Statistics Administration, Census Bureau, *Statistical Abstract 2012*, 415.

Chapter 9 "Occupations Suitable for Women"

1. Conk, "Accuracy, Efficiency and Bias," 70.

2. Conk, *United States Census and Labor Force Change*, 9.

3. Conk, "Accuracy, Efficiency, and Bias," 65.

4. U.S. Interior Department, *Manufactures of the United States in 1860,* clxxiii.

5. Geib-Gunderson, *Uncovering the Hidden Work,* 3.

6. Rotella, *From Home to Office,* 123–24.

7. Conk, *United States Census and Labor Force Change,* 15.

8. Conk, "Accuracy, Efficiency, and Bias," 67.

9. Ibid., 68.

10. Ibid., 68.

11. Ibid., 68.

12. U.S. Commerce and Labor Department, Census Bureau, *Statistics of Women at Work,* 31.

13. Ibid., 32–33.

14. Ibid., 97.

15. U.S. Commerce Department, Census Bureau, *Alphabetical Index to Occupations 1920,* 3.

16. Conk, "Accuracy, Efficiency, and Bias," 68.

17. Meyer, "Who Had an Occupation?" 157.

18. Edwards, "Social-Economic Groups of the United States," 653.

19. U.S. Commerce Department, Census Bureau, *Thirteenth Census: Volume IV,* 22–23.

20. U.S. Commerce Department, Census Bureau, *Alphabetical Index to Occupations 1920,* 11. "Ladler" is out of order in the original.

21. U.S. Commerce Department, Census Bureau, *Women in Gainful Occupations, 1870 to 1920,* 46.

22. U.S. Commerce Department, Census Bureau, *Fifteenth Census: 1930, Population: Volume V,* 30.

23. Ibid., 132.

24. U.S. Commerce Department, Census Bureau, *Alphabetical Index to Occupations 1930,* 11.

25. U.S. Commerce Department, Census Bureau, *Fifteenth Census: 1930, Population: Volume V,* 6.

26. Ibid., 6.

27. U.S. Labor Department, Women's Bureau, *"Equal Pay" for Women,* 2.

28. U.S. Labor Department, Women's Bureau, *Occupational Progress of Women,* 12.

29. U.S. Interior Department, Education Office, *Symposium on Home and Family Life,* 2.

30. Conk, "Accuracy, Efficiency, and Bias," 69.

31. U.S. Commerce Department, Census Bureau, *Population Comparative Occupation Statistics,* 23.

32. Conk, "Accuracy, Efficiency, and Bias," 69–70.

33. U.S. Commerce Department, Census Bureau, *Population Comparative Occupation Statistics,* 175.

34. U.S. Government Reports Office, Information Service, *U.S. Government Manual July 1940,* 315.

35. U.S. Labor Department, Employment Service, *Occupations Suitable for Women,* vii.

36. Ibid., vii.

37. U.S. Labor Department, Employment Service, *Dictionary of Occupational Titles. Part I,* xvi.

38. U.S. Labor Department, Employment Service, *Occupations Suitable for Women,* viii.

39. Ibid., 9–47.

40. Ibid., 51–73.

41. U.S. Commerce Department, Census Bureau, *U.S. Census of Population: 1950, Occupational Characteristics,* 15–22.

42. Strober, "Comments," 35; U.S. Commerce Department, Census Bureau, *Census of Population: 1970. Occupational Characteristics,* ix.

43. U.S. Commerce Department, Census Bureau, *Census of Population: 1970. Occupational Characteristics,* ix.

44. Ibid., ix.

45. Conk, "Accuracy, Efficiency, and Bias," 70.

46. U.S. Commerce Department, Federal Statistical Policy and Standards Office, *Standard Occupational Classification Manual.*

47. U.S. Treasury Department, Statistics Bureau, *Statistical Abstract 1895,* 12.

48. U.S. Treasury Department, Statistics Bureau, *Statistical Abstract 1902,* 495–98.

Chapter 10 Gainful Employment

1. U.S. Labor Department, Women's Bureau, *Women's Occupations through Seven Decades,* 53.

2. U.S. Interior Department, Census Office, *Compendium of the Ninth Census,* 594.

3. U.S. Interior Department, Census Office, *Ninth Census Volume I,* 660.

4. U.S. Interior Department, Census Office, *Compendium of the Ninth Census,* 650.

5. U.S. Interior Department, Census Office, *Ninth Census Volume I,* 660–61.

6. U.S. Interior Department, Census Office, *Compendium of the Ninth Census,* 650.

7. Anderson, "History of Women," 23.

8. U.S. Interior Department, Census Office, *Ninth Census Volume I,* 660–61.

9. Ibid., 660.

10. U.S. Interior Department, Census Office, *Ninth Census Volume 3,* 375.

11. Anderson, "History of Women," 26.

12. Ciancanelli, *Women's Transition to Wage Labor,* 41–43.

13. Geib-Gunderson, *Uncovering the Hidden Work,* 24.

14. Ciancanelli, *Women's Transition to Wage Labor,* 52.

15. Goldin, "Household and Market Production," 14.

16. U.S. Commerce Department, Economics and Statistics Administration, Census Bureau, *Measuring America,* 51.

17. U.S. Labor Department, Women's Bureau, *Family Status of Breadwinning Women,* 1.

18. Ibid., 5–6.

19. U.S. Commerce and Labor Department, Census Bureau, *Special Reports: 1900,* 439–40.

20. Ibid., 442.

21. Ciancanelli, *Women's Transition to Wage Labor,* 62.

22. U.S. Commerce and Labor Department, Census Bureau, *Statistics of Women at Work,* 9.

23. Ciancanelli, *Women's Transition to Wage Labor,* 71; Wells, *Consumerism and the Movement,* 8.

24. U.S. Commerce Department, Census Bureau, *Thirteenth Census, Volume IV,* 26–28.

25. Ibid., 27.

26. Durand, "Development of the Labor Force Concept," 80.

27. Ciancanelli, *Women's Transition to Wage Labor,* 18.

28. Jaffe, "Trends in the Participation," 560.

29. Smuts, "Female Labor Force," 73.

30. Ciancanelli, *Women's Transition to Wage Labor,* 17.

31. U.S. Commerce Department, Census Bureau, *Abstract of the Fourteenth Census 1920,* 480.

32. U.S. Commerce Department, Census Bureau, *Women in Gainful Occupations,* 2.

33. Ibid., 30.

34. U.S. Commerce Department, Census Bureau, *Sixteenth Census: Comparative Occupation Statistics,* 139.

35. U.S. Commerce Department, Census Bureau, *Sixteenth Census: Comparative Occupation Statistics,* 137–39.

36. Smuts, "Female Labor Force," 74.

37. U.S. Commerce Department, Census Bureau, *Sixteenth Census: Comparative Occupation Statistics,* 90.

38. Folbre and Abel, "Women's Work and Women's Households," 549.

39. U.S. Commerce Department, Census Bureau, *Sixteenth Census: Comparative Occupation Statistics,* 7.

40. Ciancanelli, *Women's Transition to Wage Labor,* 41.

41. U.S. Treasury Department, Statistics Bureau, *Statistical Abstract 1902,* 495–98.

42. U.S. Commerce Department, Census Bureau, *Statistical Abstract 1944/5,* 121–22.

43. U.S. Commerce Department, Census Bureau, *Statistical Abstract 1960,* 202.

44. U.S. Commerce Department, Economics and Statistics Administration, Census Bureau, *Statistical Abstract 2003,* 375.

Chapter 11 Income

1. Allen, "Rochester Teachers Convention of 1847," 534. Allen was an eye-witness to the event that, in spite of the title, actually occurred in 1853.

2. Shepela and Viviano, "Some Psychological Factors," 47.

3. Walker, "American Industry in the Census," 694–95.

4. U.S. Labor Commissioner, *Working Women in Large Cities,* 70.

5. Ibid., 72.

6. Ibid., 73.

7. U.S. Labor Department, Bureau of Labor Statistics, *First Hundred Years,* 30–31.

8. Ibid., 26.

9. U.S. Labor Commissioner, *Work and Wages,* 516.

10. Ibid., 28.

11. Wright, "Why Women Are Paid," 634–35.

12. Ibid., 637.

13. U.S. Congress, House, Committee, *Statistics of Income 1916,* 6.

14. U.S. Labor Department, Bureau of Labor Statistics, *Summary of the Report,* 24.

15. Ibid., 23.

16. Ibid., 20.

17. Anderson, *Woman at Work,* 139.

18. U.S. Labor Department, Women's Bureau, *What the Wage Earning Woman,* 1.

19. Ibid., 2.

20. Ibid., 5.

21. Ibid., 10.

22. Ibid., 11.

23. U.S. Labor Department, Bureau of Labor Statistics, *Handbook of Labor Statistics 1924–26,* 37.

24. Ibid., 648.

25. Ibid., 339.

26. U.S. Labor Department, Women's Bureau, *Differences in the Earnings,* unnumbered page.

27. Ibid., 4.

28. Ibid., 8.

29. U.S. Commerce Department, Census Bureau, *200 Years of Census Taking,* 5.

30. U.S. Commerce Department, Census Bureau, *Sixteenth Census: 1940. Population. Volume III. Part I,* 12.

31. Truman, "The President's First Economic Report," 31.

32. *Equal Pay Act,* §§206(d).

33. Nelson and Bridges, *Legalizing Gender Equality,* 12.

34. *Civil Rights Act of 1964,* §§2000e et seq.

35. U.S. General Accounting Office, *Options for Conducting,* ii.

36. U.S. National Commission on the Observance of International Women's Year, *American Women Today and Tomorrow,* 17 and 14.

37. Jaffe and Spirer, *Misused Statistics,* 182.

38. Bell, "Comparative Worth," 5.

39. Ibid., 6–7.

40. *American Federation of State, County, and Municipal Employees v. Washington,* 578 F. Supp. 846, rev'd 770 F. 2d. 1401 (1985).

41. U.S. General Accounting Office, *Response to Questions,* 1.

42. U.S. Commerce Department, Economics and Statistics Administration, Census Bureau, *Evidence from Census 2000,* 12.

43. Ibid., 12.

44. Ibid., 21.

45. See, for example, U.S. Labor Department, Bureau of Labor Statistics, *Highlights of Women's Earnings,* 1; U.S. Labor Department, Women's Bureau, *Equal Pay,* 14; U.S. Civil Rights Commission, *Comparable Worth,* 2; U.S. Commerce Department, Economics and Statistics Administration, Census Bureau, *Evidence from Census 2000,* 11; U.S. Executive Office of the President, Council of Economic Advisers, *Gender Pay Gap,* 1.

46. U.S. Congress, Joint Economic Committee, *Gender Pay Inequality,* 12–20.

47. U.S. Commerce Department, Census Bureau, *Statistical Abstract 1964,* 340.

48. U.S. Commerce Department, Census Bureau, *Statistical Abstract 1967,* 336.

49. Ibid., 240.

50. U.S. Commerce Department, Census Bureau, *Statistical Abstract 1969,* 327.

51. U.S. Commerce Department, Census Bureau, *Statistical Abstract 1970,* 333.

52. U.S. Commerce Department, Social and Economic Statistics Administration, Census Bureau, *Statistical Abstract 1973,* 333.

Chapter 12 Unemployment during the Great Depression

1. Cortada, *All the Facts,* 135.

2. Jaffe and Spirer, *Misused Statistics,* 117–18.

3. Ibid., 118–19.

4. U.S. Labor Department, Women's Bureau, *Occupational Progress of Women,* 2.

5. Hartmann et al., *Women and Men in the Recovery,* 1–2.

6. U.S. Commerce Department, Census Bureau, *Sixteenth Census: 1940: Population: Estimates of Labor Force,* 3.

7. Rayman, "Women and Unemployment," 355–56.

8. Wandersee, *Women's Work and Family Values,* 92–93.

9. U.S. Labor Department, Women's Bureau, *Employment Fluctuations,* 1.

10. U.S. Commerce Department, Census Bureau, *Abstract of the Fifteenth Census: 1930,* 459–60.

11. U.S. Labor Department, Women's Bureau, *Employment Fluctuations,* 5.

12. U.S. Labor Department, Bureau of Labor Statistics, *Handbook of Labor Statistics 1936*, 1095.

13. U.S. Labor Department, Women's Bureau, *Employment Fluctuations*, 19.

14. U.S. Labor Department, Bureau of Labor Statistics, *Handbook of Labor Statistics 1936*, 1093.

15. Ibid., 1093.

16. Rayman, "Women and Unemployment," 359.

17. U.S. Commerce Department, Census Bureau, *Sixteenth Census: 1940. Population Volume IV. Part 1*, 179.

18. Ibid., 179–80.

19. U.S. Commerce Department, Census Bureau, *Sixteenth Census: 1940: Usual Occupation*, 2.

20. U.S. Commerce Department, Census Bureau, *Sixteenth Census: 1940: Population: Estimates of Labor Force*, 17.

21. Ibid., 17.

22. U.S. Commerce Department, Foreign and Domestic Commerce Bureau, *Statistical Abstract 1931*, 365–68.

23. U.S. Commerce Department, Foreign and Domestic Commerce Bureau, *Statistical Abstract 1935*, 326.

Chapter 13 The Bureau of Labor Statistics and the Women's Bureau

1. U.S. Labor Department, Bureau of Labor Statistics, *First Hundred Years*, 4–5.

2. Ibid., 3.

3. Ibid., 9.

4. Wright, "Why Women Are Paid," 629.

5. Ibid., 630–31.

6. Anderson, "Census and the Federal Statistical System," 157–58.

7. U.S. Labor Department, Bureau of Labor Statistics, *BLS History*.

8. U.S. Labor Department, Bureau of Labor Statistics, *First Hundred Years*, 62–69.

9. Schiffman, "Marital Status of Workers," 1.

10. U.S. Labor Department, Bureau of Labor Statistics, *First Hundred Years*, 164.

11. Finlay, *George W. Bush*, 50–51.

12. Institute for Women's Policy Research, *Statement by IWPR*.

13. Groves, "News and Views," 199.

14. U.S. Labor Department, Bureau of Labor Statistics, *Reconstruction of the Women Worker Series*.

15. U.S. Labor Department, Bureau of Labor Statistics, *Bureau of Labor Statistics*.

16. U.S. Labor Department, Bureau of Labor Statistics, *First Hundred Years*, 67.

17. Ibid., 87.

18. U.S. Congress, Senate, "Bureau of Woman Labor," 4.

19. U.S. Labor Department, Women in Industry Service, *First Annual Report*, 6.

20. Ibid., 25.

21. U.S. Labor Department, Women's Bureau, *Our History*.

22. "Federal Standards for the Employment," 216.

23. Ibid., 217–18.

24. U.S. Labor Department, Women's Bureau, *Our History*.

25. 29 U.S.C. § 12 (2016).

26. U.S. Labor Department, Women's Bureau, *Milestones*, 1.

27. U.S. Labor Department, Women's Bureau, *Fourth Annual Report*, 15.

28. Woloch, *Class by Herself*, 112 and 130.

29. U.S. Labor Department, Women's Bureau, *Eleventh Annual Report*, 13.

30. U.S. Labor Department, Women's Bureau, *Milestones*, 31.

31. Woloch, *Class by Herself*, 186–87.

32. U.S. Labor Department, Workplace Standards Administration, Women's Bureau, *Underutilization of Women Workers*, iii.

33. U.S. Labor Department, Women's Bureau, *Women's Bureau: Meeting*, 1.

34. Finlay, *George W. Bush*, 17.

35. National Council for Research on Women, *Missing*, 12.

36. Ibid., 5.

37. Ibid., 14.

38. Ibid., 13.

39. U.S. Labor Department, Women's Bureau, *Overview*.

40. U.S. Commerce and Labor Department, Statistics Bureau, *Statistical Abstract 1904*, 39.

41. U.S. Commerce and Labor Department, Statistics Bureau, *Statistical Abstract 1905*, 122.

42. U.S. Commerce Department, Foreign and Domestic Commerce Bureau, *Statistical Abstract 1913*, 249, etc.

43. U.S. Commerce Department, Foreign and Domestic Commerce Bureau, *Statistical Abstract 1923*, 693.

44. U.S. Commerce Department, Census Bureau, *Statistical Abstract 1956*, 991.

Chapter 14 Employment

1. U.S. Congress, Senate, *Report on Condition of Woman: Volume 9*, 11.

2. Wright, *History and Growth*, 310.

3. Ibid., 37.

4. Hunt, "Federal Census of Occupations," 469.

5. Ibid., 470.

6. U.S. Interior Department, *Ninth Census Volume 1*, 375.

7. U.S. Interior Department, Census Office, *Compendium 1880, Volume 2*, 1344.

8. U.S. Interior Department, Census Office, *Statistics of the Population 1880,* 1345.

9. Carter and Sutch, "Fixing the Facts," no page numbers.

10. Ibid.

11. Ibid.

12. Geib-Gunderson, *Uncovering the Hidden Work,* 21.

13. U.S. Commissioner of Labor, *Working Women in Large Cities,* 9.

14. Ibid., 9–10.

15. Ibid., 62.

16. Ibid., 63.

17. Ibid., 64.

18. Ibid., 67.

19. Ibid., 64.

20. Goldin, *Understanding the Gender Gap,* 228.

21. Conk, "Accuracy, Efficiency and Bias," 65.

22. U.S. Interior Department, Census Office, *Report on Population: 1890, Part II,* cxxxi.

23. U.S. Interior Department, Census Office, *Statistical Atlas, 1890,* 46.

24. Goldin, *Understanding the Gender Gap,* 43 and 45.

25. Ciancanelli, *Women's Transition to Wage Labor,* 61.

26. U.S. Commerce Department, Census Bureau, *Thirteenth Census: Volume IV,* 16.

27. Abbott, *Women in Industry,* 356.

28. U.S. Commerce Department, Census Bureau, *Thirteenth Census, Volume IV,* 27.

29. U.S. Commerce Department, Census Bureau, *Thirteenth Census, Volume IV,* 62; U.S. Labor Department, Women's Bureau, *Women's Occupations through Seven Decades,* 179; U.S. Labor Department, Bureau of Labor Statistics, *Women in Domestic Work,* 17.

30. U.S. Congress, Senate, *Report on Condition of Woman: Volume 5,* 5.

31. U.S. Labor Department, Bureau of Labor Statistics, *First Hundred Years,* 64.

32. U.S. Labor Department, Bureau of Labor Statistics, *Summary of the Report.*

33. Ibid., 14.

34. Ibid., 209–10.

35. U.S. Congress, Senate, *Report on Condition of Woman: Volume 5,* 11.

36. Ibid., 53.

37. U.S. Labor Department, Bureau of Labor Statistics, *Summary of the Report,* 224.

38. Folbre and Abel, "Women's Work and Women's Households," 561.

39. U.S. Commerce and Labor Department, Census Bureau, *Statistics of Women at Work,* 7.

40. Ibid., 31.

41. Ibid., 9–10.

42. Ibid., 11.

43. Ibid., 11.

44. U.S. Labor Department, Bureau of Labor Statistics, *Summary of the Report,* 14.

45. U.S. Labor Department, Bureau of Labor Statistics, *First Hundred Years,* 36.

46. Smith, "Survey of Employment Conditions," 173.

47. U.S. Labor Department, Women's Bureau, *Night-Work Laws,* 2.

48. Ibid., 3.

49. Ibid., 4.

50. *Adkins v. Children's Hospital,* 261 U.S. 525.

51. U.S. Labor Department, Bureau of Labor Statistics, *Handbook of Labor Statistics 1924–26,* 639.

52. Ibid., 788.

53. U.S. Labor Department, Women's Bureau, *Occupational Progress of Women,* 3.

54. Ibid., 2.

55. Ciancanelli, *Women's Transition to Wage Labor,* 49.

56. Geib-Gunderson, *Uncovering the Hidden Work,* 20.

57. Ciancanelli, *Women's Transition to Wage Labor,* 61–62.

58. U.S. Labor Department, Bureau of Labor Statistics, *CES Overview;* U.S. Labor Department, Bureau of Labor Statistics, *First Hundred Years,* 164.

59. U.S. Commerce Department, Census Bureau, *Social-Economic Grouping,* 8.

60. U.S. Commerce Department, Census Bureau, *Census of Population: 1940. Characteristics of Persons,* 8.

61. U.S. Commerce Department, Census Bureau, *Sixteenth Census 1940: Comparative Occupation Statistics,* 92.

62. U.S. Labor Department, Bureau of Labor Statistics, *Handbook of Labor Statistics 1941 Volume 1,* 1960.

63. Ibid., 961.

64. Ibid., 61.

65. Ibid., 971–72.

66. U.S. Labor Department, Women's Bureau, *Women Workers in Their Family Environment,* 1.

67. Ibid., 5.

68. Ibid., 13.

69. U.S. Labor Department, Bureau of Labor Statistics, *Tables of Working Life for Women, 1950,* iii.

70. Ibid., 1–2.

71. Ibid., 7.

72. U.S. Commerce Department, Social and Economic Statistics Bureau, Census Bureau, *Census of Population: 1970. Procedural History,* 12–80.

73. U.S. Labor Department, Bureau of Labor Statistics, *Handbook of Labor Statistics 1985,* 38–39.

74. Nixon, *Economic Report of the President, 1973,* 90.

75. Ibid., 89–112.

76. Ibid., 89.

77. Ibid., 92–93.

78. U.S. Labor Department, Employment and Training Administration, *Women in Traditionally Male Jobs,* 9.

79. U.S. Health, Education, and Welfare Department, Public Health Service, Health Resources Administration, Office of Health Resources Opportunity, *Study of the Participation,* i.

80. U.S. Labor Department, Women's Bureau, *Milestones,* 34.

81. U.S. National Advisory Committee on Women's Education Programs, *Working Women Speak,* 1.

82. Oppenheimer, *Female Labor Force,* 70, 67.

83. Barrett, "Data Needs for Evaluating," 12.

84. Ibid., 16.

85. U.S. Labor Department, Bureau of Labor Statistics, *Women in the Labor Force,* 4.

86. Ibid., 4.

87. Ibid., 4.

88. U.S. Merit Systems Protection Board, *Question of Equity,* ix.

89. Ibid., 19.

90. U.S. White House Council on Women and Girls, *Keeping America's Women Moving Forward,* i.

91. U.S. Treasury Department, Statistics Bureau, *Statistical Abstract 1895,* 12.

92. U.S. Commerce and Labor Department, Statistics Bureau, *Statistical Abstract 1907,* 184–85.

93. U.S. Commerce Department, Census Bureau, *Statistical Abstract 1960,* 214.

94. U.S. Commerce Department, Social and Economic Statistics Administration, Census Bureau, *Statistical Abstract 1972,* iii–iv.

95. U.S. Commerce Department, Social and Economic Statistics Administration, Census Bureau, *Statistical Abstract 1972,* 218; U.S. Commerce Department, Census Bureau, *Statistical Abstract 1962,* 226.

Chapter 15   Women Factory Workers

1. U.S. Congress, Senate, *Report on Condition of Woman, Volume 9,* 17.

2. Ibid., 19.

3. Wright, *History and Growth,* 310.

4. U.S. Interior Department, Census Office, *Ninth Census Volume 3,* 801.

5. U.S. Interior Department, Census Office, *Compendium 1880,* 1349.

6. Ibid., xviii.

7. U.S. Interior Department, Census Office, *Statistics of the Population 1880,* 1344.

8. U.S. Interior Department, Census Office, *Report on the Manufactures 1880,* xxxiv.

9. Wright, "Report on the Factory System," 20.

10. Ibid., 20.

11. Ibid., 23.

12. Ibid., 24–26.

13. U.S. Labor Department, Bureau of Labor Statistics, *Commissioners: Carroll D. Wright.*

14. U.S. Labor Commissioner, *Working Women in Large Cities,* 10.

15. Ibid., 9.

16. Ibid., 24.

17. Ibid., 387–91.

18. U.S. Labor Department, Bureau of Labor Statistics, *First Hundred Years,* 30–31.

19. U.S. Labor Commissioner, *Work and Wages,* 18.

20. Ibid., 30.

21. Ibid., 30–31.

22. U.S. Labor Department, Bureau of Labor Statistics, *Summary of the Report,* 28–29.

23. U.S. Labor Department, Bureau of Labor Statistics, *First Hundred Years,* 68.

24. Ibid., 68.

25. U.S. Congress, Senate, *Report on Condition of Woman: Volume 1,* 289–90.

26. Ibid., 540–41.

27. Ibid., 358–67.

28. Ibid., 590.

29. U.S. Commerce and Labor Department, *Report on Condition of Woman, Volume 15,* 10.

30. U.S. Labor Department, Bureau of Labor Statistics, *Handbook of Labor Statistics 1924–26,* 642.

31. Ibid., 581.

32. U.S. Labor Department, Bureau of Labor Statistics, *Handbook of Labor Statistics 1941,* 483–85.

33. U.S. Treasury Department, Statistics Bureau, *Statistical Abstract 1895,* 12.

34. U.S. Treasury Department, Statistics Bureau, *Statistical Abstract 1902,* 495–98.

Chapter 16 "Farm Females"

1. U.S. Agriculture Department, Statistics Bureau, *Wages of Farm Labor,* 71.

2. Ibid., 72.

3. Ibid., 72.

4. U.S. Agriculture Department, *Report of the Commissioner 1871,* 336.

5. Ibid., 336–46.

6. U.S. Commerce and Labor Department, Census Bureau, *Statistics of Women at Work,* 122–23.

7. Ibid., 126.

8. U.S. Congress, Senate, *Report of the Country Life Commission,* 3.

9. Gilman, "That Rural Home Inquiry," 120–21.

10. Knowles, "It's Our Turn Now," 305.

11. U.S. Congress, Senate, *Report of the Country Life Commission,* 47.

12. U.S. Commerce Department, Census Bureau, *Thirteenth Census: 1910, Volume IV*, 27.

13. Ciancanelli, *Women's Transition*, 72.

14. U.S. Commerce Department, Census Bureau, *Thirteenth Census: 1910, Volume IV*, 27.

15. Social Explorer, *Census Questionnaires and Instructions*.

16. U.S. Commerce Department, Census Bureau, *Thirteenth Census: 1910, Volume IV*, 27.

17. Folbre and Abel, "Women's Work and Women's Households," 552.

18. Ciancanelli, *Women's Transition*, 73.

19. Holmes, "Supply and Wages," 192–93.

20. U.S. Agriculture Department, Statistics Bureau, *Supply of Farm Labor*, 13–16.

21. U.S. Agriculture Department, Statistics Bureau, *Wages of Farm Labor*, 70.

22. Poe, "Clarence Hamilton Poe"; U.S. Agriculture Department, Information Office, *Social and Labor Needs*, 5.

23. U.S. Agriculture Department, Information Office, *Social and Labor Needs*, 7.

24. Ibid., 11.

25. Ibid., 8.

26. Ibid., various pages.

27. Knowles, "It's Our Turn Now," 308.

28. Ibid., 308–9.

29. U.S. Agriculture Department, National Institute of Food and Agriculture, *Cooperative Extension History*.

30. U.S. Agriculture Department, *Farm Woman's Problems*, 3.

31. Ibid., 6.

32. Ibid., 7.

33. Ibid., 7–9.

34. Ibid., 10.

35. Ibid., 11.

36. Ibid., 14.

37. U.S. Commerce Department, Census Bureau, *Fourteenth Census: 1920, Volume II*, 1383–84.

38. U.S. Commerce Department, Census Bureau, *Women in Gainful Occupations*, 16–17.

39. Ciancanelli, *Women's Transition*, 77.

40. Kneeland, "Leisure of Home Makers," 562.

41. Ibid., 563.

42. University of Minnesota, Minnesota Population Center, "1940 Census: Instructions."

43. U.S. Commerce Department, Census Bureau, *Women in Gainful Occupations*, 26.

44. Social Science Research Council, *Labor Force Definition*, 26–27.

45. Ducoff and Bancroft, "Experiment in the Measurement," 208–9.

46. Ibid.

47. U.S. Commerce Department, Census Bureau, *Census of Agriculture 1954: Volume II*, 233–35.

48. U.S. Commerce Department, Census Bureau, *Census of Agriculture 1959: Statistics by Subject*, XXXII.

49. Rosenfeld, *Farm Women*, 36–37.

50. Jones and Rosenfeld, *American Farm Women*, i.

51. Ibid., i–iii.

52. Ibid., iii.

53. Ibid., iii and 53.

54. Rosenfeld, *Farm Women*, 245; Jones and Rosenfeld, *American Farm Women*, 64.

55. Jones and Rosenfeld, *American Farm Women*, iii.

56. Scholl, "Household and Farm," 8.

57. "Survey of American Women," 10.

58. U.S. Agriculture Department, Economic Research Service, *Agricultural Work Force of 1987*, 8–9.

59. U.S. Commerce Department, Economics and Statistics Administration, Census Bureau, *Residents of Farms*, 3.

60. U.S. Agriculture Department, *2012 Census Highlights*.

61. U.S. Treasury Department, *Statistical Abstract 1878*, 115 and other pages.

62. U.S. Treasury Department, Statistics Bureau, *Statistical Abstract 1895*, 12.

63. U.S. Treasury Department, Statistics Bureau, *Statistical Abstract 1902*, 495.

64. U.S. Commerce and Labor Department, Statistics Bureau, *Statistical Abstract 1907*, 180.

65. U.S. Commerce Department, Census Bureau, *Statistical Abstract 1985*, 634.

Chapter 17   Women Business Owners, Women-Owned Businesses

1. U.S. Labor Department, Women's Bureau, *Women in Industry*, 76.

2. Martelle, *Blood Passion*, 178.

3. U.S. Labor Department, Women's Bureau, *Occupational Progress*, 22.

4. U.S. Labor Department, Women's Bureau, *Women's Occupations*, 196.

5. U.S. Labor Department, Women's Bureau, *Changes in Women's Occupations*, 68.

6. U.S. Labor Department, Women's Bureau, *1958 Handbook*, 14–15.

7. Ibid., 132.

8. U.S. Commerce Department, Census Bureau, *Women-Owned Businesses, 1972*, 1.

9. U.S. Labor Department, Women's Bureau, *1975 Handbook*, 109.

10. Ibid., 108.

11. U.S. Congress, Senate, Small Business Select Committee, *Women and the Small Business Administration*, 2.

12. Ibid., 3.

13. Ibid., 49.

14. Ibid., 52.

15. "Packwood Resignation."

16. U.S. Commerce Department, Census Bureau, *Women-Owned Businesses*, 4.

17. U.S. Commerce Department, Census Bureau, *Selected Characteristics*, 1 and 5.

18. Brannen, *Women-Owned Businesses*.

19. U.S. Commerce Department, Census Bureau, *Occupation by Industry*, 1.

20. Ibid., 2.

21. U.S. Commerce Department, Census Bureau, *Place of Work*.

22. U.S. Labor Department, Women's Bureau, *Time of Change*, 68.

23. Ibid., 4.

24. U.S. Small Business Administration, *Status Report*, no page number.

25. U.S. Small Business Administration, Office of Advocacy, *Women in Business*, 16.

26. *Women's Business Ownership Act of 1988*, Public Law 100-533; U.S. Statutes at Large 102 *(1988)*: 2689.

27. U.S. National Women's Business Council, *Compendium 1994*.

28. Griffin, "Lost Count," 28.

29. Ibid., 28.

30. U.S. National Women's Business Council, *Compendium: Executive Summary and Data Report*, 1–2.

31. Ibid., ES-6.

32. U.S. Commerce Department, Economic and Statistics Administration, *Women-Owned Businesses*, 33.

33. Ibid., 1.

34. Ibid., 24.

35. U.S. National Women's Business Council, *Women-Owned Firms*, 2.

36. U.S. Commerce Department, Census Bureau, *Statistical Abstract 1948*, 295.

37. U.S. Commerce Department, Census Bureau, *Statistical Abstract 1961*, 187.

38. U.S. Commerce Department, Census Bureau, *Statistical Abstract 1963*, 215, 216, and 323.

39. U.S. Commerce Department, Census Bureau, *Statistical Abstract 1976*, 222, 236, and 343.

40. U.S. Commerce Department, Economics and Statistics Administration, Census Bureau, *Statistical Abstract, 2012*, 511.

41. Ibid., 769.

42. Ibid., 768.

Chapter 18   Non-Reproductive Health Issues

1. Huls, *United States Government Documents on Women, Volume I*, 174.

2. U.S. Health and Human Services Department, Office on Women's Health, *Century of Women's Health*, 1.

3. U.S. Census Superintendent, *Seventh Census: Report 1852*, 24–25.

4. U.S. Congress, House, *Mortality Statistics of the Seventh Census: 1850*, 12.

5. U.S. Congress, Senate, *Preliminary Report on the Eighth Census, 1860*, 116.

6. U.S. Treasury Department, Public Health Service, *Healthy Happy Woman-hood,* 2.

7. Ibid., 13.

8. U.S. Health and Human Services Department, Centers for Disease Control and Prevention, National Center for Health Statistics, *National Health Interview Survey;* U.S. Health and Human Services Department, Centers for Disease Control and Prevention, National Center for Health Statistics, *About the National Health Interview Survey.*

9. U.S. Health and Human Services Department, Centers for Disease Control and Prevention, National Center for Health Statistics, *NHIS Surveys Available on the Internet.*

10. U.S. Health, Education, and Welfare Department, Public Health Service, *Smoking and Health,* 31.

11. Ibid., 39.

12. U.S. Health and Human Services Department, Public Health Service. Office of the Assistant Secretary for Health, Office on Smoking and Health, *Health Consequences of Smoking for Women,* 271.

13. Ibid., 275.

14. Ibid., 54.

15. U.S. Health and Human Services Department, Public Health Service, Office of the Surgeon General, *Women and Smoking,* iii.

16. Muller, "Data Needs Related to Women's Health," 99–102.

17. U.S. Health, Education and Welfare Department, National Center for Health Services Research, *Women and Their Health.*

18. U.S. Health, Education, and Welfare Department, Public Health Service, Office of Health Research, Statistics and Technology, National Center for Health Statistics, *Office Visits by Women,* 1.

19. Ibid., 2.

20. Ibid., 33.

21. Ibid., 38.

22. U.S. Health and Human Services Department, Public Health Service, Health Resources Administration, *Woman and Health 1980,* 3.

23. Ibid., no page number.

24. Ibid., 81.

25. U.S. Health, Education, and Welfare Department, Public Health Service, *Women's Health,* 5.

26. Woods et al., "Women's Health," 123.

27. U.S. Congress, Office of Technology Assessment, Health Program, *Breast Cancer Screening for Medicare Beneficiaries,* 14.

28. U.S. General Accounting Office, *National Institutes of Health,* 1.

29. Ibid., 2–3.

30. Slaughter, "Remarks," viii.

31. U.S. Health and Human Services Department, Public Health Service, National Institutes of Health, Office of Research on Women's Health, *Report of the Advisory Committee,* 6.

32. Ibid., 7.

33. *"Pneumocystis* Pneumonia," 250.

34. "Update on Kaposi's Sarcoma," 294.

35. U.S. Health and Human Services Department, Office on Women's Health, *Who We Are.*

36. U.S. Health and Human Services Department, Centers for Disease Control and Prevention, National Center for Health Statistics, *Women: Work and Health,* 1.

37. Ibid., iii.

38. U.S. Health and Human Services Department, National Institutes of Health, Office of Research on Women's Health, *Highlights of NIH Women's Health,* 59.

39. U.S. Health and Human Services Department, Centers for Disease Control and Prevention, National Center for Health Statistics, *Women's Health.*

40. U.S. Government Accountability Office, *Breast Cancer Education.*

41. U.S. Commerce Department, Foreign and Domestic Commerce Bureau, *Statistical Abstract 1925,* 68.

42. U.S. Commerce Department, Census Bureau, *Statistical Abstract 1960,* 84.

43. U.S. Commerce Department, Census Bureau, *Statistical Abstract 1961,* 70.

44. U.S. Commerce Department, Census Bureau, *Statistical Abstract 1963,* 797.

45. U.S. Commerce Department, Census Bureau, *Statistical Abstract 1968,* 81–82.

46. U.S. Commerce Department, Census Bureau, *Statistical Abstract 1967,* 84–45.

47. U.S. Commerce Department, Census Bureau, *Statistical Abstract 1968,* 69; U.S. Commerce Department, Census Bureau, *Statistical Abstract 1967,* 74.

48. U.S. Commerce Department, Census Bureau, *Statistical Abstract 1970,* 65.

49. U.S. Commerce Department, Social and Economic Statistics Administration, Census Bureau, *Statistical Abstract 1972,* 81.

50. U.S. Commerce Department, Social and Economic Statistics Administration, Census Bureau, *Statistical Abstract 1974,* 81.

51. U.S. Commerce Department, Census Bureau, *Statistical Abstract 1975,* 88.

52. Ibid.

53. U.S. Commerce Department, Census Bureau, *Statistical Abstract 1976,* 89.

54. U.S. Commerce Department, Census Bureau, *Statistical Abstract 1977,* 107 and 112.

55. U.S. Commerce Department, Census Bureau, *Statistical Abstract 1979,* 126.

56. U.S. Commerce Department, Census Bureau, *Statistical Abstract 1980,* 127 and 128.

57. U.S. Commerce Department, Census Bureau, *Statistical Abstract 1982–3,* 122.

58. U.S. Commerce Department, Census Bureau, *Statistical Abstract 1984,* 116.

59. U.S. Commerce Department, Census Bureau, *Statistical Abstract 1986,* 101.

60. U.S. Commerce Department, Census Bureau, *Statistical Abstract 1987,* 103.

61. U.S. Commerce Department, Census Bureau, *Statistical Abstract 1988,* 107 and 109.

62. U.S. Commerce Department, Census Bureau, *Statistical Abstract 1989,* 106 and 108.

63. Ibid., 117.

64. U.S. Commerce Department, Census Bureau, *Statistical Abstract 1990,* 121.

65. Ibid., 132, 144, and 126.

66. U.S. Commerce Department, Economics and Statistics Administration, Census Bureau, *Statistical Abstract 1997,* 147.

67. Ibid., 132 and 133.

68. U.S. Commerce Department, Economics and Statistics Administration, Census Bureau, *Statistical Abstract 1998,* 155 and 268.

69. U.S. Commerce Department, Economics and Statistics Administration, Census Bureau, *Statistical Abstract 2007,* 127–28.

70. U.S. Commerce Department, Economics and Statistics Administration, Census Bureau, *Statistical Abstract 2008,* 141.

71. U.S. Commerce Department, Economics and Statistics Administration, Census Bureau, *Statistical Abstract 2011,* 128.

72. U.S. Commerce Department, Economics and Statistics Administration, Census Bureau, *Statistical Abstract 2012,* 126.

Chapter 19 Contraception

1. U.S. Congress, Senate, Judiciary Committee, *Birth Control, Hearings on S. 4582,* 2.

2. *Griswold v. Connecticut,* 381 U.S. 479 (1965).

3. *Eisenstadt v. Baird,* 405 U.S. 438 (1972).

4. Schoen, *Choice and Coercion,* 57–58.

5. Kennedy, *Birth Control in America,* 266–67.

6. "Achievements in Public Health," no page numbers.

7. Schoen, *Choice and Coercion,* 58.

8. U.S. Health, Education, and Welfare Department, *Report on Family Planning,* iv.

9. U.S. Health, Education, and Welfare Department, *Family Planning,* 7.

10. Haupt, "The National Reporting System," 637.

11. U.S. Health and Human Services Department, Public Health Service, Health Services and Mental Health Administration, Center for Disease Control, *Family Planning Services Annual Summary 1971,* ii.

12. U.S. Health and Human Services Department, National Institutes of Health, National Library of Medicine, National Center for Biotechnology Information, *Family Planning Digest.*

13. Ibid., 1.

14. Dryfoos, "National Reporting System," 192.

15. U.S. Health and Human Services Department, Centers for Disease Control and Prevention, National Center for Health Statistics, *About the National Survey of Family Growth.*

16. U.S. Health and Human Services Department, Centers for Disease Control and Prevention, National Center for Health Statistics, *Series 23.*

17. U.S. Health and Human Services Department, Centers for Disease Control and Prevention, National Center for Health Statistics, *Key Statistics.*

18. U.S. Health, Education, and Welfare Department, Human Resources Administration, National Center for Health Statistics, *Health, United States 1975,* 212.

19. Ibid., 213.

20. U.S. Health and Human Services Department, Centers for Disease Control and Prevention, National Center for Health Statistics, *Health, United States 2015,* 79.

21. Ibid., 81–82.

22. Dryfoos, "National Reporting System," 193.

23. U.S. Health, Education, and Welfare Department, Public Health Service, National Center for Health Statistics, *National Inventory of Family Planning Services,* 1.

24. Ibid., 2.

25. Martinez and Abma, *Sexual Activity,* 1.

26. U.S. Commerce Department, Census Bureau, Center for Economic Studies, *Fifty Years of Family Planning,* 1.

27. U.S. Commerce Department, Census Bureau, *Statistical Abstract 1976,* 57; U.S. Census Bureau, *Statistical Abstract 1975,* 58.

28. U.S. Commerce Department, Census Bureau, *Statistical Abstract 1986,* 65.

29. Ibid., 63 and 65.

Chapter 20 Abortion

1. Jacobson, "Jon Kyl Says."

2. U.S. Congress, *Congressional Record.* 157. April 8, 2011. S2289.

3. *Roe v. Wade,* 410 U.S. 113 (1973).

4. Casey, "Elective Abortion."

5. U.S. Health, Education and Welfare Department, Public Health Service, Centers for Disease Control, *Family Planning Evaluation,* 36.

6. U.S. Congress, Senate, Committee, *Birth Control: S. 4582,* 12.

7. U.S. Congress, Senate, Committee, *Birth Control: S. 4436,* 34.

8. U.S. Interior Department, Census Office, *Report on the Defective,* xxxix.

9. Ibid., 506–9.

10. U.S. Interior Department, Census Office, *Report on Vital and Social Statistics: 1890, Part IV,* 114.

11. U.S. Commerce and Labor Department, Census Bureau, *Mortality Statistics: 1910,* 225.

12. U.S. Commerce Department, Census Bureau, *Mortality Statistics: 1931–2,* 75.

13. U.S. Commerce Department, Census Bureau, *Birth, Stillbirth, and Infant Mortality 1931,* 165.

14. Ibid., 164.

15. U.S. Commerce Department, Census Bureau, *Vital Statistics 1940,* 31; U.S. Social Security Administration, Children's Bureau, *Further Progress in Reducing,* 17.

16. U.S. Health, Education, and Welfare Department, Public Health Service, *Vital Statistics 1950, Volume 1,* 134.

17. U.S. Health, Education, and Welfare Department, Public Health Service, *Vital Statistics 1950, Volume 3,* 124.

18. U.S. Health, Education, and Welfare Department, Public Health Service, *Vital Statistics 1960, Volume II, Mortality, Part A,* 5–27; U.S. Health, Education, and Welfare Department, Public Health Service, National Center for Health Statistics, *Vital Statistics 1970, Volume II, Mortality, Part A,* 1–72.

19. U.S. Health, Education, and Welfare Department, Public Health Service, National Center for Health Statistics, *Vital Statistics 1980, Volume II, Mortality, Part A,* 64.

20. U.S. Health, Education, and Welfare Department, Public Health Service, National Center for Health Statistics, *Infant, Fetal, and Maternal Mortality,* 55.

21. Williams and McIntosh, "National Resource Requirements," 440.

22. U.S. Health, Education and Welfare Department, Public Health Service, Center for Disease Control, *Family Planning Evaluation,* 36.

23. Ibid., 36.

24. Whitcomb, "Abortion Surveillance," 112.

25. U.S. Health, Education and Welfare Department, Public Health Service, Center for Disease Control, *Family Planning Evaluation,* 3.

26. Ibid., 3.

27. Bourne et al., "Surveillance of Legal Abortions," 19.

28. U.S. Health, Education and Welfare Department, Public Health Service, Center for Disease Control, *Family Planning Evaluation,* 1.

29. Bourne et al., "Surveillance of Legal Abortions," 25.

30. Smith and Bourne, "Abortion Surveillance Program," 256.

31. U.S. Health, Education, and Welfare Department, Public Health Service, Health Services and Mental Health Administration, *Effect of Changes,* 2.

32. Ibid., 5.

33. Ibid., 3–4.

34. U.S. National Commission for the Observance of International Women's Year, ... *To Form a More Perfect Union,* 106.

35. U.S. Health, Education, and Welfare Department, Public Health Service, Health Services and Mental Health Administration, *Effect of Changes,* 12.

36. Ibid., 10.

37. Smith and Bourne, "Abortion Surveillance Program," 256.

38. Korenbrot et al., *Trends in Rates of Live Births,* 555.

39. U.S. Health and Human Services Department, Public Health Service, Centers for Disease Control and Prevention, *CDCs [sic] Abortion Surveillance System FAQs.*

40. Matt Conens, e-mail message to the author, October 14, 2015.

41. U.S. Health and Human Services Department, Public Health Service, Centers for Disease Control and Prevention, U.S. *Abortion Surveillance—United States, 1998.*

42. U.S. Health and Human Services Department, Public Health Service, Centers for Disease Control and Prevention, National Center for Health Statistics, *Trends in Pregnancies*, 1.

43. Guttmacher Institute, "History of the Guttmacher Institute."

44. U.S. Health and Human Services Department, Public Health Service, Centers for Disease Control and Prevention, National Center for Health Statistics, *Health, United States 2014*, 392.

45. U.S. Health and Human Services Department, Public Health Service, Centers for Disease Control and Prevention, National Center for Health Statistics, *Trends in Pregnancies*, 3–4.

46. U.S. Health, Education, and Welfare Department, Public Health Service, Centers for Disease Control and Prevention National Center for Health Statistics, *Health, United States 2014*, 358.

47. Ibid., 392.

48. University at Albany, School of Criminal Justice, Hindelang Criminal Justice Research Center, *Sourcebook of Criminal Justice Statistics*.

49. Jacobs, "Sourcebook of Criminal Justice Statistics."

50. U.S. Justice Department, Law Enforcement Assistance Administration, National Criminal Justice Information and Statistics Service, *Sourcebook of Criminal Justice Statistics 1973*, 481.

51. U.S. Justice Department, Law Enforcement Assistance Administration, National Criminal Justice Information and Statistics Service, *Sourcebook of Criminal Justice Statistics 1995*, 675.

52. U.S. Justice Department, Law Enforcement Assistance Administration, National Criminal Justice Information and Statistics Service, *Sourcebook of Criminal Justice Statistics 1975*, 580.

53. U.S. Justice Department, Law Enforcement Assistance Administration, National Center for Crime Information and Statistics Service, *Sourcebook of Criminal Justice Statistics 1994*, 366.

54. U.S. Justice Department, Law Enforcement Assistance Administration, National Criminal Justice Information and Statistics Service, *Sourcebook of Criminal Justice Statistics 1975*, 278.

55. University at Albany, School of Criminal Justice, Hindelang Criminal Justice Research Center, *Sourcebook of Criminal Justice Statistics*.

56. U.S. Health and Human Services Department, Centers for Disease Control and Prevention, National Center for Health Statistics, *Key Statistics*.

57. U.S. Commerce Department, Census Bureau, *Statistical Abstract 1975*, 58.

58. U.S. Commerce Department, Census Bureau, *Statistical Abstract 1976*, 58.

59. U.S. Commerce Department, Census Bureau, *Statistical Abstract 1975*, 58.

60. U.S. Commerce Department, Census Bureau, *Statistical Abstract 1976*, 58.

61. U.S. Commerce Department, Census Bureau, *Statistical Abstract 1990*, 72.

62. Ibid., 71.

63. U.S. Commerce Department, Economics and Statistics Administration, Census Bureau, *Statistical Abstract 1995*, 81–82.

64. U.S. Commerce Department, Economics and Statistics Administration, Census Bureau, *Statistical Abstract 2012,* 75–76.

Chapter 21   Women as Criminals

1. U.S. Census Office, *Statistical View,* 133.

2. Ibid., 166.

3. Ibid., 167.

4. Wines, *American Prisons,* 8–9.

5. Ibid., 16.

6. U.S. Commerce and Labor Department, Census Bureau, *Special Reports: 1900,* 440.

7. U.S. Justice Department, Bureau of Justice Statistics, *Historical Corrections Statistics,* 40.

8. U.S. Congress, Senate, *Report on Condition of Woman: Volume 15,* 10.

9. Ibid., 14.

10. Ibid., 55.

11. Ibid., 30.

12. Ibid., 23.

13. Ibid., 42.

14. Ibid., 55–56.

15. Ibid., 59 and 76.

16. Ibid., 75.

17. Ibid., 16.

18. Ibid., 16–17.

19. Ibid., 21.

20. Ibid., 81.

21. Ibid., 89–91.

22. Ibid., 91–92.

23. U.S. Justice Department, Bureau of Justice Statistics, *Federal Justice Statistics,* 1.

24. Simpson, "Private Losses," 378.

25. U.S. National Commission on Law Observance and Enforcement, *Report on Penal Institutions,* 249.

26. Gora, *New Female Criminal,* 21.

27. Grana, *Women and Justice,* 62.

28. *Uniform Crime Reports,* 3 (4), 13.

29. Ibid., 14.

30. *Uniform Crime Reports,* 13 (1), 90.

31. U.S. Justice Department, Law Enforcement Assistance Administration, *Report of the LEAA Task Force,* 14–18.

32. Ibid., 4.

33. Ibid., 4.

34. Ibid., 7–8.

35. U.S. Justice Department, Law Enforcement Assistance Administration, National Institute of Law Enforcement and Criminal Justice, *National Study of Women's Correctional Programs,* foreword and xvii.

36. U.S. Justice Department, National Institute of Corrections, *Women in Jail,* 2.

37. Ibid., 4.

38. U.S. Justice Department, Bureau of Justice Statistics, *Data Collection.*

39. Holleran and Vandiver, "U.S. Homicides," 33.

40. U.S. Commerce Department, Census Bureau, Foreign and Domestic Commerce Bureau, Census Bureau, *Statistical Abstract of the United States 1926,* 70.

41. U.S. Commerce Department, Census Bureau, *Statistical Abstract 1944/5,* 101–6.

42. U.S. Commerce Department, Census Bureau, *Statistical Abstract 1965,* 157.

43. U.S. Commerce Department, Census Bureau, *Statistical Abstract 1990,* 177.

Chapter 22 Prostitution

1. U.S. Congress, Senate, *Report on Condition of Woman: Volume 15,* 82 and 11.

2. Ibid., 95–96.

3. U.S. Health and Human Services Department, Centers for Disease Control and Prevention, *HIV Risk.*

4. U.S. Interior Department, Census Office, *Ninth Census Volume I,* 659.

5. U.S. Interior Department, Census Office, *Report on the Defective, 1880 Census,* liv–lv.

6. "Occupational Coding," *IPUMSusa.*

7. U.S. Commissioner of Labor, *Working Women in Large Cities,* 10.

8. Ibid., 73–74.

9. Ibid., 76. Wright made a similar point in his 1883 Census Office publication "Report on the Factory System," 31–33.

10. U.S. Commerce and Labor Department, Census Bureau, *Marriage and Divorce, Part I,* 30 and 80.

11. Bankston, "Dillingham Commission."

12. U.S. Congress, Senate, *Dictionary of Races.*

13. U.S. Congress, Senate, *Importing Women,* 3.

14. Ibid., 3.

15. Ibid., 14.

16. Ibid., 12.

17. Beckman, "White Slave Traffic Act," 85.

18. *White Slave Traffic Act. Chapter 395. U.S. Statutes at Large* 36 (1910) 825.

19. *United States v. Holte,* 236 U.S. 140 (1915).

20. Beckman, "White Slave Traffic Act," 91–92.

21. U.S. Congress, Senate, *Report on Condition of Woman: Volume 15,* 97.

22. U.S. Interdepartmental Social Hygiene Board, *Manual for the Various Agents*, 8.

23. Pivar, "Cleansing the Nation," 33.

24. Storey, "Evaluation of Governmental Aid," 4.

25. Pivar, "Cleansing the Nation," 38.

26. U.S. Interdepartmental Social Hygiene Board, *Manual for the Various Agents*, 19–20.

27. U.S. Interdepartmental Social Hygiene Board, *Detention Houses and Reformatories*, 74.

28. Reilly, *Sex without Spheres*, 156.

29. U.S. Interdepartmental Social Hygiene Board, *Manual for the Various Agents*, 84.

30. Ibid., 75.

31. Reilly, *Sex without Spheres*, 193.

32. Ibid., 82.

33. Ibid., 78.

34. *Uniform Crime Reports*, 4 (3) 15–16, 18.

35. *Uniform Crime Reports*, 5 (1), 21.

36. U.S. Justice Department, Federal Bureau of Investigation, *Estimated Number of Arrests*.

37. U.S. Federal Security Agency, Office of Community War Services, Social Protection Division, *Meet Your Enemy*, iii.

38. Ibid., 16.

39. U.S. Labor Department, Women's Bureau, *Trafficking in Persons*.

40. U.S. Commerce Department, Foreign and Domestic Commerce Bureau, *Statistical Abstract 1921*, 270.

41. U.S. Commerce Department, Census Bureau, *Statistical Abstract 1943*, 96–97.

42. U.S. Commerce Department, Economics and Statistics Administration, Census Bureau, *Statistical Abstract 1991*, 196.

Chapter 23 Women as Crime Victims

1. Mikulski, "Challenge I," 115 and 117.

2. U.S. Justice Department, Justice Programs Office, Bureau of Justice Statistics, *Redesign of the National Crime Survey*, 5.

3. U.S. Justice Department, Law Enforcement Assistance Administration, National Criminal Justice Information and Statistics Service, *Criminal Victimization 1973*, 7.

4. Ibid., 47.

5. See, for example, U.S. Civil Rights Commission, *Silent Victims*.

6. U.S. Civil Rights Commission, *Under the Rule of Thumb*, 1.

7. U.S. Justice Department, Bureau of Justice Statistics, *Family Violence*, 1–3.

8. Brozan, "An Expert Looks."

9. U.S. Justice Department, Attorney General's Task Force on Family Violence, *Final Report,* 84.

10. U.S. Justice Department, Bureau of Justice Statistics, *Preventing Domestic Violence,* 1.

11. Bachman, *Violence against Women: Synthesis,* 1.

12. Ibid., 9.

13. Kearns, "Down for the Count," 9.

14. U.S. Commerce Department, Economics and Statistics Administration, Census Bureau, *1990 Census: Social and Economic Characteristics,* B-11.

15. U.S. Commerce Department, Economics and Statistics Administration, Census Bureau, *1990 Census: History. Part A,* 6–50.

16. U.S. Commerce Department, Economics and Statistics Administration, Census Bureau, *Emergency and Transitional Shelter,* 4.

17. Social Explorer, *Data Dictionary.*

18. U.S. Justice Department, Justice Programs Office, Bureau of Justice Statistics, *Criminal Victimization 1992,* 149.

19. Ford et al., *Controlling Violence,* 1.

20. *Violence against Women Act,* U.S. Code 42 sections §§13701 et seq.

21. U.S. Justice Department, Justice Programs Office, Bureau of Justice Statistics, *Violence against Women,* 1.

22. Bachman, *Incidence Rates of Violence,* no page numbers. This report also compared the NCVS to the National Family Violence Survey, which was paid for by the National Institute of Mental Health, but not published by the government.

23. Ibid., 1.

24. U.S. Justice Department, Justice Programs Office, Bureau of Justice Statistics, *Intimate Partner Violence,* 6.

25. U.S. Health and Human Services Department, Centers for Disease Control and Prevention, National Center for Injury Prevention and Control, *Costs of Intimate Partner Violence,* 1.

26. Ibid., 2.

27. Ibid., 5.

28. U.S. Health and Human Services Department, Centers for Disease Control and Prevention, National Center for Injury Prevention and Control, *Intimate Partner Violence—2010,* 1.

29. U.S. Justice Department, Justice Programs Office, National Institute of Justice, *Annual Report 1996,* 27.

30. U.S. Justice Department, Justice Programs Office, National Institute of Justice, *Stalking in America,* 2.

31. U.S. Justice Department, Justice Programs Office, Office of Violence against Women, *Stalking and Domestic Violence,* 1.

32. Ibid., 18.

33. U.S. Justice Department, Justice Programs Office, Bureau of Justice Statistics, *Special Report: Stalking Victimization,* 10.

34. Ibid., 1.

35. Ibid., 3.

36. U.S. Justice Department, Justice Programs Office, Bureau of Justice Statistics, *Stalking Victims—Revised,* 4–5.

37. U.S. Government Accountability Office, *Sexual Violence Data, no page number.*

38. U.S. Commerce Department, Census Bureau, *Statistical Abstract 1943,* 95.

39. U.S. Commerce Department, Census Bureau, *Statistical Abstract 1967,* 152.

40. U.S. Commerce Department, Census Bureau, *Statistical Abstract 1958,* 142.

41. U.S. Commerce Department, Census Bureau, *Statistical Abstract 1975,* 153.

42. U.S. Commerce Department, Economics and Statistics Administration, Census Bureau, *Statistical Abstract 2001,* 190.

43. U.S. Commerce Department, Economics and Statistics Administration, Census Bureau, *Statistical Abstract 2010,* 293.

Chapter 24 Rape

1. U.S. National Commission on the Causes and Prevention of Crime, *Crimes of Violence,* 224. The quotation is from George Meredith's poem "Love's Grave."

2. Ibid., 224.

3. Ibid., 3.

4. U.S. Interior Department, Census Office, *Report on the Defective, 1880,* 508.

5. U.S. Justice Department, Bureau of Justice Statistics, *Historical Corrections Statistics,* 11.

6. Baron and Straus, *Four Theories of Rape,* 26.

7. *Uniform Crime Reports,* 1 (1) 1930, 7–19.

8. U.S. Commerce Department, Census Bureau, *Statistical Abstract 1960,* 139.

9. U.S. Justice Department, Federal Bureau of Investigation, Criminal Justice Information Services Division, *Crime in the United States 2014. Rape.*

10. U.S. National Commission on the Causes and Prevention of Crime, *Crimes of Violence,* 219.

11. Ibid., 219.

12. Ibid., 220.

13. Ibid., 245.

14. Hindelang and Davis, "Forcible Rape: A Statistical Profile," 90–99.

15. U.S. Justice Department, Justice Programs Office, Bureau of Justice Statistics, *Criminal Victimization 1993,* 150.

16. Ibid., 150.

17. Brownmiller, *Against Our Will,* 15.

18. Ibid., 174.

19. Ibid., 77.

20. U.S. Justice Department, Law Enforcement Assistance Administration, National Institute of Law Enforcement and Criminal Justice, *Forcible Rape: Police,* iii.

21. Ibid., 15.

22. Ibid., 48.

23. U.S. Justice Department, Law Enforcement Assistance Administration, National Institute of Law Enforcement and Criminal Justice, *Forcible Rape: Prosecutors,* 4.

24. Ibid., 32.

25. U.S. Justice Department, Law Enforcement Assistance Administration, National Criminal Justice Information and Statistics Service, *Rape Victimization,* 2.

26. U.S. Justice Department, Justice Programs Office, Bureau of Justice Statistics, *Sourcebook of Criminal Justice Statistics 2003,* 606.

27. U.S. Justice Department, Bureau of Justice Statistics, *Crime of Rape,* 1–2.

28. Baron and Straus, *Four Theories of Rape,* 29.

29. U.S. Justice Department, Justice Programs Office, National Institute of Justice, *Extent, Nature, and Consequences of Intimate,* 9–10 and 13.

30. U.S. Justice Department, Justice Programs Office, National Institute of Justice, *Extent, Nature, and Consequences of Rape,* 9.

31. U.S. Justice Department, Justice Programs Office, National Institute of Justice, *Sexual Victimization of College Women,* 3.

32. Ibid., 10.

33. Ibid., 18.

34. Ibid., 19.

35. U.S. Health and Human Services Department, Centers for Disease Control and Prevention, National Center for Health Statistics, *Unwanted Sexual Intercourse.*

36. U.S. Health and Human Services Department, Centers for Disease Control and Prevention, National Center for Health Statistics, *Nonvoluntary Sexual Intercourse.*

37. Kilpatrick et al., *Understanding National Rape Statistics,* 7–8.

38. U.S. Justice Department, Justice Programs Office, Bureau of Justice Statistics, *Female Victims of Sexual Violence, 1994,* 1.

39. U.S. Commerce Department, Census Bureau, *Statistical Abstract 1943,* 95.

40. U.S. Commerce Department, Census Bureau, *Statistical Abstract 1950,* 136.

41. U.S. Commerce Department, Census Bureau, *Statistical Abstract 1943,* 95.

42. U.S. Commerce Department, Census Bureau, *Statistical Abstract 1967,* 152.

43. U.S. Commerce Department, Census Bureau, *Statistical Abstract 1977,* 171.

44. U.S. Commerce Department, Census Bureau, *Statistical Abstract 1979,* 185.

45. U.S. Commerce Department, Census Bureau, Statistical *Abstract 1978,* 186.

46. U.S. Commerce Department, Census Bureau, Statistical *Abstract 1990,* 175.

Chapter 25   Rosie the Riveter: Civilian Women during the World Wars

1. Conner, "Mothers of the Race," 32.

2. U.S. Labor Department, Women's Bureau, *Women Street Car Conductors,* 34.

3. Orleck, *Common Sense,* 137–38.

4. Conner, "Mothers of the Race," 31.

5. Ibid., 51.

6. Ibid., 36.

7. Ibid., 34.

8. U.S. Labor Department, Women's Bureau, *Women Street Car Conductors,* 8.

9. Conner, "Mothers of the Race," 51.

10. U.S. Civil Service Commission, *First Year,* 30.

11. Ibid., 27.

12. U.S. Labor Department, Women's Bureau, *New Position of Women,* 24, 116, 121, 134, 148, and 149.

13. Ibid., 20.

14. Anderson, *Woman at Work,* 94.

15. Cortada, *All the Facts,* 230.

16. *War Organization of the Government.*

17. Straub, "United States Government Policy," 242.

18. U.S. Selective Service, *Selective Service in Wartime: Second Report,* 391.

19. "Women Who Can Work," 3.

20. U.S. Labor Department, Women's Bureau, *Effective Use of Women,* 2–3.

21. "Women's Chances," 3.

22. Scheer, *Governor Lady,* 251.

23. U.S. Civil Service Commission, *First Year,* 5.

24. Ibid., 17.

25. U.S. Civil Service Commission, *Second Year,* 15.

26. U.S. Civil Service Commission, *First Year,* 17–19.

27. U.S. Civil Service Commission, *Second Year,* 1.

28. Ibid., 13–14 and 28. Slightly modified.

29. Ibid., 44.

30. U.S. Labor Department, Bureau of Labor Statistics, *Handbook of Labor Statistics 1941 Volume 1,* 147–48.

31. U.S. Federal Security Agency, Social Security Board, Bureau of Employment Security, United States Employment Service, Occupational Analysis Section, *Occupations Suitable for Women,* viii.

32. Schwartztrauber, "Make-Up, America," 7.

33. U.S. Selective Service, *Selective Service in Wartime: Second Report,* 388.

34. Ibid., 388–89.

35. Ibid., 411.

36. Anderson, *Woman at Work,* 64.

37. U.S. Labor Department, Women's Bureau, *Negro Women War Workers,* 1.

38. U.S. Labor Department, Women's Bureau, *Choosing Women,* 2.

39. U.S. Labor Department, Women's Bureau, *Women's Occupations,* 1.

40. U.S. Labor Department, Women's Bureau, *Employing Women in Shipyards,* 1 and 18.

41. U.S. Labor Department, Women's Bureau, *Women Workers,* 3.

42. U.S. Labor Department, Women's Bureau, *Community Services,* 3.

43. U.S. Labor Department, Women's Bureau, *Employing Women in Shipyards,* 23–24.

44. U.S. Labor Department, Women's Bureau, *Negro Women War Workers,* 8.

45. U.S. Labor Department, Women's Bureau, *Women's Emergency Farm Service,* 5.

46. U.S. Labor Department, Women's Bureau, *"Equal Pay" for Women,* 1.

47. Ibid., 15.

48. U.S. Labor Department, Women's Bureau, *Employing Women in Shipyards,* 32.

49. Stapleford, "Housewife versus Economist," 89.

50. Ibid., 109.

51. Ibid., 90.

52. Ibid., 105.

53. Ibid., 106.

54. U.S. Labor Department, Women's Bureau, *Women Workers in Ten,* vii.

55. Ibid., 1.

56. U.S. Labor Department, Women's Bureau, *Women's Wartime Hours,* 1–2.

57. Anderson, *Wartime Women,* 10.

58. U.S. Commerce Department, Foreign and Domestic Commerce Bureau, *Statistical Abstract 1917,* 677–87.

59. U.S. Commerce Department, Foreign and Domestic Commerce Bureau, *Statistical Abstract 1918,* 764.

60. U.S. Commerce Department, Foreign and Domestic Commerce Bureau, *Statistical Abstract 1919,* 735.

61. Ibid., 738.

62. U.S. Commerce Department, Census Bureau, *Statistical Abstract 1946,* 174–75.

Chapter 26   Women in the Military

1. Huls, *United States Government Documents on Women, Volume I,* 230.

2. U.S. Defense Department, Army Department, Office of the Chief of Military History, *Women's Army Corps,* 4.

3. U.S. Civil War Centennial Commission, *Our Women of the Sixties,* 17.

4. U.S. Defense Department, *Military Women,* 1.

5. U.S. Defense Department, Marine Corps, History and Museum Division, *Women Marines in World War I,* 3.

6. Ibid., 4.

7. U.S. Defense Department, Army Department, Office of the Chief of Military History, *Women's Army Corps,* 17.

8. Ibid., 6.

9. U.S. Defense Department, Army, *Women in the Army.*

10. U.S. Defense Department, Army Department, Office of the Chief of Military History, *Women's Army Corps,* xi.

11. Tilley, *History of Women,* 3.

12. U.S. Defense Department, Marine Corps, History and Museum Division, *Free a Marine,* 2.

13. Ibid., 7.

14. U.S. Defense Department, *Military Women,* 1.

15. Ibid., 1.

16. National Women's Law Center, *Assignment Policies for Military Women,* 1.

17. Mahoney, *Downgrading of DACOWITS,* 1.

18. U.S. Defense Department, *Military Women,* 1.

19. U.S. General Accounting Office, *Job Opportunities for Women,* 1.

20. U.S. Commerce Department, Census Bureau, *1980 Census Users' Guide. Part A. Text,* 12.

21. U.S. Veteran's Administration, Statistical Policy and Research Service, *Female Veteran Population,* 1–2.

22. U.S. Veteran's Administration, Statistical Policy and Research Service, *Aging Female Veteran,* 2–5.

23. U.S. Veteran's Administration, Statistical Policy and Research Service, *Survey of Female Veterans,* i.

24. Ibid., ii.

25. U.S. Veterans Affairs Department, National Center for Veterans Analysis and Statistics, *Profile of Women Veterans 2014,* 3.

26. U.S. Defense Department, *Military Women,* ii.

27. U.S. Defense Department, "Women in Defense," 1.

28. U.S. Defense Department, Defense Manpower Data Center, *Sexual Harassment in the Military: 1988,* xiii.

29. U.S. Defense Department, *Annual Report on Sexual Assault 2012, Volume 2,* 1.

30. U.S. Defense Department, Inspector General, *Tailhook '91: Part 2,* 1.

31. U.S. Defense Department, Defense Manpower Data Center, *2004 Sexual Harassment Survey,* iv.

32. U.S. Defense Department, *Annual Report on Sexual Harassment 2006–2007,* 6.

33. U.S. Defense Department, *Annual Report on Sexual Assault 2011,* 1.

34. U.S. Defense Department, Office of the Undersecretary for Personnel and Readiness, *Annual Report FY2015. Appendix B,* 9.

35. U.S. Defense Department, Office of the Undersecretary for Personnel and Readiness, *Annual Report on Sexual Assault FY2015,* 7.

36. U.S. Defense Department, Inspector General's Office, *Consolidated Listing of Reports.*

37. U.S. Defense Department, Inspector General's Office, *Air Force Academy Sexual Assault Survey,* 2–3.

38. U.S. Defense Department, Inspector General's Office, *Consolidated Listing of Reports.*

39. U.S. Government Accountability Office, *Search.*

40. U.S. Government Accountability Office, *Military Personnel.*

41. U.S. Defense Department, Defense Advisory Committee on Women in the Services, *2009 Report,* i.

42. Mahoney, *Downgrading of DACOWITS,* 2.

43. U.S. Defense Department, Defense Advisory Committee on Women in the Services, *DACOWITS Reports.*

44. Mahoney, *Downgrading of DACOWITS,* 2.

45. U.S. Defense Department, Defense Advisory Committee on Women in the Services, *2010 Report,* i and 20.

46. U.S. Commerce Department, Foreign and Domestic Commerce Bureau, *Statistical Abstract 1921,* 814.

47. U.S. Commerce Department, Census Bureau, *Statistical Abstract 1943,* 161.

48. U.S. Commerce Department, Census Bureau, *Statistical Abstract 1962,* 263.

49. U.S. Commerce Department, Census Bureau, *Statistical Abstract 1963,* 270.

50. U.S. Commerce Department, Census Bureau, *Statistical Abstract 1967,* 270–78.

51. U.S. Commerce Department, Economic and Statistics Administration, Census Bureau, *Statistical Abstract 2000,* 372.

Chapter 27 Conclusion

1. MacLean, "Sybilla Masters."

2. *Adkins v. Children's Hospital,* 261 U.S. 525 (1923).

3. Center for Military Readiness, *Summary and Overview.*

4. Scott, *Census, U.S.A.,* 20.

5. Dinan, "EXCLUSIVE: Minn. Lawmaker Vows."

6. Smith, "Information Cancelled."

7. Jaffe, *Misused Statistics,* 117–18.

8. U.S. Commerce Department, Census Bureau, *Thirteenth Census: Volume IV,* 22–23.

9. Griffin, "Lost Count," 28.

10. Mikulski, "Challenge I," 117.

11. U.S. Health and Human Services Department, National Institutes of Health. Office of Research on Women's Health, *Highlights of NIH Women's Health,* 59.

12. U.S. White House Council on Women and Girls, *Keeping America's Women Moving Forward,* i.

13. Kreps, "Changing Roles of Women," 4.

14. U.S. Commerce Department, Patent and Trademark Office, *Buttons to Biotech,* 1.

Bibliography

In some of the following records, a string of letters and numbers with a colon in it appear in parentheses. For example: (VA 1.2:F 34/5). This is the Sudoc (Superintendent of Documents) number for a government publication. Many libraries use these numbers for filing the publications.

Abbott, Edith. *Women in Industry: A Study in American Economic History*. New York: D. Appleton, 1910.

"Achievements in Public Health, 1900–1999: Family Planning." *Morbidity and Mortality Weekly Report* 48, no. 47 (December 3, 1999): 1073–1080.

Adkins v. Children's Hospital, 261 U.S. 525 (1923).

Adkinson, Florence M. "The Industrial Progress of Woman." *Thirty-Third Annual Report of the Indiana State Board of Education*. Indianapolis: W.R. Burford, 1884. 220–225. http://tinyurl.com/hszxh9a

Allen, Abigail Maxson. "The Rochester Teachers Convention of 1847." *The Sabbath Recorder*. 70. August 24, 1893. 534.

American Federation of State, County, and Municipal Employees v. Washington, 578 F. Supp. 846, rev'd 770 F 2d. 1401 (1985).

Anderson, Karen. *Wartime Women: Sex Roles, Family Relations, and the Status of Women during World War II*. Westport, CT: Greenwood Press, 1981.

Anderson, Margo. "The Census and the Federal Statistical System: Historical Perspectives." *The Annals of the American Academy of Political and Social Science* 631 (September 2010): 152–162.

Anderson, Margo. "The History of Women and the History of Statistics." *Journal of Women's History* 4, no. 1 (1992): 14–36.

Anderson, Mary, as told to Mary N. Winslow. *Woman at Work*. Minneapolis: University of Minnesota Press, 1951. http://tinyurl.com/jjycwc4

Association for the Advancement of Women. *Historical Account of the Association for the Advancement of Women, 1873–1893*. Dedham, MA: Transcript Steam Job Print, 1893.

Aughinbaugh, Alison, and Maury Gittleman. *Maternal Employment and Adoles-cent Risky Behavior.* Working Paper 366. Washington, D.C.: U.S. Labor Department, Bureau of Labor Statistics, Office of Compensation and Working Conditions. 2003. http://tinyurl.com/md4rpyj

Bachman, Ronet. *Incidence Rates of Violence against Women: A Comparison of the Redesigned National Crime Victimization Survey and the 1985 National Family Violence Survey.* Harrisburg, PA: National Resource Center on Domestic Violence, 1998. http://tinyurl.com/mwmgysm

Bachman, Ronet. *Violence against Women: Synthesis of Research for Criminal Justice Policymakers.* NCJ 199579. Washington, D.C.: U.S. Justice Department, National Institute of Justice, 2000.

Bankston, Carl L. "Dillingham Commission." *Immigration to the United States.* http://tinyurl.com/h7oxwnc

Barlow, E.R. "She Looketh Well to the Ways of Her Household." *Arthur's Illustrated Home Magazine* 44, no. 11 (November 1876): 620–621. http://tinyurl.com/zmve4se

Baron, Larry and Murray A. Straus. *Four Theories of Rape in American Society: A State-Level Analysis.* New Haven, CT: Yale University Press, 1989.

Barrett, Nancy Smith. "Data Needs for Evaluating the Labor Market Status of Women." *Census Bureau Conference on Issues in Federal Statistical Needs Relating to Women.* P-23. No. 83. Washington, D.C.: Census Bureau, 1979. 10–19. (C 3.186:P-23/83) http://tinyurl.com/glv2hnl

Beckman, Marlene D. "The White Slave Traffic Act: Historical Impact of a Federal Crime Policy on Women." *Women & Politics* 4, no. 3 (1984): 83–101.

Bell, Carolyn Shaw. "Comparative Worth: How Do We Know It Will Work?" *Monthly Labor Review* 108, no. 12 (December 1985): 5–12.

Bourne, Judith P., James B. Kahn, S. Beach Conger, and Carl Tyler Jr. "Surveillance of Legal Abortions in the United States, 1970." *Public Health Resources.* Paper 237 (1972). http://tinyurl.com/juaf24j

Brannen, Kathleen C. *Women-Owned Businesses 1972–1982: A View of the Statistics.* Conway, AR: Small Business Institute Director's Association, 1989. http://tinyurl.com/kucyfcl

Bricker, Jesse, Lisa J. Dettling, Alice Henriques, Joanne W. Hsu, Kevin B. Moore, John Sabelhaus, Jeffrey Thompson, and Richard A. Windle. "Changes in U.S. Family Finances from 2010 to 2013: Evidence from the Survey of Consumer Finances." *Federal Reserve Bulletin* 100, no. 4 (September 2014). http://tinyurl.com/l3wqnan

Brownmiller, Susan. *Against Our Will: Men, Women, and Rape.* New York: Simon and Schuster, 1975.

Brozan, Nadine. "An Expert Looks at Family Violence." *New York Times.* May 20, 1984. http://tinyurl.com/j9yzzg2

Carter, Susan B. and Richard Sutch. "Fixing the Facts: Editing of the 1880 United States Census of Occupations with Implications for Long-Term

Labor-Force Trends and the Sociology of Official Statistics." *Historical Methods* 29, no. 1 (Winter 1996): 5–24.

Carucci, P.M. and S. Prasad. "Comparison of Mothers' Occupations Reported on Live Birth Certificates and on a Survey Questionnaire." *Public Health reports* 94, no. 5 (September–October 1979): 432–437. http://tinyurl.com/zqg4lzs

Casey, Frances E. "Elective Abortion." *Medscape.* http://tinyurl.com/c7gwu8h

Center for Military Readiness. *Summary and Overview: Discontinue the DACOW-ITS.* January 28, 2002. http://tinyurl.com/z8p86w6

Ciancanelli, Penelope. *Women's Transition to Wage Labor: A Critique of Labor Force Statistics and Reestimation of the Labor Force Participation of Married Women in the United States 1900 to 1930.* New York: School for Social Research, 1984.

Civil Rights Act of 1964, as amended in 1972, Title VII, U.S. Code 42 (2012), §§2000e et seq.

Conk, Margo Anderson. "Accuracy, Efficiency and Bias: The Interpretation of Women's Work in the U.S. Census of Occupations, 1890–1940." *Historical Methods* 14, no. 2 (1981): 65–72.

Conk, Margo Anderson. *The United States Census and Labor Force Change: A History of Occupation Statistics, 1870–1940.* Ann Arbor, MI: UMI Research Press, 1980.

Conner, Valerie J. " 'The Mothers of the Race' in World War I: The National War Labor Board and Women in Industry." *Labor History* 21, no. 1 (Winter 1979/80): 31–54.

Cortada, James W. *All the Facts: A History of Information in the United States since 1870.* New York: Oxford University Press, 2016.

Cutright, Phillips. "Illegitimacy and Income Supplements." U.S. Congress. Joint Economic Committee. Fiscal Policy Subcommittee. *The Family, Poverty, and Welfare Programs: Factors Influencing Family Instability.* Paper No. 12 (Part 1). Washington, D.C.: JEC, 1973. 90–138. http://tinyurl.com/j92fngn

Dinan, Stephen. "EXCLUSIVE: Minn. Lawmaker Vows Not to Complete Census." *The Washington Times.* June 17, 2009. http://tinyurl.com/nuqr9n

Dryfoos, Joy G. "The National Reporting System for Family Planning Services—A New Look." *Family Planning Perspectives* 12, no. 4 (July–August 1980): 193–201.

Ducoff, Louis and Gertrude Bancroft. "Experiment in the Measurement of Unpaid Family Labor in Agriculture." *Journal of the American Statistical Association* 40, no. 230 (June 1945): 205–207.

Durand, John D. "Development of the Labor Force Concept, 1930–40." Social Science Research Council. *Labor Force Definition and Measurement: Recent Experience in the United States.* New York: SSRC (no year). 80–90.

Eckler, A. Ross. *The Bureau of the Census.* New York: Praeger, 1972.

Edwards, Alba M. "Social-Economic Groups of the United States: Gainful Workers of United States, Classified by Social-Economic Groups or Strata." *Quarterly Publications of the American Statistical Association* 15 (June 1917): 643–661. http://tinyurl.com/grkojh8

Eisenstadt v. Baird, 405 U.S. 438 (1972).

Equal Pay Act, U.S. Code 29 (2012), §§206 et seq.

Executive Order 10980 of December 14, 1961, Establishing the President's Commission on the Status of Women. *Code of Federal Regulations, title 3* (1961): 138–139. http://tinyurl.com/znglw8t

"Federal Standards for the Employment of Women in Industry." *Monthly Labor Review* 8, no. 1 (January 1919): 216–219.

FedStats. "Agencies." http://tinyurl.com/z5oogk8

FedStats. "Showcase." http://tinyurl.com/zmjtzva

Finlay, Barbara. *George W. Bush and the War on Women: Turning Back the Clock on Women's Progress.* New York: Zed Books, 2006.

Folbre, Nancy and Marjorie Abel. "Women's Work and Women's Households: Gender Bias in the U.S. Census." *Social Research* 56, no. 3 (Autumn 1989): 545–569.

Ford, David A., Ronet Bachman, Monika Friend, and Michelle Meloy. *Controlling Violence against Women: A Research Perspective on the 1994 VAWA's Criminal Justice Impacts.* NCJ 197137. Washington, D.C.: U.S. Justice Department, National Institute of Justice, 2002.

Frankel, Todd C. "Why the CDC Still Isn't Researching Gun Violence, Despite the Ban Being Lifted Two Years Ago." *Washington Post.* January 14, 2015. http://tinyurl.com/ptlq3hc

Geib-Gunderson, Lisa. *Uncovering the Hidden Work of Women in Family Businesses: A History of Census Undernumeration.* New York: Garland, 1998.

Gilman, Charlotte Perkins. "That Rural Home Inquiry: Why Are There No Women on the President's Commission?" *Good Housekeeping* 48, no. 1 (January 1901): 120–122. http://tinyurl.com/hl79tzo

Goldin, Claudia. "Household and Market Production of Families in a Late Nineteenth Century City." *Explorations in Economic History* 16, no. 2 (April 1979): P111–131.

Goldin, Claudia. *Understanding the Gender Gap.* New York: Oxford University Press, 1990.

Gora, JoAnn Gennaro. *The New Female Criminal: Empirical Reality or Social Myth?* New York: Praeger, 1982.

Grana, Sheryl J. *Women and Justice.* Second edition. Lanham, MD: Rowman and Littlefield, 2010.

Griffin, Cynthia E. "Lost Count." *Entrepreneur.* July 2001. 28. http://tinyurl.com/jgx8ltm

Griswold v. Connecticut, 381 U.S. 479 (1965).

Groves, Sharon. "News and Views." *Feminist Studies* 31, no. 1 (Spring 2005): 199. http://tinyurl.com/h7plvdb

Guttmacher Institute. *History of the Guttmacher Institute.* http://tinyurl.com/lmje392

Hacker, Meg. "When Saying 'I Do' Meant Giving Up Your U.S. Citizenship." *Prologue* 46, no. 1 (Spring 2014): 56–61.

Hartmann, Heidi, Elyse Shaw, and Rachel O'Connor. *Women and Men in the Recovery: Where the Jobs Are: Women Recover Jobs Lost in Recession in Year Five.* Briefing Paper IWPR #C426. Washington, D.C.: Institute for Women's Policy Research, 2014.

Haupt, Barbara J. "The National Reporting System for Family Planning Services." *Health Services Reports* 88, no. 7 (August–September 1973): 637–639. http://tinyurl.com/zkcw4yg

Hautaniemi, Susan. "Technology, Women's Labor, and Compensation." *The Population of the United States.* Edited by Anderton, Douglas L., Richard E. Barrett, and Donald J. Bogue. Third Edition. New York: Free Press, 1997. 111–112.

Hindelang, Michael J. and Bruce J. Davis. "Forcible Rape in the United States: A Statistical Profile." *Forcible Rape: The Crime, the Victim, and the Offender.* Edited by Duncan Chappell, Robley Geis, and Gilbert Geis. New York: Columbia University Press, 1977. 87–114.

Holleran, Lisa L. and Donna M. Vandiver. "U.S. Homicides: Multi-Offenders and the Presence of Female Offenders." *Violence and Gender* 3, no. 1 (2016): http://tinyurl.com/hros4pm

Holmes, George K. "Supply and Wages of Farm Labor." *Yearbook of the United States Department of Agriculture 1910.* Washington, D.C.: Agriculture Department, 1911. 189–200.

Huls, Mary Ellen. *United States Government Documents on Women, 1800–1990: A Comprehensive Bibliography. Volume I: Social Issues. Volume II: Labor.* Westport, CT: Greenwood Press, 1993.

Hunt, William C. "The Federal Census of Occupations." *American Statistical Association.* New Series 86. June 1909. 467–485.

Institute for Women's Policy Research. *Statement by IWPR on the BLS Decision to Discontinue Data Collection on Women's Employment.* IWPR, 2004. http://tinyurl.com/h8ee6fp

Jacobs, James R. "Sourcebook of Criminal Justice Statistics: Another Defunded Publication." *Free Government Information.* June 29, 2012. http://tinyurl.com/gmlfgz7

Jacobson, Louis. "Jon Kyl Says Abortion Services Are 'Well Over 90 Percent of What Planned Parenthood Does.'" @politifact, 2011. http://tinyurl.com/3pk3f4s

Jaffe, A.J. "Trends in the Participation of Women in the Working Force." *Monthly Labor Review* 79, no. 5 (May 1956): 559–565.

Jaffe, A.J. and Herbert F. Spirer. *Misused Statistics: Straight Talk for Twisted Numbers.* New York: Marcel Dekker, 1987.

Johnson, Beverly L. and Elizabeth Waldman. "Most Women Who Maintain Families Receive Poor Labor Market Returns." *Monthly Labor Review* 106, no. 12 (December 1983): 30–34.

Jones, Calvin and Rachel A. Rosenfeld. *American Farm Women: Findings from a National Survey.* NORC Report no. 130. Chicago: National Opinion Research Center, 1981. http://tinyurl.com/jmx9wrm

Kearns, Brendan. "Down for the Count: Overcoming the Census Bureau's Neglect of the Homeless." National Coalition for the Homeless. http://tinyurl.com/jedx9uu

Kennedy, David M. *Birth Control in America: The Career of Margaret Sanger.* New Haven, CT: Yale University Press, 1970.

Kilpatrick, Dean, Jenna McCauley, and Grace Mattern. *Understanding National Rape Statistics.* Harrisburg, PA: National Online Resource Center on Violence against Women, 2009. http://tinyurl.com/gwp3e6b

Kneeland, Hildegarde. "Is the Modern Housewife a Lady of Leisure?" *Family Economics Review* 3 (1982): 34–35.

Kneeland, Hildegarde. "Leisure of Home Makers Studied for Light on Standards of Living." *Yearbook of Agriculture* (1932): 562–564.

Knowles, Jane B. "'It's Our Turn Now': Rural American Women Speak Out, 1900–1920." *Women and Farming: Changing Roles, Changing Structures.* Edited by Wava G. Haney and Jane B. Knowles. Boulder, CO: Westview Press, 1988. 303–318.

Kohlhell, Jacob. "Calif. Students Now Given Six 'Gender Identity' Choices on College Admission Applications." *The College Fix.* July 27, 2015. http://tinyurl.com/jnxkshx

Korenbrot, Carol C., Claire Brindis, and Fran Priddy. "Trends in Rates of Live Births and Abortions Following State Restrictions on Public Funding of Abortion." *Public Health Reports* 105, no. 6 (November–December 1990): 555–562.

Krause, Harry D. "Child Welfare, Parental Responsibility, and the State." U.S. Congress. Joint Economic Committee. Fiscal Policy Subcommittee. *The Family, Poverty, and Welfare Programs: Factors Influencing Family Instability.* Paper No. 12 (Part 2). Washington, D.C.: JEC, 1973. 255–274.

Kreider, Rose M. "Differences in Statistics about Births to Unmarried Women." *Random Samplings.* May 1, 2013. http://tinyurl.com/d8muxtp

Kreps, Juanita M. "Changing Roles of Women and Statistical Policy." *Census Bureau Conference on Issues in Federal Statistical Needs Relating to Women.* P-23. No. 83. Washington, D.C.: Census Bureau, 1979. 3–5. (C 3.186: P-23/83). http://tinyurl.com/glv2hnl

Kyrk, Hazel. "Family Responsibilities of Earning Women." *Report on 1948 Women's Bureau Conference.* Bulletin 224. Washington, D.C.: Women's Bureau, 1948. 59–68. (L 13.3:224)

Lewis, Jamie L., Nancy Bates, and Matthew Streeter. *Measuring Same-Sex Couples: The What and Who of Misreporting on Relationship and Sex.* SEHSD Working Paper 2015–12. Census Bureau, 2015. http://tinyurl.com/hggzc2q

Love, Keith. "How Do You Put a Price Tag on a Housewife's Work?" *New York Times.* January 13, 1976. 40.

MacLean, Maggie. "Sybilla Masters." *History of American Women*. http://tinyurl .com/grt6web

Mahoney, Carolyn B. *The Downgrading of DACOWITS: How President Bush Has Failed America's Women in Uniform*. Washington, D.C.: Congresswoman Maloney's Office, 2004. http://tinyurl.com/hdzomlg

Martelle, Scott. *Blood Passion: The Ludlow Massacre and Class War in the American West*. New Brunswick, NJ: Rutgers University Press, 2007.

Martinez, Gladys M. and Joyce C. Abma. *Sexual Activity, Contraceptive Use, and Childbearing of Teenagers Aged 15–19 in the United States*. NCHS Data Brief. 209, 2015. http://tinyurl.com/o859586

Meyer, Peter B. "Who Had an Occupation? Changing Boundaries in Historical U.S. Census Data." *Historical Social Research* 34, no. 3 (2009): 149–167.

Mikulski, Barbara M. "Challenge I." *Census Bureau Conference on Issues in Federal Statistical Needs Relating to Women*. P-23. No. 83. Washington, D.C.: Census Bureau, 1979. 115–119. (C 3.186:P-23/83). http://tinyurl.com /glv2hnl

Moore, Kristin A. "Nonmarital Childbearing in the United States." U.S. Health and Human Services Department. Centers for Disease Control and Prevention. National Center for Health Statistics. *Report to Congress on Out-of-Wedlock Childbearing* (PHS) 95-1257. Hyattsville, MD: NCHS, 1995. V–xxii. http://tinyurl.com/jqebcyk

Mosher, William D. "Fertility and Family Planning in the 1970s: The National Survey of Family Growth." *Family Planning Perspectives* 14, no. 6 (November–December 1982): 314–320.

Muller, Charlotte. "Data Needs Related to Women's Health." *Census Bureau Conference on Issues in Federal Statistical Needs Relating to Women*. P-23. No. 83. Washington, D.C.: Census Bureau, 1979. 94–105. (C 3.186:P-23/83) http://tinyurl.com/glv2hnl

National Council for Research on Women. *Missing: Information about Women's Lives*. New York: NCRW, 2004. http://tinyurl.com/hvz3sms

National Women's Law Center. *Assignment Policies for Military Women: History and Status*. Washington, D.C.: NWLC, 2016. http://tinyurl.com/juoazeg

Nelson, Robert L. and William P. Bridges. *Legalizing Gender Equality: Courts, Markets, and Unequal Pay for Women in America*. New York: Cambridge University Press, 1999.

Nixon, Richard M. *Economic Report of the President, 1973*. Washington, D.C.: President, 1973.

Norwood, Janet L. "New Approaches to Statistics on the Family." *Monthly Labor Review* 100, no. 31 (July 1977): 31–34.

"Occupational Coding in the 1880 Public Use Microdata Sample." IPUMSusa. http://tinyurl.com/jt8efbj

Oppenheimer, Valerie Kincade. *The Female Labor Force in the United States*. Westport, CT: Greenwood Press, 1970.

Orleck, Annelise. *Common Sense and a Little Fire: Women and Working Class Politics in the United States, 1900–1965.* Chapel Hill: University of North Carolina Press, 1995.

"The Packwood Resignation." *New York Times.* September 8, 1995. http://tinyurl.com/z4lwvd4

Pivar, David J. "Cleansing the Nation: The War on Prostitution, 1917–1921." *Prologue* 12, no. 1 (Spring 1980): 29–40.

"*Pneumocystis* Pneumonia—Los Angeles." *Morbidity and Mortality Weekly Report.* 30. June 5, 1981. 250–252.

Poe, Charles A. "Clarence Hamilton Poe, 1881–." *Dictionary of North Carolina Biography.* Edited by William S. Powell. Reprinted in *Documenting the American South.* http://tinyurl.com/h7ebgvj

Presser, Harriet B. "Decapitating the U.S. Census Bureau's 'Head of Household': Feminist Mobilization in the 1970s." *Feminist Economics* 4, no. 3 (1998). doi:10.1080/135457098338356. http://tinyurl.com/hhdfgqr

Rayman, Paula. "Women and Unemployment." *Social Research* 54, no. 2 (Summer 1987): 355–376.

Reilly, Kimberley A. *Sex without Spheres: Labor, Marriage, and Citizenship in the Era of the New Woman.* Chicago: University of Chicago, 2008.

Rhoads, Steven A. *Incomparable Worth: Pay Equity Meets the Market.* New York: Cambridge University Press, 1993.

Robbins, Warren D. "Report of Nez Percé Agency." *Sixteenth Annual Report of the Commissioner of Indian Affairs to the Secretary of the Interior 1890.* Washington, D.C.: Commissioner of Indian Affairs, 1890. 232–234.

Roe v. Wade, 410 U.S. 113 (1973).

Rosenfeld, Rachel Ann. *Farm Women: Work, Farm, and Family in the United States.* Chapel Hill: University of North Carolina Press, 1985.

Rotella, Elyce J. *From Home to Office: U.S. Women at Work, 1870–1930.* Ann Arbor MI: UMI Research Press, 1981.

S., F.P. "A Record of Broken Vows." *The New York Times.* March 31, 1889. 16. http://nyti.ms/2bMrbNv

Scheer, Teva J. *Governor Lady: The Life and Times of Nellie Tayloe Ross.* Columbia: University of Missouri Press, 2005.

Schiffman, Jacob. "Marital Status of Workers, 1959." *Monthly Labor Review* 83, no. 3 (March 1960): 257–261.

Schmeckebier, Laurence F. *The Statistical Work of the National Government.* Baltimore, MD: Johns Hopkins Press, 1925.

Schoen, Johanna. *Choice and Coercion: Birth Control, Sterilization, and Abortion in Public Health and Welfare.* Chapel Hill, NC: University of North Carolina Press, 2005.

Scholl, Kathleen K. "Household and Farm Task Participation of Women." *Family Economics Review* 3 (1982): 3–9.

Scott, Ann Herbert. *Census, U.S.A.* New York: Seabury Press, 1968.

Schwartztrauber, Evelyn. "Make-Up, America 'Pick Up' Morale." *Domestic Commerce* 31, no. 21 (August 1943): 7–8, 24.

Shepela, Sharon Toffee and Ann T. Viviano. "Some Psychological Factors Affecting Job Segregation and Wages." *Comparable Worth and Wage Discrimination: Technical Possibilities and Political Realities.* Edited by Helen Remick. Philadelphia: Temple University Press, 1984. 47–58.

Simpson, Sidney P. "Private Losses Due to Criminal Acts." U.S. National Commission on Law Observance and Enforcement. *Report on the Cost of Crime.* Washington, D.C.: NCLOE, 1931. http://tinyurl.com/zdcea97

Slaughter, Louise M. "Remarks." U.S. Health and Human Services Department. Public Health Service. National Institutes of Health. Office of Research on Women's Health. *Recruitment and Retention of Women in Clinical Studies.* NIH Publication 95-3756. ORWH, 1995. http://tinyurl.com/jfc6jkx

Smith, Christopher E. "Information Cancelled." *OGJ Newsletter.* November 28, 2011. No page number. http://tinyurl.com/gl3y78v

Smith, George Otis. "Survey of Employment Conditions: The Weaker Sex." *Women and the National Experience: Primary Sources in American History.* Second edition. Edited by Ellen Skinner. New York: Longman, 2003. 172–174.

Smith, Jack C. and Judith P. Bourne. "Abortion Surveillance Program of the Center for Disease Control." *Health Service Reports* 88, no. 3 (March 1973): 255–259.

Smith, Sandra S. "NCHS Dataline." *Public Health Reports* 126, no. 1 (January–February 2011): 136–138. http://tinyurl.com/hwota5e

Smuts, Robert W. "The Female Labor Force: A Case Study in the Interpretation of Historical Statistics." *Journal of the American Statistical Association* 55, no. 289 (March 1960): 71–79.

Snow, Michael. "Census Pop Culture through the Decades." *Random Samplings.* March 19, 2012. http://tinyurl.com/8xmwzyy

Social Explorer. *Census Questionnaires and Instructions: 1790 to 2000.* http://tinyurl.com/j8s3v6e

Social Explorer. *Data Dictionary: Census 2010.* http://tinyurl.com/hbvnklo

Social Science Research Council. *Labor Force Definition and Measurement: Recent Experience in the United States.* New York: SSRC, no year.

Stapleford, Thomas A. "'Housewife versus Economist': Gender, Class, and Domestic Economic Knowledge in Twentieth-Century America." *Labor: Studies in Working Class Histories of the Americas* 1, no. 2 (2004): 89–112.

Statistics Canada. *Statistics Canada.* http://tinyurl.com/c9q7b3

Storey, Thomas A. "Evaluation of Governmental Aid to Detention Houses and Reformatories." U.S. Interdepartmental Social Hygiene Board. *Detention Houses and Reformatories as Protective Social Agencies in the Campaign of the United States Government against Venereal Diseases,* by Mary Macey Dietzler. Washington, D.C.: ISHB, 1922. 3–9.

Straub, Eleanor F. "United States Government Policy toward Civilian Women during World War II." *Prologue* 5, no. 4 (Winter 1973): 240–254.

Strober, Myra H. "Comments." *Census Bureau Conference on Issues in Federal Statistical Needs Relating to Women*. Washington, D.C.: Census Bureau, 1979. 35–39. (C 3.186:P-23/83). http://tinyurl.com/glv2hnl

"Survey of American Women." *Family Economics Review* 3 (1982): 9–10.

Tilley, John A. *A History of Women in the Coast Guard*, 1996. http://tinyurl.com /hd9ufeh

Truman, Harry S. "The President's First Economic Report. January 8, 1947." *Public Papers of the Presidents of the United States: Harry S. Truman 1947*. Washington, D.C.: Office of the Federal Register, 1965. 13–38.

29 U.S.C. § 12 (2016).

Uniform Crime Reports. 1 (1) 1930.

Uniform Crime Reports. 3 (4) 1933.

Uniform Crime Reports. 4 (3) 1933.

Uniform Crime Reports. 5 (1) 1934.

Uniform Crime Reports. 13 (1) 1942.

United States v. Holte, 236 U.S. 140 (1915).

University at Albany. School of Criminal Justice. Hindelang Criminal Justice Research Center. *Sourcebook of Criminal Justice Statistics*. http://www .albany.edu/sourcebook/

University of Minnesota. Minnesota Population Center. "1940 Census: Instructions to Enumerators." IPUMS USA. http://tinyurl.com/jcwe4ke

"Update on Kaposi's Sarcoma and Opportunistic Infections in Previously Healthy Person—United States." *Morbidity and Mortality Weekly Report* 31 (June 11, 1982): 294–310.

U.S. Agriculture Department. *2012 Census Highlights: Farm Demographics—U.S. Farmers by Gender, Age, Race, Ethnicity, and More*. ACH12-3. Washington, D.C.: NASS, 2014. http://tinyurl.com/hzo3s7s

U.S. Agriculture Department. *The Farm Woman's Problems*, by Florence E. Ward. Department of Agriculture Circular 148. Washington, D.C.: Agriculture Department, 1920. http://tinyurl.com/hoqfskr

U.S. Agriculture Department. *Report of the Commissioner of Agriculture for the Year 1871*. Washington, D.C.: Agriculture Department, 1872. http://tinyurl .com/zfe4hq5

U.S. Agriculture Department. Economic Research Service. *Agricultural Work Force of 1987: A Statistical Profile*, by Victor J. Oliveira and E. Jane Cox. Report 609. Washington, D.C.: ERS, 1989. http://tinyurl.com/zn6z6tv

U.S. Agriculture Department. Information Office. *Social and Labor Needs of Farm Women*. Report 103. Washington, D.C.: Information Office, 1915.

U.S. Agriculture Department. National Agricultural Statistics Service. *About NASS: History of Agricultural Statistics*, 2016. http://tinyurl.com/jk4gd2j

U.S. Agriculture Department. National Institute of Food and Agriculture. *Cooperative Extension History*. http://tinyurl.com/hhsnrg3

U.S. Agriculture Department. Statistics Bureau. *Supply of Farm Labor,* by George K. Holmes. Bulletin 94. Washington, D.C.: Statistics Bureau, 1912. http://tinyurl.com/hrrgpsh

U.S. Agriculture Department. Statistics Bureau. *Wages of Farm Labor,* by George K. Holmes. Bulletin 99. Washington, D.C.: Statistics Bureau, 1912. http://tinyurl.com/zwv8o84

U.S. American Indian Policy Review Commission. Alcohol and Drug Abuse Task Force. *Report on Alcohol and Drug Abuse,* by Stephen LaBoueff Jr., Reuben Snake, and George Hawkins. Washington, D.C.: AIPRC, 1976.

U.S. Census Office. *Statistical View of the United States,* by J.D.B. De Bow. Washington, D.C.: A.O.P. Nicholson, 1854. http://tinyurl.com/zu4wv6a

U.S. Census Office. *Statistics of the United States (Including Mortality, Property, etc.) in 1860.* Washington, D.C.: Census Office, 1866. http://tinyurl.com/h2a59kc

U.S. Census Superintendent. *The Seventh Census: Report of the Superintendent of the Census for December 1, 1852.* Washington, D.C.: Robert Armstrong, 1853.

U.S. Civil Rights Commission. *Battered Women: Issues of Public Policy.* Washington, D.C.: CRC, 1978. (CR 1.2:W 84/3). http://tinyurl.com/httmej9

U.S. Civil Rights Commission. *Comparable Worth: Issues for the 80s. Volume 2: Proceedings.* CRC, 1984. http://tinyurl.com/zo5xxhr

U.S. Civil Rights Commission. *The Silent Victims: Denver's Battered Women.* Washington, D.C.: CRC, 1977. (CR 1.2:W 84/2). http://tinyurl.com/jyna6g8

U.S. Civil Rights Commission. *Under the Rule of Thumb: Battered Women and the Administration of Justice.* Washington, D.C.: CRC, 1982. (CR 1.2:W 84/10). http://tinyurl.com/htfwnq5

U.S. Civil Rights Commission. *The Unfinished Business: Twenty Years Later . . .* Washington, D.C.: CRC, 1977. (CR 1.2: Un 2)

U.S. Civil Service Commission. *The First Year: A Study of Women's Participation in Federal Defense Activities,* by Lucille Foster McMillin. Washington, D.C.: CSC, 1941. (CS 1.2:W 84/2). http://tinyurl.com/ox3pu87

U.S. Civil Service Commission. *The Second Year: A Study of Women's Participation in War Activities of the Federal Government,* by Lucille Foster McMillin. Washington, D.C.: CSC, 1943. (CS 1.2:W 84/2/942). http://tinyurl.com/joq5f2o

U.S. Civil War Centennial Commission. *Our Women of the Sixties,* by Sylvia G.L. Dannett and Katharine M. Jones. Washington, D.C.: CWCC, 1963. (Y 3.C 49/2:2 W 84) http://tinyurl.com/j3oyept

U.S. Commerce and Labor Department. Census Bureau. *Census 1910. Volume III. Population.* Washington, D.C.: Census Bureau, 1913.

U.S. Commerce and Labor Department. Census Bureau. *Marriage and Divorce 1867–1906, Part I.* Washington, D.C.: Census Bureau, 1909. http://tinyurl.com/jtvrqql

U.S. Commerce and Labor Department. Census Bureau. *Marriage and Divorce 1887–1906.* Bulletin 96. Second edition. Washington, D.C.: Census Bureau, 1914. http://tinyurl.com/zhrrjhm

U.S. Commerce and Labor Department. Census Bureau. *Mortality Statistics: 1910.* Bulletin 109. Washington, D.C.: Census Bureau, 1912. http://tinyurl .com/kjeqbnb

U.S. Commerce and Labor Department. Census Bureau. *Special Reports: Supplementary Analysis and Derivative Tables: Twelfth Census of the United States: 1900.* Washington, D.C.: Census Bureau, 1906.

U.S. Commerce and Labor Department. Census Bureau. *Statistics of Women at Work Based on Unpublished Information Derived from the Schedules of the Twelfth Census: 1900.* Washington, D.C.: Census Bureau, 1907. http:// tinyurl.com/h348roo

U.S. Commerce and Labor Department. Foreign and Domestic Commerce Bureau. *Statistical Abstract of the United States 1912.* Washington, D.C.: Statistics Bureau, 1913. http://tinyurl.com/ha93jc5

U.S. Commerce and Labor Department. Statistics Bureau. *Statistical Abstract of the United States 1904.* Washington, D.C.: Statistics Bureau, 1905.

U.S. Commerce and Labor Department. Statistics Bureau. *Statistical Abstract of the United States 1905.* Washington, D.C.: Statistics Bureau, 1906.

U.S. Commerce and Labor Department. Statistics Bureau. *Statistical Abstract of the United States 1907.* Washington, D.C.: Statistics Bureau, 1908. http:// tinyurl.com/zlevwc3.

U.S. Commerce and Labor Department. Statistics Bureau. *Statistical Abstract of the United States 1908.* Washington, D.C.: Statistics Bureau, 1909.

U.S. Commerce and Labor Department. Statistics Bureau. *Statistical Abstract of the United States 1910.* Washington, D.C.: Statistics Bureau, 1911.

U.S. Commerce Department. Census Bureau. *200 Years of Census Taking: Population and Housing Questions, 1790–1990.* Washington, D.C.: Census Bureau, 1989. http://tinyurl.com/ja9j6aq

U.S. Commerce Department. Census Bureau. *The 1950 Censuses: How They Were Taken.* Washington, D.C.: Census Bureau, 1955.

U.S. Commerce Department. Census Bureau. *1950 United States Census of Population: Fertility.* Volume 4, Part 5C. Washington, D.C.: Census Bureau, 1955. http://tinyurl.com/gnd3938

U.S. Commerce Department. Census Bureau. *1970 Census of Population: Subject Reports: Childspacing and Current Fertility.* PC2-3(B). Washington, D.C.: Census Bureau, 1975. (C 3.970/2:Pt. 3B). http://tinyurl.com/gma8bkk

U.S. Commerce Department. Census Bureau. *1980 Census of Population. Occupation by Industry.* Washington, D.C.: Census Bureau, 1984. (C 3.223/10:980 v.2 pt.7c)

U.S. Commerce Department. Census Bureau. *1980 Census of Population. Place of Work.* Washington, D.C.: Census Bureau, 1984. (C 3.223/10:980 v.2 pt.6e)

U.S. Commerce Department. Census Bureau. *1980 Census of Population and Housing. Users' Guide. Part A. Text.* Washington, D.C.: Census Bureau, 1982.

U.S. Commerce Department. Census Bureau. *Abstract of the Fifteenth Census of the United States: 1930.* Washington, D.C.: Census Bureau, 1933. http://tinyurl.com/hzd9onr

U.S. Commerce Department. Census Bureau. *Abstract of the Fourteenth Census of the United States 1920.* Washington, D.C.: Census Bureau, 1923.

U.S. Commerce Department. Census Bureau. *Alphabetical Index to Occupations.* Washington, D.C.: Census Bureau, 1920. http://tinyurl.com/zomgvc8

U.S. Commerce Department. Census Bureau. *Alphabetical Index to Occupations.* Washington, D.C.: Census Bureau, 1930. http://tinyurl.com/jdh45av

U.S. Commerce Department. Census Bureau. *Birth, Stillbirth, and Infant Mortality Statistics 1931.* Washington, D.C.: Census Bureau, 1934. http://tinyurl.com/hrv9fkc

U.S. Commerce Department. Census Bureau. *Census '80: Continuing the Factfinder Tradition,* by Charles P. Kaplan and Thomas L. Van Valey. Washington, D.C.: Census Bureau, 1980.

U.S. Commerce Department. Census Bureau. *Census of Population: 1940. Characteristics of Persons Not in the Labor Force.* Washington, D.C.: Census Bureau, 1943. http://tinyurl.com/hj53834

U.S. Commerce Department. Census Bureau. *Census of Population: 1970. Volume 1. Characteristics of the Population. Part 1. United States Summary—Section 1.* Washington, D.C.: Census Bureau, 1973.

U.S. Commerce Department. Census Bureau. *Differential Fertility 1940 and 1910: Women by Number of Children Ever Born.* Washington, D.C.: Census Bureau, 1945.

U.S. Commerce Department. Census Bureau. *Divorce, Child Custody, and Child Support.* Washington, D.C.: Census Bureau, 1979.

U.S. Commerce Department. Census Bureau. *Families Maintained by Female Householders 1970–79,* by Steve W. Rawlings. P-23. No. 107. Washington, D.C.: Census Bureau, 1980. (C 3.186:P-23/107). http://tinyurl.com/zy2p92a

U.S. Commerce Department. Census Bureau. *Female Family Heads.* Series P-23, No. 50. Washington, D.C.: Census Bureau, 1974.

U.S. Commerce Department. Census Bureau. *Fifteenth Census of the United States: 1930, Population: Volume V, General Report on Occupations,* by Alba M. Edwards. Washington, D.C.: Census Bureau, 1933. http://tinyurl.com/jugudpu

U.S. Commerce Department. Census Bureau. *Fourteenth Census of the United States: 1920, Volume II, Population, General Report and Analytical Tables.* Washington, D.C.: Census Bureau, 1922.

U.S. Commerce Department. Census Bureau. *Marriage, Divorce, Widowhood, and Remarriage by Family Characteristics, June 1975.* Series P-20, No. 312. Washington, D.C.: Census Bureau, 1977. http://tinyurl.com/hmxjnbf

U.S. Commerce Department. Census Bureau. *Mortality Statistics: 1931–2.* Washington, D.C.: Census Bureau, 1934. http://tinyurl.com/hqhgp8m

U.S. Commerce Department. Census Bureau. *Perspectives on American Husbands and Wives.* Series P-23, No. 77. Washington, D.C.: Census Bureau, 1978.

U.S. Commerce Department. Census Bureau. *Population: Differential Fertility 1940 and 1910. Fertility by Duration of Marriage.* Washington, D.C.: Census Bureau, 1947. http://tinyurl.com/j4ej8du

U.S. Commerce Department. Census Bureau. *Premarital Fertility,* by Wilson H. Grabill. Series P-23, No. 63. Washington, D.C.: Census Bureau, 1976. (C 3.186:P-23/63)

U.S. Commerce Department. Census Bureau. "Remarriage among Women in the United States: 1985," by Arthur J. Norton and Louisa F. Miller. *Studies in Household and Family Formation.* P-23. No. 169. Washington, D.C.: Census Bureau, 1990.

U.S. Commerce Department. Census Bureau. *Selected Characteristics of Women-Owned Businesses, 1977.* Washington, D.C.: Census Bureau, 1980. (C 3.250:77-2). http://tinyurl.com/hgu2qeq

U.S. Commerce Department. Census Bureau. *Sixteenth Census of the United States: 1940: Population: Comparative Occupation Statistics 1870 to 1940.* Washington, D.C.: Census Bureau, 1943. http://tinyurl.com/gvdz9xc

U.S. Commerce Department. Census Bureau. *Sixteenth Census of the United States: 1940: Population: Estimates of Labor Force, Employment, and Unemployment.* Washington, D.C.: Census Bureau, 1944. http://tinyurl.com/hujpzmo

U.S. Commerce Department. Census Bureau. *Sixteenth Census of the United States: 1940. Population: Labor Force (Sample Statistics) Usual Occupation.* Washington, D.C.: Census Bureau, 1943.

U.S. Commerce Department. Census Bureau. *Sixteenth Census of the United States: 1940. Population. Volume III. The Labor Force. Occupation, Industry, Employment, and Income. Part I. The United States Summary.* Washington, D.C.: Census Bureau, 1943.

U.S. Commerce Department. Census Bureau. *Sixteenth Census of the United States: 1940. Population Volume IV. Characteristics by Age, Marital Status, Relationship, Education, and Citizenship. Part 1, United States Summary.* Washington, D.C.: Census Bureau, 1943. http://tinyurl.com/hkuyl82

U.S. Commerce Department. Census Bureau. *Sixteenth Census of the United States: 1940. Population Volume IV. Characteristics by Age, Marital Status, Relationship, Education, and Citizenship. Part 3, Maine—North Dakota.* Washington, D.C.: Census Bureau, 1943.

U.S. Commerce Department. Census Bureau. *A Social-Economic Grouping of the Gainful Workers of the United States,* by Alba M. Edwards. Washington, D.C.: Census Bureau, 1938. (C 3.2:So 1/938-2)

U.S. Commerce Department. Census Bureau. *Statistical Abstract of the United States 1940.* Washington, D.C.: Census Bureau, 1941. (C 3.134: 940). http://tinyurl.com/hxsxnad

U.S. Commerce Department. Census Bureau. *Statistical Abstract of the United States 1943.* Washington, D.C.: Census Bureau, 1944. (C 3.134: 944)

U.S. Commerce Department. Census Bureau. *Statistical Abstract of the United States. 1944/5.* Washington, D.C.: Census Bureau, 1945. (C 3.134: 944/5)

U.S. Commerce Department. Census Bureau. *Statistical Abstract of the United States 1946.* Washington, D.C.: Census Bureau, 1946. (C 3.134: 946)

U.S. Commerce Department. Census Bureau. *Statistical Abstract of the United States. 1947.* Washington, D.C.: Census Bureau, 1947. (C 3.134: 947)

U.S. Commerce Department. Census Bureau. *Statistical Abstract of the United States. 1948.* Washington, D.C.: Census Bureau, 1948. (C 3.134: 948)

U.S. Commerce Department. Census Bureau. *Statistical Abstract of the United States 1950.* Washington, D.C.: Census Bureau, 1950. (C 3.134: 950)

U.S. Commerce Department. Census Bureau. *Statistical Abstract of the United States. 1951.* Washington, D.C.: Census Bureau, 1951. (C 3.134: 951)

U.S. Commerce Department. Census Bureau. *Statistical Abstract of the United States. 1952.* Washington, D.C.: Census Bureau, 1952. (C 3.134: 952)

U.S. Commerce Department. Census Bureau. *Statistical Abstract of the United States 1953.* Washington, D.C.: Census Bureau, 1953. (C 3.134: 953). http://tinyurl.com/jqzq369

U.S. Commerce Department. Census Bureau. *Statistical Abstract of the United States 1954.* Washington, D.C.: Census Bureau, 1954. (C 3.134: 954)

U.S. Commerce Department. Census Bureau. *Statistical Abstract of the United States 1955.* Washington, D.C.: Census Bureau, 1955. (C 3.134: 955)

U.S. Commerce Department. Census Bureau. *Statistical Abstract of the United States 1956.* Washington, D.C.: Census Bureau, 1956. (C 3.134: 956). http://tinyurl.com/hcnoqb2

U.S. Commerce Department. Census Bureau. *Statistical Abstract of the United States 1957.* Washington, D.C.: Census Bureau, 1957. (C 3.134: 957)

U.S. Commerce Department. Census Bureau. *Statistical Abstract of the United States 1958.* Washington, D.C.: Census Bureau, 1958. (C 3.134: 958). http://tinyurl.com/jo9xq3q

U.S. Commerce Department. Census Bureau. *Statistical Abstract of the United States 1960.* Washington, D.C.: Census Bureau, 1960. (C 3.134: 960). http://tinyurl.com/zolxpf4

U.S. Commerce Department. Census Bureau. *Statistical Abstract of the United States. 1961.* Washington, D.C.: Census Bureau, 1961. (C 3.134: 961)

U.S. Commerce Department. Census Bureau. *Statistical Abstract of the United States 1962.* Washington, D.C.: Census Bureau, 1962. (C 3.134: 962)

U.S. Commerce Department. Census Bureau. *Statistical Abstract of the United States. 1963.* Washington, D.C.: Census Bureau, 1963. (C 3.134: 963). http://tinyurl.com/guhprgo

U.S. Commerce Department. Census Bureau. *Statistical Abstract of the United States 1964.* Washington, D.C.: Census Bureau, 1964. (C 3.134: 964)

U.S. Commerce Department. Census Bureau. *Statistical Abstract of the United States 1965.* Washington, D.C.: Census Bureau, 1965. (C 3.134: 965)

U.S. Commerce Department. Census Bureau. *Statistical Abstract of the United States 1966*. Washington, D.C.: Census Bureau, 1966. (C 3.134: 966)

U.S. Commerce Department. Census Bureau. *Statistical Abstract of the United States 1967*. Washington, D.C.: Census Bureau, 1967. (C 3.134: 967)

U.S. Commerce Department. Census Bureau. *Statistical Abstract of the United States 1968*. Washington, D.C.: Census Bureau, 1968. (C 3.134: 968). http://tinyurl.com/jzc2u55

U.S. Commerce Department. Census Bureau. *Statistical Abstract of the United States 1969*. Washington, D.C.: Census Bureau, 1969. (C 3.134: 969)

U.S. Commerce Department. Census Bureau. *Statistical Abstract of the United States 1970*. Washington, D.C.: Census Bureau, 1970. (C 3.134: 970)

U.S. Commerce Department. Census Bureau. *Statistical Abstract of the United States 1975*. Washington, D.C.: Census Bureau, 1975. (C 3.134: 975). http://tinyurl.com/h8mj9c4

U.S. Commerce Department. Census Bureau. *Statistical Abstract of the United States 1976*. Washington, D.C.: Census Bureau, 1976. (C 3.134: 976)

U.S. Commerce Department. Census Bureau. *Statistical Abstract of the United States 1977*. Washington, D.C.: Census Bureau, 1977. (C 3.134: 977). http://tinyurl.com/h5mbk7p

U.S. Commerce Department. Census Bureau. *Statistical Abstract of the United States 1978*. Washington, D.C.: Census Bureau, 1978. (C 3.134: 978). http://tinyurl.com/jomupns

U.S. Commerce Department. Census Bureau. *Statistical Abstract of the United States 1979*. Washington, D.C.: Census Bureau, 1979. (C 3.134: 979). http://tinyurl.com/zhp5bt2

U.S. Commerce Department. Census Bureau. *Statistical Abstract of the United States 1980*. Washington, D.C.: Census Bureau, 1980. (C 3.134: 980). http://tinyurl.com/zswgprh

U.S. Commerce Department. Census Bureau. *Statistical Abstract of the United States 1982–3*. Washington, D.C.: Census Bureau, 1982. C 3.134: 982-3). http://tinyurl.com/hhfvjzz

U.S. Commerce Department. Census Bureau. *Statistical Abstract of the United States 1984*. Washington, D.C.: Census Bureau, 1983. C 3.134: 984). http://tinyurl.com/jphzv5k

U.S. Commerce Department. Census Bureau. *Statistical Abstract of the United States 1986*. Washington, D.C.: Census Bureau, 1985. C 3.134: 986) http://tinyurl.com/hq3fjud

U.S. Commerce Department. Census Bureau. *Statistical Abstract of the United States 1987*. Washington, D.C.: Census Bureau, 1986. C 3.134: 987)

U.S. Commerce Department. Census Bureau. *Statistical Abstract of the United States 1988*. Washington, D.C.: Census Bureau, 1987. C 3.134: 988). http://tinyurl.com/j8653uw

U.S. Commerce Department. Census Bureau. *Statistical Abstract of the United States 1989*. Washington, D.C.: Census Bureau, 1989. C 3.134: 989). http://tinyurl.com/hvmy33q

U.S. Commerce Department. Census Bureau. *Statistical Abstract of the United States 1990.* Washington, D.C.: Census Bureau, 1990. C 3.134: 990). http://tinyurl.com/j7d8okc

U.S. Commerce Department. Census Bureau. *Thirteenth Census of the United States: 1910, Volume IV, Population, Occupation Statistics.* Washington, D.C.: Census Bureau, 1914. http://tinyurl.com/hxrbjts

U.S. Commerce Department. Census Bureau. *Thirteenth Census of the United States, Volume I, Population, 1910, General Report and Analysis.* Washington, D.C.: Census Bureau, 1913. http://tinyurl.com/hpywr5s

U.S. Commerce Department. Census Bureau. *Trends in Child Care Arrangements of Working Mothers,* by Marjorie Lueck, Ann C. Orr, and Martin O'Connell. P-23. No. 117. Washington, D.C.: Census Bureau, 1982. (C 3.186:P-23/117) http://tinyurl.com/zddavy5

U.S. Commerce Department. Census Bureau. *Urban Enumerators Reference Manual: 1950 Census.* Washington, D.C.: Census Bureau, 1950.

U.S. Commerce Department. Census Bureau. *U.S. Census of Agriculture 1954: Volume II, General Report, Statistics by Subjects.* Washington, D.C.: Census Bureau, 1958. (C 3.31/9: 954/v.2/pt.2)

U.S. Commerce Department. Census Bureau. *U.S. Census of Agriculture 1959: Statistics by Subject. General Report Vol. II.* Washington, D.C.: Census Bureau, 1961. (C 3.31/9:959)

U.S. Commerce Department. Census Bureau. *U.S. Census of Population 1950. Volume IV. Duration of Current Marital Status.* Special Reports. Part 2. Chapter E. Washington, D.C.: Census Bureau, 1955. http://tinyurl.com/hupwzyg

U.S. Commerce Department. Census Bureau. *U.S. Census of Population: 1950, Volume IV, Special Reports, Part 1, Chapter B, Occupational Characteristics.* Washington, D.C.: Census Bureau, 1953.

U.S. Commerce Department. Census Bureau. *U.S. Census of Population 1950. Volume IV. Special Reports, Part 2, Chapter B, General Characteristics of Families.* Washington, D.C.: Census Bureau, 1953. http://tinyurl.com/ja7ewd4

U.S. Commerce Department. Census Bureau. *U.S. Census of Population 1960: Subject Reports: Employment Status and Work Experience.* Final Report PC (2)-6A. Washington, D.C.: Census Bureau, 1963.

U.S. Commerce Department. Census Bureau. *U.S. Census of Population 1960: Subject Reports: Marital Status.* Final Report PC (2)-4E. Washington, D.C.: Census Bureau, 1966.

U.S. Commerce Department. Census Bureau. *U.S. Census of Population 1960: Subject Reports: Women by Children under 5 Years Old.* PC2-3(B). Washington, D.C.: Census Bureau, 1968.

U.S. Commerce Department. Census Bureau. *Vital Statistics of the United States. 1940. Part I.* Washington, D.C.: Census Bureau, 1943.

U.S. Commerce Department. Census Bureau. *Women in Gainful Occupations, 1870 to 1920,* by Joseph A. Hill. Census Monograph IX. Washington, D.C.: Census Bureau, 1929. http://tinyurl.com/h2f9fzn

U.S. Commerce Department. Census Bureau. *Women-Owned Businesses, 1972.* Washington, D.C.: Census Bureau, 1972. (C 3.250:72)

U.S. Commerce Department. Census Bureau. *Women-Owned Businesses, 1977.* Washington, D.C.: Census Bureau, 1980. (C 3.250:77-1)

U.S. Commerce Department. Census Bureau. Center for Economic Studies. *Fifty Years of Family Planning: New Evidence on the Long-Run Effects of Increasing Access to Contraception,* by Martha Bailey. Washington, D.C.: CES, 2014. http://tinyurl.com/h4yzrpb

U.S. Commerce Department. Economics and Statistics Administration. *Women-Owned Businesses in the 21st century.* Washington, D.C.: ESA, 2010. http://tinyurl.com/hdf4fap

U.S. Commerce Department. Economics and Statistics Administration. Census Bureau. *1790 Overview.* http://tinyurl.com/jh54sbn

U.S. Commerce Department. Economics and Statistics Administration. Census Bureau. *1990 Census of Population and Housing: History. Part A.* Washington, D.C.: Census Bureau, 1993. (C 3.223/22:1990 CPH-R-2A). http://tinyurl.com/z2tlxjq

U.S. Commerce Department. Economics and Statistics Administration. Census Bureau. *1990 Census of Population: Social and Economic Characteristics: United States.* Washington, D.C.: Census Bureau, 1993.

U.S. Commerce Department. Economics and Statistics Administration. Census Bureau. *Age and Sex Composition 2010,* by Lindsay M. Howden and Julie A. Meyer. C2010BR-03. Washington, D.C.: Census Bureau, 2011. (C 3.205/8:C 2010 BR-03). http://tinyurl.com/mv8vswn

U.S. Commerce Department. Economics and Statistics Administration. Census Bureau. *Changes to the American Community Survey between 2007 and 2008 and Their Potential Effect on the Estimates of Same-Sex Couple Households,* by Martin O'Connell and Daphne Lofquist. Washington, D.C.: Census Bureau, 2009. http://tinyurl.com/z7yhyfg

U.S. Commerce Department. Economics and Statistics Administration. Census Bureau. *Characteristics of Same Sex Couple Households: Historic Tables.* Census Bureau. http://tinyurl.com/zj27uzd

U.S. Commerce Department. Economics and Statistics Administration. Census Bureau. *Emergency and Transitional Shelter Population 2000,* by Annetta C. Smith and Denise L. Smith. Report CENSR/01-2 Washington, D.C.: Census Bureau, 2001. (C 3.205/8-3:01-2). http://tinyurl.com/je76xne

U.S. Commerce Department. Economics and Statistics Administration. Census Bureau. *Evidence from Census 2000 about Earnings by Detailed Occupation for Men and Women,* by Daniel H. Weinberg. CENSR-15. Washington, D.C.: Census Bureau, 2004. (C 3.205/8-3:15). http://tinyurl.com/lt92kl9

U.S. Commerce Department. Economics and Statistics Administration. Census Bureau. *Frequently Asked Questions about Same-Sex Couple Households.* Census Bureau, 2013. http://tinyurl.com/jdr67ay

U.S. Commerce Department. Economics and Statistics Administration. Census Bureau. *Households and Families: 2010,* by Daphne Lofquist, Terry Lugaila, Martin O'Connell, and Sarah Feliz. C2010BR-14. Washington, D.C.: Census Bureau, 2012.

U.S. Commerce Department. Economics and Statistics Administration. Census Bureau. *Households, Families, and Children: A 30-Year Perspective,* by Terry Lugaila. P23-181. Washington, D.C.: Census Bureau, 1992. (C 3.186: P23-181)

U.S. Commerce Department. Economics and Statistics Administration. Census Bureau. *Marital Events of Americans 2009,* by Diana B. Elliott and Tavia Simmons. ACS-13. Washington, D.C.: Census Bureau, 2011. http://tinyurl.com/6u7mnx6

U.S. Commerce Department. Economics and Statistics Administration. Census Bureau. *Measuring America: The Decennial Censuses from 1790 to 2000.* Washington, D.C.: Census Bureau, 2002. http://tinyurl.com/joeu4w2

U.S. Commerce Department. Economics and Statistics Administration. Census Bureau. *Residents of Farms and Rural Areas: 1991,* by Laami T. Dacquel and Donald C. Dahmann. P20-472. Washington, D.C.: Census Bureau, 1993. http://tinyurl.com/gmbrfv3

U.S. Commerce Department. Economics and Statistics Administration. Census Bureau. *Same-Sex Couple Households,* by Daphne Lofquist. ACSBR/10-03. Washington, D.C.: Census Bureau, 2011. (C 3.297/3:10-03). http://tinyurl.com/6m2urtu

U.S. Commerce Department. Economics and Statistics Administration. Census Bureau. *Same Sex Couples Main.* http://tinyurl.com/z9jucf4

U.S. Commerce Department. Economics and Statistics Administration. Census Bureau. *Statistical Abstract of the United States 1991.* Washington, D.C.: Census Bureau, 1991. (C 3.134: 991)

U.S. Commerce Department. Economics and Statistics Administration. Census Bureau. *Statistical Abstract of the United States, 1992.* Washington, D.C.: Census Bureau, 1992. (C 3.134: 992)

U.S. Commerce Department. Economics and Statistics Administration. Census Bureau. *Statistical Abstract of the United States 1995.* Washington, D.C.: Census Bureau, 1995. (C 3.134: 995)

U.S. Commerce Department. Economics and Statistics Administration. Census Bureau. *Statistical Abstract of the United States 1996.* Washington, D.C.: Census Bureau, 1996. (C 3.134: 996). http://tinyurl.com/z92dpzm

U.S. Commerce Department. Economics and Statistics Administration. Census Bureau. *Statistical Abstract of the United States 1997.* Washington, D.C.: Census Bureau, 1997. (C 3.134: 997). http://tinyurl.com/zwd9b4g

U.S. Commerce Department. Economics and Statistics Administration. Census Bureau. *Statistical Abstract of the United States 1998.* Washington, D.C.: Census Bureau, 1998. (C 3.134: 998)

U.S. Commerce Department. Economics and Statistics Administration. Census Bureau. *Statistical Abstract of the United States 2000.* Washington, D.C.: Census Bureau, 2000. (C 3.134: 2000)

U.S. Commerce Department. Economics and Statistics Administration. Census Bureau. *Statistical Abstract of the United States 2001.* Washington, D.C.: Census Bureau, 2001. (C 3.134: 2001)

U.S. Commerce Department. Economics and Statistics Administration. Census Bureau. *Statistical Abstract of the United States 2002.* Washington, D.C.: Census Bureau, 2002. (C 3.134: 2000)

U.S. Commerce Department. Economics and Statistics Administration. Census Bureau. *Statistical Abstract of the United States 2003.* Washington, D.C.: Census Bureau, 2003. (C 3.134: 2003). http://tinyurl.com/j6o8q2m

U.S. Commerce Department. Economics and Statistics Administration. Census Bureau. *Statistical Abstract of the United States 2007.* Washington, D.C.: Census Bureau, 2007. (C 3.134: 2007)

U.S. Commerce Department. Economics and Statistics Administration. Census Bureau. *Statistical Abstract of the United States 2008.* Washington, D.C.: Census Bureau, 2007. (C 3.134: 2008)

U.S. Commerce Department. Economics and Statistics Administration. Census Bureau. *Statistical Abstract of the United States 2010.* Washington, D.C.: Census Bureau, 2010. (C 3.134: 2010)

U.S. Commerce Department. Economics and Statistics Administration. Census Bureau. *Statistical Abstract of the United States 2011.* Washington, D.C.: Census Bureau, 2010. (C 3.134: 2011). http://tinyurl.com/zu9b7vt

U.S. Commerce Department. Economics and Statistics Administration. Census Bureau. *Statistical Abstract of the United States 2012.* Washington, D.C.: Census Bureau, 2012. (C 3.134: 2012). http://tinyurl.com/nnhmabf

U.S. Commerce Department. Economics and Statistics Administration. Census Bureau. *Subject Index to Current Population Reports and other Population Report Series,* by Linda Morris. P23-192. Washington, D.C.: Census Bureau, 1996. (C 3.186:P-23/192). http://tinyurl.com/lroxjb9

U.S. Commerce Department. Economics and Statistics Administration. Census Bureau. *Trends in Marital Status of U.S. Women at First Birth: 1930 to 1994,* by Amara Bachu. Working Paper POP-WP020. Washington, D.C.: Census Bureau, 1998. http://tinyurl.com/hkqucfj

U.S. Commerce Department. Economics and Statistics Administration, and U.S. Executive Office of the President. Office of Management and Budget. *Women in America: Indicators of Social and Economic Well-Being.* Washington, D.C.: ESA, 2011.

U.S. Commerce Department. Federal Statistical Policy and Standards Office. *Standard Occupational Classification Manual.* Washington, D.C.: OFSPS, 1977.

U.S. Commerce Department. Foreign and Domestic Commerce Bureau. *Statistical Abstract of the United States 1913.* Washington, D.C.: FDCB, 1914.

U.S. Commerce Department. Foreign and Domestic Commerce Bureau. *Statistical Abstract of the United States 1917.* Washington, D.C.: FDCB, 1918.

U.S. Commerce Department. Foreign and Domestic Commerce Bureau. *Statistical Abstract of the United States 1918.* Washington, D.C.: FDCB, 1919.

U.S. Commerce Department. Foreign and Domestic Commerce Bureau. *Statistical Abstract of the United States 1919.* Washington, D.C.: FDCB, 1920.

U.S. Commerce Department. Foreign and Domestic Commerce Bureau. *Statistical Abstract of the United States 1921.* Washington, D.C.: FDCB, 1922. http://tinyurl.com/he4oypu

U.S. Commerce Department. Foreign and Domestic Commerce Bureau. *Statistical Abstract of the United States 1922.* Washington, D.C.: FDCB, 1923.

U.S. Commerce Department. Foreign and Domestic Commerce Bureau. *Statistical Abstract of the United States 1923.* Washington, D.C.: FDCB, 1924.

U.S. Commerce Department. Foreign and Domestic Commerce Bureau. *Statistical Abstract of the United States 1925.* Washington, D.C.: FDCB, 1926. http://tinyurl.com/zdzcgrj

U.S. Commerce Department. Foreign and Domestic Commerce Bureau. *Statistical Abstract of the United States 1926.* Washington, D.C.: FDCB, 1927. http://tinyurl.com/hak8wtv

U.S. Commerce Department. Foreign and Domestic Commerce Bureau. *Statistical Abstract of the United States 1931.* Washington, D.C.: FDCB, 1931.

U.S. Commerce Department. Foreign and Domestic Commerce Bureau. *Statistical Abstract of the United States 1934.* Washington, D.C.: FDCB, 1934.

U.S. Commerce Department. Foreign and Domestic Commerce Bureau. *Statistical Abstract of the United States 1935.* Washington, D.C.: FDCB, 1935.

U.S. Commerce Department. Office of Public Affairs. *Uncle Sam Counts: Census '70.* Washington, D.C.: Commerce Department, 1969.

U.S. Commerce Department. Patent and Trademark Office. *Buttons to Biotech: 1996 Update Report with Supplemental Data through 1998: U.S. Patenting by Women, 1977 to 1996.* Washington, D.C.: USPTO, 1999. http://tinyurl.com/h3po7de

U.S. Commerce Department. Social and Economic Statistics Administration. Census Bureau. *Census of Population: 1970. Occupational Characteristics.* Subject Report PC (2)-7A. Washington, D.C.: Census Bureau, 1973. http://tinyurl.com/hvghwtl

U.S. Commerce Department. Social and Economic Statistics Administration. Census Bureau. *Census of Population: 1970. Procedural History.* Washington, D.C.: Census Bureau, 1976. http://tinyurl.com/jj2v48o

U.S. Commerce Department. Social and Economic Statistics Administration. Census Bureau. *Statistical Abstract of the United States 1972.* Washington, D.C.: Census Bureau, 1972. (C 56.243: 1972). http://tinyurl.com/h5l38jz

U.S. Commerce Department. Social and Economic Statistics Administration. Census Bureau. *Statistical Abstract of the United States 1973.* Washington,

D.C.: Census Bureau, 1973. (C 56.243: 1973). http://tinyurl.com /hykshqu

U.S. Commerce Department. Social and Economic Statistics Administration. Census Bureau. *Statistical Abstract of the United States 1974.* Washington, D.C.: Census Bureau, 1974. (C 56.243: 1974). http://tinyurl.com/j9dp5kw

U.S. Congress. *Congressional Record.* 157. April 8, 2011. S2289. http://tinyurl .com/zkcjkhp

U.S. Congress. House. *Mortality Statistics of the Seventh Census: 1850,* by J.D.B. De Bow. 33rd Cong., 2d sess., 1855. Ex. Doc. 98.

U.S. Congress. House. Ways and Means Committee. *2004 Green Book: Background Material and Data on the Programs within the Jurisdiction of the Committee on Ways and Means.* WMCP: 108-6. Washington, D.C.: WMC, 2004. http://tinyurl.com/z7g2tjw

U.S. Congress. House. Ways and Means Committee. *Statistics of Income 1916.* 65th Cong., 2d sess., 1918. H. Doc. 1169, serial 7338.

U.S. Congress. Joint Economic Committee. *Gender Pay Inequality: Consequences for Women, Families and the Economy: A Report by the Joint Economic Committee Democratic Staff.* Washington, D.C.: JEC, 2016. http://tinyurl.com /z669qj9

U.S. Congress. Office of Technology Assessment. Health Program. *Breast Cancer Screening for Medicare Beneficiaries: Effectiveness, Costs to Medicare and Medical Resources Required.* OTA, 1987. http://tinyurl.com/hvmzuhx

U.S. Congress. Senate. "Bureau of Woman Labor," by Flora McDonald Thompson. 63rd Cong., 1st sess., 1913. S. Doc. 38. Serial 6535. http://tinyurl .com/gltzmlm

U.S. Congress. Senate. *Dictionary of Races or Peoples.* 61st Cong., 3d sess., 1911. S. Doc. 662. http://tinyurl.com/znyuv57

U.S. Congress. Senate. *Importing Women for Immoral Purposes.* 61st Cong., 2d sess., 1909. S. Doc. 196. http://tinyurl.com/hauabzj

U.S. Congress. Senate. *Memorial of Mary F. Eastman, Henrietta L.T. Woolcott, and Others, Officers of the Association for the Advancement of Women.* 45th Cong., 2d sess., 1878. S. Misc. Doc. 84. Serial 1786. http://tinyurl.com/z7skf6f

U.S. Congress. Senate. *Preliminary Report on the Eighth Census, 1860.* Washington, D.C.: Senate, 1862.

U.S. Congress. Senate. *Report of the Country Life Commission.* 60th Cong., 2d sess., 1909. S. Doc. 705. http://tinyurl.com/hn4cp9p

U.S. Congress. Senate. *Report on Condition of Woman and Child Wage-Earners in the United States. Volume 1: Cotton Textile Industry.* 61st Cong., 2d sess., 1910. S. Doc. 645.

U.S. Congress. Senate. *Report on Condition of Woman and Child Wage-Earners in the United States. Volume 5: Wage-Earning Women in Stores and Factories.* 61st Cong., 2d sess., 1910. S. Doc. 645.

U.S. Congress. Senate. *Report on Condition of Woman and Child Wage-Earners in the United States. Volume 9: History of Women in Industry in the United States,* by Helen L. Sumner. 61st Cong., 2d sess., 1910. S. Doc. 645. http://tinyurl.com/z5ohqlc

U.S. Congress. Senate. *Report on Condition of Woman and Child Wage-Earners in the United States. Volume 15: Relation between Occupation and Criminality of Women,* by Mary Conyngton. 61st Cong., 2d sess., 1911. S. Doc. 645.

U.S. Congress. Senate. *Report on Condition of Woman and Child Wage-Earners in the United States. Volume 16: Family Budgets of Typical Cotton-Mill Workers.* 61st Cong., 2d sess., 1911. S. Doc. 645.

U.S. Congress. Senate. Judiciary Committee. *Birth Control, Hearings on S. 4436.* May 12, 19–20, 1932.

U.S. Congress. Senate. Judiciary Committee. *Birth Control, Hearings on S. 4582.* February 13–14, 1931. http://tinyurl.com/j8mepb4

U.S. Congress. Senate. Judiciary Committee. Constitutional Rights Subcommittee. *Individual Rights and the Federal Role in Behavior Modification: Staff Report.* 93rd Cong., 2d sess., 1974. http://tinyurl.com/gt3vrcl

U.S. Congress. Senate. Small Business Select Committee. *Women and the Small Business Administration: Hearing. February 24, 1976.* Washington, D.C.: Small Business Select Committee, 1976.

U.S. Const. Art. I, § 2.

U.S. Defense Department. *Annual Report on Sexual Assault in the Military: Fiscal Year 2011.* Washington, D.C.: Defense Department, 2012.

U.S. Defense Department. *Annual Report on Sexual Assault in the Military: Fiscal Year 2012, Volume 2.* Washington, D.C.: Defense Department, 2013.

U.S. Defense Department. *Annual Report on Sexual Harassment and Violence at the U.S. Military Service Academies: Academic Year 2006–2007.* Washington, D.C.: Defense Department, 2007. http://tinyurl.com/jxdeahk

U.S. Defense Department. *Military Women in the Department of Defense: Manpower, Reserve Affairs & Logistics.* Washington, D.C. Defense Department, 1983.

U.S. Defense Department. "*Women in Defense—DoD Leading the Way.*" Defense Department, 1996. (D 1.2:W84/6)

U.S. Defense Department. Army. *Women in the Army.* http://tinyurl.com/jnjulr8

U.S. Defense Department. Army Department. Office of the Chief of Military History. *The Women's Army Corps,* by Mattie E. Treadwell. Washington, D.C.: OCMH, 1954. http://tinyurl.com/gonfaah

U.S. Defense Department. Defense Advisory Committee on Women in the Services. *2003 Report.* Washington, D.C.: DACOWITS, 2003. http://tinyurl.com/hellczc

U.S. Defense Department. Defense Advisory Committee on Women in the Services. *2004 Report.* Washington, D.C.: DACOWITS, 2004. http://tinyurl.com/hrst5av

U.S. Defense Department. Defense Advisory Committee on Women in the Services. *2005 Report.* Washington, D.C.: DACOWITS, 2004. http://tinyurl.com/jldpbpy

U.S. Defense Department. Defense Advisory Committee on Women in the Services. *2006 Report*. Washington, D.C.: DACOWITS, 2007. http://tinyurl.com/hrcnomm

U.S. Defense Department. Defense Advisory Committee on Women in the Services. *2007 Report*. Washington, D.C.: DACOWITS, 2008. http://tinyurl.com/hem8ehn

U.S. Defense Department. Defense Advisory Committee on Women in the Services. *2008 Report*. Washington, D.C.: DACOWITS, 2008. http://tinyurl.com/gmug3df

U.S. Defense Department. Defense Advisory Committee on Women in the Services. *2009 Report*. Washington, D.C.: DACOWITS, 2010.

U.S. Defense Department. Defense Advisory Committee on Women in the Services. *2010 Report*. Washington, D.C.: DACOWITS, 2011.

U.S. Defense Department. Defense Advisory Committee on Women in the Services. *2011 Report*. Washington, D.C.: DACOWITS, 2012. http://tinyurl.com/hyrd52z

U.S. Defense Department. Defense Advisory Committee on Women in the Services. *2012 Report*. Washington, D.C.: DACOWITS, 2013. http://tinyurl.com/hjxclmo

U.S. Defense Department. Defense Advisory Committee on Women in the Services. *2013 Report*. Washington, D.C.: DACOWITS, 2014.

U.S. Defense Department. Defense Advisory Committee on Women in the Services. *2014 Report*. Washington, D.C.: DACOWITS, 2014. http://tinyurl.com/zdldv3g

U.S. Defense Department. Defense Advisory Committee on Women in the Services. *2015 Report*. Washington, D.C.: DACOWITS, 2016.

U.S. Defense Department. Defense Advisory Committee on Women in the Services. *DACOWITS Reports and Meeting Documents*. http://tinyurl.com/hlh85vg

U.S. Defense Department. Defense Advisory Committee on Women in the Services. *Defense Advisory Committee on Women in the Armed Services*. http://dacowits.defense.gov

U.S. Defense Department. Defense Manpower Data Center. *2004 Sexual Harassment Survey of Reserve Component Members,* by Rachel N. Lipari and Anita R. Lancaster. Arlington, VA: DMDC, 2004.

U.S. Defense Department. Defense Manpower Data Center. *Sexual Harassment in the Military: 1988,* by Melanie Martindale. Arlington, VA: MDC, 1990.

U.S. Defense Department. Inspector General's Office. *Consolidated Listing of Reports*. http://tinyurl.com/hp2hp5o

U.S. Defense Department. Inspector General's Office. *Interim Report on the United States Air Force Academy Sexual Assault Survey*. Project No. 2003C004 DOD IG, 2003. http://tinyurl.com/z4ynj7b

U.S. Defense Department. Inspector General's Office. *Tailhook '91: Part 2: Events at the 35th Annual Tailhook Symposium*. Washington, D.C.: Inspector General, 1993.

U.S. Defense Department. Marine Corps. History and Museum Division. *Free a Marine to Fight: Women Marines in World War II,* by Mary V. Stremlow. Washington, D.C.: Marine Corps, 1994. http://tinyurl.com/gsljofo

U.S. Defense Department. Marine Corps. History and Museum Division. *Women Marines in World War I,* by Hewitt, Linda L. Washington, D.C.: Marine Corps, 1974. http://tinyurl.com/k5t9av7

U.S. Defense Department. Office of the Undersecretary for Personnel and Readiness. *Annual Report on Sexual Assault in the Military FY2015.* Washington, D.C.: OSD P&R, 2016. http://tinyurl.com/z6dd7se

U.S. Defense Department. Office of the Undersecretary for Personnel and Readiness. *Annual Report on Sexual Assault in the Military FY2015. Appendix B. Statistical Data on Sexual Assault.* Washington, D.C.: OSD P&R, 2016. http://tinyurl.com/z2t4a5v

U.S. Education Department. Institute of Education Sciences. National Center for Educational Statistics. *Education Statistics and Education Policy: The American Experience,* by Pascal D. Forgione. Washington, D.C.: NCES, 1998. http://tinyurl.com/h2xk24m

U.S. Education Department. National Center for Education Statistics. *Fathers' and Mothers' Involvement in Their Children's Schools by Family Type and Resident Status,* by Christine Winquist Nord and Jerry West. NCES 2001-032. Washington, D.C.: NCES, 2001.

U.S. Employment Service. *Dictionary of Occupational Titles. Part I. Definitions of Titles.* Washington, D.C.: USES, 1939. http://tinyurl.com/gvww96l

U.S. Energy Department. Energy Information Administration. *About EIA: Legislative Timeline.* Washington, D.C.: EIA. http://tinyurl.com/zgsp99q

U.S. Executive Office of the President. Council of Economic Advisers. *Gender Pay Gap: Recent Trends and Explanations.* Issue Brief. Washington, D.C.: CEA, 2015. http://tinyurl.com/knmn2pr

U.S. Federal Reserve System. *Janet L. Yellen.* http://tinyurl.com/hjm5ufv

U.S. Federal Security Agency. Office of Community War Services. Social Protection Division. *Meet Your Enemy: Venereal Disease.* OCWS, 1944. http://tinyurl.com/joqymf8

U.S. Federal Security Agency. Social Security Board. Bureau of Employment Security. United States Employment Service. Occupational Analysis Section. *Occupations Suitable for Women.* Washington, D.C.: USES, 1942. http://tinyurl.com/hbjn8lx

U.S. General Accounting Office. *Job Opportunities for Women in the Military: Progress and Problems.* FPCD-76-26. Washington, D.C.: GAO, 1976. http://tinyurl.com/hsactyz

U.S. General Accounting Office. *National Institutes of Health: Problems in Implementing Policy on Women in Study Populations.* T-HRD-90-50. Washington, D.C.: GAO, 1990. http://tinyurl.com/zca3ko4

U.S. General Accounting Office. *Options for Conducting a Pay Equity Study of Federal Pay and Classification Systems.* GGD-85-37. Washington, D.C.: GAO, 1985.

U.S. General Accounting Office. *Response to Questions Related to Comparable Worth and Sex-Based Wage Discrimination.* GGD-85-40. Washington, D.C.: GAO, 1985.

U.S. Government Accountability Office. *Breast Cancer Education: HHS Has Implemented Initiatives Aimed at Young Women.* GAO-17-19. Washington, D.C.: GAO, 2016. http://tinyurl.com/hxyul7r

U.S. Government Accountability Office. *Military Personnel: Actions Needed to Address Sexual Assaults of Male Servicemembers.* GAO-15-284. Washington, D.C.: GAO, 2015. http://tinyurl.com/njvxajg

U.S. Government Accountability Office. *Search.* http://tinyurl.com/golvmv2

U.S. Government Accountability Office. *Sexual Violence Data: Actions Needed to Improve Clarity and Address Differences Across Federal Data Collection Efforts.* Washington, D.C.: GAO, 2016. (GA 1.13:GAO-16-54)

U.S. Government Reports Office. Information Service. *U.S. Government Manual July 1940.* Washington, D.C.: USIS, 1940.

U.S. Health and Human Services Department. Centers for Disease Control and Prevention. *Abortion Surveillance—United States, 1998.* Atlanta, GA.: CDC, 2002. http://tinyurl.com/jfd2fxj

U.S. Health and Human Services Department. Centers for Disease Control and Prevention. *CDCs [sic] Abortion Surveillance System FAQs.* Atlanta, GA: CDC, 2017. http://tinyurl.com/2flqa4t

U.S. Health and Human Services Department. Centers for Disease Control and Prevention. *First Premarital Cohabitation in the United States: 2006–2010 National Survey of Family Growth,* by Casey E. Copen, Kimberly Daniels, and William D. Mosher. Number 64. Hyattsville, MD: NCHS, 2013.

U.S. Health and Human Services Department. Centers for Disease Control and Prevention. *HIV Risk among Adult Sex Workers in the United States.* Atlanta, GA.: CDC, 2016. http://tinyurl.com/hx6awuk

U.S. Health and Human Services Department. Centers for Disease Control and Prevention. *PRAMS.* Atlanta, GA.: CDC, 2017. https://www.cdc.gov /prams

U.S. Health and Human Services Department. Centers for Disease Control and Prevention. National Center for Health Statistics. *About the National Health Interview Survey.* Atlanta, GA.: CDC, 2016. http://tinyurl.com /zhktyzw

U.S. Health and Human Services Department. Centers for Disease Control and Prevention. National Center for Health Statistics. *About the National Survey of Family Growth.* Atlanta, GA.: CDC, 2016. http://tinyurl.com /hk73vwt

U.S. Health and Human Services Department. Centers for Disease Control and Prevention. National Center for Health Statistics. *Cohabitation, Marriage, Divorce, and Remarriage in the United States,* by Matthew D. Bramlett and William D. Mosher. Series 23. Number 22. Hyattsville, MD: NCHS, 2002. http://tinyurl.com/jelzqfq

U.S. Health and Human Services Department. Centers for Disease Control and
    Prevention. National Center for Health Statistics. *Health, United States
    2000.* Hyattsville, MD: NCHS, 2000. http://tinyurl.com/jcu8r25

U.S. Health and Human Services Department. Centers for Disease Control and
    Prevention. National Center for Health Statistics. *Health, United States
    2005.* Hyattsville, MD: NCHS, 2005. http://tinyurl.com/zyrulj7

U.S. Health and Human Services Department. Centers for Disease Control and
    Prevention. National Center for Health Statistics. *Health, United States
    2010.* DHHS 2011-1232. Hyattsville, MD: NCHS, 2011.

U.S. Health and Human Services Department. Centers for Disease Control and
    Prevention. National Center for Health Statistics. *Health, United States
    2015.* Hyattsville, MD: NCHS, 2016. http://tinyurl.com/zb7g9oe

U.S. Health and Human Services Department. Centers for Disease Control and
    Prevention. National Center for Health Statistics. *Key Statistics from the
    National Survey of Family Growth.* Atlanta, GA: CDC, 2012. http://tinyurl
    .com/hp5sd9a

U.S. Health and Human Services Department. Centers for Disease Control and
    Prevention. National Center for Health Statistics. *Mean Age of Mothers Is
    on the Rise: United States, 2000–2014,* by T.J. Mathews and Brady E. Ham-
    ilton. Data Brief 232. Atlanta, GA: NCHS, 2016. http://tinyurl.com
    /h9fl7oe

U.S. Health and Human Services Department. Centers for Disease Control and
    Prevention. National Center for Health Statistics. *National Health Inter-
    view Survey.* Atlanta, GA: CDC, 2017. http://tinyurl.com/zh4bpp3

U.S. Health and Human Services Department. Centers for Disease Control and
    Prevention. National Center for Health Statistics. *NHIS Surveys Available
    on the Internet.* Atlanta, GA: CDC. 2011. http://tinyurl.com/jg6m7je

U.S. Health and Human Services Department. Centers for Disease Control and
    Prevention. National Center for Health Statistics. *Nonvoluntary Sexual
    Intercourse.* Atlanta, GA: CDC, 2015. http://tinyurl.com/hsyezaj

U.S. Health and Human Services Department. Centers for Disease Control and
    Prevention. National Center for Health Statistics. *Report to Congress on
    Out-of-Wedlock Childbearing* (PHS) 95-1257. Hyattsville, MD: NCHS,
    1995. http://tinyurl.com/jqebcyk

U.S. Health and Human Services Department. Centers for Disease Control and
    Prevention. National Center for Health Statistics. *Series 23. Data from the
    National Survey of Family Growth.* Atlanta, GA: CDC, 2011. http://tinyurl
    .com/zbbq4kd

U.S. Health and Human Services Department. Centers for Disease Control and
    Prevention. National Center for Health Statistics. *Unmarried Childbearing*
    Atlanta, GA: CDC. 2017. http://tinyurl.com/hyv4ce4

U.S. Health and Human Services Department. Centers for Disease Control and
    Prevention. National Center for Health Statistics. *Unwanted Sexual Inter-
    course.* Atlanta, GA: CDC. 2015. http://tinyurl.com/hlvsm2z

U.S. Health and Human Services Department. Centers for Disease Control and
    Prevention. National Center for Health Statistics. *Vital and Health Statis-
    tics Series*. Atlanta, GA: CDC, 2011. http://tinyurl.com/3vxlev9
U.S. Health and Human Services Department. Centers for Disease Control and
    Prevention. National Center for Health Statistics. *Women: Work and
    Health,* by Diane K. Wagener, Jane Walstedt, Lynn Jenkins, Carol Bur-
    nett, Nina Lalich, and Marilyn Fingerhut. Vital and Health Statistics
    Series 3. Number 31. Hyattsville, MD: NCHS, 1997. http://tinyurl.com
    /j6lvgbj
U.S. Health and Human Services Department. Centers for Disease Control and
    Prevention. National Center for Health Statistics. *Women's Health*. Atlanta,
    GA: CDC, 2017. http://tinyurl.com/hxtwtnp
U.S. Health and Human Services Department. Centers for Disease Control and
    Prevention. National Center for Injury Prevention and Control. *Costs of
    Intimate Partner Violence against Women in the United States*. Atlanta, GA:
    NCIPC, 2003. http://tinyurl.com/7f5dx8w
U.S. Health and Human Services Department. Centers for Disease Control and
    Prevention. National Center for Injury Prevention and Control. *Intimate
    Partner Violence in the United States—2010,* by M.J. Breiding, J. Chen, and
    M.C. Black. Atlanta, GA: NCIPC, 2014. http://tinyurl.com/h3g55sy
U.S. Health and Human Services Department. Health Resources and Services
    Administration. Maternal and Child Health Bureau. *Title V: A Snapshot of
    Maternal and Child Health 2000*. Washington, D.C.: MCHB, 2000. http://
    tinyurl.com/jtqtyv4
U.S. Health and Human Services Department. National Institutes of Health.
    National Library of Medicine. National Center for Biotechnology Infor-
    mation. *Family Planning Digest*. Bethesda, MD: NLM. http://tinyurl.com
    /gsta3kt
U.S. Health and Human Services Department. National Institutes of Health.
    Office of Research on Women's Health. *Highlights of NIH Women's Health
    and Sex Differences Research 1990–2010*. NIH 10-7606-D. NIH, 2010.
U.S. Health and Human Services Department. Office on Women's Health. *A Cen-
    tury of Women's Health, 1900–2000*. Washington, D.C.: OWH, 2002.
    http://tinyurl.com/gp4egee
U.S. Health and Human Services Department. Office on Women's Health. *Who
    We Are*. Washington, D.C.: OWH, 2016. http://tinyurl.com/z8armrn
U.S. Health and Human Services Department. Public Health Service. *Progress
    Report: Violent and Abusive Behavior. PHS,* November 26, 1996. http://
    tinyurl.com/jq42n5s
U.S. Health and Human Services Department. Public Health Service. Centers for
    Disease Control and Prevention. National Center for Health Statistics.
    Handbook on the Reporting of Induced Termination of Pregnancies. DHHS
    Publication (PHS) 98-1117. Hyattsville, MD: NCHS, 1998. http://tinyurl
    .com/j5ccrx8

U.S. Health and Human Services Department. Public Health Service. Centers for Disease Control and Prevention. National Center for Health Statistics. *Health Aspects of Pregnancy and Childbirth: United States, 1982–88.* Series 23. Number 18. Hyattsville, MD: NCHS, 1995. http://tinyurl.com/zxybzay

U.S. Health and Human Services Department. Public Health Service. Centers for Disease Control and Prevention. National Center for Health Statistics. *Health, United States 1990* (PHS) 91-1232. Washington, D.C.: NCHS, 1991.

U.S. Health and Human Services Department. Public Health Service. Centers for Disease Control and Prevention. National Center for Health Statistics. *Health, United States 2014.* Washington, D.C.: NCHS, 2014.

U.S. Health and Human Services Department. Public Health Service. Centers for Disease Control. National Center for Health Statistics. *Remarriages and Subsequent Divorces, United States,* by Barbara Foley Wilson. Series 21. Number 45. Hyattsville, MD: NCHS, 1989. (HE 20.6209: 21/45)

U.S. Health and Human Services Department. Public Health Service. Centers for Disease Control and Prevention. National Center for Health Statistics. *Trends in Pregnancies and Pregnancy Rates by Outcome: Estimates for the United States, 1976–96,* by S.J. Ventura, W.D. Mosher, S.C. Curtin, J.C. Abma, and S. Henshaw. Series 21. Number 56. Washington, D.C.: CDC, 2000. http://tinyurl.com/za9tqqt

U.S. Health and Human Services Department. Public Health Service. Health Resources Administration. *Woman and Health 1980,* by Emily C. Moore. Supplement to September/October issue of *Public Health Reports.* Hyattsville, MD: PHS, 1980.

U.S. Health and Human Services Department. Public Health Service. Health Resources Administration. National Center for Health Statistics. *100 Years of Marriage and Divorce Statistics, United States, 1867–1967,* by Alexander A. Plateris. Series 21. Number 24. Hyattsville, MD: NCHS, 1973.

U.S. Health and Human Services Department. Public Health Service. National Center for Health Statistics. *Health, United States 1985.* PHS 86-1232. Hyattsville, MD: PHS, 1985. http://tinyurl.com/j327b2f

U.S. Health and Human Services Department. Public Health Service. National Center for Health Statistics. *Health, United States 1995.* Hyattsville, MD: PHS, 1996. http://tinyurl.com/gt9wxv6

U.S. Health and Human Services Department. Public Health Service. National Center for Health Statistics. *Midwife and Out-of-Hospital Deliveries, United States,* by Selma Taffel. Series 21. Number 40. Washington, D.C.: NCHS, 1984.

U.S. Health and Human Services Department. Public Health Service. National Center for Health Statistics. *Trends in Teenage Childbearing United States 1970–1981,* by Stephanie J. Ventura. Series 21. Number 41. Hyattsville, MD: NCHS, 1984. (HE 20.6209:21/41)

U.S. Health and Human Services Department. Public Health Service. National Center for Health Statistics. *Vital Statistics of the United States: 1980, Volume II—Mortality, Part A* (HRA) 75-1101. Hyattsville, MD: NCHS, 1985.

U.S. Health and Human Services Department. Public Health Service. National Institutes of Health. Office of Research on Women's Health. *Report of the Advisory Committee on Research on Women's Health, Fiscal Years 2009–2010.* Bethesda, MD: ORWH, 2011.

U.S. Health and Human Services Department. Public Health Service. Office of the Assistant Secretary for Health. Office on Smoking and Health. *The Health Consequences of Smoking for Women.* Washington, D.C.: PHS, 1980. (HE 20.2:Sm 7/5)

U.S. Health and Human Services Department. Public Health Service. Office of the Surgeon General. *Women and Smoking: A Report of the Surgeon General.* Rockville, MD: OSG, 2001. http://tinyurl.com/zzjocby

U.S. Health, Education, and Welfare Department. *Family Planning: Nationwide Opportunities for Action.* Washington, D.C.: HEW, 1968. http://tinyurl .com/jbm2jc6

U.S. Health, Education, and Welfare Department. *Report on Family Planning.* Washington, D.C.: HEW, 1966. http://tinyurl.com/zbb8ygq

U.S. Health, Education, and Welfare Department. Education office. *Management Problems of Homemakers Employed Outside the Home,* by Mildred Weigley Wood, Alberta Hill, and Mary Resh. Washington, D.C.: Education Office, 1961. (FS 5.283: 83009). http://tinyurl.com/gtrnsdb

U.S. Health, Education, and Welfare Department. Human Resources Administration. National Center for Health Statistics. *Health, United States 1975.* HRA 76-1232. Rockville, MD: PHS, 1975. (HE 20.6202:H 34/3/975)

U.S. Health, Education and Welfare Department. National Center for Health Services Research. *Women and Their Health: Research Implications for a New Era,* edited by Virginia Olesen (HRA) 77-3138. Washington, D.C.: NCHSR, 1977. (HE 20.6512/3:W 84)

U.S. Health, Education, and Welfare Department. Public Health Service. *Smoking and Health: Report of the Advisory Committee to the Surgeon General.* Washington, D.C.: PHS, 1964. (HE 20.2:SM 7/20). http://tinyurl.com/jbfy54g

U.S. Health, Education, and Welfare Department. Public Health Service. *Vital Statistics of the United States 1950. Volume 1.* Washington, D.C.: PHS, 1954. http://tinyurl.com/hvc9qkx

U.S. Health, Education, and Welfare Department. Public Health Service. *Vital Statistics of the United States 1950. Volume 3.* Washington, D.C.: PHS, 1954. http://tinyurl.com/gq9ey3e

U.S. Health, Education, and Welfare Department. Public Health Service. *Vital Statistics of the United States: 1960, Volume II—Mortality, Part A.* Washington, D.C.: PHS, 1963.

U.S. Health, Education, and Welfare Department. Public Health Service. *Women's Health: Report of the Public Health Service Task Force on Women's Health Issues. Volume 1&2.* PHS, 1985. (HE 20.2:W 84/2/v.1 and v.2).

U.S. Health, Education and Welfare Department. Public Health Service. Center for Disease Control. *Family Planning Evaluation: Abortion Surveillance*

Report—Legal Abortions, United States Annual Summary, 1970. Washington, D.C.: CDC, 1973.

U.S. Health, Education, and Welfare Department. Public Health Service. Health Resources Administration. National Center for Health Statistics. *Trends in Illegitimacy United States 1940–1965.* Series 21. Number 15. Rockville, MD: NCHS, 1974. http://tinyurl.com/j8rphfc

U.S. Health, Education, and Welfare Department. Public Health Service. Health Resources Administration. National Center for Health Statistics. *Wanted and Unwanted Births Reported by Mothers 15–44 Years of Age: United States, 1973.* Hyattsville, MD: NCHS, 1977. http://tinyurl.com/h8ssg28

U.S. Health, Education, and Welfare Department. Public Health Service. Health Resources Administration. Office of Health Resources Opportunity. *A Study of the Participation of Women in the Health Care Industry Labor Force: Executive Summary.* Washington, D.C.: OHRO, 1977. (HE 20.6002:W 84). http://tinyurl.com/juy832s

U.S. Health, Education, and Welfare Department. Public Health Service. Health Services and Mental Health Administration. *The Effect of Changes in the State Abortion Laws,* by Edward A. Duffy. Rockville, MD: HSMHA, 1971. (HE 20.2752:Ab 7)

U.S. Health, Education, and Welfare Department. Public Health Service. Health Services and Mental Health Administration. Center for Disease Control. *Family Planning Services Annual Summary 1971* (HSM) 73-8220. Atlanta, GA: CDC, 1973. http://tinyurl.com/z6dkdlc

U.S. Health, Education, and Welfare Department. Public Health Service. Health, Statistics, and Technology Office. National Center for Health Statistics. *Trends in Breast Feeding among American Mothers,* by Charles Hirschman. Washington, D.C.: NCHS, 1979. (HE 20.6209:23/3). http://tinyurl.com/jdgoyyh

U.S. Health, Education, and Welfare Department. Public Health Service. National Center for Health Statistics. *Infant, Fetal, and Maternal Mortality, United States 1963.* Washington, D.C.: NCHS, 1966.

U.S. Health, Education, and Welfare Department. Public Health Service. National Center for Health Statistics. *The National Inventory of Family Planning Services: 1978 Survey Results.* By Edmund Graves. Series 14. Number 26. Hyattsville, MD: NCHS, 1982. (HE 20.6209:14/26)

U.S. Health, Education, and Welfare Department. Public Health Service. National Center for Health Statistics. *Vital Statistics of the United States: 1970, Volume II—Mortality, Part A* (HRA) 75-1101. Rockville, MD: NCHS, 1974.

U.S. Health, Education, and Welfare Department. Public Health Service. Office of Health Research, Statistics and Technology. National Center for Health Statistics. *Office Visits by Women: The National Ambulatory Medical Care Survey: United States, 1977* (PHS 80-1976). Hyattsville, MD: NCHS, 1980. (HE 20.6209:13/45). http://tinyurl.com/hjrpbqa

U.S. Health, Education, and Welfare Department. Public Health Service. Office of Health Research, Statistics and Technology. National Center for Health Statistics. National Center for Health Services Research. *Health, United States, 1970* (PHS 81-1232). Hyattsville, MD: NCHS, 1980. http://tinyurl .com/h9kdppq

U.S. Health, Education, and Welfare Department. Public Health Service. Office of Health Research, Statistics and Technology. National Center for Health Statistics. National Center for Health Services Research. *Health, United States, 1980* (PHS 81-1232). Hyattsville, MD: NCHS, 1980. http://tinyurl .com/h9kdppq

U.S. Interdepartmental Social Hygiene Board. *Detention Houses and Reformatories as Protective Social Agencies in the Campaign of the United States Government against Venereal Diseases,* by Mary Macey Dietzler. Washington, D.C.: ISHB, 1922.

U.S. Interdepartmental Social Hygiene Board. *Manual for the Various Agents.* Washington, D.C.: ISHB, 1920. http://tinyurl.com/jcd77eb

U.S. Interior Department. *Manufactures of the United States in 1860; Compiled from the Original Returns of the Eighth Census.* Washington, D.C.: Interior Department, 1865. http://tinyurl.com/hlrvvso

U.S. Interior Department. *Statistical Atlas of the United States Based on the Results of the Ninth Census 1870,* by Francis A. Walker. Washington, D.C.: Interior Department, 1874. http://tinyurl.com/znzwjsy

U.S. Interior Department. *Statistics of the United States (Including Mortality, Property, &c.) in 1860.* Washington, D.C.: Interior Department, 1866. http:// tinyurl.com/gmdce8m

U.S. Interior Department. Census Office. *Compendium of the Eleventh Census, 1890: Part II.* Washington, D.C.: Census Office, 1894.

U.S. Interior Department. Census Office. *Compendium of the Eleventh Census: 1890. Part III.* Washington, D.C.: Census Office, 1897. http://tinyurl.com /jtt9t3l

U.S. Interior Department. Census Office. *A Compendium of the Ninth Census, 1870,* by Francis A. Walker. Washington, D.C.: Census Office, 1872.

U.S. Interior Department. Census Office. *Compendium of the Tenth Census. 1880, Volume 2.* Washington, D.C.: Census Office, 1883. http://tinyurl.com/zk8jcac

U.S. Interior Department. Census Office. *Ninth Census Volume I. The Statistics of the Population of the United States 1870,* by Francis Amasa Walker. Washington, D.C.: Interior Department, 1872. http://tinyurl.com/zpbypmd

U.S. Interior Department. Census Office. *Ninth Census Volume 3. The Statistics of the Wealth and Industry of the United States 1870,* by Francis Amasa Walker. Washington, D.C.: Interior Department, 1872. http://tinyurl.com/z47wa4x

U.S. Interior Department. Census Office. *Report on Crime, Pauperism, and Benevolence, Eleventh Census 1890, Part II,* by Frederick H. Wines. Washington, D.C.: Census Office, 1895. http://tinyurl.com/z25477w

U.S. Interior Department. Census Office. *Report on Population of the United States at the Eleventh Census, 1890, Part 1.* Washington, D.C.: Census Office, 1895.

U.S. Interior Department. Census Office. *Report on Population of the United States at the Eleventh Census: 1890. Part II.* Washington, D.C.: Census Office, 1897. http://tinyurl.com/zjresa7

U.S. Interior Department. Census Office. *Report on the Defective, Dependent, and Delinquent Classes, 1880 Census,* by Frederick Howard Wines. Washington, D.C.: Census Office, 1888. http://tinyurl.com/hbksde4

U.S. Interior Department. Census Office. *Report on the Manufactures of the United States at the Tenth Census 1880.* Washington, D.C.: Census Office, 1883.

U.S. Interior Department. Census Office. *Report on Vital and Social Statistics in the United States at the Eleventh Census: 1890: Part IV: Statistics of Deaths,* by John S. Billings. Washington, D.C.: Census Office, 1895.

U.S. Interior Department. Census Office. *Statistical Atlas of the United States, 1890 Census,* by Henry Gannett. Washington, D.C.: Census Office. 1890 Census, 1898.

U.S. Interior Department. Census Office. *Statistics of the Population of the United States at the Tenth Census 1880.* Washington, D.C.: Census Office, 1883.

U.S. Interior Department. Census Superintendent. *Population of the United States in 1860,* by Joseph C.G. Kennedy. Washington, D.C.: Interior Department, 1864.

U.S. Interior Department. Education Office. *Symposium on Home and Family Life in a Changing Civilization,* by William John Cooper, Karl E. Leib, Arthur J. Todd, and William E. Lancelot. Washington, D.C.: Education Office, 1931. http://tinyurl.com/go2y82u

U.S. Justice Department. *A Community Checklist: Important Steps to End Violence against Women.* Washington, D.C.: Justice Department, 1996. (J 1.2:V 81/7). http://tinyurl.com/gqm4oql

U.S. Justice Department. Attorney General's Task Force on Family Violence. *Final Report.* Washington, D.C.: AGTFFV, 1984. (J 1.2:F 21/2)

U.S. Justice Department. Bureau of Justice Statistics. *The Crime of Rape.* Washington, D.C.: BJS, 1985. (J 29.11:985/3)

U.S. Justice Department. Bureau of Justice Statistics. *Data Collection: National Incident-Based Reporting System (NIBRS).* http://tinyurl.com/hdf7anu

U.S. Justice Department. Bureau of Justice Statistics. *Family Violence,* by Patsy A. Klaus and Michael R. Rand. Washington, D.C.: BJS, 1984. (J 29.13:F 21)

U.S. Justice Department. Bureau of Justice Statistics. *Federal Justice Statistics.* Washington, D.C.: BJS, 1982. (J 29.11:982/2)

U.S. Justice Department. Bureau of Justice Statistics. *Historical Corrections Statistics in the United States, 1850–1984,* by Margaret Werner Cahalan. NCJ-102529. Washington, D.C.: BJS, 1986. (J 29.2:C 81/850-984). http://tinyurl.com/gr8sje3

U.S. Justice Department. Bureau of Justice Statistics. *Preventing Domestic Violence against Women,* by Patrick A. Langan. Washington, D.C.: BJS, 1986. (J 29.13:V 81/2). http://tinyurl.com/jtg3vpo

U.S. Justice Department. Bureau of Justice Statistics. *Sourcebook of Criminal Justice Statistics 1983.* NCJ-91534. Washington, D.C.: Bureau of Justice Statistics, 1983. (J 29.9:SD-SB-11)

U.S. Justice Department. Federal Bureau of Investigation. *Estimated Number of Arrests: United States: 2014.* FBI. http://tinyurl.com/j3b3hp5

U.S. Justice Department. Federal Bureau of Investigation. Criminal Justice Information Services Division. *Crime in the United States 2014. Offenses Known to Law Enforcement: Rape.* http://tinyurl.com/hurrc7j

U.S. Justice Department. Justice Programs Office. Bureau of Justice Statistics. *About the Bureau of Justice Statistics.* BJS. http://tinyurl.com/hfqbwpl

U.S. Justice Department. Justice Programs Office. Bureau of Justice Statistics. *Criminal Victimization in the United States 1992.* NCJ-145125. Washington, D.C.: BJS, 1994. http://tinyurl.com/hq9flvg

U.S. Justice Department. Justice Programs Office. Bureau of Justice Statistics. *Criminal Victimization in the United States 1993,* by Craig A. Perkins, Patsy A. Klaus, Lisa D. Bastian, and Robyn L. Cohen. NCJ-151657. Washington, D.C.: BJS, 1996. http://tinyurl.com/zet6wy7

U.S. Justice Department. Justice Programs Office. Bureau of Justice Statistics. *Criminal Victimization in the United States, 2003 Statistical Tables.* NCJ 207811. Washington, D.C.: BJS, 2005.

U.S. Justice Department. Justice Programs Office. Bureau of Justice Statistics. *Criminal Victimization in the United States—Statistical Tables Index: Rape/Sexual Assault.* BJS. http://tinyurl.com/glphtcj

U.S. Justice Department. Justice Programs Office. Bureau of Justice Statistics. *Female Victims of Sexual Violence, 1994–2010,* by Michael Planty, Lynn Langton, Christopher Krebs, Marcus Berzofsky, and Hope Smiley-McDonald. NCJ 240655. Washington, D.C.: BJS, 2013.

U.S. Justice Department. Justice Programs Office. Bureau of Justice Statistics. *Intimate Partner Violence and Age of Victim, 1993–99,* by Callie Marie Rennison. NCJ 187635. Washington, D.C.: BJS, 2001.

U.S. Justice Department. Justice Programs Office. Bureau of Justice Statistics. *Redesign of the National Crime Survey.* NCJ-111457. Washington, D.C.: BJS, 1989.

U.S. Justice Department. Justice Programs Office. Bureau of Justice Statistics. *Sourcebook of Criminal Justice Statistics 1993.* NCJ-148211. Washington, D.C.: Bureau of Justice Statistics, 1993. (J 29.9/6:993). http://tinyurl.com/h2kke7r

U.S. Justice Department. Justice Programs Office. Bureau of Justice Statistics. *Sourcebook of Criminal Justice Statistics 2003.* NCJ 208756. Washington, D.C.: Bureau of Justice Statistics, 2003. (J 29.9/6:2003)

U.S. Justice Department. Justice Programs Office. Bureau of Justice Statistics. *Special Report: Stalking Victimization in the United States,* by Katrina Baum, Shannan Catalano, and Michael Rand. NCJ 224527. Washington, D.C.: BJS, 2009.

U.S. Justice Department. Justice Programs Office. Bureau of Justice Statistics. *Stalking Victims in the United States—Revised,* by Shannan Catalano. NCJ 224527. Washington, D.C.: BJS, 2012. http://tinyurl.com/o58rd3u

U.S. Justice Department. Justice Programs Office. Bureau of Justice Statistics. *Violence against Women: Estimates from the Redesigned Survey,* by Ronet Bachman and Linda E. Saltzman. NCJ-154348. BJS, 1995. http://tinyurl .com/hehpsdy

U.S. Justice Department. Justice Programs Office. National Institute of Justice. *Annual Report to Congress 1996.* Washington, D.C.: NIJ, 1997.

U.S. Justice Department. Justice Programs Office. National Institute of Justice. *Extent, Nature, and Consequences of Intimate Partner Violence: Findings from the National Violence against Women Survey,* by Pamela Tjaden and Nancy Thoennes. NCJ 181867. Washington, D.C.: NIJ, 2000. http://tinyurl.com /oj7nxql

U.S. Justice Department. Justice Programs Office. National Institute of Justice. *Extent, Nature, and Consequences of Rape Victimization: Findings from the National Violence against Women Survey,* by Patricia Tjaden and Nancy Thoennes. NCJ 210346. Washington, D.C.: NIJ, 2006. http://tinyurl.com /8n7th4t

U.S. Justice Department. Justice Programs Office. National Institute of Justice. *The Sexual Victimization of College Women,* by Bonnie S. Fisher, Francis T. Cullen, and Michael G. Turner. NCJ 182369. Washington, D.C.: NIJ, 2000. (J 28.24/3:V 81/3)

U.S. Justice Department. Justice Programs Office. National Institute of Justice. *Stalking in America: Findings from the National Violence against Women Survey,* by Patricia Tjaden and Nancy Thoennes. Washington, D.C.: NIJ, 1998. http://tinyurl.com/hpuc2wt

U.S. Justice Department. Justice Programs Office. Office of Violence against Women. *Stalking and Domestic Violence: Report to Congress.* Washington, D.C.: OVW, 2001. http://tinyurl.com/h737arc

U.S. Justice Department. Law Enforcement Assistance Administration. *Report of the LEAA Task Force on Women.* Washington, D.C.: LEAA, 1975. http:// tinyurl.com/jptcou8

U.S. Justice Department. Law Enforcement Assistance Administration. National Criminal Justice Information and Statistics Service. *Criminal Victimization in the United States 1973.* SD-NCP-N-4. Washington, D.C.: NCJISS, 1976.

U.S. Justice Department. Law Enforcement Assistance Administration. National Criminal Justice Information and Statistics Service. *Rape Victimization in 26 Cities,* by M. Joan McDermott. Analytic Report SC-VAD-6. Washington, D.C.: NCJISS, 1979.

U.S. Justice Department. Law Enforcement Assistance Administration. National Criminal Justice Information and Statistics Service. *Sourcebook of Criminal Justice Statistics 1973.* Criminal Justice Research Center. Albany, NY: CJRC, 1973.

U.S. Justice Department. Law Enforcement Assistance Administration. National Criminal Justice Information and Statistics Service. *Sourcebook of Criminal*

Justice Statistics 1975, by Michael J. Hindelang, Christopher S. Dunn, L. Paul Sutton, and Alison L. Aumick. Washington, D.C.: NCJISS, 1976.

U.S. Justice Department. Law Enforcement Assistance Administration. National Criminal Justice Information and Statistics Service. *Sourcebook of Criminal Justice Statistics 1994.* Edited by Kathleen Maguire and Ann L. Pastore. Criminal Justice Research Center. Albany, NY: CJRC, 1995.

U.S. Justice Department. Law Enforcement Assistance Administration. National Criminal Justice Information and Statistics Service. *Sourcebook of Criminal Justice Statistics 1995.* Edited by Kathleen Maguire and Ann L. Pastore. Criminal Justice Research Center. Albany, NY: CJRC, 1996.

U.S. Justice Department. Law Enforcement Assistance Administration. National Institute of Law Enforcement and Criminal Justice. *Forcible Rape: A National Survey of the Response by Police: Police Volume I.* Washington, D.C.: LEAA, 1977. (J 1.2:R 18/2 V.1)

U.S. Justice Department. Law Enforcement Assistance Administration. National Institute of Law Enforcement and Criminal Justice. *Forcible Rape: A National Survey of the Response by Prosecutors: Prosecutors Volume I.* Washington, D.C.: LEAA, 1977. (J 1.2:R 18 V.1)

U.S. Justice Department. Law Enforcement Assistance Administration. National Institute of Law Enforcement and Criminal Justice. *National Study of Women's Correctional Programs,* by Ruth M. Glick and Virginia V. Neto. Washington, D.C.: NILECJ, 1977.

U.S. Justice Department. National Institute of Corrections. *Women in Jail: Classifications Issues,* by Tim Brennan and James Austin. Washington, D.C.: NIC, 1997. (J 16.102:W 84)

U.S. Labor Commissioner. *A Report on Marriage and Divorce in the United States, 1867 to 1886,* by Carroll D. Wright. Washington, D.C.: Labor Commissioner, 1889. http://tinyurl.com/gv3btvq

U.S. Labor Commissioner. *Work and Wages of Men, Women, and Children.* Annual Report 1895–6. Washington, D.C.: Labor Commissioner, 1897. http://tinyurl.com/j4vxdtr

U.S. Labor Commissioner. *Working Women in Large Cities.* Washington, D.C.: Labor Commissioner, 1889. http://tinyurl.com/h9eg7p3

U.S. Labor Department. Bureau of Labor Statistics. *BLS History.* Washington, D.C.: BLS, 2012. http://tinyurl.com/hvggd9d

U.S. Labor Department. Bureau of Labor Statistics. *Children of Working Mothers,* by Allyson Sherman Grossman. Bulletin 2158. Washington, D.C.: BLS, 1983.

U.S. Labor Department. Bureau of Labor Statistics. *Commissioners: Carroll D. Wright.* Washington, D.C.: BLS, 2014. http://tinyurl.com/hw4xq84

U.S. Labor Department. Bureau of Labor Statistics. *The First Hundred Years of the Bureau of Labor Statistics.* Washington, D.C.: BLS, 1985. http://tinyurl.com/gwd3wd8

U.S. Labor Department. Bureau of Labor Statistics. *Handbook of Labor Statistics 1924–26.* Bulletin 439. Washington, D.C.: BLS, 1927. http://tinyurl.com/je5n4yp

U.S. Labor Department. Bureau of Labor Statistics. *Handbook of Labor Statistics 1936.* Bulletin 616. Washington, D.C.: BLS, 1936. http://tinyurl.com/gmpy7wx

U.S. Labor Department. Bureau of Labor Statistics. *Handbook of Labor Statistics 1941, Volume 1.* Bulletin 694. Washington, D.C.: BLS, 1942. http://tinyurl.com/zfoe6nv

U.S. Labor Department. Bureau of Labor Statistics. *Handbook of Labor Statistics 1985.* Bulletin 2217. Washington, D.C.: BLS, 1985.

U.S. Labor Department. Bureau of Labor Statistics. *Highlights of Women's Earnings in 2013.* Report 1051. Washington, D.C.: BLS, 2014.

U.S. Labor Department. Bureau of Labor Statistics. *Summary of the Report on Condition of Woman and Child Wage Earners in the United States.* Bulletin 175. Washington, D.C.: GPO, 1916. http://tinyurl.com/gwtgcsm

U.S. Labor Department. Bureau of Labor Statistics. *Tables of Working Life for Women, 1950.* Bulletin 1204. Washington, D.C.: BLS, 1956. (L 2.3:1204)

U.S. Labor Department. Bureau of Labor Statistics. *Women in Domestic Work: Yesterday and Today,* by Allyson Sherman Grossman. Special Labor Force Report 242. Washington, D.C.: BLS, 1981. (L 2.98:242)

U.S. Labor Department. Bureau of Labor Statistics. *Women in the Labor Force: Some New Data Series 1979,* by Janet L. Norwood and Elizabeth Waldman. Washington, D.C.: BLS, 1979. (L2.71:575). http://tinyurl.com/zp8q6rd

U.S. Labor Department. Bureau of Labor Statistics. Division of Current Employment Statistics. *CES Overview.* Washington, D.C.: BLS, 2017. http://tinyurl.com/hhcparr

U.S. Labor Department. Bureau of Labor Statistics. Division of Current Employment Statistics. *Reconstruction of the Women Worker Series for the Current Employment Statistics Survey.* Washington, D.C.: BLS, 2006. http://tinyurl.com/huglv9b

U.S. Labor Department. Children's Bureau. *Children of Illegitimate Birth and Measures for Their Protection,* by Emma O. Lundberg. No. 166. Washington, D.C.: Children's Bureau, 1926. http://tinyurl.com/j2x2qdt

U.S. Labor Department. Children's Bureau. *Children of Illegitimate Birth Whose Mothers Have Kept Their Custody.* No. 190. Washington, D.C.: Children's Bureau, 1928. (L 5. 20:190)

U.S. Labor Department. Children's Bureau. *Maternal Mortality from All Conditions Connected with Childbirth in the United States and Certain Other Countries,* by Grace L. Meets. Miscellaneous Series 6. Bureau Publication 19. Washington, D.C.: Children's Bureau, 1917. http://tinyurl.com/znfvkfh

U.S. Labor Department. Children's Bureau. *Mothers' Aid, 1931.* Bureau Publication 220. Washington, D.C.: Children's Bureau, 1933. http://tinyurl.com/grz8luj

U.S. Labor Department. Employment and Training Administration. *Women in Traditionally Male Jobs: The Experiences of Ten Public Utility Companies.* Washington, D.C.: ETA, 1978. http://tinyurl.com/zbe9epw

U.S. Labor Department. Naturalization Bureau. *Annual Report of the Commissioner of Naturalization.* Washington, D.C.: Naturalization Bureau, 1923. http://tinyurl.com/hprvp3r

U.S. Labor Department. Women in Industry Service. *First Annual Report.* Washington, D.C.: WIS, 1919.

U.S. Labor Department. Women's Bureau. *1952 Handbook of Facts on Women Workers.* Bulletin 242. Washington, D.C.: Women's Bureau, 1952. http://tinyurl.com/h2yfkdf

U.S. Labor Department. Women's Bureau. *1958 Handbook on Women Workers.* Bulletin 266. Washington, D.C.: Women's Bureau, 1958. (L 13.3: 266). http://tinyurl.com/zzogzqr

U.S. Labor Department. Women's Bureau. *1975 Handbook on Women Workers.* Bulletin 297. Washington, D.C.: Women's Bureau, 1975. (L13.3:297)

U.S. Labor Department. Women's Bureau. *1993 Handbook on Women Workers Trends and Issues.* Washington, D.C.: Women's Bureau, 1994. http://tinyurl.com/hjea8b4

U.S. Labor Department. Women's Bureau. *Changes in Women's Occupations, 1940–1950.* Bulletin 253. Washington, D.C.: Women's Bureau, 1954. (L 13.3:253). http://tinyurl.com/zwqnyon

U.S. Labor Department. Women's Bureau. *Choosing Women for War-Industry Jobs.* Special Bulletin 12. Washington, D.C.: Women's Bureau, 1943. (L 13.10:12). http://tinyurl.com/hh3moc4

U.S. Labor Department. Women's Bureau. *Community Services for Women War Workers,* by Kathryn Blood. Special Bulletin 15. Washington, D.C.: Women's Bureau, 1944. (L 13.10:15)

U.S. Labor Department. Women's Bureau. *Differences in the Earnings of Women and Men,* by Mary Elizabeth Pidgeon. Bulletin 152. Washington, D.C.: Women's Bureau, 1938. http://tinyurl.com/jj6g2lo

U.S. Labor Department. Women's Bureau. *Domestic Employment: A Digest of Current Information.* Washington, D.C.: Women's Bureau, 1946. http://tinyurl.com/gl8ryoz

U.S. Labor Department. Women's Bureau. *Effective Use of Women in the Defense Program.* Special Bulletin 1. Washington, D.C.: Women's Bureau, 1940. (L 13.10:1)

U.S. Labor Department. Women's Bureau. *Eleventh Annual Report.* Washington, D.C.: Women's Bureau, 1929. http://tinyurl.com/jzu2nrs

U.S. Labor Department. Women's Bureau. *Employing Women in Shipyards,* by Dorothy K. Newman. Bulletin 192-6. Washington, D.C.: Women's Bureau, 1944. (L 13.3:192/6). http://tinyurl.com/hp9llkz

U.S. Labor Department. Women's Bureau. *Employment Fluctuations and Unemployment of Women: Certain Indications from Various Sources, 1928–31,* by Mary Elizabeth Pidgeon. Washington, D.C.: Women's Bureau, 1933. (L 13.3:113). http://tinyurl.com/hrytpqe

U.S. Labor Department. Women's Bureau. *Equal Pay: A Thirty-five Year Perspective.* Washington, D.C.: Women's Bureau, 1998.

U.S. Labor Department. Women's Bureau. *"Equal Pay" for Women in War Industries,* by Mary Elizabeth Pidgeon. Bulletin 196. Washington, D.C.: Women's Bureau, 1942. (L 13.3:196)

U.S. Labor Department. Women's Bureau. *Facts about Women Heads of Households and Families.* Washington, D.C.: Women's Bureau, 1979. http://tinyurl .com/zssgyao

U.S. Labor Department. Women's Bureau. *The Family Status of Breadwinning Women: A Study of Material in the Census Schedules of a Selected Locality 1922.* Washington, D.C.: Women's Bureau, 1922. (L 13.3:23). http:// tinyurl.com/jeu3tyj

U.S. Labor Department. Women's Bureau. *Family Status of Breadwinning Women in Four Selected Cities.* Bulletin 41. Washington, D.C.: Women's Bureau, 1925.

U.S. Labor Department. Women's Bureau. *Fourth Annual Report.* Washington, D.C.: Women's Bureau, 1922.

U.S. Labor Department. Women's Bureau. *Handbook on Women Workers 1965.* Washington, D.C.: Women's Bureau, 1966. http://tinyurl.com/h2yfkdf

U.S. Labor Department. Women's Bureau. *Milestones: The Women's Bureau Celebrates 65 Years of Women's Labor History.* Washington, D.C.: Women's Bureau, 1985.

U.S. Labor Department. Women's Bureau. *Negro Women War Workers.* Bulletin 205. Washington, D.C.: Women's Bureau, 1945. (L 13.3:205)

U.S. Labor Department. Women's Bureau. *The New Position of Women in American Industry.* Bulletin 124. Washington, D.C.: Women's Bureau, 1920. (L 13.3:12). http://tinyurl.com/hmelkwl

U.S. Labor Department. Women's Bureau. *Night-Work Laws in the United States.* Bulletin 7. Washington, D.C.: Women's Bureau, 1920. (L 13.3:7)

U.S. Labor Department. Women's Bureau. *The Occupational Progress of Women, 1910 to 1930,* by Mary V. Dempsey. Bulletin 104. Washington, D.C.: Women's Bureau, 1933. (L 13.3:104). http://tinyurl.com/j5fnms3

U.S. Labor Department. Women's Bureau. *Our History.* Washington, D.C.: Women's Bureau. http://tinyurl.com/glcjto4

U.S. Labor Department. Women's Bureau. *Overview.* http://www.dol.gov/wb /overview_14.htm

U.S. Labor Department. Women's Bureau. *Report on 1948 Women's Bureau Conference.* Bulletin 224. Washington, D.C.: Women's Bureau, 1948. (L 13.3:224)

U.S. Labor Department. Women's Bureau. *Third Annual Report.* Washington, D.C.: Women's Bureau, 1921.

U.S. Labor Department. Women's Bureau. *Time of Change: 1983 Handbook on Women Workers.* Washington, D.C.: Women's Bureau, 1984. (L 36.103: 298), http://tinyurl.com/gqof3vw

U.S. Labor Department. Women's Bureau. *Trafficking in Persons: A Guide for Non-Governmental Organizations.* Washington, D.C.: Women's Bureau, 2002. http://tinyurl.com/h5k8g2f

U.S. Labor Department. Women's Bureau. *Twelfth Annual Report.* Washington, D.C.: Women's Bureau, 1930.

U.S. Labor Department. Women's Bureau. *What the Wage Earning Woman Contributes to Family Support,* by Agnes L. Peterson. Bulletin 75. Washington, D.C.: Women's Bureau, 1929.

U.S. Labor Department. Women's Bureau. *Women in Industry: A Series of Papers to Aid Study Groups,* by Mary Elizabeth Pidgeon. Bulletin 164. Washington, D.C.: Women's Bureau, 1938. (L 13.3:164). http://tinyurl.com/guxzz4t

U.S. Labor Department. Women's Bureau. *Women Street Car Conductors and Ticket Agents.* Bulletin 11. Washington, D.C.: Women's Bureau, 1921.

U.S. Labor Department. Women's Bureau. *Women Workers in Ten War Production Areas and Their Postwar Employment Plans,* by Sylvia R. Weissbrodt. Bulletin 209. Washington, D.C.: Women's Bureau, 1946. (L 13.3:209). http://tinyurl.com/juemcek

U.S. Labor Department. Women's Bureau. *Women Workers in Their Family Environment.* Bulletin 183. Washington, D.C.: 1941, http://tinyurl.com/jjr7mzr

U.S. Labor Department. Women's Bureau. *Women's Bureau: Meeting the Challenges of the 80's.* Washington, D.C.: Women's Bureau, 1985. (L 36.102:C 35)

U.S. Labor Department. Women's Bureau. *Women's Emergency Farm Service on the Pacific Coast in 1943.* Bulletin 204. Washington, D.C.: Women's Bureau, 1945. (L 13.3:204)

U.S. Labor Department. Women's Bureau. *Women's Occupations through Seven Decades,* by Janet M. Hooks. Bulletin 218. Washington, D.C.: Women's Bureau, 1947. (L 13.3:218). http://tinyurl.com/hb3l8sr

U.S. Labor Department. Women's Bureau. *Women's Wartime Hours of Work: The Effect on Their Factory Performance and Home Life,* by Margaret Kay Anderson. Bulletin 208. Washington, D.C.: Women's Bureau, 1947. (L 13.3:208). http://tinyurl.com/j23yof3

U.S. Labor Department. Workplace Standards Administration. Women's Bureau. *Underutilization of Women Workers.* Washington, D.C.: Women's Bureau, 1971 (Revised).

U.S. Merit Systems Protection Board. *A Question of Equity: Women and the Glass Ceiling.* Washington, D.C.: MSPB. 1992.

U.S. National Academies of Science, Engineering and Medicine. Behavioral and Social Sciences and Education Division. Committee on National Statistics. *Coordinating and Sustaining Federal Statistics.* Washington, D.C.: NASEM, 2016. http://tinyurl.com/z5cayw5.

U.S. National Advisory Committee on Women's Education Programs. *Working Women Speak: Education, Training, Counseling Needs,* by Cynthia Harrison. Washington, D.C.: NACWEP, 1979. http://tinyurl.com/zzk6sbm

U.S. National Archives and Records Administration. *Records of the Bureau of Economic Analysis.* NARA, 2016. http://tinyurl.com/jaycrzs

U.S. National Archives and Records Administration. *Records of the Economic Research Service.* NARA, 2016. http://tinyurl.com/c3ascm3

U.S. National Archives and Records Administration. Federal Register Office. *U.S. Government Manual 1988/89.* Washington, D.C.: NARA, 1988. (AE 2.108/2:988/89)

U.S. National Commission on Law Observance and Enforcement. *Report on Penal Institutions: Probation and Patrol.* Washington, D.C.: NCLEO, 1931. http://tinyurl.com/jd56sk2

U.S. National Commission on the Causes and Prevention of Crime. *Crimes of Violence, Volume 11, a Staff Report,* by Donald J. Mulvihill and Melvin M. Tumin, with Lynn A. Curtis. Washington, D.C.: NCCPC, 1970. http://tinyurl.com/grpg8ey

U.S. National Commission on the Observance of International Women's Year. *American Women Today and Tomorrow,* by Barbara Everitt Bryant. Washington, D.C.: NCOIWY, 1977.

U.S. National Commission on the Observance of International Women's Year. *The Legal Status of Homemakers in Colorado,* by Joyce S. Steinhardt. Washington, D.C.: NCOIWY, 1976.

U.S. National Council on the Observance of International Women's Year 1975. *... To Form a More Perfect Union: Justice for American Women.* Washington, D.C.: NCOIWY, 1975.

U.S. National Commission on the Observance of International Woman's Year. Homemaker's Committee. *The Legal Status of Women in Missouri,* by Joan M. Krauskopf. Washington, D.C.: Homemaker's Committee, 1976.

U.S. National Science Foundation. *A Minor Miracle: An Informal History of the National Science Foundation.* Washington, D.C.: NSF, 1975. (NS 1.2: M 66/3)

U.S. National Women's Business Council. *A Compendium of National Statistics on Women-Owned Businesses in the U.S.* Washington, D.C.: NWBC, 1994. http://tinyurl.com/zzto9vz

U.S. National Women's Business Council. *A Compendium of National Statistics on Women-Owned Businesses in the U.S. Executive Summary and Data Report.* Washington, D.C.: NWBC, 2001. http://tinyurl.com/kqkykh7

U.S. National Women's Business Council. *Women-Owned Firms in the U.S.* Washington, D.C.: NWBC, 2012. http://tinyurl.com/ksr9rx9

U.S. President's Commission on the Status of Women. *Report of the Committee on Civil and Political Rights.* Washington, D.C.: PCSW, 1963.

U.S. President's Commission on the Status of Women. *Report of the Committee on Home and Community.* Washington, D.C.: PCSW, 1963.

U.S. Selective Service. *Selective Service in Wartime: Second Report of the Director of Selective Service 1941–1942.* Washington, D.C.: Selective Service, 1943.

U.S. Small Business Administration. *A Status Report to Congress: Statistical Information on Women in Business.* Washington, D.C.: SBA, 1990. (SBA 1.2:W 84/8)

U.S. Small Business Administration. Office of Advocacy. *Women in Business.* Washington, D.C.: SBA, 1998.

U.S. Social Security Administration. *Economic Value of a Housewife,* by Wendyce H. Brody. Research Note No. 9. Washington, D.C.: SSA, 1975.

U.S. Social Security Administration. Children's Bureau. *Further Progress in Reducing Maternal and Infant Mortality: The Record of 1945 and 1946,* by George Wolff and Eleanor P. Hunt. Statistical Series 4. Washington, D.C.: Federal Security Agency, 1949.

U.S. Superintendent of the United States Census. *Statistical View of the United States, Being a Compendium of the Seventh Census,* by J.D.B. De Bow. Washington, D.C.: Census Superintendent, 1854. http://tinyurl.com/ho5chfp

U.S. Transportation Department. Bureau of Transportation Statistics. *About BTS.* Washington, D.C.: BTS, 2016. http://tinyurl.com/z8mdrbg

U.S. Treasury Department. *Statistical Abstract of the United States 1878.* Washington, D.C.: Treasury Department, 1878.

U.S. Treasury Department. *Statistical Abstract of the United States 1879.* Washington, D.C.: Treasury Department, 1879.

U.S. Treasury Department. *Statistical Abstract of the United States 1898.* Washington, D.C.: Treasury Department, 1899.

U.S. Treasury Department. Internal Revenue Service. *Publication 501, Exemptions, Standard Deduction, and Filing Information.* Washington, D.C.: IRS, 2015. http://tinyurl.com/hz4772s

U.S. Treasury Department. Public Health Service. *Healthy Happy Womanhood: A Pamphlet for Girls and Young Women.* Washington, D.C.: PHS, 1920. http://tinyurl.com/jh472dt

U.S. Treasury Department. Statistics Bureau. *Statistical Abstract of the United States 1885.* Document 793. Washington, D.C.: Statistics Bureau, 1886.

U.S. Treasury Department. Statistics Bureau. *Statistical Abstract of the United States 1888.* Document 1209. Washington, D.C.: Statistics Bureau, 1889.

U.S. Treasury Department. Statistics Bureau. *Statistical Abstract of the United States 1889.* Document 1310. Washington, D.C.: Statistics Bureau, 1890.

U.S. Treasury Department. Statistics Bureau. *Statistical Abstract of the United States 1895.* Washington, D.C.: Statistics Bureau, 1896.

U.S. Treasury Department. Statistics Bureau. *Statistical Abstract of the United States 1902.* Washington, D.C.: Statistics Bureau, 1903. http://tinyurl.com/zwwce7w

U.S. Treasury Department. Tax Analysis Office. *Joint Filing by Same-Sex Couples after Windsor: Characteristics of Married Tax Filers in 2013 and 2014,* by Robin Fisher, Geof Gee, and Adam Looney. Working Paper 108. Washington, D.C.: OTA, 2016. http://tinyurl.com/jaf9cvb

U.S. USA.gov USA.gov. https://www.usa.gov

U.S. Veterans Affairs Department. National Center for Veterans Analysis and Statistics. *Profile of Women Veterans 2014.* NCVAS, 2016. http://tinyurl.com/zznb86v

U.S. Veteran's Administration. Statistical Policy and Research Service. *The Aging Female Veteran: Follow-Up Analysis from the Survey of Aging Veterans.* SAV 70 84-1. Washington, D.C.: VA, 1984. (VA 1.2:V 64/10). http://tinyurl.com/jzcyq7x

U.S. Veteran's Administration. Statistical Policy and Research Service. *The Female Veteran Population,* by Mark S. Russell. Washington, D.C.: VA, 1984. (VA 1.2:F 34). http://tinyurl.com/zql7f4o

U.S. Veteran's Administration. Statistical Policy and Research Service. *Survey of Female Veterans: A Study of the Needs, Attitudes and Experiences of Women Veterans.* Washington, D.C.: VA, 1985. (VA 1.2:F 34/5). http://tinyurl.com/j6ywnnb

U.S. White House. *The Structure of the Federal Statistical System* White House. http://tinyurl.com/lml3w57

U.S. White House Council on Women and Girls. *Keeping America's Women Moving Forward: The Key to an Economy Built to Last.* Washington, D.C.: WHCWG, 2012.

Violence against Women Act, U.S. Code 42 §§13701 et seq.

Waldman, Elizabeth and Robert Whitmore. "Children of Working Mothers, March 1973." *Monthly Labor Review* 97, no. 5 (May 1974): 50–58.

Walker, Francis Amasa. "American Industry in the Census." *Atlantic Monthly.* December 1869. 689–701. http://tinyurl.com/nd3jzmp

Wandersee, Winifred D. *Women's Work and Family Values, 1920–1940.* Cambridge, MA: Harvard University Press, 1981.

War Organization of the Government. CQ Researcher. http://tinyurl.com/z2s5snr

Waring, Marilyn. *If Women Counted: A New Feminist Economics.* San Francisco: HarperSanFrancisco. 1990.

Wells, David R. *Consumerism and the Movement of Housewives into Wage Work.* Brookfield, VT: Ashgate, 1998.

Whitcomb, David J. "Abortion Surveillance: Trends, Characteristics, and the Necessity of Data Collection." *AWHONNS Lifelines* 8, no. 2 (2004): 112–115.

White Slave Traffic Act. Chapter 395. U.S. Statutes at Large 36 (1910) 825.

"Why—and How—We Should Queer the Census." *Between the Lines* 1750, no. 642 (December 10, 2009): 10.

Williams, S.J. and E.N. McIntosh. "National Resource Requirements for Abortion Services." *Public Health Reports* 89, no. 5 (September–October 1974): 440–446.

Wines, Frederick Howard. *American Prisons in the Tenth United States Census.* New York: G.P. Putman and Sons: The Knickerbocker Press, 1888.

Woloch, Nancy. *A Class by Herself: Protective Laws for Women Workers, 1890s-1990s.* Princeton, NJ: Princeton University Press, 2015.

"Women Who Can Work in Defense Industries." *Woman Worker* 20, no. 5 (September 1940): 3.

Women's Business Ownership Act of 1988. Public Law 100-533. U.S. Statutes at Large 102 (1988): 2689. http://tinyurl.com/mc9l9pd

"Women's Chances for Defense Jobs." *Woman Worker* 21, no. 1 (January 1941): 3.

Woods, Cara M., Bethany Applebaum, Yvonne Green, Deborah L. Kallgren, and Evelyn Kappeler. "Women's Health: 30 Years of Progress in the U.S. Department of Health and Human Services." *Public Health Reports* 130, no. 20 (March–April 2015): 123–127.

Worldcat. Worldcat.org.

Wright, Carroll D. *The History and Growth of the United States Census.* Washington, D.C.: Senate Committee on the Census, 1900. http://tinyurl.com /hqovmpq

Wright, Carroll D. "Report on the Factory System of the United States." U.S. Interior Department. Census Office. *Report on the Manufactures of the United States at the Tenth Census 1880.* Washington, D.C.: Census Office, 1883. http://tinyurl.com/jd88bhf

Wright, Carroll D. "Why Women Are Paid Less Than Men." *Forum.* July 1892. 629–639. http://tinyurl.com/zu5ae5y

Index

Abbott, Edith, 114
Abel, Marjorie, 49, 54, 58, 81, 117
Abortion, 159, 179–88; as cause of
    death, 181, 182, 183–85; as crime,
    179–83, 187; California, 186; laws,
    179, 182–83; legal, 182–88; New
    York, 182; non-Whites, 188
Adkinson, Florence M., 54–55
*Adkins v. Children's Hospital of
    Washington, D.C.*, 119
"Adrift," women, 116–17
African Americans, 64; abortions,
    184; lynchings, 220; married, 23,
    27; occupations, 114; population,
    16, 18; prisoners, 191, 200; rape,
    221; women, by number of
    children, 30; working women, 233
Against Our Will, 222
Age, 15–19; consent for marriage, 21;
    heaping, 16; lying about, 16, 18;
    military, 15–16; voting, 16–17, 19
AIDS, 168, 170, 171
Alcoholism, 22, 24, 170, 192, 198
American Community Survey, 9,
    25, 26
American Statistical Association, 89,
    105, 111
Anderson, Karen, 238
Anderson, Margo, 76; Conk, Margo
    A., 64, 69, 72, 74

Anderson, Mary, 86, 105, 233, 236
Anthony, Susan B., 83
Armed forces, 241–48; academies,
    244–45; sexual assault, 244–45,
    247; sexual harassment, 244–45;
    venereal disease, 207, 208

Bachmann, Michele, 9, 252
Bailey, Martha J., 176
Bancroft, Gertrude, 145
Barlow, E. R., 54
Barrett, Nancy Smith, 46, 58, 124–25
Battered women. *See* Domestic
    violence
Beckman, Marlene D., 206
Beetham, Gwendolyn, 109
Bell, Carolyn Shaw, 58, 89
Bergmann, Barbara, 46
Birth control. *See* Contraception
Births, 32–33, 34, 35; out-of-hospital,
    32; unmarried, 35–39; unwanted,
    32, 34, 176; wanted, 32
Blind people, 17, 160, 170
Boarders, 44, 51, 77
Boardinghouse keepers, 77, 79, 113
Brannen, Kathleen C., 153
Breadwinners, 78, 147; men, 27, 31,
    44, 147; women, 26–27, 44, 55,
    117,118, 126, 147
Breast feeding, 32, 34

Brody, Wendyce, 57–58
Brothels, 195, 203–4
Brownmiller, Susan, 222
Bush, George W., 102, 108–9,
    245–47
Business owners, female, 149–56

Cancer, 170; breast, 167, 169, 171;
    lung, 161–62, 163
Carter, Susan B., 102, 108
Census of Agriculture, 147
Census of Manufactures, 129
Census of Population: bias in
    employment statistics, 58, 63, 64,
    65–66, 97, 112, 114; bias in job-
    seeking statistics, 94;
    "decapitation," 45–47; false
    responses in, 8, 18, 22, 23, 36, 52,
    53; inaccuracies, 54, 63, 66, 69,
    71–72, 76, 79, 111–12, 145;
    processing, 64, 65, 66, 69, 70, 112,
    113, 252; questions, proposed, 7, 9;
    resistance to, 8, 9, 251–52;
    undercounts, 17, 94, 97, 112,
    129–30, 203–4
Census of Population of 1790, 15
Census of Population of 1820, 16,
    63, 111
Census of Population of 1830, 112
Census of Population of 1840, 129
Census of Population of 1850, 8, 15,
    43, 63, 75, 160, 191
Census of Population of 1860, 16, 29,
    63, 75, 112, 161
Census of Population of 1870, 16;
    criminals undercounted, 203–4;
    criticism, 52; gainful employment,
    75–76; occupations of women, 50;
    working women undercounted,
    112, 129
Census of Population of 1880:
    abortion, 180; boarders, 77; clerical
    workers, 63; crime, 191; gainful
    employment, 77; factory work, 129,

130–31; heads of households, 44;
    homemakers, 50; housekeepers, 50,
    52; marital status, 21, 112; mental
    retardation, 180; occupations, 63;
    prisoners, 191; prostitution, 204;
    rape, 215; working women, 112
Census of Population of 1890: births,
    unmarried, 35; farm labor, 147;
    homemakers, 50; housewives, 50;
    mothers, 29, 35; naturalization, 23;
    processing, 64, 113; *Statistical Atlas*,
    114; working women, 53
Census of Population of 1900: age, 15,
    18; criminals undercounted, 195;
    criticism, 78–79, 114, 194–95; farm
    labor, 141, 144; gainful
    employment, 77, 79; homemakers,
    50, 53; housekeepers, 50; marital
    status, 22; men undercounted, 17;
    occupations, 65, 114; processing,
    64; recount, 17; self-employed, 77;
    working women, 44
Census of Population of 1910: age, 19;
    boarders, 77; consensual marriage,
    24; controversy, 79–81, 115, 141,
    144; farm labor, 81, 141, 144;
    gainful employment, 54, 79;
    homemakers, 50–51; housewives,
    50–51; Indians, 24; men, more
    than women, 18; occupations, 3,
    51, 114; working women, 79–80,
    112, 115
Census of Population of 1920,120;
    farm labor, 81, 144; gainful
    employment, 77; homemakers, 51,
    54; housewives, 51; occupations,
    66–69, 70; working women, 79,
    80, 94
Census of Population of 1930,
    119–20; farm labor, 145; gainful
    employment, 81; heads of families,
    44; homemakers, 51; housekeepers,
    51, 54; occupations, 66, 69–70;
    professionals, 55–56; seasonal

workers, 96–97; unemployment, 94–95, 97; working women, 80
Census of Population of 1940: farm labor, 145; fertility, 30, 36; gainful employment, 56; homemakers, 51; housekeepers, 51; income, 88; labor force, 81, 96, 145; long form, 9; occupations, 71–72, 80; private households, 44; railroad workers, 63; seasonal workers, 96–97; unemployment, 97; working women undercounted, 71–72, 122
Census of Population of 1950, 24, 30, 44, 51–52, 57, 73
Census of Population of 1960, 9, 30, 36, 52, 73
Census of Population of 1970, 24, 36, 45, 52, 73, 123, 214
Census of Population of 1980, 37, 52, 89, 153, 243
Census of Population of 1990, 25, 52, 214
Census of Population of 2000, 9, 52, 90, 214
Census of Population of 2010, 9, 19, 52, 214, 252
Census of Unemployment, 95
Census-takers. *See* Enumerators
Children: adopted, 30; delinquents, 207; of prisoners, 191; of single mothers, 22, 35, 36, 37, 39; of working women, 33; prisoners, 191, 200; step, 30, 33. *See also* Working children
Chinese, 18
Ciancanelli, Penelope, 76–77, 78, 82, 114, 121, 144
Citizenship, 18, 23
Clerks and clerical workers, 63–64, 65, 118, 121, 122, 135, 241
Cohabitation, 25–26, 27
Comparable worth, 88–90
Conk, Margo A., 64, 69, 72, 74; Margo Anderson, 76

Constitution, 7, 179
Contraception, 37, 159, 173–88; methods, 175–76, 179–88; teenage, 176
Conyngton, Mary, 134, 195–97, 203, 206–7
Cooper, William J., 71
Corporations, women-owned, 153–54
Crime, 191–218; abortion as, 179–83, 187; sexual assault, 152, 228, 244, 245, 247; sexual harassment, 107, 244–45. *See also* Rape
Crime victims, 211–28
Criminal Victimization in the United States, 47, 212, 214, 226–27, 228
Current Population Reports, 24, 25, 30–31, 46, 102
Current Population Survey, 25, 26, 46, 58
Cutright, Phillips, 37
Cyberstalking, 217–18

Daughters, grown, 50–52, 76
Deaths: abortions as cause, 181, 182, 183–85; in childbirth, 29, 30; children, 131, 176; smokers, 162; statistics, 29, 30, 58, 160, 181; violent, 161
De Bow, J.D.B., 8, 16, 160
Dempsey, Mary V., 70, 94, 120
Department store workers, 117, 196–97, 203, 206–7
Dictionary of Occupational Titles, 72, 235
Differences in the Earnings of Women and Men, 87–88
Dillingham Commission, 205–6
Discrimination: employment, 88, 89, 91, 118; sex, 88, 89, 91, 118; wage, 86, 88, 89, 91
Divorce, 21–27, 32, 78; causes, 22, 24, 205
Domestic violence, 211–16, 225, 253; changes in terminology, 212–13;

costs of, 126, 216, 218, 219; sexual assault, 152, 228, 244, 245, 247. *See also* Rape

Draft, 235–36, 242

Dryfoos, Joy G., 175

Ducoff, Louis, 145

Duffy, Edward A., 183

Durand, John D., 80

Education, 83; parents' involvement in, 32–33; prisoners, 196; women, 138

Edwards, Alba M., 65–72, 79, 81, 121, 252

Employment, 105, 111–27; concepts of, 63–97; definition, 40–41; household, 56–57, 115; married women, 63, 112, 122. *See also* Factory workers; Farm laborers; Gainful employment; War industries; Working mothers; Working women

Employment policies of companies, 122

Enumerators, 8, 9, 18, 80, 94, 97, 145; inaccuracy, 54, 56, 57, 76, 79, 94, 112, 114, 123;

Enumerators' instructions: 1870 Census, 50, 75; 1880 Census, 50; 1890 Census, 50, 53; 1900 Census, 50, 79–80, 141; 1910 Census, 50–51, 54, 77, 79–80, 81, 115, 141; 1920 Census, 51, 66–69, 80–81, 144; 1930 Census, 51, 69–70, 94; 1940 Census, 51, 96; 1950 Census, 30, 44, 51; 1960 Census, 52; 1970 Census, 36, 52; 1980 Census, 52; 1990 Census, 52; 2000 Census, 52; 2010 Census, 52

Equal Rights Amendment, 105, 119, 242

Factory system, 101, 130–31

Factory workers, 101; children, 129, 130–31, 132, 134; health, 132;

moral standards, 134; women, 122, 129–36

Families, 32–33, 34, 56, 125; aid to, 31, 37, 97; broken, 32, 45, 123; headed by women, 44, 45, 47–48, 106, 122, 237; heads of, 43–48; military, 245–46, 248; single parent, 38; traditional, 29, 123, 125

Family businesses, 70; workers, 51, 57, 59, 76, 82, 97, 121

Family planning services, 174–76, 177

Family violence. *See* Domestic violence

Farmers, 80, 140, 141, 142, 143, 145, 146, 147; Female reluctance to be called, 139, 147

Farmer's wives, 138, 140–43, 145, 146

"Farm females," 137, 147

Farm laborers (not farmers), 65, 80, 81, 96–97, 141–42, 144, 145

Farm operators, 145–47

Farm Woman's Problems, 143

Farm women, 79, 137–47; complaints of, 142–44; criticized, 141–42; insanity, alleged, 137–38; surveyed, 146–47

Federal employees, female civilian, 8, 113, 125, 132, 205, 232–33

Federal Reserve Bulletin, 47

Fertility, 30, 31, 36, 37, 162, 164, 225; by duration of marriage, by, 30; differential, 30, 35; premarital, 37; unwanted, 34

Firefighters, 64, 70, 72, 73

Folbre, Nancy, 49, 54, 58, 81

Foreign-born persons, 29, 132

Gainful employment, 52, 54, 55, 75–82, 97, 114, 145

Gardner, John W., 174

Gay men, 27, 43, 168; homosexuals, 25, 43, 187; same-sex couples, 47

Geib-Gunderson, Lisa, 77, 112

Gender identity, 15
Gilman, Charlotte Perkins, 140
Glick, Paul, 45
Goldin, Claudia, 114
Great Depression, 31, 81, 93–97, 119, 252
Griffin, Cynthia E., 154
Guttmacher Institute, 186–87, 188–89

Handbook of Labor Statistics, 87, 95, 119, 121, 134–35, 235
Handbook on Women Workers, 105–7, 110, 151, 152, 153
Hautaniemi, Susan, 56
Heads of family, 43–48; age, 44; controversy, 45–47; female, 44, 122–23; unemployed, 95
Heads of Household, 8, 15, 43–48; controversy, 45–47; female, 45; occupations, 45
Health, United States, 16–166, 175, 183–85; criticism of, 162
Health issues, 59, 132, 159–88
Hill, Joseph A., 54–55, 69, 144
Historical Corrections Statistics in the United States, 220
History of Women in Industry in the United States, 109, 111
Holleran, Lisa L. 200
Holmes, George K., 137–38, 141–42
Home and Family Life in a Changing Civilization, 71
Home housekeeper, 54–55
Homemakers, 49–60, 65, 144; farm, 144; treated as nonworkers by census, 50–52, 78
Homes for unwed mothers, 35, 39
Home work. *See* Piecework
Homosexuals, 25, 27, 43, 187; gay men, 168; lesbians, 26, 43, 167; transgendered persons, 32
Hoover, Herbert, 93, 197
Householders, 46–47; female, 34

Households, 43–48, 103, 169; biracial, 43; with boarders, 77; same-sex, 26; unmarried partner, 27
Housekeepers, paid, 5–52, 52–53, 54, 59, 65
Housewives, 49–60, 76, 77, 80, 81; causes of death, 58–59; cost-of-living controversy, 237–38; economic status, 78; employed women counted as, 80; farm women, 146; unemployed women counted as, 94
Housework, 50–52, 54–57, 59–60, 77, 96, 118, 144; not gainful employment, 52, 54–56, 81; working women doing, 113, 134
Howe, Louise Kapp, 124
Huls, Mary Ellen, 159, 248
Hyde Amendment, 185

Illegitimacy. *See* Births: unmarried; Children: of single mothers
Immigrants, 115, 205–6
Income, 83–92; family, 91; median, 91; percentage earned by women, 85; by sex, 91
Index to Occupations, 66, 69
Insanity: farm women, alleged, 137–38; race, 160; slaves, 160
Intercourse: first experience, 176, 208, 225–26; premarital, 37–38, 197–98
Intimate partner violence. *See* Domestic violence
Issues in Federal Statistical Needs Relating to Women, 46, 58, 124, 162, 211–12

Jaffe, A. J., 80, 93–94
Javits, Jacob, 152
Job seeking, 81, 94, 96, 120, 123

Kennedy, Anthony, 89
Knowles, Jane, 140, 143

Krause, Harry D., 37
Kreps, Juanita M., 253
Kyl, Jon, 179
Kyrk, Hazel, 57

Labor force, 127, 234; definition, 79, 93–94, 96; gainful employment, change from, 56, 81, 82, 145; people counted incorrectly, 58, 97, 112, 121; unpaid workers in, 57; World War II, 234, 236
Laun, Louis F., 152
Laundresses, male, 72
Lenroot, Katharine, 173
Leopold, Alice K., 107
Lesbians, 26, 27, 43, 167; homosexuals, 25, 187; same-sex couples, 47
Lynchings, 220

Mahoney, Carolyn B., 245
Mann Act, 206, 209
Marital status of women, 21–27, 34, 39, 44, 48, 127, 128; abortions by, 188; domestic violence victims, 215; mothers, 35–39; occupations, 63, 113; rape victims, 221, 227; working, 63, 87, 102, 106, 132, 152, 184, 188
Marriage, 21–27, 85, 87, 117–18; age at, 27; age of consent, 21; biracial, 27, 43; common-law, 24, 37; consensual, 24, 37; duration, 24; immigrants, 23; as prostitution, 85; remarriage, 25; same-sex, 25, 26, 43; unbroken, 30. *See also* Housewives
Married women, 21–27, 30, 44, 45, 46, 77, 79, 80; "adrift," 116–17; African American, 23, 27; business owners, 151, 153; citizenship, 23; companies' policies on employing, 122; contraceptive use, 175–76, 177; factory workers, 131–35; farm

women, 146; income, 85–86; maiden names, 39; occupations, 53, 63, 77, 113; prostitutes, 208; unemployed, 94; White, 27, 53; working, 58, 79–80, 95, 112, 122, 131, 135; working undercounted, 77, 79–80, 94, 112, 121. *See also* Domestic violence; Housewives
Masters, Sybilla, 249, 251
McMillan, Lucille Foster, 234
Meets, Grace L., 30–31
Men, 16, 17, 19, 60, 76, 79, 124; African American, 18; age, 18; criminals, 191, 194–95, 198; deaths, 161; farmers, 140, 142, 143, 145, 146, 147; health, 161, 166, 169, 170, 171, 175; income, 90, 91; married, 22–23; Mulattoes, 18; occupations, 63, 64, 72, 73, 90; prisoners, 191, 194–95, 200–201, 219; taking women's jobs, 133; unemployed, 95, 97, 112, 123; White, 15; working, 75, 88, 89,123
Mental retardation, 160, 180
Merriam, William. R., 8
Midwives, 32, 65, 74, 192
Mikulski, Barbara A., 211–12
Miller, Frieda S., 49
Mill workers, 102, 119, 130, 134, 196
Miners, 63, 149–50
Minimum wage, 118, 119
Mommy penalty, 91
Moore, Emily C., 167
Moore, Kristin A., 38
Motherhood, 29–39, 159
Mothers, 29–39; age, 33; employment status, 30, 91; health, 159; occupations, 30; single, 22, 35–39; teenage, 37–38. *See also* Working mothers
Mulattoes, 18. *See also* African Americans
Muller, Charlotte, 162

National Council for Research on Women, 108

National Crime Victimization Survey, 212, 213, 214, 215, 222, 225, 228

National Health Interview Survey, 161, 162

National Household Education Survey, 32–33

National Incident-Based Reporting System, 200, 214

National Intimate Partner and Sexual Violence Survey, 216

National Opinion Research Center, 146, 218

National Reporting System for Family Planning Services, 175–76

National Survey of Family Growth, 25, 32, 175, 187, 225

National Survey of Small Business Finance, 153–54

National Violence against Women Survey, 216, 225

Native Americans, 24

Native-born persons (i.e., not foreign-born), 18, 30, 114, 132, 206

New York State Teachers Association, 83

Night work, 105, 118–19, 134, 231

Norton, Arthur, 45–46

Norwood, Janet L., 46

Nurses, 65, 89, 115, 163, 239, 241, 242, 248

Obama, Barack, 109, 125, 246–48, 252

Occupational Progress of Women, 1910–1930, 70–71, 94

Occupations, 63–74, 80, 113, 126, 150; crime, related to, 195, 205; fathers', 30; men's, 64, 112, 135, 147; women's, 63–74, 112, 117, 135, 147; "peculiar" for women, 3, 66; suitable for women, 235

Oppenheimer, Valerie Kincade, 124

Packwood, Robert, 152

Pay equity, 88–89

Perkins, Frances, 97

Peterson, Agnes L., 86–87

Pidgeon, Mary Elizabeth, 88, 95

Piecework, 77, 83, 104, 121, 136

Pink-collar jobs, 124

"Pin money," 83, 86, 122

Planned Parenthood, 179, 186

Police: domestic violence, 214; female, 199; National Incident-Based Reporting System, and, 200; prostitution, 204; rape, 222–23; stalking, 217; *Uniform Crime Reports,* 198, 220, 225

Population, 15–19

Pregnancy, 159, 180, 188; attitudes toward, 32; policies on employment during, 122, 243; smoking during, 161; teenage, 187

Prenatal care, 32, 165, 166

Presser, Harriet B., 45–46

Prisoners, 191–96; juveniles, 191, 201; male compared to female, 195, 200; men, 191, 194, 200, 219; older, 191; race, 191; slaves, 191; women, 191–94, 199, 200, 206

Prisons, 191, 196, 198, 199, 206

Prosecutors, 217, 222–23

Prostitutes, 203–9; department store workers and, 206–7; juvenile, 206–7, 209; married, 208; World War I, 207–8; World War II, 208–9

Railroad workers, 63, 65, 71–72, 231–32

Rape, 193–94, 198, 219–28, 244, 245; college students, 225; intoxication-facilitated, 226; "lower classes," 221; male victims, 225, 228; racial statistics, 220, 221; terminology difficulties, 218, 223, 225

Rayman, Paula, 95

Red Cross, 238–39, 241, 248

Reilly, Kimberley A., 207
Relation between Occupation and Criminality of Women, 134, 195–97, 203, 206–7
Report of the Commissioner of Agriculture, 138–40
Report on Condition of Woman and Child Wage-Earners in the United States, 116; Census supplement, 79, 117–18; consequences, 86, 102–3, 118; controversy, 134; cotton mills, 133–34; men taking women's jobs, 133; origin, 115; "women adrift," 116–17; women's earnings, 86. See also *Relation between Occupation and Criminality of Women*
Report on Cost of Crime, 197–98
Report on the Defective, Dependent, and Delinquent Classes, 180, 191–94, 204
"Report on the Factory System," 130–31
Roche, Josephine, 149
Roe v. Wade, 34, 179, 183
Roosevelt, Franklin D., 93, 97, 173, 234
Roosevelt, Theodore, 114
Rosie the Riveter, 105, 231, 240

Saleswomen, 95, 115, 117, 206, 207; morality, 74, 206–7
Same-sex couples, 25, 26, 47
Sanger, Margaret, 173
Seasonal workers, 87, 96–97
Self-employed, 121, 153, 156; men, 77; women, 82, 150–51, 153, 155
Seneca Falls Convention, 49
Sex-segregated occupations, 95, 103
Sexual assault, 152, 228, 244, 245, 247. *See also* Rape
Sexual harassment, 107, 244–45
Sexual identity, 27
Shelters for abused women, 214–16
Shepela, Sharon Toffee, 83
Simpson, Sidney O., 197–98

Skill levels of occupations, 65–66, 71–72, 121, 122, 133
Slaves, 5, 15; insanity, 160; prisoners, 191
Smoking, 169–70; sex differences, 161–62
Smuts, Robert W., 53, 80, 81
Social Scientists in Population Research, 45
Sourcebook of Criminal Justice Statistics, 187, 223–25
Spirer, Herbert F., 93–94
Stalking, 216–18
Standard Occupational Classification Manual, 74
Standards for the Employment of Women in Industry, 104
Stapleford, Thomas A., 237
Statistical Abstract, 4, 11–12, 252; abortion, 186, 187; age, 19; cohabitation, 27; contraception, 177; crime victims, 218, 228; criminals, 200–201, 209; divorce, 27; factory workers, 135; farm women, 147; gainful employment, 82; heads of families or households, 47–48; health issues, 169; homemakers, 59–60; housekeepers, 59; housewives, 59; income, 91; Mann Act, 209; marriage, 26–27; motherhood, 33–34, 39; occupations, 74; population, 19; prostitution, 209; rape, 228; self-employed persons, 156; single mothers, 39; unemployment, 97; U.S. Bureau of Labor, 109–10; U.S. Women's Bureau, 127; veterans, 248; war industries, 239; "white slavery," 209; women in the military, 248; women-owned businesses, 156; World War I, 238–39, 248; World War II, 239, 248
Statistics Canada, 10

Statistics of Women at Work, 64, 65, 79, 117, 140
Sumner, Helen L., 109
Sutch, Richard, 52, 112

Tailhook, 244
Tailors and tailoresses, 63
Taxation, 26, 47, 85, 146, 152
Teachers, 73, 83
Technical change, 56, 113, 133, 143
Teenagers: contraceptive use, 176; mothers, 34; pregnant, 37–38, 167, 187; risky behavior, 33; sexually active, 37
Telephone workers, 65, 73, 74, 115, 135, 231
Trafficking in persons, 209
Transportation workers, 73, 115, 135
Truman, Harry S., 49, 88

Unemployment, 93–97
Uniform Crime Reports, 180, 198–99; criticism, 198, 221; domestic violence, 213–14; prostitution, 208; rape, 222, 225, 226
Unions, 107; cost-of-living controversy, 237–38; married working women, 135; mining, 149–50; opposing working women, 133, 232; strike benefits, 87; women's trade, 105; World War I, 232
Unmarried partners, 25, 27
Unpaid family workers, 56–57, 59–60, 76–77, 79, 82; farm work, 145; moving to paid work, 111
USA.gov, 35
U.S. Agriculture Department, 41, 137, 138, 142–44, 146, 147
U.S. Bureau of Justice Statistics: domestic violence, 213, 214, 215; historical statistics, 220; rape, 222, 225, 228; stalking, 217
U.S. Bureau of Labor Statistics, 125; cost-of-living controversy, 237–38;

Current Employment Statistics, 121; heads of households, 46–47; length of working life, 123; origin, 10–11, 101–3; unemployment, 93; working mothers, 31–32, 33; working women, 125. See also *Handbook of Labor Statistics; Report on Condition of Woman and Child Wage-Earners in the United States*
U.S. Census Bureau: controversies, 46–47, 79–81; heads of households, 43, 45–47; housekeepers, 53–54; occupations of women, 65–71, 74; origin, 8–9; shelters for battered women, 214; unpaid family workers, 57; women farm workers, 79–81, 141, 144; women-owned businesses, 152, 154–55; working women, 64–65, 79–82, 117–18, 140. *See also* Census of Agriculture; Census of Manufactures; Census of Population; Census of Unemployment
U.S. Center for Disease Control, 25, 168, 182, 183, 203, 216, 217
U.S. Centers for Disease Control and Prevention, 32, 168, 203, 216
U.S. Children's Bureau, 30, 35, 103, 173
U.S. Civil Rights Commission, 212
U.S. Civil Service Commission, 232, 234–35
U.S. Coast Guard, 242, 248
U.S. Commerce and Labor Department, 9–10, 101, 103, 115, 133
U.S. Commerce Department, 153, 235
U.S. Commission on Immigration, 205
U.S. Congress, 8, 103, 171, 211
U.S. Country Life Commission, 140–41
U.S. Defense Advisory Committee on Women in the Services, 242, 243, 245–47, 251

U.S. Defense Department, 243–44
U.S. Employment Service, 72, 97, 235
U.S. Federal Bureau of Investigation, 198–99, 200, 211, 214, 221
U.S. Federal Reserve Board, 47, 153–54
U.S. General Accounting Office, 88–89, 90, 167–68
U.S. Government Accountability Office, 169, 185, 218, 245
U.S. Health and Human Services Department, 38, 169, 225
U.S. Health, Education, and Welfare Department, 212; contraception policy, 174
U.S. Health Services and Mental Health Administration, 183
U.S. House of Representatives, 7, 38
U.S. Interdisciplinary Social Hygiene Board, 207
U.S. Interior Department, 8, 11, 101, 118
U.S. Internal Revenue Service, 47, 85, 152
U.S. Joint Economic Committee, 36, 90
U.S. Justice Department, 187, 211
U.S. Labor Bureau, 101, 109–10
U.S. Labor Department, 80, 89, 101–2, 123, 134
U.S. Law Enforcement Assistance Administration, 199–200, 211, 221
U.S. Marine Corps, 241, 242, 248
U.S. National Center for Health Statistics: abortion, 182, 183, 186; family planning clinics, 175; housewives and causes of death, 58–59; National Survey of Family Growth, 32, 175–76; teenage childbearing, 37–38; unmarried childbearing, 35, 37; *Vital and Health Statistics,* 159, 175, 186; working women's health, 168–69

U.S. National Commission on Law Observation and Enforcement, 197
U.S. National Commission on the Causes and Prevention of Violence, 219, 222
U.S. National Commission on the Observance of International Women's Year, 89, 183
U.S. National Institute of Justice, 216, 217, 225, 226
U.S. National Institute of Mental Health, 211, 253
U.S. National Institutes of Health, 168, 169
U.S. National War Labor Board, 232
U.S. National Women's Business Council, 154–55
U.S. Navy, 237, 241, 242, 244, 248
U.S. Office of Research on Women's Health, 168, 169
U.S. Office on Women's Health, 159, 168
U.S. Public Health Service, 58, 161, 167, 168, 173
U.S. Selective Service, 235–36
U.S. Senate, 152, 179, 180
U.S. Small Business Administration, 152, 153–54
U.S. Social Security Administration, 46, 57, 152
U.S. Supreme Court, 119, 173, 179, 187–88, 206, 251
U.S. Surgeon General, 161–62
U.S. Veterans Administration, 243
U.S. White House Council on Women and Girls, 125, 155, 253
U.S. Women Accepted for Volunteer Emergency Service, 242
U.S. Women in Industry Service, 104, 232
U.S. Women's Army Corps, 242
U.S. Women's Bureau: gainful employment, 77; *Handbook on Women Workers,* 105–7;

housekeepers, 56–57; marital status of workers, 87, 121; mission statement, 104, 108–9; origin and history, 103–10; protective legislation, 118–19; women-owned businesses, 149–50; women's earnings, 87–88; women supporting families, 86–87, 122–23, 237; World War II, 233–34, 236, 237, 238

Vandiver, Donna M., 200
Van Kleeck, Mary, 232
Venereal disease, 161, 207, 208
Veterans, 34, 243, 248
"Victim precipitation," 219
Violence against Women Act, 215, 216
Vital and Health Statistics, 159–60, 175, 186
Vital Statistics, 25, 159–60, 181
Viviano, Ann T., 83

Wagener, Diane K., 58
Walker, Francis Amasa, 16, 52, 75–76, 84, 112, 203; alleged misconduct by, 112
Wandersee, Winifred D., 95
Ward, Florence E., 143
War industries, women in, 57, 72, 105, 121, 173, 231–39
Waring, Marilyn, 59
"War on Women," 108–9
Washington, George, 8, 251–52
Welfare programs, 31, 37, 93–94, 97, 118
"White slavery," 205, 209. *See also* Trafficking in persons
"Why Women Are Paid Less than Men," 85, 101
Wickersham Commission, 197–98
Wines, Frederick Howard, 180, 191, 194, 204
Wives. *See* Housewives; Married women

Woman Worker, 234, 235
Women: "adrift," 116–17; African American, 30; armed forces, 241–48; business owners, 149–56; contributing to family income, 46, 77, 84, 86, 87, 91, 123, 127, 144; crime victims, 211–28; criminals, 191–209; divorced, 22–25, 78; doctor's visits, 162, 166; factory workers, 122, 129–36; farm, 137–47; heads of families or households, 44, 45, 122–23; medical research subjects, 162, 167–68, 253; not gainfully employed, 53, 75–82, 123; by number of children, 30; occupations, 63–74; older, 112, 166; "peculiar occupations" for, 3, 66–72; rapists, 228; single, 87, 113, 123, 132, 135; unemployed, 94, 123; veterans, 243, 248; voting, 19, 104; wartime industrial work, 57, 72, 105, 121, 173, 231–39; White, 15, 30, 166. *See also* Married women; Working women
Women and Their Health, 162, 166
Women in Gainful Occupations, 1870 to 1920, 54, 69
"Women in Industry," 119–20, 121
Women-owned businesses, 149–56, 252–53
Womanpower, 236, 245
Working children, 115; African American, 114; efficiency, 85; factory, 129–34; not counted, 112; unusual occupations, 70
Working mothers, 91, 106, 126; factory, 131, 134; newborns, 34; occupations, 30; risky behavior of children, 33; trends, 30, 32, 33
Working women, 55, 119; "adrift," 116–17; African-American, 114, 233, 236; armed forces, 241–48; criminal tendencies, 195–97, 205;

divorced, 78; efficiency compared to men, 85, 124, 139, 233, 235, 237; factory workers, 101, 122, 129–36; gainful employment, 75–82; health issues, 132, 168–69; housework (done by) 113, 134; income, 83–92, 232; legal issues, 105; low status, 53, 58, 76; marital status, 27, 63, 87, 102, 112, 113, 132; moral standards, 134; obstacles, 95, 122–23, 236–37; standards for, 104, 233; statistics, 75, 79, 114–15; supporting families, 116–17, 122–23, 237, 238; temporarily unemployed, 94; undercounted, 112, 114, 121; war industries, 105, 231–39; White, 141–42. *See also* Working mothers

Working Women in Large Cities, 84, 113, 132, 205
World War I, 81, 104, 120, 207, 229–31, 238–39, 241
World War II, 56, 71, 105, 199, 208, 222, 234–39, 241–42, 248
Wright, Carroll D.: Bureau of Labor, 101; factory work, 101, 130–32; marriage and divorce, 21–23; working women in cities, 84–86, 113, 205
Wright Report (on marriage and divorce), 21–23

Yearbook of Agriculture, 141–42, 144
Yellen, Janet B., 47

About the Author

Robert Lopresti has been a government information librarian for 40 years, most of them at Western Washington University. His scholarly articles cover such subjects as citation accuracy in environmental journals and the scandal in the House of Representatives Library at the start of the Civil War. He is also the author of 2 mystery novels and more than 60 short stories, including winners of the Derringer and Black Orchid Novella Awards.